EYEWITNESS TRAVEL

BERLIN

AROUND UNTER DEN LINDEN
See pp54–69

NORTH OF THE CENTRE
See pp98–111

EAST OF THE CENTRE
See pp86–97

North of the Centre

East of the Centre

Around Unter den Linden

Museum Island

Tiergarten

Kreuzberg

KREUZBERG
See pp136–145

| 0 metres | 1000 |
| 0 yards | 1000 |

MUSEUM ISLAND
See pp70–85

EYEWITNESS TRAVEL

BERLIN

MAIN CONTRIBUTOR: MAŁGORZATA OMILANOWSKA

LONDON, NEW YORK,
MELBOURNE, MUNICH AND DELHI
www.dk.com

Produced by Wydawnictwo Wiedza i Życie, Warsaw

MANAGING EDITOR Ewa Szwagrzyk
SERIES EDITOR Joanna Egert
DTP DESIGNER Paweł Pasternak
CONSULTANT Nils Meyer
ILLUSTRATIONS Andrzej Wielgosz,
Lena Maminajszwili, Dorota Jarymowicz
PHOTOGRAPHY Dorota and Mariusz Jarymowicz
CORRECTION Bożena Leszkowicz
PRODUCTION Anna Kożurno-Królikowska, Ewa Roguska

Dorling Kindersley Limited
EDITORS Nancy Jones, Esther Labi, Hugh Thompson
SENIOR EDITOR Helen Townsend

CONTRIBUTORS Małgorzata Omilanowska,
Jürgen Scheunemann, Christian Tempel
MAPS Maria Wojciechowska, Dariusz Osuch (D. Osuch i spółka)

Reproduced by Colourscan, Singapore
Printed and bound by South China Co. Ltd., China

First published in Great Britain in 2000
by Dorling Kindersley Limited
80 Strand, London, Great Britain WC2R 0RL

**Reprinted with revisions 2002, 2003, 2004, 2005, 2006, 2008,
2009, 2011 (001)**

Copyright 2000, 2011 © Dorling Kindersley Limited, London
A Penguin Company

A CIP CATALOGUE RECORD IS AVAILABLE FROM THE BRITISH LIBRARY.

ISBN 978-1-4053-5880-4

FLOORS ARE REFERRED TO THROUGHOUT IN ACCORDANCE WITH BRITISH
USAGE, IE THE "FIRST FLOOR" IS THE FLOOR ABOVE GROUND LEVEL.

Front cover main image: Dome of the Reichstag

MIX
Paper from
responsible sources
FSC
www.fsc.org   FSC™ C018179

◁ **Berliner Dom from Schlossebrücke**

CONTENTS

HOW TO USE
THIS GUIDE **6**

**A child's drawing of Fernsehturm,
Siegessäule and Funkturm**

INTRODUCING
BERLIN

FOUR GREAT DAYS IN
BERLIN **10**

PUTTING BERLIN ON
THE MAP **12**

THE HISTORY OF
BERLIN **18**

BERLIN AT A GLANCE **30**

BERLIN THROUGH
THE YEAR **48**

**Bomb-damaged Kaiser-Wilhelm-
Gedächtnis-Kirche (see pp152–3)**

The Spree river passing by the Nikolaiviertel *(see pp88–9)*

A selection of German sausages *(see pp232–233)*

Modern architecture by the former Checkpoint Charlie *(see p141)*

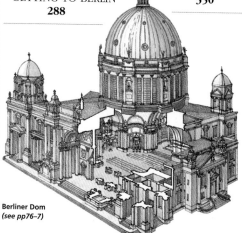

Berliner Dom *(see pp76–7)*

HOW TO USE THIS GUIDE

This Dorling Kindersley travel guide helps you to get the most from your visit to Berlin. It provides detailed practical information and expert recommendations. *Introducing Berlin* maps the city and the region, and sets it in its historical and cultural context, and describes events through the entire year. *Berlin at a Glance* is an overview of the city's main attractions. *Berlin Area by Area* starts on page 52. This is the main sightseeing section, which covers all of the important sights, with photographs, maps and illustrations. *Greater Berlin* covers the nearby historic city of Potsdam, as well as three walking tours. Information about hotels, restaurants, shops and markets, entertainment and sports is found in *Travellers' Needs*. The *Survival Guide* has advice on everything from using Berlin's medical services, telephones and post offices to the public transport system.

FINDING YOUR WAY AROUND THE SIGHTSEEING SECTION

Each of eight sightseeing areas in Berlin is colour-coded for easy reference. Every chapter opens with an introduction to the area of the city it covers, describing its history and character, and has a *Street-by-Street* map illustrating typical parts of that area. Finding your way around the chapter is made simple by the numbering system used throughout. The most important sights are covered in detail in two or more full pages.

Each area has colour-coded thumb tabs.

1 Introduction to the area
For easy reference, the sights in each area are numbered and plotted on an area map. To help the visitor, this map also shows U- and S-Bahn stations, main bus and tram stops and parking areas. The area's key sights are listed by category, such as Museums.

Locator map

A locator map shows where you are in relation to other areas in the city centre.

A suggested route takes in some of the most interesting and attractive streets in the area.

2 Street-by-Street map
This gives a bird's-eye view of interesting and important parts of each sightseeing area. The numbering of the sights ties up with the area map and the fuller description of the entries on the pages that follow.

Stars indicate the features that no visitor should miss.

BERLIN AREA MAP

The coloured areas shown on this map *(see inside front cover)* are the eight main sightseeing areas used in this guide. Each is covered in a full chapter in *Berlin Area by Area (see pp52–205)*. They are highlighted on other maps throughout the book. In *Berlin at a Glance*, for example, they help you locate the top sights. They are also used to help you find the position of three walks *(see pp207–213)*.

Numbers refer to each sight's position on the area map and its place in the chapter.

Practical information provides everything you need to know to visit each sight. Map references pinpoint the sight's location on the *Street Finder* map *(see pp300–323)*.

3 Detailed information
All the important sights in Berlin are described individually. They are listed in order following the numbering on the area map at the start of the section. Practical information includes a map reference, opening hours and telephone numbers. The key to the symbols is on the back flap.

The visitors' checklist gives all the practical information needed to plan your visit.

Story boxes provide information about historical or cultural topics relating to the sights.

4 Berlin's major sights
Historic buildings are dissected to reveal their interiors; museums and galleries have colour-coded floorplans to help you find the most important exhibits.

The list of star sights recommends the places that no visitor should miss.

INTRODUCING BERLIN

FOUR GREAT DAYS IN BERLIN

As Berlin is laid out on an epic scale, these four days are organized so that you can take in as much of the city as possible. They guide you to all the interesting monuments, museums and art collections Berlin has to offer, as well as giving you ideas for family

Sanssouci statue

fun and where to go shopping. There's a lot of things to do each day, but nothing is rigid and as all the places mentioned are cross-referenced, you can look up the details and tailor the day to suit your stamina. The price guides include cost of travel, food and admission fees.

HISTORY AND CULTURE

- See Brandenburger Tor
- Walk along Wilhelmstrasse
- Lunch at a brasserie
- Zeughaus/Museum Island
- Checkpoint Charlie

TWO ADULTS allow at least €89

Morning
Start on the Unter den Linden at the city's most famous landmark, **Brandenburger Tor** *(see p67)*, one of the few remaining historic city gates. Continue east on Unter den Linden and turn right into Wilhelmstrasse, where the **Reich's Chancellery** and **Hitler's office** *(see p66)* were to your left at No. 77 Vossstrasse. Another grim reminder of Germany's Nazi past is round

The Rotunda gallery of the Altes Museum, Museum Island

the corner. **The Topographie des Terrors** *(see p140)*, at the site of the former Gestapo and SS HQ, details crimes at the excavated torture cells. An original section of the Berlin Wall that used to run just behind Neo-Renaissance **Martin-Gropius-Bau** building is nearby *(see p140)*. From here, walk back along Wilhelmstrasse to 39 Unter den Linden for lunch at the brasserie **Dressler** *(see p236)*.

Afternoon
Tour the German history exhibit at the **Zeughaus (Deutsches Historisches Museum)** *(see pp58–9)*. Then head north along the canal to **Museum Island** *(see pp71–85)*, a world-class museum complex, and explore the Altes Museum or the Pergamonmuseum with its famous Pergamon Altar. Detour to Kreuzberg by walking south on Friedrichstrasse to **Checkpoint Charlie**, the former allied border crossing, and visit the museum **Haus am Checkpoint Charlie** *(see p141)*.

Children and animals at the Zoologischer Garten, Berlin

A FAMILY DAY

- Visit the zoo
- A quick self-service lunch
- Hands-on technology fun
- Studio tour at the Filmpark

FAMILY OF FOUR allow at least €197

Morning
Start at the **Zoo Berlin** *(see p150)*, one of Germany's oldest and biggest zoos. Leave the zoo via the Hardenbergplatz exit and walk east towards the Kaiser-Wilhelm-Gedächtniskirche on bustling Breitscheidplatz. Enjoy the jugglers and street artists on the square, then pop in to see the heavenly blue light in the church's modern section. Lunch at the Marché Mövenpick, set up like a street market on the elegant **Kurfürstendamm** *(see pp147–155)*.

Afternoon
Catch a bus on Kurfürstendamm to the **Deutsches Technikmuseum**

(see p144), with its planes, vintage cars, trains, boats and hands-on experiments to try. Bus back to Zoologischer Garten and then take the S-Bahn to Potsdam-Babelsberg to its **Filmpark Babelsberg** for a tour of Germany's biggest studio complex *(see p205)*. You can get a simple dinner in Kreuzberg or Neukölln.

A SHOPPING DAY

- Shop at KaDeWe
- Stroll to Savignyplatz
- Snack on the go
- Friedrichstadtpassagen chic

TWO ADULTS allow at least €43 (cost of lunch and travel only)

Morning
Begin at **Kaufhaus des Westens**, called KaDeWe by Berliners, Europe's second biggest department store *(see p155)*. Then explore the Tauentzienstrasse, a popular, affordable shopping avenue, and continue on Kurfürsten-damm – the further west you go, the more elegant the shops and boutiques. Take detours into even more chic side streets such as **Fasanen-, Meineke-, Uhland-, Bleibtreu-** and **Schlüterstrasse** as you head to **Savignyplatz** *(see p154)* with its many boutiques and eateries.

Afternoon
Take the S-Bahn from Savignyplatz towards the east and exit at Friedrichstrasse. Walk north; once over Unter

Gardens of Sanssouci palace, in Park Sanssouci

The impressive French department store, Galeries Lafayette

den Linden, you'll find the huge complexes of the **Frie-drichstadtpassagen** including the French **Galeries Lafayette** and the über-luxurious **Quartier 206**, alongside top designers Gucci, Versace and Donna Karan. If not yet shopped out, walk back north on Friedrichstrasse and then east on Oranienburger Strasse to **Hackescher Markt**. This is a hip area of mostly alterna-tive-style, young fashion, as well as clubs, bars and pubs.

BERLIN OUTDOORS

- A walk to Grunewald forest
- Boat trip to Pfaueninsel
- The Tiergarten
- Schloss Bellevue

TWO ADULTS allow at least €100

Morning
From the S-Bahn station Grunewald walk south (about 60 minutes) to **Jagdschloss Grunewald** *(see pp212–13)*, a lovely hunting palace with an art gallery,

past fine historic villas. Continue through the forest to **Wannsee lake** *(see p181)* or walk back to the S-Bahn and get off at Wannsee station. Take a bus ride to the ferry for a walk on **Pfaueninsel**, a nature reserve *(see pp208–209)*. Head back to the S-Bahn to Potsdam-Hauptbahnhof to enjoy the lovely **Park Sanssouci** with its beautiful palace – a gem of Prussian Rococo architecture *(see pp192–6)*.

Afternoon
From Potsdam, take the S-Bahn to the green lung of Berlin, the vast **Tiergarten** *(see pp113–35)*. Follow the Strasse des 17. Juni east and climb the **Siegessäule** *(see pp132–33)*, the victory column with a great view of the city. Follow Spreeweg to **Schloss Bellevue** *(see p133)*, the official Presidential seat. To finish, walk southwest to **Neuer See**, a pretty lake in the park. Rent a boat at the Café am Neuen See and return there for supper.

Putting Berlin on the Map

Berlin, the capital of the Federal Republic of
Germany, has a population of approximately 3.4
million and covers 889 sq km (343 sq miles). Situated
in the eastern part of the country, in the middle of the
Brandenburg region, Berlin occupies the flatlands on
the banks of the Havel and Spree rivers, which merge
in the Spandau district. The whole city is
criss-crossed with numerous canals.

EUROPE

KEY

☐ Berlin and Environs

- - Ferry route

–·– National border

✈ Airport

═ Autobahn (motorway)

═ Major road

– Railway

⚓ Ferry terminal

An aerial view of the centre of Berlin, showing the Tiergarten and Unter den Linden (see p14)

Berlin and Environs

Tourist attractions in central Berlin are described on pages 54–165, and there is also a Streetfinder on pages 300–323 to help you find the sights. Places of interest in the outer districts of Berlin and in Potsdam are described on pages 166–205.

Greater Berlin

Berlin in its present form was created in 1920, through an amalgamation of several towns and villages surrounding the historic centre. It now consists of 12 administrative districts, some of which were formerly separate municipalities, such as Spandau. The city is surrounded by recreational areas, including lakes and woodlands. To the southwest lies the city of Potsdam with its splendid palaces, which can be reached easily by public transport.

Hamburg

Oranienburg

REINICKENDORF

Flughafen Tegel

111 E26

SPANDAU

Haselhorst

Siemensstadt

Spandau

Spree

100

Moabit

TIERGARTEN

Nauen

2/5

Olympiastadion

CHARLOTTENBURG

TIERGART

Landwehrkanal

Zoologischer Garten

Charlottenburg

Halensee

TEUFELSBERG

BERLINER

Grunewald

Grunewald

100

WILMERSDORF

Havela

Schmargendorf

SCHÖNEBER

FORST

Friedenau

1

HAVELBERG

GRUNEWALD

Dahlem

STEGLITZ

115 E51

Schlachtensee

ZEHLENDORF

Lichterfelde

Lankwitz

Schlachtensee

Nikolassee

1

Potsdam

Leipzig

Kleinmachnow

Schönow

Teltow

Teltowkanal

Marienfelde

Central Berlin

Central Berlin is divided into eight colour-coded sightseeing areas. The historic core is located along the eastern and northern banks of the Spree river, around the grand boulevard Unter den Linden and on Museum Island. West of the centre is the sprawling green Tiergarten. To the south is Kreuzberg, an area renowned for its alternative lifestyle. Further west is Kurfürstendamm, the centre of former West Berlin. Finally, at the edge of the city centre is the summer residence of the Prussian kings, the Schloss Charlottenburg.

Around Schloss Charlottenburg
The Baroque Charlottenburg Palace, named after Sophie Charlotte (wife of Friedrich III), is one of Berlin's greatest tourist attractions. Its magnificent rooms contain many beautiful objects (see pp156–65).

Kulturforum, Tiergarten
The Kulturforum is a cluster of interesting museums and libraries. It is also the home of the Berlin Philharmonic (see pp112–35).

KEY

▩	Major sight
🚉	Railway station
Ⓤ	U-Bahn
Ⓢ	S-Bahn
🅿	Parking
✝	Church
✡	Synagogue
ℹ	Tourist information

Around Kurfürstendamm
The Kurfürstendamm, or Ku'damm as it is often called, is the main thoroughfare of western Berlin. This area contains numerous shops, restaurants, bars and cinemas (see pp146–55).

Berliner Dom, Museum Island
*On this island are Berlin's Protestant
cathedral, with its Neo-Baroque interior
and massive dome, and
a museum complex
(see pp70–85).*

**Rotes Rathaus,
East of the Centre**
*This monumental
town hall, which
replaces the former
medieval Rathaus,
dates from the 1860s.
It is decorated with
terracotta bas-reliefs,
(see pp86–97).*

**Galeries Lafayette,
Friedrichstrasse**
*This department store
combines history
with ultra-modern
architecture (see
pp54–69).*

Viktoriapark, Kreuzberg
*This park is situated on a hill in the
Kreuzberg district, whose inhabitants include many Turks and
eccentric artists (see pp136–45).*

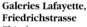

| 0 metres | 500 |
| 0 yards | 500 |

THE HISTORY OF BERLIN

Berlin is one of the younger European capitals. The first written reference to the small fishing settlement of Cölln appeared in the year 1237. Together with the equally insignificant settlement of Berlin on the opposite bank of the Spree river, it was to become first a successful trading city under the control of the Margraves of Brandenburg, then capital of Prussia, and finally, the capital of Germany. Following World War II and the 1949 armistice, Berlin became a central arena for the Cold War. In 1991, after the fall of the Berlin Wall, the city became the capital of the newly-united Federal Republic of Germany.

EARLY SETTLEMENTS

During the first centuries AD the banks of the Spree and Havel rivers were inhabited by various tribes, most notably the Germanic Semnones. By the end of the 6th century the Semnones were competing for land with Slavic tribes, who built forts at what are now the Berlin suburbs of Köpenick (see p175) and Spandau (see p185). Five hundred years later the Slavic tribes were finally defeated following the arrival of the warlike Saxon, Albrecht the Bear of the House of the Ascanians, who became the first *Markgraf* (Margrave, or Count) of Brandenburg. The banks of the Spree river were now resettled with immigrants from areas to the west including the Harz mountains, the Rhine valley and Franconia.

Statue of Albrecht the Bear

BEGINNINGS OF THE MODERN CITY

Berlin's written history began in the early 13th century, when the twin settlements of Berlin and Cölln grew up on opposite banks of the Spree river, around what is now the Nikolaiviertel (see p90). Trading in fish, rye and timber, the towns formed an alliance in 1307, becoming Berlin-Cölln, a deal celebrated by the construction of a joint town hall.

Following the death of the last Ascanian ruler in 1319, Brandenburg became the object of a long and bloody feud between the houses of Luxemburg and Wittelsbach, with devastating effects for the area's inhabitants. In 1411 the desperate townspeople appealed to the Holy Roman Emperor for help, receiving in response Friedrich von Hohenzollern as the town's special protector. Then in 1415 Rome duly rewarded Friedrich by naming him Elector of Brandenburg, a fateful appointment that marked the beginning of the 500-year rule of the House of Hohenzollern.

TIMELINE

1134 Investiture of Albrecht the Bear	**1197** First mention of Spandau	**1237** First written reference to Cölln	**1307** Signing of the treaty between Cölln and Berlin	**1359** Berlin and Cölln join Hanseatic League		**1415** Friedrich von Hohenzollern appointed Elector of Brandenburg
1100	**1150**	**1200**	**1250**	**1300**	**1350**	**1400**
	1209 First documented mention of Köpenick		**c.1260** Berlin is enlarged			
1157 Albrecht the Bear defeats Slavic tribes and is crowned Margrave of Brandenburg			**1244** First written reference to the settlement of Berlin			

Silver denarius of 1369

◁ Adolf von Menzel's symbolic painting *Borussia*, or *Prussia* (1868), at the Ephraim-Palais

Elector in 1486, Berlin-Cölln was formally established as the capital of the March of Brandenburg.

REFORMATION AND THE THIRTY YEARS' WAR

During the first half of the 16th century, the radical religious ideas of Martin Luther (1483–1546) spread quickly throughout the whole of Brandenburg. In 1539 the new Protestantism was adopted by the Elector, Joachim II Hector, and most of the town's aldermen.

For a time the city grew fast, boosted by the arrival of religious refugees from the Netherlands, as well as Italian artists invited by the subsequent elector, Joachim Georg. However, successive epidemics of the bubonic plague occurred in 1576, 1598 and 1600, checking the town's growth. The effect was compounded by the advent of the Thirty Years' War which raged from 1618 to 1648, turning the whole of the Holy Roman Empire into a bloody battlefield. In 1627 the Elector of Brandenburg had fled, relocating his court to the less exposed town of Königsberg. By 1648 the population of Berlin-Cölln had fallen to just 6,000, its population being decimated by famine and disease.

Deposition from the Cross (c.1520), a pane of a Gothic polyptych from the time of the Reformation

THE EARLY HOHENZOLLERNS

In 1432 Berlin and Cölln were formally unified. By 1443 Elector Friedrich II, son of Friedrich I, had begun construction of the town's first castle, the future Stadtschloss *(see p71)*. This was part of his plan to make Berlin-Cölln the capital of Brandenburg and to reduce the powers and privileges of its citizens. Despite fierce opposition from the local population, the castle was built. By 1448 all opposition had been violently crushed, and in 1451 the castle became the Elector's official residence. To symbolize the consolidation of Hohenzollern power, he added an iron chain and padlock around the neck of the city's heraldic bear. By the time Friedrich's nephew Johann Cicero became

BERLIN UNDER THE GREAT ELECTOR

The fortunes of Berlin were turned by the arrival of Friedrich Wilhelm von Hohenzollern, who ascended the Brandenburg throne in 1640. Under the rule of this man, later known as the Great Elector, Berlin experienced a period of an unprecedented growth. The city's population

A falconer on a 16th-century tile

TIMELINE

	1432 Unification of Cölln and Berlin	1486 Elector Johann Cicero makes Berlin his permanent residence	1539 Elector Joachim II converts to the Protestant faith
1415	**1465**	**1515**	**1565**
	1447–8 Berlin rebellion against the Elector		1594 Building of the Spandau citadel completed
	1442 Construction begins on the royal castle in Cölln		

Tankard in the shape of Berlin's heraldic bear (1562)

The former Stadtschloss (Berlin Castle), with Lange Brücke in the foreground, c.1685

rose to 20,000 by 1688 at the end of Friedrich Wilhelm's long reign.

In 1648 work started on the modern fortification of the city. The Lustgarten (see p74) was established opposite the Stadtschloss and the road later to become known as Unter den Linden (see p60) was planted with lime trees. The city's economic power increased following the building of the canal linking the Spree and Oder rivers, which turned Berlin into the hub of all Brandenburg trade.

Berlin began to expand in all directions with the creation of new satellite towns – first Friedrichswerder, then Dorotheenstadt and Friedrichstadt, all between 1650 and 1690. They would all be absorbed into a unified city of Berlin in 1709.

In 1671 several wealthy Jewish families expelled from Vienna settled in Berlin, while following the 1685 Edict of Potsdam, large numbers of French Huguenots flocked to Brandenburg, forced out of their homeland after Louis XIV repealed the Edict of Nantes. Both these events came to play a major role in the future development of the city.

Friedrich II (1740–86)

THE CAPITAL OF PRUSSIA

The successor to the Great Elector, Friedrich III inherited the title in 1688. Thirteen years later he raised Brandenburg's status to that of a kingdom, and was crowned King Friedrich I of Prussia. Ambitious and with a taste for luxury, Friedrich became a powerful patron of the arts. Under his rule Berlin acquired its Academies of Fine Arts and Science. Artists transformed the castle into a Baroque palace. The Zeughaus (see pp58–9) and the summer palace or Schloss in Lietzenburg, later renamed Charlottenburg (see pp160–61), were built at this time.

The next ruler of Prussia, Friedrich Wilhelm I (1713–40), was unlike his father and soon became known as the "Soldier-King". His initiatives were practical: Berlin was further expanded and encircled with a new wall, not for defence but as a measure against the desertion of conscripted citizens. Pariser Platz (see p67), Leipziger Platz (see p126) and Mehringplatz (see p144) were all built at that time, and the population reached 90,000.

The next king was Friedrich II (1740–1786), otherwise known as Frederick the Great or "Alter Fritz" (Old Fritz). An educated man who appreciated art, he oversaw the city's transformation into a sophisticated cultural centre. He was also an aggressive empire builder, sparking the Seven Years' War of 1756–63 with his invasion of Silesia, during which Berlin was briefly occupied by Austrian and Russian troops. The city's development continued, however, and at the time of Friedrich II's death in 1786, its population numbered 150,000.

1618–48 Thirty Years' War	**1688** Establishment of the new town of Friedrichstadt	**1751–2** Friedrich II introduces conscription
1668 Opening of the Spree-Oder canal	**1701** Coronation of Friedrich III as the first king of Prussia	**1756–63** Seven Years' War
1615	**1665**	**1715**	**1765**
1685 Edict of Potsdam allows large numbers of French Huguenot refugees to settle in Berlin	**1709** Unification of Berlin	**1740** Coronation of Frederick the Great
	1696 Opening of the Academy of Fine Arts (Akademie der Künste)	

Silver chalice (1695)

The Baroque Period

Berlin's Baroque Period lasted from the second half of the 17th century to the end of the 18th, and saw the expansion of Berlin-Cölln from a small town, devastated by successive epidemics of bubonic plague and the ravages of the Thirty Years' War, into a rich and cosmopolitan metropolis. Population growth was rapid, aided by the official amalgamation of Berlin-Cölln with the previously independent communities of Dorotheenstadt, Friedrichstadt and Friedrichswerder. New city walls were built, as were many substantial buildings, including the Akademie der Künste, the Charité and Schloss Charlottenburg.

EXTENT OF THE CITY

▉ *1734* ☐ *Today*

Flute Concert
This painting by Adolf von Menzel shows the arts-loving King Friedrich II (1740–86) giving a flute recital for his guests in the music room of the Schloss Sanssouci.

Nikolaikirche

Frederick the Great
The famous French-born portrait painter, Antoine Pesne, created this portrait of Friedrich II of Prussia, heir to the Prussian throne, in 1739.

Rococo Tureen
This elaborate silver tureen, decorated with a gilded lemon, was made in the Berlin workshop of Georg Wilhelm Marggraf und Müller in 1765.

Stadtschloss
(Royal Palace)

Love in the Italian Theatre (1714)
French painter Jean-Antoine Watteau (1684–1721) was a favourite with King Friedrich II, and as a result many of his works can still be seen in Berlin.

Zeughaus (Former Arsenal)
The splendid Baroque Zeughaus was completed in 1730. Used to store weapons until 1875, it will house the Deutsches Historisches Museum. This view of it was painted in 1786 by Carl Traugott Fechhelm.

Rondell (now Mehringplatz)

Oktogon (now Leipziger Platz)

King Friedrich I
This medallion bears the likeness of the first King of Prussia (1688– 1713). The work of sculptor and architect Andreas Schlüter (1660– 1714), it adorns the king's tomb.

Quarré (now Pariser Platz)

BERLIN IN 1740

This map shows the layout of the city's 18th-century fortifications, with various landmark buildings. Contrary to today's convention, this map was drawn with the north pointing down, rather than up.

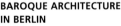

Unter den Linden

BAROQUE ARCHITECTURE IN BERLIN

Many of Berlin's Baroque buildings have been destroyed, but in the city centre some fine examples still exist. Don't miss the Zeughaus *(see pp58–9)*, two fine churches in Gendarmenmarkt – the Deutscher Dom and the Französischer Dom *(see pp64–5)* – the Parochialkirche *(see p97)* and Sophienkirche *(see p104)*. Another Baroque highlight, even though it is largely a reconstruction, is Schloss Charlottenburg *(see pp158–9)* with its delightful park.

Schloss Charlottenburg

Antique scroll depicting the grand boulevard of Unter den Linden, 1821

BEGINNINGS OF THE MODERN ERA

By the time Friedrich Wilhelm II (1786–97) ascended the throne of Prussia, the country's era of absolute rulers was nearing an end. New trends associated with Romanticism were gaining popularity, and there was an explosion of ideas from outstanding personalities such as writers Gotthold Ephraim Lessing (1729–81) and Friedrich and August-Wilhelm von Schlegel.

Throughout Europe, French Emperor Napoleon Bonaparte (1769–1821) was waging war, defeating the Prussians in 1806 at the battles of Jena and Austerlitz. As French troops moved in to occupy Berlin, Friedrich Wilhelm took his court to Königsberg, while Berlin's pride, the horse-drawn chariot (*Quadriga*) crowning the Brandenburg Gate, was dismantled and taken to Paris.

By the end of 1809 the royal court had returned to Berlin, and, having received huge reparations, Napoleon and his troops finally left the city. In 1814 the *Quadriga* was returned to Berlin, and a year later Napoleon was defeated at Waterloo. Granted the mineral-rich lands of the Rhineland and Westphalia at the subsequent Congress of Vienna, Prussia enjoyed rapid industrialization during the next 30 years, particularly in Berlin. By 1837 August

Borsig had opened his locomotive factory in the city, and in 1838 the first train ran on the Berlin–Potsdam railway.

Many outstanding buildings were designed at this time by Karl Friedrich Schinkel *(see p187)*, including the Neue Wache *(see p60)* and the Schauspielhaus, renamed the Konzerthaus *(see p64)*. Berlin University (now Humboldt Universität) was established in 1810 and became a major seat of learning, attracting famous lecturers such as philosophers Georg Hegel (1770–1831) and Arthur Schopenhauer (1788–1860).

In 1844, however, recession hit Europe, leaving a quarter of all Prussians in poverty. Hunger riots rocked the city in April 1847 and by 1848 Berlin saw a people's uprising in which over 250 demonstrators were shot dead by the Prussian army.

BUILDING AN EMPIRE

In 1861 Friedrich Wilhelm IV (1840–1861) was forced by madness to cede the throne to his brother, Wilhelm (1861–1888). Otto von Bismarck was soon appointed Chancellor, with a foreign policy to install Prussia in Austria's place at the head of all German-speaking states. In 1864 Prussia declared war on Denmark, and successfully acquired Schleswig-Holstein.

Portrait of Friedrich Wilhelm IV

TIMELINE

1791 Building of the Brandenburg Gate completed	**1799** Foundation of the Bauakademie	**1810** Berlin University established	**1831** Cholera epidemic breaks out	**1844** Opening of the Berlin zoo (Zoologischer Garten)

1785	1800	1815	1830	1845

Enamelled box, mid-18th century

1806 Beginning of the 2-year French occupation of Berlin

1830 Opening of the Altes Museum

1838 Opening of the Berlin–Potsdam railway line

In 1866, following war with Austria, Prussia established dominance over the North German Confederation, an association of 22 states and free towns. In 1870 Prussia went to war with France, annexing the provinces of Alsace and Lorraine. Bismarck's next move was the proclamation of a German Empire on 18 January 1871, with Berlin as its capital and King Wilhelm I as Kaiser (Emperor). Thanks to the colossal reparations paid by France, and the abolition of trade barriers, Berlin now entered another period of rapid industrial growth, accompanied by a population explosion. By 1877 Berlin's population had grown to one million; by 1905 it was two million.

Poster advertising the Berlin Secession Exhibition of 1900, by Wilhelm Schulz

TRIUMPH AND DISASTER

The late 19th century saw an explosion of scientific and cultural achievement in the city, including the completion of a new sewage system in 1876, dramatically improving public health. By 1879 electric lamps lit the streets

Berlin's original Reichstag (parliament) building, constructed in 1894

and in 1881 the first telephones were installed. A year later the first urban train line, the S-Bahn, was opened. Berlin's cultural and scientific life flourished, headed by such outstanding personalities as writer Theodor Fontane, painter Adolf von Menzel and bacteriologist Robert Koch. In 1898 Max Liebermann *(see p67)* founded the hugely influential Berlin Secessionist movement, with members including Käthe Kollwitz and Max Slevogt.

As the city prospered, political developments in Germany and throughout Europe were moving towards the stalemate of 1914. Initially, the outbreak of World War I had little effect on the life of Berlin, but the subsequent famine, strikes and total German defeat led to the November Revolution in 1918, and the abdication of Kaiser Wilhelm II.

The Berlin Congress of 1878 by Anton von Werner

Capital of the German Empire

On 18 January 1871, Berlin became the capital of the newly-established German Empire, fulfilling the expansionist ambitions of the Prussian Chancellor Otto von Bismarck. Bringing together many previously independent German-speaking regions, the new Empire stretched beyond the borders of present-day Germany, into what are now France, Poland, Russia and Denmark. Massive reparations paid by France after her defeat in the Franco-German war of 1870 stimulated the rapid growth of a fast-industrializing Berlin, accompanied by an explosion of scientific and artistic invention. Standing at just 300,000 in 1850, by 1900 the city's population had reached 1.9 million.

EXTENT OF THE CITY

▨ 1800   ☐ Today

House of Hohenzollern
Mosaics depicting the Hohenzollern rulers decorate the bombed remains of the Kaiser-Wilhelm-Gedächtnis-kirche (see pp152–3), completed in 1895.

The Stadtschloss
The Stadtschloss was the royal residence at the declaration of the Prussian Empire in 1871. Decorating the Rathausbrücke, in the foreground, was the magnificent statue of the Great Elector, now in the courtyard of Schloss Charlottenburg (see pp160–61).

Prussian nobles

Members of Parliament

Riehmers Hofgarten
In the late 19th century a huge number of buildings were erected, from tenement blocks to grand buildings like this one.

Neptunbrunnen
This exuberant fountain (see p92) created by sculptor Reinhold Begas in 1891 was a present to Wilhelm II from the Berlin town council.

Hackescher Markt Station
Formerly called Bahnhof Börse, this is one of Berlin's first S-Bahn stations, built to a design by Johannes Vollmer and opened in 1902.

Vase with Portrait of Wilhelm II
Designed by Alexander Kips and bearing a portrait of Kaiser Wilhelm II, this vase was mass-produced at the Berlin Königliche-Porzellan-Manufaktur. Pieces were often presented to visiting heads of state.

Empress Augusta Victoria

Heir to the throne, Wilhelm

Black mourning clothes for women and black armbands for men were obligatory after the deaths of the two Kaisers, Wilhelm I and Friedrich III, in 1888.

Diplomatic corps

Prussian Chancellor Otto von Bismarck

Kaiser Wilhelm II

OPENING OF THE REICHSTAG
This enormous canvas, painted by Anton von Werner in 1893, portrays Kaiser Wilhelm II giving a speech to the Members of Parliament, nobles and other dignitaries at the official opening of the Reichstag. This important event took place only 11 days after the coronation of the new Kaiser.

Charlotte Berend
The arts flourished in the years before World War I. This 1902 portrait of an actress is by Berlin artist Lovis Corinth.

The burning of one of the thousands of buildings belonging to Jews on *Kristallnacht*, November 1938

THE WEIMAR REPUBLIC

On 9 November 1918 two politicians simultaneously proclaimed the birth of two German Republics. Social democrat Philipp Scheidemann announced the founding of a Democratic Republic, while hours later Karl Liebknecht, founder of the German communist movement, declared the Free Socialist Republic of Germany. Rivalries between the two groups erupted in January 1919 in a week of rioting, crushed by the Freikorps army who also brutally murdered communist leaders Karl Liebknecht and Rosa Luxemburg.

In February 1919 the National Assembly elected Social Democrat Friedrich Ebert President of the German Republic. In 1920 urban reform dramatically increased the size of Berlin, causing the population to swell to 3.8 million. Berlin, like the rest of the country, fell on hard times, with rising unemployment and rampant hyper-inflation.

At the same time, the city became the centre of a lively cultural life. Leading figures in theatre included Max Reinhardt and Bertolt

Brecht, while from the UFA film studio came such classics as *The Cabinet of Dr Cagliari* and *Metropolis*. Jazz was popular, and the Berlin Philharmonic gained worldwide fame. Architecture flourished with Walter Gropius and Bruno Taut, while Berlin scientists Albert Einstein, Carl Bosch and Werner Heisenberg were all awarded the Nobel Prize.

THE THIRD REICH

The world stock-market crash of October 1929 and the ensuing Depression put the fragile German democracy under great pressure, paving the way for extremist politicians. On 30 January 1933 Adolf Hitler was appointed Chancellor. The Reichstag fire in February was used as a pretext to arrest communist and liberal opponents, and by March 1933 Hitler's Nazi (National Socialist German Workers) Party was in control of the Reichstag. Books by "un-German" authors were burned, and works of art deemed as "degenerate" removed from museums.

Inferno (1946), Fritz Koelle

The 1936 Olympic Games in Berlin were meant as a showcase for Aryan supremacy. Although Germany won 33 gold medals, the real hero was the black US athlete Jesse Owens.

The effects of the Nazi regime were felt particularly by Jews and intellectuals, many of whom were forced to emigrate. On the night of 9–10 November

Ein Volk, ein Reich, ein Führer!

Nazi propoganda poster of Hitler, printed in 1938

TIMELINE

1919 Proclamation of the Weimar Republic	**1926** The Funkturm (radio tower) is opened	**1938** Kristallnacht on the night of 9–10 November	**1945** Germany surrenders on 8 May		**1961** Construction of the Berlin Wall on 13 August
	1930 Opening of the Pergamonmuseum		**24 June 1948–12 May 1949** Soviet blockade of Berlin		
1920	**1930**	**1940**	**1950**		**1960**
1928 Premiere of *The Threepenny Opera* by Bertolt Brecht	**1933** Hitler accedes to power	**1942** Wannsee Conference	*Poster depicting the German race*		**1971** "Basic Treaty" allows travel fro. West to East Berl
1920 Urban reform creates Greater Berlin	**1939** Outbreak of World War II on 1 September				

1938, known as *Kristallnacht* (Night of the Broken Glass), thousands of synagogues, cemeteries, Jewish homes and shops were looted and burned.

WORLD WAR II

Hitler's invasion of Poland on 1 September 1939 signalled the start of World War II. For the citizens of Berlin, food shortages were followed in August 1940 by British air raids. By 1941 the goverment policy of the mass deportation of Jews to concentration camps had begun. Other groups targeted included homosexuals, priests and Romany gypsies. In January 1942, following a conference at Wannsee *(see p181)* the systematic extermination of all European Jews began. The unsuccessful attempt to assassinate Hitler in 1944 led to Nazis murdering many members of the German resistance.

After nearly four years of bitter warfare, the tide began to turn against the Germans. In April 1945 more than 1.5 million Soviet soldiers invaded Berlin. On 30 April Hitler committed suicide, and Germany conceded defeat.

BERLIN DIVIDED

The Potsdam Conference of 1945 *(see p199)* divided Berlin into four sectors, occupied respectively by Soviet, US, British and French troops, putting the city at the centre of the Cold War. On 24 June 1948 the Soviet authorities, in their attempt to annex the whole city, introduced a blockade of its Western sectors. The Allies responded with the Berlin Airlift, which thwarted the Soviet plans. On 12 May 1949 the blockade was lifted. The same year saw the birth of the Federal Republic of Germany, with its capital in Bonn, and the German Democratic Republic (GDR), with the

Historic buildings at the Gendarmenmarkt destroyed by British and American bombs, 1945–6

capital in East Berlin. West Berlin remained as a separate enclave. On 17 June 1953 workers' strikes in the GDR and East Berlin turned into an uprising which was bloodily crushed. In 1961, the GDR authorities surrounded West Berlin with a wall, and shot at any refugees attempting to cross it.

REUNIFICATION

The political changes which occurred all over Eastern Europe in 1989 led to the fall of the Berlin Wall. On 3 October 1990, Germany was officially reunified and Berlin once again became the capital. The government moved here in 1991.

Today, Berlin's cutting-edge culture attracts visitors from all over the world, bolstered by the images of a festive, happy Berlin celebrating the World Cup at the Brandenburg Gate in 2006.

Celebrations as the Berlin Wall falls, 9 November 1989

1987 Celebration of Berlin's 750th anniversary

1990 Official reunification of Germany, 3 October

1991 Berlin becomes the German capital, 20 June

1994 Allies leave Berlin

2008 Opening of new embassy on Pariser marks complete restoration of the square

1980	1990	2000	2010	2020

Trabant – the most popular car in the GDR

1989 Fall of the Berlin Wall, 9 November

1999 The Federal German Parliament assembles at the rebuilt Reichstag in April

2009 Celebrated the 20th anniversary of the fall of the Berlin Wall

2006 Berlin hosted the World Cup

2004 Re-opening of the Olympiastadion Berlin

BERLIN AT A GLANCE

More than 150 places of interest are described in the *Area by Area* section of this book. These include a range of sights from historic monuments, such as the Nikolaikirche *(see p90)*, to modern landmarks like the ambitious showcase architecture of the new Potsdamer Platz district *(see p126);* from the peace of the Botanical Garden *(see p177)* to the noisier charms of Berlin's long-established zoo *(see p150)*. To help you make the most of your stay, the following 16 pages provide a time-saving guide to the very best that Berlin has to offer. Museums and galleries, historic buildings, parks and gardens, modern architecture, the legacy of the divided city and famous Berliners all feature in this section. Below is a top ten selection of attractions that no visitor should miss.

BERLIN'S TOP TEN ATTRACTIONS

Pergamonmuseum
See pp80–83.

Schloss Charlottenburg
See pp160–61.

Kungstgewerbe-museum
See pp118–21.

Gemäldegalerie
See pp122–5.

Nikolaiviertel
See pp88–9.

Zoo Berlin
See p150.

Fernsehturm
See p93.

Brandenburger Tor
See p67.

Reichstag
See p134.

Kaiser-Wilhelm-Gedächt-nis-Kirche See pp152–3.

◁ Interior of the Reichstag *(see p134)*, with its new dome designed by Sir Norman Foster

Berlin's Best: Museums and Galleries

Ancient Greek vase

Berlin boasts some of the finest museum collections in the world. Since 1990 most of the collections previously split between East and West Berlin have been brought together in new venues. One example is the Gemäldegalerie collection, a magnificent collection of Old Master paintings. Berlin's major museum complexes are located on Museum Island, around Schloss Charlottenburg, at the Kulturforum and at Dahlem.

Kunstgewerbemuseum
The arts and crafts collection at the Kunstgewerbemuseum (see pp118–21) is among the most interesting in Europe. One of its many treasures is this 17th-century gold elephant-shaped vessel.

Around Schloss Charlottenburg

Tiergarten

Around Kurfürstendamm

Gemäldegalerie
This world-famous collection illustrates the history of European painting from the 13th to the 18th centuries. Originally part of a triptych, The Adoration of the Magi (1470) was painted by Hugo van der Goes (see pp122–5).

Museen Dahlem
This huge complex houses several museums devoted to ethnography and non-European art (see p178).

| 0 metres | 750 |
| 0 yards | 750 |

Hamburger Bahnhof
Featuring artists such as Joseph Beuys and Andy Warhol, as well as the renowned Flick Collection, this museum of modern art is housed in the former Hamburger railway station (see pp110–11).

Deutsches Historisches Museum
The Baroque Zeughaus contains the Museum of German History. Everyday objects as well as works of art are used to illustrate historical events (see pp58–9).

North of the Centre

East of the Centre

Around Unter den Linden

Museum Island

Pergamonmuseum
This museum owes its name to the reconstructed Pergamon Zeus altar, which stands in its main hall (see pp80–83).

Altes Museum
The ground floor of Karl Friedrich Schinkel's Neo-Classical building has been used since 1998 to exhibit a collection of Greek and Roman antiquities (see p75).

Kreuzberg

Deutsches Technikmuseum
The development of a range of industrial technologies, from locomotive-building to brewing, is illustrated in this entertaining museum (see pp144–5).

Jüdisches Museum
Berlin's Jewish museum was designed by Daniel Libeskind, an American architect of Jewish descent. The form of the building is based on the Star of David (see p141).

Exploring Berlin's Museums

Majolica plate,
Kunstgewerbe-
museum

Despite being damaged during World War II, Berlin's numerous museums are still among the finest, and the most heavily subsidized, in the world. Many collections were split up when the city was partitioned in 1946, and although the process of bringing them together again is almost complete, a few collections are still scattered around different sites, and many of the older museums are being refurbished.

Picasso's *Head of the Faun* (1937)
in the Museum Berggruen

ANCIENT ART

The art of ancient Egypt is shown at the **Ägyptisches Museum** (Egyptian Museum). The jewel of this museum, which is currently housed in the **Neues Museum**, is the bust of Queen Nefertiti. The 19th century **Altes Museum** contains a large Greek and Roman antiquities collection, as does the **Pergamonmuseum**, where visitors can see several reconstructed architectural wonders, including the Pergamon Zeus altar and the Market Gate from Miletus. The museum also holds an impressive collection of Middle Eastern art, including a reconstruction of the Babylonian Ishtar Gate.

Bust of Nefertiti,
Ägyptisches
Museum

German and Italian sculpture is housed in the **Bodemuseum**, while the **Alte Nationalgalerie** (Old National Gallery) displays 18th- and 19th-century art, including paintings by the German Romantics, amongst which are famous landscapes by Caspar David Friedrich.

A collection of sculpture from the late-16th to the mid-19th centuries can be seen in the **Schinkel-Museum**. The **Neue Nationalgalerie** (New National Gallery) is filled with late 19th- and early 20th-century paintings and sculpture. Art Nouveau and Art Deco works are featured at the **Bröhan-Museum**, while works by modern greats, such as Pablo Picasso, Paul Klee

and Georges Braque, are on show at the **Museum Berggruen** (Berggruen Museum).

The **Brücke-Museum** displays the works of German Expressionists, and contemporary art is exhibited in the **Hamburger Bahnhof**.

Arts and crafts, from the Middle Ages to the present, are displayed at the **Kunstgewerbemuseum** (Museum of Applied Arts). The **Bauhaus-Archiv** displays applied arts from the influential inter-war Bauhaus movement.

Two recent additions are the **Newton-Sammlung**, which contains the life's work of 20th-century photographer Helmut Newton, while the reopened **Berlinische Galerie** shows the city's collection of modern art and architecture.

FINE ART AND DESIGN

Berlin's largest collection of 13th- to 18th-century European painting is displayed in the **Gemäldegalerie** (Picture Gallery). Here are works by old masters including Dürer, Rembrandt, Titian, Botticelli and Caravaggio. In the same museum complex is the **Kupferstichkabinett**, with drawings and prints from the Middle Ages to the present.

Old masters can also be seen in the **Jagdschloss Grunewald**, a Renaissance palace home to German and Dutch paintings from the 14th to 19th centuries. A large collection of predominantly 17th-century paintings is housed in the **Bildergalerie** (Gallery of Paintings) in Potsdam.

Étienne Chevalier with St Stephen by Jean Fouquet, Gemäldegalerie

NON-EUROPEAN ART

Those interested in Asian art should visit the **Museen Dahlem**. This complex houses three large collections: the Museum für Asiatische Kunst (Museum of Asian Art), the Ethnologisches Museum (Museum of Ethnography), which explores the heritage of non-European nations, and the Museum Europäischer Kulturen (Museum for European Cultures). The **Museum für Islamische Kunst** (Museum of Islamic Art) is located in the same building as the Pergamonmuseum.

Totem pole, Ethnologisches Museum

HISTORY

The collection of the **Deutsches Historisches Museum** (Museum of German History) traces German history from the Middle Ages to the present. The **Hugenotten-museum** (Huguenot Museum), located in the tower of the Französischer Dom, charts the history of the city's Huguenots.

The **Centrum Judaicum** (Jewish Centre) in the Neue Synagogue (New Synagogue), and the **Jüdisches Museum** (Jewish Museum), in a new building by Daniel Libeskind, are devoted to Jewish history and cultural heritage.

Berlin has several museums associated with World War II. The **Topographie des Terrors** (Topography of Terror) exhibition is displayed at the site of the former Gestapo and SS headquarters. A deeply shocking collection of documents concerning the Holocaust is kept at the **Haus der Wannsee-Konferenz**. The tools of terror used on the citizens of the German Democratic Republic can be seen at the **Stasi-Museum**, while the **Haus am Checkpoint Charlie** (House at Checkpoint Charlie) museum tells the stories of those who crossed the Berlin Wall. The **Alliiertenmuseum** focuses on life during the Cold War.

TECHNOLOGY AND NATURAL HISTORY

The **Museum für Natur-kunde** (Museum of Natural History) contains the world's biggest dinosaur skeleton. Also popular with visitors is the **Deutsches Technik-museum** (German Technology Museum), which is situated in a large site around a former railway station. German movie history (including props, clips and original costumes worn by divas such as Marlene Dietrich) is presented at the **Filmmuseum Berlin**. Those interested in technology should also visit the **Museum für Kommunikation** (Museum of Communications).

SPECIALIST SUBJECTS

Berlin is not short of specialist museums. There are museums devoted to laundry, sugar and even hemp. Lovers of theatre and literature can visit the one-time home of Bertolt Brecht (1898–1956), now the **Brecht-Weigel Gedenkstätte** (Brecht-Weigel Memorial). Worth a visit to see the magnificent Wurlitzer organ alone is the **Musikinstrumenten-Museum** (Musical Instruments Museum). The outdoor **Domäne Dahlem** (Dahlem Farm Museum) shows 300 years of local farm life and exhibits old-fashioned tools.

FINDING THE MUSEUMS

A wide array of exhibits in the Musikinstrumenten-Museum

Berlin's Best: Historic Architecture

Berlin is a relatively new city. It expanded
slowly until the first half of the 19th century, and
then grew with increasing rapidity from around
1850 onwards. Although many of the city's finest
architectural treasures were destroyed by World
War II bombing, it is still possible to discover
many interesting historic buildings
(for more information, *see pp38–9*). In nearby
Potsdam *(see pp190–205)* you can visit the
splendid Schloss Sanssouci. Set in magnificent
parkland, the palace was built for Friedrich II
(1740–1786) and extended by subsequent rulers.

Schloss Charlottenburg
*The construction of this
Baroque royal palace at
Charlottenburg was begun in
1695. Subsequent extension
works took place throughout the
18th century (see pp160–61).*

*Around Schloss
Charlottenburg*

Tiergarten

*Around
Kurfürstendamm*

Schloss Bellevue
*This Rococo palace
by Philipp Daniel
Boumann is now the
official residence of the
President of the Federal
Republic of Germany.*

The Reichstag
*This massive Neo-
Renaissance building
was designed in 1884
by Paul Wallot. Its
elegant new dome is
the work of British
architect Norman
Foster (see p134).*

Schloss Sanssouci
*This small palace was the favourite
residence of Friedrich II.*

Neues Palais
*The Neues Palais combines elements of
Baroque and Neo-Classical style.*

**POTSDAM
PALACES**

The summer palace
of Schloss Sanssouci
gives its name to
Potsdam's Park
Sanssouci, a royal
complex with
highlights including
the grand 18th-
century Neues Palais
and the small but
charming Schloss
Charlottenhof.

| 0 metres | 750 |
| 0 yards | 750 |

Zeughaus
This Baroque arsenal houses the Deutsches Historisches Museum (see pp58–9). Its courtyard contains masks of dying warriors by sculptor Andreas Schlüter (1660–1714).

Brandenburger Tor
This Neo-Classical gate stands at the end of Unter den Linden. Crowned by a Quadriga (chariot) driven by the Goddess of Victory, it is the symbol of Berlin (see p67).

Marienkirche
This Gothic church, founded in the 13th century, contains a striking 15th-century mural. It is one of the city's oldest buildings (see pp94–5).

North of the Centre

East of the Centre

Around Unter den Linden

Museum Island

Rotes Rathaus
Berlin's main Town Hall is named "red" after the colour of its brick exterior, not the political persuasion of the Mayor (see p90).

Kreuzberg

Berliner Dom
This enormous cathedral, built between 1894 and 1905, is an example of the Neo-Renaissance style in Berlin (see pp76–7).

Konzerthaus
Built in 1820 to replace a theatre destroyed by fire, this beautiful building on the Gendarmenmarkt was designed by Karl Friedrich Schinkel (see pp64–5).

Exploring Berlin's Historic Architecture

Until the industrial revolution of the late 19th century, Berlin was little more than a small town surrounded by villages. As a result, the city's oldest buildings are concentrated in the central core around Unter den Linden and along the Spree river, an area which suffered heavy damage during World War II. Older country residences, however, as well as some important more recent buildings, can be seen in former villages such as Wedding and Charlottenburg, which now form part of Greater Berlin.

14th-century Gothic doorway of the Nikolaikirche in the Nikolaiviertel

MIDDLE AGES AND RENAISSANCE

The **Nikolaikirche** is the oldest building in central Berlin. The base of its massive front tower is Romanesque and dates back to about 1230, although the church itself is Gothic and was built between 1380 and 1450. The second Gothic church in the city centre is the **Marienkirche**. Nearby are the ruins of a **Franciscan friary**, and the **Heiliggeistkapelle**. Many medieval churches outside the city centre have survived the war. Among the most beautiful is the late-Gothic **Nikolaikirche** in Spandau, dating

from the early 15th century. A further ten village churches, most dating from the 13th century, can be found hidden among high-rise apartment buildings. **St Annen-Kirche** in Dahlem, however, still enjoys an almost rural setting.

The few surviving secular structures include fragments of the **city walls** in the city centre, and the **Julius-turm** in Spandau, a huge, early 13th-century tower which stands in the grounds of the Spandau Citadel. Berlin's only surviving Renaissance buildings are the **Ribbeckhaus** with its four picturesque gables, the **Jagdschloss-Grunewald**, a modest hunting lodge designed by Casper Theyss in 1542, and the **Spandau Citadel** (or fortress), a well-preserved example of Italian-style military defence architecture. Finished in 1592, the construction of the Citadel was begun in 1560 by Christoph Römer using plans by Italian architect Francesco Chiaramella da Gandino. It was brought to completion by Rochus Guerrini Graf zu Lynar (the Count of Lynar).

Detail of the Zeughaus

BAROQUE EXPANSION

The Thirty Years' War (1618–48) put a temporary stop to the town's development, and it was not until the Peace of 1648 that new building work in the Baroque style began. One of the first of the city's Baroque buildings is the late 17th-century **Schloss Köpenick**. More buildings followed, many of which survive today. They include the **Parochialkirche**, the **Deutscher Dom** and the **Französischer Dom**, as well as the magnificent **Zeughaus**, built between 1695 and 1730. During this period Andreas Schlüter (1664–1714) designed the now-demolished Stadtschloss (Royal Palace), while Johann Arnold Nering (1659–95) designed **Schloss Charlottenburg**. Other surviving Baroque palaces include **Palais Podewils** and **Schloss Niederschönhausen**. One of the few buildings dating from the reign of Friedrich Wilhelm I (1713–40) is the **Kollegienhaus** at Lindenstrasse No. 14, designed by Philipp Gerlach and built in 1733. During the reign of Friedrich II (1740–86), many buildings were erected in the late Baroque and Rococo styles. These include **Schloss Sanssouci** in Potsdam and the **Alte Bibliothek** building on Unter den Linden, which completed the Forum Friedericianum project, now better known as Bebelplatz (*see pp56–7*).

NEO-CLASSICISM AND ROMANTICISM

The Neo-Classical architecture of the late-18th and early-19th centuries has given Berlin much of its basic form. One dominant figure of this period was Carl Gotthard Langhans (1732–1808), creator of the **Brandenburg Gate** and of **Schloss Bellevue**. Even more influential, however, was Karl

Renaissance-style defence, the Citadel building at Spandau

Friedrich Schinkel *(see p187)*. His work includes some of Berlin's most important public buildings, including the **Neue Wache**, the **Altes Museum** and the **Konzerthaus**. Many of Schinkel's residential commissions are also still standing, with some such as **Schloss Klein Glienicke** and **Schloss Tegel** open to the public. Schinkel's Neo-Gothic work includes **Schloss Babelsberg** and the **Friedrichswerdersche Kirche**.

Elegant Neo-Classicism at Karl Friedrich Schinkel's Schloss Klein Glienicke

INDUSTRIALIZATION AND THE MODERN AGE

The second half of the 19th century was a time of rapid development for Berlin. After Schinkel's death, his work was continued by his students, Ludwig Persius (1803–45) and Friedrich August Stüler (1800–65). Stüler designed the Neo-Classical **Alte Nationalgalerie** between 1866 and 1876. Some splendid Neo-Romanesque and Neo-Gothic churches and several notable public buildings in various styles were also produced at this time. The spirit of the Italian Neo-Renaissance is seen in the **Rotes Rathaus** designed by Hermann Friedrich Waesemann, and in the **Martin-Gropius-Bau**, by Martin Gropius in 1877. Late Neo-Renaissance features are used in Paul Wallot's **Reichstag** building and in Ernst von

Decorative frieze on the Martin-Gropius-Bau

Ihne's **Statsbibliothek** building. Julius Raschdorff's **Berliner Dom** shows Neo-Baroque influences. Much of the religious architecture of the period continued in the Neo-Gothic style, while Franz Schwechten designed the **Kaiser-Wilhelm-Gedächtnis-Kirche** in the Neo-Romanesque style. Many structures of this period are built in the modernist style inspired by the industrial revolution, the textbook example being the huge power station, **AEG-Turbinenhalle**, designed by Peter Behrens in the 1890s.

BETWEEN THE TWO WORLD WARS

The greatest architectural achievements of this period include a number of splendid housing estates, such as the **Hufeisensiedlung** designed by Bruno Taut and Martin Wagner in 1924, and **Onkel-Toms-Hütte** in Zehlendorf. An interesting example of the Expressionist style is Erich Mendelsohn's **Einsteinturm** in Potsdam. Art Deco is represented by Hans Poelzig's **Haus des Rundfunks**, the country's first Broadcasting House. Hitler's rise to power in the 1930s marked a return to the classical forms which dominated German architecture of the Fascist period. Representatives of this period include the **Tempelhof Airport** Terminal building and the **Olympia-Stadion**, built for the 1936 Olympic Games.

20th-century Neo-Renaissance detail of the massive Berliner Dom

Reminders of the Divided City

In 1945, as part of the post-war peace, Berlin was divided into four zones of occupation: Soviet, American, British and French. Hostilities erupted in June 1948, when the Soviets blockaded West Berlin in an attempt to bring the area under their control. The ensuing year-long standoff marked the start of the Cold War. By the 1950s, economic problems in the East had led to bloodily-suppressed riots and a mass exodus to the West. In 1961 the East German government constructed the infamous Berlin Wall *(die Mauer)* to contain its citizens. Between this time and reunification at the end of 1989, more than 180 people were shot trying to cross the Wall.

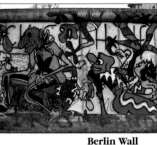

Berlin Wall
Protected to the east by land mines, the Wall, known by the East German authorities as the "Anti-Fascist Protection Wall", surrounded West Berlin and was 155 km (95 miles) long (see p168).

Memorial to Soviet Soldiers
Part of West Berlin, the area around this monument to Red Army troops killed in the 1945 Battle of Berlin was closed for many years due to attacks on its Soviet guards (see p135).

Around Schloss Charlottenburg

Tiergarten

Around Kurfürstendamm

0 km _____ 1

0 miles _____ 0.5

KEY

━ Berlin Wall

BERLIN BEFORE REUNIFICATION

The Wall cut the city in half, severing its main transport arteries, the S-Bahn and U-Bahn lines. West Berliners were excluded from the centre of the city. Running along the Wall was a no-man's-land.

KEY

━ Berlin Wall

━ Sector boundaries

✈ Airport

French Sector

British Sector

Soviet Sector

American Sector

Tränenpalast (Palace of Tears)

Until 1989 the Tränenpalast, next to the final S-Bahn station in East Berlin, was a border checkpoint for S-Bahn passengers heading west.

Checkpoint Charlie

This border crossing between the American and Soviet sectors was used by foreign citizens and diplomats. It was the location of many dramatic events during the years of the Cold War.

North of the Centre

East of the Centre

Around Unter den Linden

Museum Island

East Side Gallery

The longest remaining section of the Berlin Wall became an open-air gallery in 1990, covered with an eclectic mixture of paintings by 118 artists (see p173).

Kreuzberg

Luftbrücke

This striking memorial commemorates those who died during the Berlin Airlift of 1948–9. Allied planes delivered 2.3 million tons of supplies to West Berlin in the face of the year-long Soviet blockade (see p145).

Haus am Checkpoint Charlie

This museum holds photos and other Wall memorabilia, including a selection of escape vehicles (see p140).

Berlin's Best: Modern Architecture

Following Berlin's devastation in World War II, intense post-war reconstruction turned the city into a giant building site. With the help of architects from several countries the city acquired many modern structures and estates, ranked among the best in the world. The city's reunification in 1990 and the reinstatement of Berlin as the main seat of government gave rise to a second wave of building activity, carried out on a scale unprecedented in Europe. The architectural elite are participating in the design of the new Berlin, and the sites in the city centre that stood empty until 1990 are being filled with buildings at an incredible rate.

Bauhaus-Archiv
This cubist structure was completed in 1978 to house the Bauhaus museum. It was designed much earlier by Walter Gropius (1883–1969), director of the Bauhaus art school from 1919 to 1928.

Around Schloss Charlottenburg

Tiergarten

Around Kurfürstendamm

Kant-Dreieck
This building, with its pure forms and the eccentric sail-like structure mounted on the roof, is the work of Josef Paul Kleihues.

Nordische Botschaften
Built between 1997 and 1999, the five interconnected embassies of the Scandinavian countries are an example of daring architectural design. The building's green shutters adjust to the intensity and direction of available sunlight.

Kammermusiksaal
Both the Berliner Philharmonie building
(1961) and the adjacent Kammermusiksaal, or chamber music hall (1987), were
designed by Hans Scharoun. The latter
was built posthumously by Edgar
Wisniewski, Scharoun's pupil.

Galeries Lafayette
This elegant
department store in
Friedrichstrasse,
designed by Jean
Nouvel, brings
Parisian chic to the
heart of Berlin.

*North of
the Centre*

East of the Centre

Quartier Schützenstrasse
This part of the city features
the work of Italian architect
Aldo Rossi. With high-rise
blocks and bold colour
schemes, the area shows
modernity and classical
forms standing side by side.

*Around Unter
den Linden*

*Museum
Island*

Kreuzberg

0 metres	750
0 yards	750

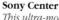

Gemäldegalerie
The Gemäldegalerie, designed by
the Hilmer and Sattler Partnership,
opened in June 1998. The main
hall is particularly elegant.

Sony Center
This ultra-modern steel-and-glass building was
designed by German-American architect Helmut
Jahn. It houses offices, entertainment venues, the
Kaisersaal and Sony's European headquarters.

Exploring Berlin's Modern Architecture

Around the world architects are forever designing buildings with innovative and interesting structures, but in Berlin this creative process is happening on an unprecedented scale. The city is a vast melting pot of trends and styles, where the world's greatest architects scramble for commissions and where the buildings compete with each other in the originality of their form and in their use of the latest technology.

Haus der Kulturen der Welt in the Tiergarten

FROM 1945 TO 1970

World War II exacted a heavy price from Berlin. The centre was reduced to rubble and the partitioning of the city made it impossible to carry out any co-ordinated reconstruction. In 1952, East Berlin decided to develop **Karl-Marx-Allee** in the Socialist-Realist style. In reply, West Berlin employed the world's greatest architects to create the **Hansaviertel** estate. Le Corbusier built one of his *unités d'habitation*, while the American architect, Hugh A Stubbins, built the Kongress-halle (now the **Haus der Kulturen der Welt**). The West's response to the cultural venues inherited by the East Berliners, including the opera, the library and the museums, was the **Kulturforum** complex. The complex included such magnificent buildings as the **Philharmonie**, designed by Hans Scharoun, and the **Neue Nationalgalerie**, designed by Mies van der Rohe. While West Berlin acquired its huge "trade temple"– the **Europa-Center**, constructed in 1965, East Berlin boasted its **Fernsehturm** (television tower), built in 1969.

FROM 1970 TO 1990

The continuing rivalry, as each part of the city tried to outdo the other, resulted in the construction of East Berlin's now demolished **Palast der Republic** in 1976. The West replied with the ultramodern **Internationales Congress Centrum** in 1979. The Kulturforum complex was further extended with designs by Scharoun, including the **Kammermusik-saal** and the **Staatsbibliothek** (library). The impressive **Bauhaus-Archiv** was developed from a design by Walter Gropius. In 1987 Berlin celebrated its 750th anniversary, which in the East saw the completion of the huge **Nikolaiviertel** development, with its pre-war allusions. In the West, the IBA's 1987 scheme gave the town its enormous post-modernist housing estates in Kreuzberg and also in the **Tegel** area.

POST-REUNIFICATION ARCHITECTURE

The government district was constructed within the bend of the Spree river. Its designers include Charlotte Frank and Axel Schultes. The **Reichstag** building has been famously remodelled by Norman Foster. **Pariser Platz** has been filled with designs by Günther Behnisch, Frank O Gehry, Josef Paul Kleihues and others. The magnificent **Friedrichstadtpassagen** complex became the scene of rivalry between Jean Nouvel and Oswald M Ungers. Many interesting office buildings have sprung up around town, including **Ludwig-Erhard-Haus** by Nicholas Grimshaw and the nearby **Kant-Dreieck** by Josef Paul Kleihues. Housing has also been transformed, with perhaps the most original example being Aldo Rossi's **Quartier Schützen-strasse**. The city has also acquired some fine museums, including the **Gemäldegalerie** designed by the Hilmer and Sattler Partnership, and the Deconstructivist style **Jüdisches Museum**, designed by Daniel Libeskind.

Neue Nationalgalerie at Kulturforum designed by Mies van der Rohe

Potsdamer Platz

Between 1993 and 1998, a financial, business and entertainment district was erected on the once vast and empty wasteland around Potsdamer Platz. It boasts splendid constructions designed by Renzo Piano, Arata Isozaki and Helmut Jahn. As well as office blocks, the area has many public buildings, including cinemas and a theatre, as well as a huge shopping centre – the Arkaden, plus luxury hotels, restaurants and several bars.

The Beisheim Center is a mix of exclusive apartments and international hotels.

The Sony Center

POTSDAMER PLATZ

POTSDAMER STRASSE

BEN–GURION–STRASSE

The Sony Tower
designed by Helmut Jahn, is the most modern building in Potsdamer Platz and is curved on one side and flat on the other.

This office building, which is the tallest in Potsdamer Platz, was designed by the architects Kollhoff & Timmermann Partnership.

Arkaden, opened in autumn 1998, immediately became one of the city's favourite shopping centres.

0 metres	100
0 yards	100

The Debis House
designed by Italian architect Renzo Piano.

LANDWEHRKANAL

Berlin's Best: Parks and Gardens

Berlin is undoubtedly one of Europe's greenest
capital cities, with the sprawling Tiergarten
at its centre. However, most of Berlin's districts
have their own smaller parks and gardens, too,
some of them with children's play areas and
nature trails. To the west of the city is the vast
Grunewald, a beautiful area of forest which
contains mountain bike trails and scenic paths
for walkers and cyclists. In summer, numerous
lakes, rivers and canals provide excellent
facilities for water sports.

Zoologischer Garten
*Popular with children, Berlin's
zoo has some 14,000 animals,
representing 1,400 different
species. It is the oldest zoo in
Germany (see p150).*

**Schloss
Charlottenburg**
*The well-maintained
grounds of this royal
palace were designed
in the French Baroque
style (see pp160–61).*

*Around Schloss
Charlottenburg*

*Around
Kurfürstendamm*

**Botanischer
Garten**
*Established from
1899 to 1910 in
Dahlem, this
botanical garden is
one of the biggest in
the world (see p177).*

Park Babelsberg
*This vast landscaped park was
designed by Peter Joseph Lenné,
and now lies within the Potsdam
city limits. It surrounds the
picturesque Schloss Babelsberg
(see pp210–11).*

Tiergarten
Once a hunting reserve, this was converted into a park after 1818 by landscape designer Peter Joseph Lenné (see p132).

Monbijoupark
The park once surrounded Monbijou Palace, which was destroyed during World War II (see p103).

North of the Centre

East of the Centre

Around Unter den Linden

Museum Island

Tiergarten

Kreuzberg

Tierpark Friedrichsfelde
In 1954 the park at Schloss Friedrichsfelde was converted into the East Berlin Zoological Garden (see p174).

Britzer Garten
The landscaped park with its beautiful lime-tree avenue, surrounds the early 18th-century Schloss Britz (see p176).

Viktoriapark
This large park winds around a hill with good views of Kreuzberg. At its peak stands a memorial to the wars of liberation fought against Napoleon (see p145).

0 metres	1000
0 yards	1000

BERLIN THROUGH THE YEAR

Like all major European capitals, Berlin offers a wide range of activities throughout the year. The best seasons for cultural and sporting events are spring and autumn, when the city hosts many spectacular fairs and exhibitions. During summer the city's population shrinks, as many locals head for their holiday destinations. But the weather is often pleasant, and rarely

Karneval der Kulturen

very hot, so this is a good time for serious sightseeing. In winter, although it can get quite cold, it is possible to spend time visiting museums or simply walking around the city. The streets teem with shoppers during the run up to Christmas. A more detailed programme of events can be obtained from tourist information offices *(see p278)* or on the Internet at www.visitberlin.de.

The Karneval der Kulturen in the streets of Kreuzberg

SPRING

In springtime, Berlin holds many interesting fairs and cultural events in its squares, parks and gardens, allowing the visitor to appreciate fully the beauty of the city as the trees and flowers burst into life. With the arrival of the warmer weather, another natural resource springs to life as cruise and rowing boats start operating on the Spree river and the city's canals.

MARCH

ITB-Internationale Tourismus-Börse *(mid-Mar)*. The biggest European fair devoted to tourism where representatives from all parts of the world try to attract visitors to their countries.
Rassehunde-Zuchtschau *(weekend mid-Mar)* is a huge show for pedigree dogs and pedigree dog lovers.

Berlin Motorrade Tage *(end Mar)*. Motorcyclists from all over Germany converge on Berlin for this specialist event.

APRIL

Festtage *(Apr)*. A series of popular concerts and operas performed by world-class musicians in the Philharmonie and at the Staatsoper.
Easter *(exact date varies)*. Huge markets open around the Kaiser-Wilhelm-Gedächtnis-kirche, Alexanderplatz and other central locations.
Britzer Baumblüte *(all of Apr)* is a month-long spring festival organized in Britz, a suburb in the south of the city famous for its windmills.
Neuköllner Maientage *(all of Apr)* Hasenheide. Traditional springtime festival celebrating the new season.
Köpenicker Winzerfest *(end of Apr)*. Sample top wines and gourmet food in the charming old town square of Köpenick, a district in southeast Berlin.

MAY

Theatertreffen Berlin *(May)*. This important Berlin theatre festival has been running since 1963, and provides a platform for theatre productions from German-speaking regions worldwide.
Internationales Tango Festival Berlin *(mid-May)* brings a bit of South American culture to various venues.
Karneval der Kulturen *(late May)*. For three days, the streets of Kreuzberg district are brought to life by singing and dancing in this colourful display celebrating multicultural Berlin.
Berliner Frauenlauf *(late May)* is a popular 5 km fun-run through Tiergarten – but it is reserved for women only.
Big 25 Berlin *(early May)*, formerly known as the Franzosenlauf (French run), starts at the Olympiastadion and winds through the city. All runners can participate.

Street recitation of poetry during the Theatertreffen Berlin in May

AVERAGE DAILY HOURS OF SUNSHINE

Hours

Sunshine Chart
In Berlin, the highest number of sunny days occurs in May, but June, July and August also enjoy good weather. The cloudiest month is December, followed by January and November.

SUMMER

Summertime in Berlin is marked by many open-air events. There are concerts of classical music and opera performances, jazz festivals and sports events, an annual air show, a series of open-air concerts and festivals for the young. It is also possible to take advantage of the good weather by taking a walk or bicycle ride in the Grunewald, or swimming in the lakes of Wannsee or Müggelsee.

An outdoor artist at work in the Potsdamer Platz

JUNE

Internationales Stadionfest (ISTAF) *(first week in Jun)*. International track and field event in the Olympiastadion.
Deutsch-Französisches Volksfest *(early Jun–mid-Jul)*. German-French folk festival near Kurt-Schumacher-Damm.
Jazz Across the Border *(Jun)*. This jazz festival is organized by the Haus der Kulturen der Welt and other venues.
Luft- und Raumfahrtausstellung Berlin-Brandenburg *(Jun)*. This festival and air show of civil, military, and space craft fills the skies above Schönefeld airport.

Christopher Street Day *(end Jun)* features a gay and lesbian parade with revellers in extravagant outfits, held around Ku'damm. At night, the party continues in the city's many gay clubs and kniepen.
Berliner Theatermarkt an der Deutschen Oper *(end Jun)* is a programme of open days at the opera.

JULY

Open-Air-Classic *(mid-Jul)*. A series of operas in Waldbühne with a gala finale in Gendarmenmarkt.
Konzertsommer im Englischen Garten *(early Jul–end Aug)* Open-air concerts.
Berliner Gauklerfest *(late Jul–early Aug)*. Stalls on Unter den Linden sell speciality foods, while crowds are entertained by acrobats and musicians.

AUGUST

Deutsch-Amerikanisches Volksfest *(30 Jul–22 Aug)*. A programme of entertainment

Ku'damm full of revellers on Christopher Street Day

with an American theme that always draws the crowds.
Kreuzberger Festliche Tage *(end Aug–early Sep)*. This is a large multi-event festival of traditional classical music held in Kreuzberg.
Jüdische Kulturtage *(end Aug–early Sep)*. A festival devoted to Jewish arts and culture with films, plays, concerts and lectures.

Prokofiev's *The Love of Three Oranges* performed in the Komische Oper

AVERAGE MONTHLY RAINFALL

Rainfall Chart
The lowest amount of rainfall occurs in February and again in April, as the temperature begins to rise. The amount of rain in September can dampen the enthusiasm of the unprepared visitor. Unexpectedly heavy cloudbursts can also occur during the summer months.

AUTUMN

Autumn in Berlin is marked by major cultural events. In September the city's hotels fill with visitors arriving for the Berliner Festwochen, to hear concerts given by some of the world's top artists and to make the most of the wide range of culture on offer. Autumn is also a time for major sports events, including the Berlin Marathon, the third biggest in the world after New York and London.

SEPTEMBER

Internationale Funkausstellung *(early Sep, every two years).* High-tech media and computer fair at the Internationales Congress Centrum *(see p182).*
Bach Tage Berlin *(early Sep)* features around 30 concerts of Johann Sebastian Bach's music, performed in concert halls in

Potsdam. The festival lasts nine days.
Internationales Literaturfestival *(mid-Sep).* Readings, lectures and special events featuring old and new writing from around the world.
Popkomm *(mid-Sep).* This is Europe's biggest pop music fair, which also has a very lively club and dance programme/festival.
Musikfest Berlin *(mid-Sep).* Orchestras and ensembles from across the world come to Berlin to take part in this impressive classical music event, held mostly at the Philharmonie.
Berlin-Marathon *(3rd Sun in Sep).* This international running event attracts thousands of runners and brings the city's traffic to a halt for several hours.

Participants in the September Berlin-Marathon

OCTOBER

Tag der Deutschen Einheit *(3 Oct).* Berlin celebrates the reunification of Germany by staging an annual grand parade through the streets.
Art Forum in Berlin *(early Oct).* Artists and art collectors from all over Europe gather for this five-day modern art fair.
International Salsa Festival *(early Oct).* Salsa shows and more.
Haupstadt Turnier *(late Oct).* International horse-jumping.

NOVEMBER

Jazz Fest Berlin *(early Nov).* Held annually since 1964, this respected jazz festival kicks off in the Haus der Kulturen der Welt *(see p134).*
Treffen Junge Musik-Szene *(early Nov).* Music for the younger generation.
Spielzeit Europa *(Oct–Dec).* A festival of unusual and high-quality theatre and dance, held at the Haus der Berliner Festspiele.

Marching through the Brandenburg Gate on Tag der Deutschen Einheit

AVERAGE MONTHLY TEMPERATURE

Temperature Chart
Average maximum and minimum temperatures are shown here. The warmest months are June, July and August when the temperature exceeds 20°C. Winters are cold and temperatures can drop below –5°C in January, with the chance of heavy snowfalls or extreme frost.

WINTER

Berlin's winters are usually cold and the temperature can sometimes drop to below zero, with a carpet of snow lining the streets. During December, the city prepares for Christmas with many traditional markets. January brings numerous Carnival balls, while the major event in February is the great cinema gala – the Berlin International Film Festival, Berlinale.

DECEMBER

Weihnachtsmärkte
(throughout Dec). In the month before Christmas the city is dotted with picturesque fairs and festive stalls selling Christmas gifts and regional culinary specialities.
Christmas (Weihnachten)
(25–26 Dec). As in many other European cities, Berlin's traditional celebrations include Christmas trees, present-giving, family gatherings and communal feasts.
New Year's Eve (Silvester)
(31 Dec) is celebrated in hotels, restaurants, discos, clubs and in private homes; another traditional activity is the popping of champagne corks at the Brandenburg Gate.

JANUARY

Berliner Neujahrslauf
(1 Jan). For those unaffected by the previous night's revelry, this 4-km (2.4-mile) run along the city streets starts off at the Brandenburg Gate.
Lange Nacht der Museen
(end of Jan, also held in Aug).

Berlinale – the grand festival of world cinema

A series of events organized by Berlin's museums which stay open until midnight or later.
Internationale Grüne Woche
(last week of Jan). This giant fair is devoted to agriculture and food; it provides an ideal opportunity to sample delicacies from all over the world.
Transmediale *(Jan and Feb)* is a busy festival of experimental and electronic music.

Christmas shopping in the KaDeWe department store

FEBRUARY

Sechs-Tage-Rennen *(early Feb)*. This meeting in the Velodrome features a six-day bicycle-race and other events.
Berlinale – Internationale Filmfestspiele *(2nd and 3rd week in Feb)*. This gala of cinematography attracts movie stars and the best films of the season. It is held in tandem with the **Internationales Forum des Jungen Films** which features low-budget movies (see p97).

PUBLIC HOLIDAYS

Neujahr New Year (1 Jan)
Karfreitag Good Friday
Ostermontag Easter Mon
Tag der Arbeit Labour Day (1 May)
Christi Himmelfahrt Ascension Day
Pfingsten Whitsun
Tag der Deutschen Einheit (3 Oct)
Weihnachten Christmas (25–26 Dec)

View over Potsdamer Platz and the Tiergarten beyond ▷

BERLIN AREA BY AREA

AROUND UNTER DEN LINDEN

The area around the grand avenue Unter den Linden is among the most attractive in Berlin. Its development started during the Baroque period with the establishment of Dorotheenstadt to the north and Friedrichstadt to the south. From the early 18th century, prestigious buildings began to appear here, and work started on the

Bas-relief from the Schadow-Haus, located on Schadowstrasse

Forum Friedericianum (later Bebelplatz). Over the following two centuries Unter den Linden became one of the city's most imposing avenues. World War II bombing took a heavy toll, but despite only partial reconstruction by the East German government, the area is still home to the highest concentration of historic buildings in Berlin.

SIGHTS AT A GLANCE

Churches
Deutscher Dom ⑱
Französischer Dom ⑯
Friedrichswerdersche Kirche ⑭
St-Hedwigs-Kathedrale ⑪

Museums and Galleries
Deutsche Guggenheim ⑦
Museum für Kommunikation ㉒
Zeughaus (Deutsches Historisches Museum) (pp58–9) ①

Streets and Squares
Bebelplatz ⑩
Gendarmenmarkt ⑮
Pariser Platz ㉔
Unter den Linden ②

Theatres
Admiralspalast ㉛
Komische Oper ㉙
Konzerthaus ⑰

Maxim Gorki Theater ㉜
Staatsoper Unter den Linden ⑫

Historic Buildings and Sites
Alte Bibliothek ⑨
Altes Palais ⑧
Brandenburger Tor ㉕
Holocaust Denkmal ㉖
Humboldt Universität ④
Kronprinzenpalais ⑬
Mohrenkolonnaden ⑳
Neue Wache ③
Palais am Festungsgraben ㉝
Reiterdenkmal Friedrichs des Grossen ⑤
Spittelkolonnaden ㉑
Staatsbibliothek ⑥

Others
Ehemaliges Regierungsviertel ㉓
Friedrichstadtpassagen ⑲
Hotel Adlon ㉗
Russische Botschaft ㉘
S-Bahnhof Friedrichstrasse ㉚

KEY

▨ Street-by-Street map See pp56–7

🚉 Railway station

Ⓢ S-Bahn station

Ⓤ U-Bahn station

GETTING THERE
This area is served by S-Bahn 1, 3, 5, 7 and 75; U-Bahn 6, 9 and 55; and buses 100, 200 and TXL.

0 metres   400

0 yards   400

◁ Sculpture of the personification of History on the plinth of Schiller's monument, Gendarmenmarkt

Street-by-Street: Around Bebelplatz

The section of Unter Den Linden between Schlossbrücke
and Friedrichstrasse is one of the most attractive places
in central Berlin. There are some magnificent Baroque
and Neo-Classical buildings, many of them designed by
famous architects. There are also some restored palaces
that are now used as public buildings. Of particular
interest is the beautiful Baroque building of the
Zeughaus (the former Arsenal), which now houses the
German History Museum.

Staatsbibliothek
*This Neo-Baroque
building, designed
by Ernst von Ihne,
was built between
1903 and 1914. It
houses a collection
that dates from the
17th century* ❻

Humboldt Universität
*The entrance to the courtyard
is framed by two guardroom
pavilions and is crowned
with the allegorical
figures of Dawn
and Dusk* ❹

**Equestrian Statue
of Frederick
the Great**
*The impressive
statue dates
from 1851 and
is the work of
Christian Daniel
Rauch* ❺

Deutsche Guggenheim
*The building, which was
rebuilt after World War II,
provides exhibition space for
the fifth branch of the famous
Guggenheim museum* ❼

KEY

– – – Suggested route

Altes Palais
*This Neo-Classical
palace was built between
1834 and 1837 for the
future Kaiser Wilhelm I. It
was reconstructed after
World War II* ❽

Alte Bibliothek
*The west side of Bebelplatz features a
Baroque building with an unusual
concave façade. Locals have nick-
named it the "chest of drawers"* ❾

★ Neue Wache
*Since 1993, this monu-
ment has served as a
memorial to all victims of
war and dictatorship* ❸

**★ Zeughaus (Deutsches
Historisches Museum)**
*A wing designed by I M Pei has
been added to this beautiful
Baroque building. The Zeughaus
pediment shows the Roman
goddess of wisdom* ❶

LOCATOR MAP
*See Street Finder, maps 6, 7,
15 & 16*

0 metres   100

0 yards   100

Unter den Linden
*This magnificent avenue was
replanted with four rows of
lime trees in 1946* ❷

Kronprinzenpalais
*The rear elevation of
the palace pavilion
features a magnifi-
cent portal from
the dismantled
Bauakademie
building* ❸

UNTER DEN LINDEN

HINTER DER KATH. KIRCHE

BEBELPLATZ

**Staatsoper
Unter den Linden**
*Unter den Linden's opera
house is Germany's oldest
theatre building not attached
to a palace residence* ⓬

**★ Friedrichswerdersche
Kirche**
*In this Neo-Gothic church,
designed by Karl Friedrich
Schinkel, is a museum devot-
ed to this great architect* ⓮

St-Hedwigs-Kathedrale
*Bas-reliefs (1837) by Theodore
Wilhelm Achtermann adorn
the cathedral's supports* ⓫

STAR SIGHTS

★ Zeughaus (Deutsches
   Historisches
   Museum)

★ Neue Wache

★ Friedrichswerdersche
   Kirche

Bebelplatz
*Designed in the 18th century as the
Forum Friedericianum, this square
was renamed in 1947 in honour
of social activist, August Bebel. The
Nazis burned books here in 1933* ❿

Zeughaus (Deutsches Historisches Museum) ❶

This former arsenal was built in the Baroque style in 1706 under the guidance of Johann Arnold Nering, Martin Grünberg, Andreas Schlüter and Jean de Bodt. It is a magnificent structure; its wings surrounding an inner courtyard, its exterior decorated with Schlüter's sculptures, including masks

Warrior's mask, courtyard arcade

of dying warriors in the courtyard. Since 1952 it has housed the German History Museum. Zeughaus is home to a permanent exhibition that contains more than 8,000 objects about German history in a European context. In the adjacent exhibition hall, designed by the famous architect I M Pei, are the museum's temporary exhibitions about significant historical events.

★ Martin Luther
This portrait, painted by Lucas Cranach the Elder in 1529, is the focal point of the exhibition devoted to the Reformation.

★ Gloria Victis
The death of a friend in the final days of the Franco-Prussian War (1870–71) inspired French artist Antonin Mercié to create this moving allegory.

Prisoner's Jacket
This jacket, which once belonged to a concentration camp prisoner, will be used to illustrate the horrors of the Nazi regime.

Saddle
This valuable mid-15th-century saddle is decorated with graphic carved plaques made of ivory.

First floor

VISITORS' CHECKLIST

Unter den Linden 2. **Map** 7 A3, 16 E2. **Tel** 20 30 44 44. Ⓢ & Ⓤ Friedrichstrasse. Ⓢ Hackeschermarkt. 🚌 100, 200. 🕙 10am–6pm daily. 🖳 **www**.dhm.de

Europa
A group of Meissen porcelain figurines, depicting the continents, possibly designed by Johann Joachim Kändler.

Unter den Linden
Carl Traugott Fechhelm's painting shows Berlin's grandest avenue, Unter den Linden, at the end of the 18th century.

GALLERY GUIDE
The ground floor houses exhibits from 1918 to the present. The first floor contains collections dating from early history to the beginning of the 20th century. A subterranean pathway links the Zeughaus to the temporary exhibits in the exhibition hall by I M Pei.

KEY

▢	Early Civilizations and the Middle Ages
▢	1500–1648
▢	1648–1789
▣	1789–1871
▢	1871–1918
▣	1918–1945
▢	1945–1949
▢	1949 to present day
▢	Non-exhibition rooms

Museum Cinema

Ground floor

Steam Engine
The history of the Industrial Revolution will be illustrated with exhibits such as this 1847 steam-powered engine.

STAR EXHIBITS

★ Gloria Victis

★ Martin Luther

Unter den Linden as depicted in Franz Krüger's *Opernplatz Parade* (1824–30)

Unter den Linden ❷

Map 6 E3, 6 F3, 15 A3, 16 D3.
Ⓢ & Ⓤ *Brandenburger Tor.* 🚌 *100, 200, TXL.*

One of the most famous streets in Berlin, Unter den Linden starts at Schlossplatz and runs down to Pariser Platz and the Brandenburg Gate. It was once the route to the royal hunting grounds that were later transformed into the Tiergarten. In the 17th century the street was planted with lime trees, to which it owes its name. Although removed around 1658, they were replanted in four rows in 1820.

During the 18th century, Unter den Linden became the main street of the westward-growing city. It was gradually filled with prestigious buildings that were restored after World War II. Following the reunification of Germany, Unter den Linden has acquired several cafés and restaurants, as well as many smart new shops. This street is also the venue for many interesting outdoor events; it is usually crowded with tourists and students browsing the bookstalls around the Humboldt Universität and the Staatsbibliothek.

Neue Wache ❸

Unter den Linden 4. **Map** 7 A3, 16 E2. Ⓢ *Hackescher Markt.* 🚌 *100, 200, TXL.* ⬜ *10am–6pm daily.*

This war memorial, designed by Karl Friedrich Schinkel and built between 1816 and 1818, is considered to be one of the finest examples of Neo-Classical architecture in Berlin. The front of the monument is dominated by a huge Doric portico with a frieze made up of bas-reliefs depicting goddesses of victory. The triangular tympanum above the pediment shows allegorical representations of Battle, Victory, Flight and Defeat.

The building was originally used as a royal guardhouse, but during 1930 and 1931 it was turned it into a monument to the soldiers killed in World War I. In 1960, following its restoration, Neue Wache became the Memorial to the Victims of Fascism and Militarism. Then, in 1993 it was rededicated once again, this time to the memory of all victims of war and dictatorship.

Inside the building is an eternal flame and a granite slab over the ashes of an unknown soldier, a resistance fighter and a concentration camp prisoner. Under the circular opening in the roof is a copy of the 20th century sculpture *Mother with her Dead Son*, by Berlin artist Käthe Kollwitz, who lost her own son in World War I.

Humboldt Universität ❹

HUMBOLDT UNIVERSITY

Unter den Linden 6. **Map** 7 A3, **Tel** 20930. 16 D2. Ⓢ & Ⓤ *Friedrichstrasse.* 🚌 *100, 200, TXL.*

The university building was constructed in 1753, for Prince Heinrich of Prussia, the brother of Frederick the Great. The university was founded in 1810 on the initiative of Wilhelm von Humboldt. It became the Berlin University but was renamed in von Humboldt's honour in 1949.

The overall design of the palace, with its main block and the courtyard enclosed within a pair of wings, has been extended many times. Two marble statues (1883) by Paul Otto stand at the

---

WILHELM AND ALEXANDER VON HUMBOLDT

The Humboldt brothers rank among the most distinguished Berlin citizens. Wilhelm (1767–1835) was a lawyer and politician, occupying various government posts. It was on his initiative that the Berlin University (later renamed Humboldt University) was founded, and he conducted studies in comparative and historical linguistics there. Alexander (1769–1859), a professor at the University, researched natural science, including meteorology, oceanography and agricultural science.

Statue of Alexander von Humboldt

entrance gate and represent Wilhelm von Humboldt (holding a book) and his brother Alexander (sitting on a globe), who was a famous explorer. The entrance gate leads to the courtyard, which was designed by Reinhold Begas.

Many famous scholars have worked at the University, including philosophers Fichte and Hegel, physicians Rudolf Virchow and Robert Koch and physicists Max Planck and Albert Einstein. Among its graduates are Heinrich Heine, Karl Marx and Friedrich Engels.

After World War II, the University was in the Russian sector of the divided city and the difficulties encountered by the students of the western zone led to the establishment of a new university in 1948 – the Freie Universität *(see p179).*

Humboldt University courtyard with statue of Hermann Helmholtz

Reiterdenkmal Friedrichs des Grossen **5**

EQUESTRIAN STATUE OF FREDERICK THE GREAT

Unter den Linden. **Map** 7 A3. Ⓢ & Ⓤ *Friedrichstrasse.* 🚌 *100, 200.*

This is one of the most famous monuments in Berlin, featuring a massive bronze statue 5.6 m (18.5 ft) in height and standing on the centre lane of Unter den Linden. It was designed by Christian Daniel Rauch and created between 1839 and 1851. It depicts Frederick the Great on horseback, wearing a uniform and a royal cloak. The base of the high plinth is surrounded

by statues of famous military leaders, politicians, scientists and artists. The top tier of the plinth is decorated with bas-reliefs depicting scenes from the life of Frederick the Great. Out of line with GDR ideology, the monument was removed to Potsdam, where until 1980 it stood by the Hippodrome in Park Sanssouci.

Staatsbibliothek **6**

STATE LIBRARY

Unter den Linden 8. **Map** 7 A3, 16 D2. *Tel 266 23 03.* Ⓢ & Ⓤ *Friedrichstrasse.* 🚌 *100, 200, TXL.* 🕐 *9am–6pm Mon–Fri, 9am–1pm Sat.*

The nucleus of the State Library collection was the library belonging to the Great Elector – Friedrich Wilhelm – founded in 1661 and situated in the Stadtschloss. At the end of the 18th century it was moved to the Alte Bibliothek building. Its current home was designed by Ernst von Ihne and constructed between 1903 and 1914 on the site of the Academy of Science and the Academy of Fine Arts. This impressive building was

severely damaged during World War II and underwent extensive restoration. The collection, numbering 3 million books and periodicals, was scattered during the war, including a collection of priceless music manuscripts, which ended up in the Jagiellonian Library in Cracow, Poland.

After the war only part of the collection was returned to the building in Unter den Linden, and the rest was held in West Berlin. Since reunification, both collections are once again under the same administration.

Deutsche Guggenheim **7**

Unter den Linden 13–15. **Map** 7 A3, 16 D3. *Tel 202 09 30.* 🕐 *10am–8pm daily (to 10pm Thu).* Ⓢ & Ⓤ *Friedrichstrasse.* 🚌 *100, 200, TXL.* 🏛

The Deutsche Guggenheim-building is home to the German branch of the New York-based Guggenheim Foundation. The museum does not have its own permanent collection, but is regularly used to display a variety of temporary exhibitions.

The ivy-clad Staatsbibliothek building on Unter den Linden

A window with a heraldic shield on the Altes Palais

Altes Palais ❽

THE OLD PALACE

Unter den Linden 9. **Map** 7 A3, 16 D3. Ⓢ & Ⓤ *Friedrichstrasse.* 🚌 *100, 200, TXL.* ⬤ *to the public.*

This Neo-Classical palace, near the former Opernplatz (Bebelplatz), was built for the heir to the throne – Prince Wilhelm (later Kaiser Wilhelm I). The Kaiser lived here all his life. He was able to watch the changing of the guards every day from the ground-floor window on the far left.

The palace, built from 1834 to 1837, was designed by Carl Ferdinand Langhans but its splendid furnishings were destroyed during World War II. The palace was subsequently restored, and is now used by Humboldt Universität.

Alte Bibliothek ❾

THE OLD LIBRARY

Bebelplatz. **Map** 7 A3, 16 D3. **Tel** *20 930.* Ⓢ & Ⓤ *Friedrichstrasse.* 🚌 *100, 200, TXL.*

The Old Library, known by locals as the *Kommode* or "chest of drawers" after its curved façade, is actually one of the city's most beautiful Baroque buildings. It was designed by Georg Christian Unger and built around 1775 to house the royal library collection. In fact, Unger based his design on an unrealized plan for an extension to the Hofburg complex in Vienna by Josef Emanuel Fischer von Erlach some 50 years earlier. The concave façade of the building is accentuated by the insertion of three breaks, surrounded at the top by a row of massive Corinthian pilasters. The building now houses the law faculty of Humboldt University.

Bebelplatz ❿

Map 7 A3, 16 D3. Ⓢ & Ⓤ *Friedrichstrasse.* 🚌 *100, 200, TXL.*

Once named Opernplatz (Opera Square), Bebelplatz was to be the focal point of the intended Forum Friedericianum, an area designed by Georg Wenzeslaus von Knobelsdorff to mirror the grandeur of ancient Rome. Although the initial plans were only partly implemented, many important buildings rose around the square with the passage of time.

On 10 May 1933 Opernplatz was the scene of the infamous book burning act organized by the Nazi propaganda machine. Some 25,000 books written by authors considered to be enemies of the Third Reich were burned. These included works by Thomas and Heinrich Mann, Robert Musil and Lion Feuchtwanger.

Today, a monument at the centre of the square, designed by Micha Ullman, commemorates this dramatic event. A translucent panel inserted into the road surface provides a glimpse of a room filled with empty bookshelves. Next to it is a plaque bearing the tragically prophetic words of the poet Heinrich Heine, written in 1820: "Where books are burned, in the end people will burn."

St-Hedwigs-Kathedrale ⓫

ST HEDWIG'S CATHEDRAL

Bebelplatz. **Map** 7 A4, 16 D3, E3. **Tel** *203 48 10.* Ⓢ & Ⓤ *Hausvogteiplatz.* 🚌 *100, 200, TXL.* ◻ *10am–5pm daily.*

This huge church, set back from the road and crowned with a dome, is the Catholic Cathedral of the Roman Archdiocese of Berlin. It was built to serve the Catholics of Silesia (part of present-day Poland), which became part of the Kingdom of Prussia in 1742 following defeat in the Silesian Wars of 1740–63.

The initial design, by Georg Wenzeslaus von Knobelsdorff, was similar to the Roman Pantheon. Construction began in 1747 and the cathedral was consecrated in 1773, although

The façade of St-Hedwigs-Kathedrale featuring beautiful bas-relief sculptures

work continued on and off until 1778. Its design was modified repeatedly. Later, additional work was carried out from 1886 to 1887. The cathedral was damaged during World War II, and rebuilt between 1952 and 1963.

The crypt holds the tombs of many bishops of Berlin, a 16th-century Madonna and a Pietà dating from 1420. It is also the resting place of Bernhard Lichtenberg, a priest killed in a concentration camp and beatified as a martyr by Pope John Paul II.

The imposing façade of the Kronprinzenpalais

Kronprinzenpalais

⑬ CROWN PRINCE'S PALACE

Unter den Linden 3. **Map** 7 A3, B3, 16 E3. **Ⓢ** & **Ⓤ** *Friedrichstrasse.* 100, 200, TXL. ● *to the public.*

This striking late-Neo-Classical palace takes its name from its original inhabitants – the heirs to the royal, and later to the imperial, throne. Its form is the outcome of numerous changes made to what was originally a modest house dating from 1663–9. The first extensions, designed in the late-Baroque style, were conducted by Philipp Gerlach in 1732 and 1733. Between 1856 and 1857 Johann Heinrich Strack added the second floor. These extensions were rebuilt following World War II.

The palace served the royal family until the abolition of the monarchy. From 1919 to 1937, it was used by the Nationalgalerie. Under Communist rule it was renamed Palais Unter den Linden and reserved for official government guests. It was here, on 31 August 1990, that the pact was signed paving the way for reunification.

Next to the palace, with the prestigious address of Unter den Linden 1, is where the Kommandantur, the official quarters of the city's garrison commander, once stood. Totally destroyed in the last days of World War II, the original façade was rebuilt in 2003 by the German media

company Bertelsmann, as part of their Berlin headquarters.

Joined to the main palace by an overhanging passageway is the smaller Prinzessinnenpalais (Princesses' Palace), built for the daughters of Friedrich Wilhelm III.

Friedrichswerdersche Kirche (Schinkel-Museum) **⑭**

Werderscher Markt. **Map** 7 B4, 16 E3. **Tel** 20 90 55 77. **Ⓢ** & **Ⓤ** *Friedrichstrasse.* 100, 147, 200, TXL. ○ *10am–6pm daily.*

This picturesque church, designed by Karl Friedrich Schinkel and constructed between 1824 and 1830, was the first Neo-Gothic church to be built in Berlin. The small single-nave structure, with its twin-tower façade, resembles an English college chapel.

Schinkel's original interior of the church was largely destroyed in World War II.

Following its reconstruction, the church was converted to a museum. It is currently used by the Nationalgalerie to house its permanent exhibition of sculptures from the late 16th to the mid-19th century. Highlights include a model of the famous group sculpture by Johann Gottfried Schadow, depicting the princesses Friederike and Luise (later Queen of Prussia).

Bas-relief of Apollo and Mars on the façade of the Staatsoper

Staatsoper Unter den Linden **⑫**

STATE OPERA HOUSE

Unter den Linden 7. **Map** 7 A3, 16 D3. **Tel** 20 35 45 55. **Ⓢ** & **Ⓤ** *Friedrichstrasse.* 100, 200, TXL.

The early Neo-Classical façade of the State Opera House is one of the most beautiful sights along Unter den Linden. It was built by Georg Wenzeslaus von Knobelsdorff in 1741–3 as the first building of the intended Forum Fridericianum. After a fire, the opera house was restored from 1843 to 1844 under the direction of Carl Ferdinand Langhans, who altered only its interior.

Following wartime destruction, the opera house was rebuilt from 1952 to 1955, and it is now closed for restoration until October 2013. It has played host to famous singers, musicians and artists; one of its directors and conductors was Richard Strauss, and its stage designers included Karl Friedrich Schinkel.

Princesses Luise and Friederike in the Schinkel-Museum

Gendarmenmarkt ⑮

This is one of Berlin's most beautiful squares, created at the end of 17th century as a market square for the newly established Friedrichstadt. It is named after the Regiment Gens d'Armes who had their stables here. In 1950 it was renamed Platz der Akademie; after reunification the square reverted to its original name.

Französischer Dom

JÄGERSTRASSE

GENDARMEN-MARKT

TAUBENSTRASSE

CHARLOTTENSTRASSE

Galeries Lafayette

Quartier 206

Quartier 205

Deutscher Dom

0 metres 85
0 yards 85

Schiller's Monument
The poet's monument stands in the centre of the square, in front of the Konzerthaus.

Französischer Dom ⑯

FRENCH CATHEDRAL

Gendarmenmarkt 6. **Map** 7 A4, 16 D4. **Tel** 204 15 07.
Ⓤ *Stadtmitte or Französische Strasse.* **Museum** ◻ noon–5pm Tue–Sun. 🖼 **Church** ◻ noon–5pm Tue–Sun (from 11am Sun).
🕂 9:30am & 11am Sun.

Although the two churches on the opposite sides of Schauspielhaus seem identical, they differ from each other quite considerably. Their only common feature is the front towers. The French cathedral was built for the Huguenot community, who found refuge in protestant Berlin following their expulsion from France after the revocation of the Edict of Nantes. The modest church, built between 1701

Side elevation of the Französischer Dom, built for Huguenot refugees

and 1705 by Louis Cayart and Abraham Quesnay, was modelled on the Huguenot church in Charenton, France, which was destroyed in 1688. The main entrance, on the west elevation (facing Charlottenstrasse), leads to an

uncomplicated interior with a rectangular nave and semi-circular sections on both sides. It features a late-Baroque organ from 1754.

The structure is dominated by a massive, cylindrical tower which is encircled by Corinthian porticoes at its base. The recently restored tower and porticoes were designed by Carl von Gontard and added around 1785, some 80 years after the church was built. It houses the Huguenot Museum, which details the history of the Huguenots in France and Brandenburg. Well-educated and highly skilled, they played a crucial part in Berlin's rise as a city of science, craft and commerce. The French language they brought with them survives to this day in many words used in the Berlin dialect.

The interior of the Konzerthaus, formerly the Schauspielhaus

Konzerthaus ⑰

CONCERT HALL

Gendarmenmarkt 2. **Map** 7 A4, 16 D4. **Tel** 20 30 921 01. Ⓤ Stadtmitte.

A late Neo-Classical jewel, this magnificent theatre building, formerly known as the Schauspielhaus, is one of the greatest achievements of Berlin's best-known architect, Karl Friedrich Schinkel. It was built between 1818 and 1821 around the ruins of Langhan's National Theatre, destroyed by fire in 1817. The original portico columns were retained. Schinkel was responsible for the architectural structure and for the interior design, down to the door handles. Following bomb damage in World War II, it was reconstructed as a concert hall with a different interior layout. The exterior was restored to its former glory. The Konzerthaus is home to the Konzerthausorchestra (formerly the Berlin Symphony Orchestra).

The theatre façade includes a huge Ionic portico with a set of stairs that was only used by the middle classes (the upper classes entered via a separate entrance where they could leave their horse-drawn carriages). The whole building is richly decorated with sculptures alluding to drama and music: statues of musical geniuses mounted on lions and panthers, as well as figures representing the Muses and a Bacchanal procession. The façade is crowned with the sculpture of Apollo riding a chariot pulled by griffins.

In front of the theatre stands a shining, white marble statue of Friedrich Schiller. It was sculpted by Reinhold Begas, and erected in 1869. Removed by the Nazis during the 1930s, the monument was finally returned to its rightful place in 1988. Schiller's head was copied by the sculptor from a bust of the poet created in 1794 by Johann Heinrich Dannecker. The statue is mounted on a high pedestal surrounded by allegorical figures representing Lyric Poetry, Drama, Philosophy and History.

Deutscher Dom ⑱

GERMAN CATHEDRAL

Gendarmenmarkt 1. **Map** 7 A4, 16 D4. Ⓤ Stadtmitte or Französische Strasse. **Tel** 22 73 04 31. **Exhibition** ☐ May–Sep: 10am–7pm Tue–Sun; Oct–Apr: 10am–6pm Tue–Sun.

The Cathedral at the southern end of the square, to the left of Konzerthaus, is an old German Protestant-Reformed church. It was designed by Martin Grünberg and built in 1708 by Giovanni Simonetti. The design was based on a five-petal shape, and in 1785 it acquired a dome-covered tower identical to that of the French cathedral.

Burned down in 1945, the church was finally rebuilt in 1993. Its exterior was painstakingly reconstructed, including its sculpted decorations. The interior is now modern and has been adapted as an exhibition space.

On display is "*Wege, Irrwege, Umwege*" ("Paths, Confusions, Detours"), an exhibition about Germany's parliamentary democracy.

Sculpture from the Deutscher Dom

Friedrichstadtpassagen ⑲

FRIEDRICHSTADT PASSAGES

Friedrichstrasse Quartiere 205, 206, 207. **Map** 6 F4, 15 C4. Ⓤ Französische Strasse or Stadtmitte.

This group of passages is part of a huge development of luxury shops, offices, restaurants and apartments built along Friedrichstrasse.

Quartier 207 is the famous Galeries Lafayette, a branch of the French department store occupying a charming building designed by Jean Nouvel and constructed almost entirely of glass. The building's axis is formed by an inner courtyard, which is defined by two glass cones with their bases facing each other. The highly reflective glass panes, together with the multicoloured stands that are clustered around the structure, make an extraordinary impression on the visitor.

The next passage, Quartier 206, has offices and smart luxury boutiques, and is the work of the American design team Pei, Cobb, Freed & Partners. The building owes its alluring, but somewhat nouveau-riche appearance to the use of forms inspired by Art Deco architecture, including sophisticated details and expensive stone cladding.

The southernmost building in the complex, and the largest passage, is Quartier 205, which is the work of Oswald Mathias Ungers.

The exterior and main entrance of Quartier 206

Mohren-
kolonnaden ❿

Mohrenstrasse 37b and 40/41.
Map 6 F5, 15 B5. **U** *Mohrenstrasse.*

Designed by Carl Gotthard
Langhans, these Neo-Classical
arcades resting on twin
columns were constructed in
1787. They originally surrounded a bridge that spanned
the moat around the city of
Berlin. The bridge has since
been demolished, and the
arcades have been incorporated into buildings of a much
later architectural style located
on Mohrenstrasse.

A copy of one of the original Spittelkolonnaden in Leipziger Strasse

**One of the original arcades
known as the Mohrenkolonnaden**

Spittelkolonnaden ⓴

Leipziger Strasse. **Map** 7 B5, 16 E5.
U *Spittelmarkt.*

In the vicinity of Spittelmarkt-
is a picturesque Baroque-
Neo-Classical colonnade
squeezed between several
20-storey tower blocks. These
tower blocks were erected to
obscure the view of the Axel
Springer Publishers' building,
which stood on the opposite
side of the Berlin Wall.

A pair of such semicircular
colonnades, designed by Carl
von Gontard and built in
1776, originally surrounded
Spittelmarkt. The southern
one was demolished in 1929,
and the northern one was
destroyed during World War II.

In 1979, a copy of one of the
colonnades was erected in
Leipziger Strasse, using
elements from the original.

Museum für
Kommunikation ⓴

MUSEUM OF
TELECOMMUNICATIONS

Leipziger Strasse 16. **Map** 6 F5,
15 C5. **U** *Stadtmitte.* 🚌 *148.*
Tel *20 29 40.* ⏰ *9am–8pm Tue,
9am–5pm Wed–Fri, 10am–6pm Sat–
Sun.* ⚫ *Mon, 24–25 & 31 Dec.* ♿

Founded in 1872 as the Post
Office museum, this is the
world's oldest establishment
of its kind. A dozen or so
years after it was founded, it
moved into the corner of the
huge building constructed for
the main post office. The office
wings, with their modest Neo-
Renaissance elevations,
contrast with the museum
premises, which has a grand
Neo-Baroque façade richly
decorated with sculptures.
The museum houses exhibits
that illustrate the history of
postal and telecommunication
services, including contemporary digital communications.

Ehemaliges
Regierungsviertel ㉓

Wilhelmstrasse, Leipziger Strasse,
Voss Strasse. **Map** 6 E5. **U**
Potsdamer Platz, Mohrenstrasse.

Wilhelmstrasse, and the area
situated to the west of it up to
Leipziger Platz, was the

former German government
district, where the main
departments had offices from
the mid-19th century until
1945. The building at Voss
Strasse No. 77 was once the
Reich's Chancellery and Otto
von Bismarck's office. From
1933, it served as the office of
Adolf Hitler, for whom the
building was specially
extended by Albert Speer.

In the spring of 1945 the
square was the scene of fierce
fighting, and after World War
II most of the buildings had
to be demolished. Among
those that survived are the
former Prussian Landtag
offices – the huge complex
occupying the site between
Leipziger and Niederkirchner
Strasse. This building in the
Italian Renaissance-style was
designed by Friedrich Schulz,
and constructed from 1892 to
1904. It consists of two seg-
ments: the one on the side of
Leipziger Strasse (No. 3–4)
once housed the upper
chamber of the National
Assembly (the Herrenhaus)
and is now used by the
Bundesrat. The building on
the side of Niederkirchner
Strasse (No. 5) was once the
seat of the Landtag's lower
chamber, and is now the
Berliner Abgeordnetenhaus
(House of Representatives).

The second surviving com-
plex is the former Ministry of
Aviation (Reichsluftfahrtminis-
terium), at Leipziger Strasse
No. 5, built for Hermann
Göring in 1936 by Ernst
Sagebiel. This awesome building is typical of architecture
of the Third Reich.

Pariser Platz ㉔

Map 6 E3, 15 A3. Ⓢ & Ⓤ *Brandenburger Tor.* 🚌 *100, 200.*

This square, at the end of Unter den Linden, was created in 1734. Originally called Quarrée, it was renamed Pariser Platz after 1814, when the *Quadriga* sculpture from the Brandenburg Gate was returned to Berlin from Paris.

The square, enclosed on the west by the Brandenburg Gate, saw most of its buildings, including the house of painter Max Liebermann, destroyed in 1945. Following reunification, the square was redeveloped.

Twin houses designed by Josef Paul Kleihues now flank the Brandenburg Gate. On the north side of the square are the Dresdner Bank building, the French Embassy and a museum on the Kennedy Family. On the south are the US Embassy, the DZ Bank head office and the Akademie der Künste (Academy of Fine Arts). To the east is the Adlon Hotel.

Brandenburger Tor ㉕

BRANDENBURG GATE

Pariser Platz. **Map** 6 E3, 15 A3. Ⓢ & Ⓤ *Brandenburger Tor.* 🚌 *100, 200.*

The Brandenburg Gate is the quintessential symbol of Berlin. This magnificent Neo-Classical structure, completed in 1795, was designed by Carl Gotthard Langhans and modelled on the entrance to the Acropolis

MAX LIEBERMANN (1849–1935)

One of the greatest German painters, Max Liebermann was also one of the most interesting and controversial figures of Berlin's élite circles at the start of the 20th century. A sensitive observer as well as an outstanding portraitist, Liebermann was famously stubborn – he could stand up even to the Kaiser himself. From 1920 he was president of the Akademie der Künste (Academy of Fine Arts), but in view of his Jewish origin he was removed from office in 1933. He died just two years later, alone, and his wife committed suicide to escape being sent to a concentration camp.

A frieze from the Brandenburg Gate

in Athens. A pair of pavilions, once used by guards and customs officers, frames its powerful Doric colonnade. The bas-reliefs depict scenes from Greek mythology, and the whole structure is crowned by the sculpture *Quadriga*, designed by Johann Gottfried Schadow. The *Quadriga* was originally regarded as a symbol of peace. In 1806, during the French occupation, it was dismantled on Napoleon's orders and taken to Paris. On its return in 1814, it was declared a symbol of victory, and the goddess received the staff bearing the Prussian eagle and the iron cross adorned with a laurel wreath. The Brandenburg Gate has

borne witness to many of Berlin's important events, from military parades to celebrations marking the birth of the Third Reich and Hitler's ascent to power. It was here, too, that the Russian flag was raised in May 1945, and on 17 June 1953 that 25 workers demonstrating for better conditions were killed.

The gate, in East Berlin, was restored from 1956–8, when the damaged *Quadriga* was rebuilt in West Berlin. Until 1989 it stood watch over the divided city. Between 2000 and 2002 the Brandenburg Gate was meticulously restored.

Holocaust Denkmal ㉖

HOLOCAUST MEMORIAL

Ebertstrasse. **Map** 6 E3, 15 A3. **Tel** 28 04 59 60. Ⓢ & Ⓤ *Brandenburger Tor.* 🚌 *100, 200.* 🕐 *Apr–Sep: 10am–8pm; Oct–Mar: 10am–7pm.*

In 2003 the construction of a memorial for the Jews killed by the Nazis between 1933 and 1945 began. Designed by US architect Peter Eisenmann, it covers 19,000 sq m (205,000 sq ft) next to the Brandenburg Gate. Above ground, visitors can walk through an undulating field of concrete slabs; beneath lies an information centre on the genocide.

Oskar Kokoschka's *Pariser Platz in Berlin* **(1925–6), Nationalgalerie**

The luxurious interior of the Adlon Hotel

Hotel Adlon

Unter den Linden 77. **Map** 6 E3, 6 E4, 15 A3, 15 B3. **Tel** 226 10. Ⓢ & Ⓤ *Brandenburger Tor.* 🚌 *100, 200.*

Considered the most important society venue in Berlin, the original Hotel Adlon opened its doors in 1907. Its luxurious suites were once used by the world's celebrities, including Greta Garbo, Enrico Caruso and Charlie Chaplin. The hotel suffered bomb damage in World War II, and was demolished in 1945. A building bearing the same name opened in a blaze of publicity on 23 August 1997 and was later bought and branded Hotel Adlon Kempinski.

Today, it is once again the best address in town. Comfort, discretion and interiors featuring exotic timber, marble and heavy silk tempt visitors despite high prices. Those who cannot afford to stay should at least drop in for a cup of coffee: in the main hall stands the only authentic remnant of the former Adlon Hotel, an elegant black marble fountain decorated with elephants, which once stood in the orangery.

Russische Botschaft

RUSSIAN EMBASSY

Unter den Linden 63/65. **Map** 6 F3, 15 B3. Ⓢ & Ⓤ *Brandenburger Tor.* 🚌 *100, 200.*

The monumental, white Russian Embassy building is an example of the Stalinist "wedding cake" style, or *Zuckerbäckerstil*. Built between 1948 and 1953, it was the first postwar building erected on Unter den Linden. It is built on the site of a former palace that had housed the Russian (originally Tsarist) embassy from 1837.

The work of Russian architect Anatoli Strizhevsky, this structure, with its strictly symmetrical layout, resembles the old Berlin palaces of the Neo-Classical period. The sculptures that adorn it, however, belong to an altogether different era: the gods of ancient Greece and Rome have been replaced by working-class heroes.

Statue of a worker on the Russian Embassy building

Komische Oper

COMIC OPERA

Behrenstr. 55/57. **Map** 6 F4, 15 C3. **Tel** 47 99 74 00. Ⓤ *Französische-strasse.* Ⓢ & Ⓤ *Brandenburger Tor.* 🚌 *100, 147, 200.*

Looking at the modern façade of this theatre it is hard to believe that it hides one of Berlin's most impressive interiors. Originally called the Theater Unter den Linden, the theatre was built in 1892 by the internationally famous Viennese architectural practice of Ferdinand Fellner and Hermann Helmer. It has served as a variety theatre and as the German National Theatre in the past, and has only housed the Komische Oper since World War II. The postwar reconstruction deprived the building of its former façades but the beautiful Viennese Neo-Baroque interior remained, full of stuccoes and gilded ornaments. Particularly interesting are the expressive and dynamically posed statues on the pilasters of the top balcony – the work of Theodor Friedel. The Komische Oper is one of Berlin's three leading opera companies. Its repertoire consists mainly of light opera.

Crowded balconies and the plush interior of the Komische Oper

S-Bahnhof Friedrichstrasse ㉚

Map 6 F2, 6 F3 & 15 C2.

One of the city's most famous urban railway stations, Bahnhof Friedrichstrasse used to be the border station between East and West Berlin. It was built in 1882 to a design by Johannes Vollmer. In 1925 a roof was added, covering the hall and the platforms.

The original labyrinth of passages, staircases and checkpoints no longer exists but it is possible to see a model of the station at the Stasi-Museum *(see p174)*. Now used as a theatre, the only remaining structure from the original station is the special pavilion once used as a waiting room by those waiting for emigration clearance. It earned the nickname Tränenpalast, the "Palace of Tears", as it is here that Berliners from different sides of the city would say goodbye to each other after a visit.

Admiralspalast ㉛

Friedrichstr. 101–102. **Map** 6 F2, 15 C1. **Tel** 479 97 74 99. 🇺 & Ⓢ *Friedrichstrasse.*

The Admiralspalast, built in 1911, was one of the Roaring Twenties' premier entertainment complexes in Berlin, and one of the many variety and vauderville theatres once lining Friedrichstrasse. Originally designed as an indoor swimming pool above a natural hot spring, it was later transformed into an ice-skating rink and, after heavy damage in World War II, an Operettenthater that staged light musical entertainment.

In 2006, the theatre re-opened with a much discussed production of Bertolt Brecht's *Dreigroschenoper*, and now once again serves as a vibrant entertainment complex, with a large stage, a café and a nightclub. A health spa using the natural hot spring will also be opened. Designed by Heinrich Schweitzer, the beautifully restored façade is punctuated by Doric half-columns and inlaid with slabs of Istrian

A window of the Admiralspalast decorated with marble slabs

marble. The restored façade on Planckstrasse, designed by Ernst Westphal, features exotic overlapping motifs.

Maxim Gorki Theater ㉜

Am Festungsgraben 2. **Map** 7 A3, 16 E2. **Tel** 20 22 11 15. 🇺 & Ⓢ *Friedrichstrasse.* 🚌 100, 200.

The Maxim Gorki theatre was once a singing school or *Sing-Akademie*. Berlin's oldest concert hall, it was built in 1827 by Karl Theodor Ottmer, who based his design on drawings by Karl Friedrich Schinkel. This modest Neo-Classical building, with its attractive façade resembling a Greco-Roman temple, was well known for the excellent acoustic qualities of its concert hall.

Many famous composer-musicians performed here, including violinist Niccolò Paganini and pianist Franz Liszt. In 1829, Felix Mendelssohn-Bartholdy conducted a performance of the *St Matthew*

Maxim Gorki Theater occupying the oldest concert hall in Berlin

Passion by Johann Sebastian Bach, the first since the composer's death in 1750. Following reconstruction after World War II, the building is now used as a theatre.

Palais am Festungsgraben ㉝

FESTUNGSGRABEN PALACE

Am Festungsgraben 1. **Map** 7 A3, 16 E2. Ⓢ *Friedrichstrasse.* 🚌 100, 200. 🚊 M1, 12.

The Palace in Festungsgraben is one of the few structures in this part of town that has maintained its original interior decor. Built as a small Baroque palace in 1753, it owes its present form to major extension work, carried out in 1864 in the style of Karl Friedrich Schinkel, by Heinrich Bürde and Hermann von der Hude.

The late Neo-Classical style of the building is reminiscent of Schinkel's later designs. The interior includes a magnificent double-height marble hall in the Neo-Renaissance style and modelled on the White Room in the former Stadtschloss *(see p71)*. In 1934 one of the ground-floor rooms was turned into a music salon, and many musical instruments were brought here from the 19th-century house (now demolished) of wealthy merchant and manufacturer Johann Weydinger (1773–1837).

Until 2009 the Palace in Festungsgraben housed the Museum Mitte. It is now used for private events.

MUSEUM ISLAND

The long island that nestles in the tributaries of the Spree river is the cradle of Berlin's history. It was here that the first settlements appeared at the beginning of the 13th century – Cölln is mentioned in documents dating back to 1237 and its twin settlement, Berlin, is mentioned a few years later (1244). Not a trace of Gothic and Renaissance Cölln is left now: the island's character was transformed by the construction of the Brandenburg

Bas-relief from the façade of the Berliner Dom

Electors' palace, which served as their residence from 1470. Over the following centuries, the palace was converted first into a royal and later into an imperial palace – the huge Stadtschloss. Although it was razed to the ground in 1950, some interesting buildings on the island's north side have survived, including the huge Berliner Dom (cathedral) and the impressive collection of museums that give the island its name – Museumsinsel.

SIGHTS AT A GLANCE

Museums and Galleries
Alte Nationalgalerie 7
Altes Museum p75 6
Bodemuseum 10
Galgenhaus 19
Historischer Hafen Berlin 13
Märkisches Museum 14
Neues Museum 8
Pergamonmuseum pp80–83 9

Streets, Squares and Parks
Lustgarten 5
Märkisches Ufer 15
Schlossplatz 1

Historic Buildings
Berliner Dom pp76–7 4
Ermeler-Haus 16
Gertraudenbrücke 17
Marstall 11
Nicolai-Haus 18
Ribbeckhaus 12
Schlossbrücke 3

Other Buildings
Staatsratsgebäude 2

KEY

- Street-by-Street map *See pp72–3*
- **U** U-Bahn Station
- **S** S-Bahn Station
- Bus terminus

GETTING THERE

The easiest way to get to Museum Island and Schlossplatz is to walk from Hackescher Markt S-Bahn station, or to take a bus, either the 100, 200 or TXL. The Breite Strasse district is served by buses 147 and 257, while the south end of the island can be reached by U-Bahn line 2, going to Spittelmarkt, and by buses 147, 248 and 347 to Märkisches Ufer.

0 metres 400
0 yards 400

◁ **The elegant Bodemuseum, with the Fernsehturm (Television Tower) in the background**

Street-by-Street: Museum Island

On this island are the pretty Lustgarten and the
Berliner Dom (Berlin Cathedral). It is also where you
will find some of the most important museums in
the east of the city. These include the Bodemuseum,
the Altes Museum, the Alte Nationalgalerie and the
splendid Pergamonmuseum, famous for its collection
of antiquities and visited by crowds of art-lovers
from around the world.

Bodemuseum
*The dome-covered rounded
corner of the building provides
a prominent landmark at the
tip of the island* **10**

Railway bridge,
also used by the
S-Bahn.

★ Pergamonmuseum
*The museum is famous
for its reconstruction of
fragments of ancient
towns, as well as the
original friezes from
the Pergamon Altar* **9**

AM KUPFER–GRABEN

0 metres   100

0 yards   100

BODESTRASSE

Alte Nationalgalerie
*The equestrian statue of King
Friedrich Wilhelm IV in front
of the building is the work of
Alexander Calandrelli* **7**

Neues Museum
*Re-opened in 2009 after
a renovation by David
Chipperfield, this muse-
um houses the Egyptian
Museum plus parts of
the Museum of Pre-
and Early History* **8**

STAR SIGHTS

- ★ Pergamonmuseum
- ★ Altes Museum
- ★ Berliner Dom

KEY

– – – Suggested route

★ Altes Museum
The corners of the central building feature figures of Castor and Pollux, heroes of Greek myth also known as the Dioscuri ❻

LOCATOR MAP
See Street Finder, maps 7 &16

Lustgarten
The 70-ton granite bowl was the biggest in the world when it was placed in the garden in 1828 ❺

★ Berliner Dom
The Neo-Baroque interior of the Berlin Cathedral features some extravagant late 19th-century furnishings ❹

BODESTRASSE

LUSTGARTEN

SSBRÜCKE

KARL–LIEBKNECHT STR

SCHLOSSPLATZ

Schlossbrücke
Under the GDR regime this unusual bridge was called Marx-Engels-Brücke. It features statues made of stunning white Carrara marble ❸

Schlossplatz
Excavations conducted here have unearthed the cellars of the demolished Stadtschloss ❶

Schlossplatz ❶

Map 7 B3, 16 F3. Ⓢ *Hackescher Markt.* 🚌 *100, 200.*

This square was once the site of a gigantic residential complex known as Stadtschloss (City Palace). Built in 1451, it served as the main residence of the Brandenburg Electors. It was transformed from a castle to a palace in the mid-16th century when Elector Friedrich III (later King Friedrich I) ordered its reconstruction in the Baroque style. The building works (1698–1716) were overseen initially by Andreas Schlüter and then by Johann von Göthe and Martin Heinrich Böhme.

The three-storey residence, designed around two courtyards, was the main seat of the Hohenzollern family *(see pp19–20)* for almost 500 years until the end of the monarchy. The palace was partly burned during World War II, but after 1945 it was provisionally restored and used as a museum. In 1950–51, despite protests, the palace was demolished and the square was renamed Marx-Engels-Platz under the GDR.

Now all that remains of the palace is the triumphal-arch portal that once adorned the façade on the Lustgarten side. This is now incorporated into the wall of the government building, the Staatsratsgebäude. In 1989 the square reverted to its original name. In 1993 a

The surviving Stadtschloss portal fronting a government building

full-scale model of the palace was built out of cloth stretched over scaffolding. After a lengthy debate and an architectural competition won by Franco Stella, it was decided to rebuild the palace as a museum complex that will have three reconstructed historical façades and a modern one. This Humboldt-Forum will house the Dahlem museums' overseas collections. Completion is due in 2016. Until then, a temporary "White Cube" building exhibits modern art.

Staatsratsgebäude ❷

Map 7 B3, 16 F2. Ⓢ & Ⓤ *Alexanderplatz.* 🚌 *100, 147, 200, TXL, M48.*

The former Staatsratsgebäude, once the seat of the highest state government council of East Germany, was built in 1964. It now stands alone on the southern side of the square, as all the other former Socialist state buildings that once formed the government centre in this area have long been demolished. The Staatsratsgebäude features the remaining original sculptures, including the magnificent atlantes by the famous Dresden sculptor Balthasar Permoser. Their inclusion, however, was not due to their artistic merit, but rather to their propaganda value: it was from the balcony of the portal that Karl Liebknecht proclaimed the birth of the Socialist Republic *(see p28).*

Schlossbrücke ❸

Map 7 B3, 16 E2. Ⓢ *Hackescher Markt.* 🚌 *100, 200.*

This is one of the town's most beautiful bridges, connecting Schlossplatz with Unter den Linden. It was built in 1824 to a design by Karl Friedrich Schinkel, who was one of Germany's most influential architects *(see p187).* Statues were added to the top of the bridge's sparkling

Sculptures on the Schlossbrücke

granite pillars in 1853. These figures were also created by Schinkel and made of stunning white Carrara marble. The statues depict tableaux taken from Greek mythology, for instance Iris, Nike and Athena training and looking after their favourite young warriors. The wrought-iron balustrade is decorated with intertwined sea creatures.

Berliner Dom ❹

BERLIN CATHEDRAL

See pp76–7.

Lustgarten ❺

Map 7 B3, 16 E2. Ⓢ *Hackescher Markt.* 🚌 *100, 200.*

The enchanting garden in front of the Altes Museum looks as though it has always been here, but in its present form it was established from 1998 to 1999.

Used to grow vegetables and herbs for the Stadtschloss until the late-16th century, it became a real *Lustgarten* (pleasure garden) in the reign of the Great Elector (1620–88). However, its statues, grottoes, fountains and exotic vegetation were removed when Friedrich Wilhelm I (1688–1740), known for his love of military pursuits, turned the garden into an army drill ground.

Following the construction of the Altes Museum, the ground became a park, designed by Peter Joseph Lenné. In 1831 it was adorned with a monolithic granite bowl by Christian Gottlieb Cantian, to a design by Schinkel. The 70-ton bowl, measuring nearly 7 m (23 ft) in diameter, was intended for the museum rotunda, but was too heavy to carry inside.

After 1933, the Lustgarten was paved over and turned into a parade ground, remaining as such until 1989. Its current restoration is based on Lenné's designs.

Altes Museum o

The museum building, designed by Karl Friedrich Schinkel, is undoubtedly one of the world's most beautiful Neo-Classical structures, with an impressive 87-m (285-ft) high portico supported by 18 Ionic columns. Officially opened in 1830, it was built to house the royal collection of paintings and antiquities. It now houses part of Berlin's collection of classical antiquities, with an exhibition focused on the art and culture of ancient Greece. The first floor houses a permanent exhibition of Roman and Etruscan art and sculptures.

VISITORS' CHECKLIST

Am Lustgarten (Bodestrasse 1–3). **Map** 7 B3. **Tel** 266 424 242. Ⓢ *Hackescher Markt.* 🚌 *100, 200, 348.* ⬜ *10am–6pm daily (10pm Thur).* 📷 🖼 ♿

Andochides' Amphora
The amphora is decorated with the figures of wrestlers, a common motif.

Pericles' Head
This is a Roman copy of the sculpture by Kresilas that stood at the entrance to the Acropolis in Athens.

Staircase

The monumental colonnade at the front of the building dominates the façade.

Main entrance

The stately rotunda is decorated with sculptures and ringed by a colonnade. Its design is based on the ancient Pantheon.

GALLERY GUIDE
The ground floor galleries house Greek and Roman antiquities; the first floor is used for temporary exhibitions.

Mosaic from Hadrian's Villa
(c.117–138)
This colourful mosaic depicts a battle scene between centaurs and a tiger and lion. The mosaic comes from a floor of Hadrian's Villa, near Tivoli on the outskirts of Rome.

KEY

☐ Greek and Roman antiquities

☐ Temporary exhibitions

Berliner Dom ❹

The original Berliner Dom was based on a modest Baroque design by Johann Boumann. Built between 1747 and 1750 on the site of an old Dominican church, the cathedral included the original crypt of the Hohenzollern family, one of the largest in its kind in Europe. The present Neo-Baroque structure is the work of Julius Raschdorff and dates from 1894 to 1905. The central copper dome is some 98 m (321 ft)high. Following severe World War II damage, the cathedral has now been restored in a simplified form. The Hohenzollern memorial chapel, which had originally adjoined the northern walls of the cathedral, has been dismantled.

Prussian coat of arms

Phil.d.Grossm.

Figures of the apostles

Philipp der Grossmütige (Philip the Magnanimous)
At the base of the arcade stand the statues of church reformers and those who supported the Reformation. The statue of Prince Philip the Magnanimous is the work of Walter Schott.

★ Church Interior
The impressive and richly-decorated interior was designed by Julius Raschdorff at the start of the 20th century.

Sauer's Organ
The organ, the work of Wilhelm Sauer, has an exquisitely carved case. The instrument contains some 7,200 pipes.

Main entrance

★ Hohenzollern Sarcophagi
The Imperial Hohenzollern family crypt, hidden beneath the floor of the cathedral, contains 100 richly decorated sarcophagi, including that of Prince Friedrich Ludwig.

The Four Evangelists
Mosaics depicting the Four Evangelists decorate the ceilings of the smaller niches in the cathedral. They were designed by Woldemar Friedrich.

The Resurrection
The stained glass in the windows of the apses depict scenes from the life of Jesus. They are the work of Anton von Werner.

The main altar, saved from the previous cathedral, is the work of Friedrich August Stüler. It dates from 1820.

The Pulpit
This elaborate Neo-Baroque pulpit is part of the cathedral's ornate decor dating from the early 20th century.

★ Sarcophagi of Friedrich I and his Wife
Both of these were designed by Andreas Schlüter. The sculpture on Sophie Charlotte's sarcophagus depicts death.

STAR FEATURES

★ Church Interior

★ Hohenzollern Sarcophagi

★ Sarcophagi of Friedrich I and his Wife

Arnold Böcklin's *The Island of the Dead*, 1883, Alte Nationalgalerie

Alte Nationalgalerie ❼
OLD NATIONAL GALLERY

Bodestrasse 1–3. **Map** 7 B2, 16 E1.
Tel 20 90 58 01. Ⓢ *Hackescher Markt, Friedrichstrasse.* 🚌 *100, 200.*
🚊 *M1, M4, M5, M6, 12.*
🕐 *10am–6pm daily (to 10pm Thu).* 📷

The Nationalgalerie building was erected between 1866 and 1876 and designed by Friedrich August Stüler, who took into account the sketches made by Friedrich Wilhelm IV. The building is situated on a high platform reached via a double staircase. On the top stands an equestrian statue of Friedrich Wilhelm IV, the work of Alexander Calandrelli in 1886. The façade of the building is preceded by a magnificent colonnade, which becomes a row of half-columns higher up. The decorations are in keeping with the purpose of the building – the tympanum features Germania as patroness of art, while the top is crowned with the personification of the arts.

The museum was originally meant to house the collection of modern art that had been on display since 1861 in the Akademie der Künste (*see p67*). The current collection includes works of masters such as Adolph von Menzel, Wilhelm Leibl, Max Liebermann and Arnold Böcklin.

Other works include paintings by the Nazarene Brotherhood and the French Impressionists. There is also no shortage of sculptures, including works by Christian Daniel Rauch, Johann Gottfried Schadow and Reinhold Begas. Two new exhibition halls now present paintings (formerly shown at the Schloss Charlottenburg) from the German Romantic era, as well as works by Caspar David Friedrich, Karl Friedrich Schinkel and Karl Blechen.

Neues Museum ❽
NEW MUSEUM

Bodestrasse 1–3. **Map** 7 B2, 16 E2. Ⓢ *Hackescher Markt or Friedrichstrasse.* 🚌 *100, 200.*
🚊 *M1, M4, M5, M6.*

Façade statue, Neues Museum

The Neues Museum was built on Museum Island in order to relieve the Altes Museum, which was already very crowded. The building was erected between 1841 and 1855 to a design by Friedrich August Stüler. Until World War II it housed a collection of antiquities, mainly ancient Egyptian art. The monumental building's beautiful rooms were decorated to complement the exhibitions they contained.

Wall paintings by Wilhelm von Kaulbach depicted key events in world history.

In 1945 the building was badly damaged and it took a long time to decide if it would be feasible to rebuild it. But the reconstruction effort under British architect David Chipperfield, a skilful blend of conservation, restoration and creating new spaces, was highly successful. History remains palpable in every room. The resurrected museum again houses the collection of Egyptian art (with the bust of Queen Nefertiti as its star exhibit), the Collection of Classical Antiquities and the Museum for Pre- and Early History. The latter portrays the evolution of mankind from prehistoric to medieval times, including a magnificent collection from the ancient city of Troy and gold jewellery belonging to the "Treasure of Priam".

Pergamon-museum ❾

See pp80–81.

Bodemuseum ⑩

Monbijoubrücke. (Bodestrasse 1–3).
Map 7 A2, 16 D1, 16 E1. **Tel** 20
90 55 77. Ⓢ Hackescher Markt or
Friedrichstrasse. 🚌 100, 147, 200.
🚊 M1, M4, M5, M6, 12.
⬤ 10am–6pm daily (10pm Thu). 📷

The fourth museum building
on the island was erected
between 1897 and 1904. It was
designed by Ernst von Ihne to
fit the wedge-shaped end of
the island. The interior was
designed with the help of an
art historian, Wilhelm von
Bode, who was the director
of the Berlin state museums
at the time. The museum
displayed a rather mixed
collection that included some
Old Masters. Its original name,
Kaiser Friedrich Museum, was
changed after World War II.
Following the reassembling of
the Berlin collections, all of
the paintings were put in the
Kulturforum (see pp122–3).
The Egyptian art and the
papyrus collection were
moved to the Ägyptisches
Museum (Egyptian Museum)
at Charlottenburg. They are
currently housed at the Altes
Museum (see p75).

All the collections are back
on display following renovation work. Highlights include
an outstanding coin collection
of some of the world's oldest
coins, from Athens in the 6th
century BC, as well as Roman,
medieval and 20th-century
coins. There are also sculptures
by Tilman Riemenschneider,
Donatello, Gianlorenzo Bernini
and Antonio Canova.

Marstall ⑪

THE ROYAL STABLES

Schlossplatz/Breite Strasse 36–37.
Map 7 B3, C3, C4, 16 F3.
Ⓤ Spittelmarkt. 🚌 147, 248, 347.

This huge complex, occupying the area between the
Spree and Breitestrasse, south
of Schlossplatz, is the old
Royal Stables block. The
wing on the side of Breite
Strasse is a fragment of the
old structure built in 1669. It
was designed by Michael
Matthias Smids and is the
only surviving early Baroque
building in Berlin. The wings
running along Schlossplatz
and the Spree river were built
much later, between 1898 and
1901. Although they were
designed by Ernst von Ihne,
these buildings are reminiscent
of the Berlin Baroque style –
probably because von Ihne
modelled them on designs by
Jean de Bodt from 1700.

Ribbeckhaus ⑫

RIBBECK'S HOUSE

Breite Strasse 35. **Map** 7 C4.
Ⓤ Spittelmarkt. 🚌 147, 248, 347.

Four identical, picturesque
gables crown central Berlin's
only surviving Renaissance
building. The house was built
c.1624 for Hans Georg von
Ribbeck, a court counsellor,
who sold it shortly afterwards
to Anna Sophie of Brunswick.
The architect Balthasar Benzelt
converted the house for her
in 1629. After her death in

The Ribbeckhaus, central Berlin's
only surviving Renaissance building

1659, the house passed to her
nephew Elector Friedrich
Wilhelm. As crown property,
the building later housed
various state administrative
offices. When another storey
was added, the row of gables
was retained by royal decree.

The house also has an
interesting late-Renaissance
portal, ornamented with the
date and coat of arms of the
first owners – von Ribbeck
and Katharina von Brösicke
his wife. This was replaced
in 1960 with a copy. Original
features of interest include the
beautiful wrought-iron grilles
on the ground-floor windows.

Historischer Hafen Berlin ⑬

HISTORIC PORT OF BERLIN

Märkisches Ufer. **Map** 8 D4.
Tel 213 8041. Ⓤ Märkisches Ufer.
Ⓢ Jannowitzbrücke. 🚌 240, 265.
⬤ May–Oct: 2–6pm Tue–Fri,
11am–6pm Sat & Sun. 📷

Moored on the south shore
of Museum Island, in an area
called Fischerinsel, and
opposite the Märkisches Ufer
are several examples of boats,
barges and tug-boats which
operated on the Spree river at
the end of the 19th century.
These craft constitute an open-
air museum which was once
located in the Humboldt Port.
One of the boats is now used
as a summer café, while
another, the *Renate Angelika*,
houses a small exhibition
illustrating the history of
inland waterway transport.

The Bodemuseum designed by Ernst von Ihne

Pergamonmuseum ⑨

Built between 1910 and 1930 to a design by Alfred Messels and Ludwig Hoffmann, this museum houses one of Europe's most famous collections of antiquities. It is named for the famous Pergamon Altar displayed in the main hall. The three independent collections – the Museum of Antiquities (Greek and Roman), the Museum of Near Eastern Antiquities and the Museum of Islamic Art – are the result of intensive archaeological excavations by late 19th- and early 20th- century German expeditions to the Near and Middle East. Some displays may be closed or relocated during the major renovation scheduled to end in 2015.

★ **Pergamon Altar** *(170 BC)*
This scene, featuring the goddess Athena, appears on the large frieze illustrating a battle between the gods and the giants.

Roman Mosaic *(3rd or 4th century AD)*
This ancient mosaic was found at Jerash, Jordan. A second part of it was sold to an unknown collector.

The Goddesss Athena
This enchanting Hellenistic sculpture of the goddess Athena is one of many displayed in the museum.

Temporary exhibition rooms

First floor

Ground floor

Main entrance

Assyrian Palace
Parts of this beautifully reconstructed palace interior, from the ancient kingdom of Assyria, date from the 12th century BC.

Aleppo Zimmer
(c.1601–3)
This magnificent panelled room comes from a merchant's house in the Syrian city of Aleppo.

GALLERY LAYOUT
The central section of the ground floor houses reconstructions of ancient monumental structures, and the left wing is devoted to the Antiquities of Greece and Rome. The right wing houses the Museum of Near Eastern Antiquities; the first floor of the right wing houses the Museum of Islamic Art.

Façade of the Mshatta Palace (744 AD)
This fragment is from the southern façade of the Jordanian Mshatta Palace, presented to Wilhelm II by Sultan Abdul Hamid of Ottoman in 1903.

★ Market Gate from Miletus (c.120 AD)
This gate, measuring over 16 m (52 ft) in height, opened on to the southern market of Miletus, a Roman town in Asia Minor.

★ Ishtar Gate from Babylon
(6th century BC)
Original glazed bricks decorate both the huge Ishtar gate and the impressive Processional Way that leads up to it.

STAR EXHIBITS

★ Pergamon Altar

★ Market Gate from Miletus

★ Ishtar Gate from Babylon

KEY

⬜ Antiquities (Antikensammlung)

⬜ Ancient Near East (Vorderasiatisches Museum)

⬜ Islamic Art (Museum für Islamische Kunst)

⬜ Non-exhibition rooms

Exploring the Pergamonmuseum

Opened in 1930, the Pergamonmuseum is the newest museum in the Museum Island complex and is one of Berlin's major attractions. The building was one of the first in Europe designed specifically to house big architectural exhibits. The richness of its collections is the result of large-scale excavations by German archaeologists at the beginning of the 20th century. Currently, the museum is at the heart of a redevelopment programme, due for completion in 2015, that will considerably increase the range of large-scale exhibits on display.

Bird from Mesopotamia

The Greek goddess Persephone, from Tarentum, 5th century BC

Restored entrance hall of the Athena temple from Pergamon, 2nd century BC

COLLECTION OF ANTIQUITIES

Berlin's collection of Greek and Roman antiquities (Antikensammlung) came into existence during the 17th century. Growing steadily in size, the collection was opened for public viewing in 1830, initially in the Altes Museum (see p75), and from 1930 in the new, purpose-built Pergamonmuseum. The high-light of the collection is the huge Pergamon Altar from the acropolis of the ancient city of Pergamon in Asia Minor (now Bergama, Turkey). It formed part of a larger architectural complex, a model of which is also on display in the museum. The magnificently restored altar is thought to have been built to celebrate victory in war and to have been commissioned by King Eumenes in 170 BC. Probably dedicated to the god Zeus and the goddess Athena, this artistic master-piece was discovered in a decrepit state by German archaeologist Carl Humann who, after long negotiations, was allowed to transport the surviving portions of the altar to Berlin. The front section of the building was restored at the museum, together with the so-called small frieze, which once adorned the inside of the building, and fragments of the large frieze, which origi-nally encircled the base of the colonnade. The large frieze has now been reconstructed around the interior walls of the museum and its theme is the Gigantomachy (the battle of the gods against the giants). The small frieze tells the story

of Telephos, supposed founder of the city and son of the hero Heracles. The frieze is an attempt to claim an illustrious ancestry for Pergamon's rulers.

The collection also contains fragments of other Pergamon structures from the same period, including part of the Athena temple. Also featured here are some excellent examples of Greek sculpture, both originals and Roman copies, as well as many statues of the Greek gods unearthed at Miletus, Samos and Nakosos, and various examples of Greek ceramic art.

Roman architecture is repre-sented by the striking market gate from the Roman city of Miletus, on the west coast of Asia Minor. The gate dates from the 2nd century AD, and shows strong Hellenistic influences. Discovered by a German archaeological expedition, it was transported to Berlin where it was restored in 1903. Also on display are a number of mag-nificent Roman mosaics. A huge and impressive marble

Roman marble sarcophagus depicting the story of Medea, 2nd century AD

sarcophagus dates from the 2nd century AD and is decorated with delicate bas-relief carvings depicting the story of the Greek heroine Medea.

Glazed-brick wall cladding from the palace of Darius I in Susa, capital of the Persian Empire

MUSEUM OF NEAR EASTERN ANTIQUITIES

The collection now on display in the Museum of Near Eastern Antiquities (Vorderasiatisches Museum) was made up initially of donations from individual collectors. However, hugely successful excavations, begun during the 1880s, formed the basis of a royal collection that is one of the richest in the world. It features architecture, sculpture and jewellery from Babylon, Iran and Assyria.

One striking exhibit is the magnificent Ishtar Gate and the Processional Way that leads to it. They were built during the reign of Nebuchadnezzar II (604–562 BC) in the ancient city of Babylon. The original avenue was about 180 m (590 ft) long. Many of the bricks used in its construction are new, but the lions – sacred animals of the goddess Ishtar (mistress of the sky, goddess of love and patron of the army) – are all originals. Although impressive in size, the Ishtar Gate has in fact not been reconstructed in full and a model of the whole structure shows the scale of the original complex. Only the inner gate is on display, framed by two towers. Dragons and bulls decorate the gate, emblems of the Babylonian gods, Marduk, patron of the city, and Adad, god of storms.

The collection also includes pieces from the neighbouring regions of Persia, Syria and Palestine including a gigantic basalt sculpture of a bird from Tell Halaf and a glazed wall relief of a spear bearer from Darius I's palace in Susa. Other Mesopotamian peoples, including the Assyrians and the Cassians, are represented here too, as are the inhabitants of Sumer in the southern part of the Babylonian Empire with pieces dating from the 4th century BC.

MUSEUM OF ISLAMIC ART

The history of the Museum of Islamic Art (Museum für Islamische Kunst) begins in 1904 when Wilhelm von Bode launched the collection by donating his own extensive selection of carpets. He also brought to Berlin a 45-m (150-ft) long section of the façade of a Jordanian desert palace. The façade, covered with exquisitely carved limestone cladding, was presented to Kaiser Wilhelm II in 1903 by Sultan Abdul Hamid of Ottoman. The palace was part of a group of defence fortresses and residential buildings dating from the Omayyad period (AD 661–750). These were probably built for the Caliph al-Walid II.

Another fascinating exhibit is a beautiful 13th-century *mihrab*, the niche in a

Brilliantly-glazed *mihrab* from a Kashan mosque built in 1226

mosque that shows the direction of Mecca. Made in the Iranian town of Kashan renowned for its ceramics, the *mihrab* is covered in lustrous metallic glazes that make it sparkle as if studded with sapphires and gold.

The collection's many vivid carpets come from as far afield as Iran, Asia Minor, Egypt and the Caucasus. Highlights include an early 15th-century carpet from Anatolia decorated with an unusual dragon and phoenix motif and, dating from the 14th century, one of the earliest Turkish carpets in existence.

Other rooms hold collections of miniature paintings and various objects for daily use. An interesting example of provincial Ottoman architecture is an exquisitely-panelled early 17th-century reception room, known as the Aleppo Zimmer, which was once part of a Christian merchant's house in the Syrian city of Aleppo.

17th-century carpet with flower motif from western Anatolia

The exterior of the Märkisches Museum, echoing a medieval monastery

Märkisches Museum ⑭

Am Köllnischen Park 5. **Map** 8 D4.
Tel *24 00 21 62.* Ⓤ *Jannowitzbrücke,
Märkisches Museum.* Ⓢ *Jannowitzbrücke.* 🚌 *147, 240, 248, M48.* ◯
*10am–6pm Tue, Thu–Sun; noon–8pm
Wed.* 🎵 *Presentation of mechanical
musical instruments 3pm Sun.*

This architectural pastiche
is a complex of red brick
buildings that most resembles
a medieval monastery. It was
built between 1901 and 1908
to house a collection relating
to the history of Berlin and
the Brandenburg region, from
the time of the earliest settlers
to the present. Inspired by the
brick-Gothic style popular in
the Brandenburg region, architect Ludwig Hoffmann included
references to Wittstock Castle
and to St Catherine's Church
in the city of Brandenburg. In
the entrance hall, a statue of
the hero Roland stands guard,
a copy of the 15th-century
monument in the city of
Brandenburg. The main hall
features the original Gothic
portal from the Berlin residence of the Margraves of
Brandenburg *(see pp17–19)*,
demolished in 1931. Also
featured is a horse's head from
the Schadow *Quadriga*, which
once crowned the Branden-
burg Gate *(see p67)*. A further
collection in the same building
is devoted to the Berlin theatre
during the period 1730 to 1933,
including many posters, old
programmes and stage sets.
One of the galleries houses
some charming old-time
mechanical musical instruments, which can be heard
playing during special shows.
The Märkisches Museum is
a branch of the Stadtmuseum
Berlin organization, and those

who wish to find out more
about the history of the city
can visit other affiliated
museums and monuments
such as the Nikolaikirche *(see
pp90–91)* and the Ephraim-
Palais *(see p91)*. Surrounding
the museum is the Köllnischer
Park, home to three brown
bears, the official city mascots,
and an unusual statue of
Berlin artist Heinrich Zille.

Märkisches Ufer ⑮

Map 8 D4. Ⓤ *Märkisches Museum.*
Ⓢ *Jannowitzbrücke.* 🚌 *147, 240,
248, M48.*

Once called Neukölln am
Wasser, this street, which
runs along the Spree river, is
one of the few corners of
Berlin where it is still possible
to see the town much as it
must have looked in the 18th
and 19th centuries. Eight
picturesque houses have been
meticulously conserved here.
    Two Neo-Baroque houses
at No. 16 and No. 18, known
as Otto-Nagel Haus, used to
contain a small museum
displaying paintings by Otto
Nagel, a great favourite with
the communist authorities.
The building now houses the

photographic archives for the
state museums of Berlin. A
number of picturesque garden
cafés and fashionable restaurants make this attractive area
very popular with tourists.

The Neo-Classical exterior of the
Ermeler-Haus

Ermeler-Haus ⑯

ERMELER HOUSE

Märkisches Ufer 10. **Map** 7 C4. Ⓤ
Märkisches Museum. Ⓢ *Jannowitzbrücke.* 🚌 *147, 240, 248, M48.*

With its harmonious Neo-
Classical façade, Märkisches
Ufer No. 12 stands out as one
of the most handsome villas
in Berlin. This house was
once the town residence of
Wilhelm Ferdinand Ermeler, a
wealthy merchant and shop-
keeper, who made his money
trading in tobacco. It originally
stood on Fischerinsel on the
opposite bank of the river, at
Breite Strasse No. 11, but in
1968 the house was dismantled and reconstructed on this
new site. The house was remodelled in 1825 to Ermeler's
specifications, with a decor

Barges moored alongside Märkisches Ufer

that includes a frieze alluding to aspects of the tobacco business. Restorers have recreated much of the original façade. The Rococo furniture dates from about 1760 and the notable 18th-century staircase has also been rebuilt.

A modern hotel has been built to the rear of the house facing Wallstrasse, using Ermeler-Haus as its kitchens while the first-floor rooms are used for special events.

Gertrauden-brücke ⓱

ST GERTRUDE'S BRIDGE

Map 7 B4, 16 F4.
Ⓤ *Spittelmarkt.* 🚌 143, 147.

One of Berlin's more interesting bridges, this connects Fischer Island with Spittel-markt at the point where St Gertrude's Hospital once stood. The Gertrauden-brücke was designed by Otto Stahn and built in 1894.

Standing in the middle of the bridge is a bronze statue of the hospital's patron saint, St Gertrude, by Rudolf Siemering. A 13th-century Christian mystic, St Gertrude is shown here as a Benedictine abbess.

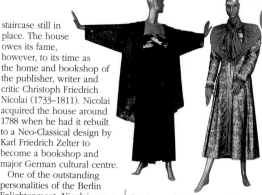

Statue of St Gertrude

Leaning over a poor youth she hands him a lily (symbol of virginity), a distaff (care for the poor), and a vessel filled with wine (love). The pedestal is surrounded by mice, a reference to the fact that Gertrude is patron saint of farmland and graves – both popular environments for mice.

Nicolai-Haus ⓲

Brüderstr. 13. **Map** 7 B4, 16 F4.
Tel 24 00 21 62. Ⓤ *Spittelmarkt.*
🚌 147, 248, 347, M48. ⓞ *by appointment only.* 📷

Built around 1670, the Nicolai-Haus is a fine example of Baroque architecture with the original, magnificent oak

staircase still in place. The house owes its fame, however, to its time as the home and bookshop of the publisher, writer and critic Christoph Friedrich Nicolai (1733–1811). Nicolai acquired the house around 1788 when he had it rebuilt to a Neo-Classical design by Karl Friedrich Zelter to become a bookshop and major German cultural centre.

One of the outstanding personalities of the Berlin Enlightenment, Nicolai was a great supporter of such talents as the Jewish philosopher Moses Mendelssohn *(see p102)* and the playwright Gotthold Ephraim Lessing (1729–81). Other regular literary visitors to the Nicolai-Haus at this period included Johann Gottfried Schadow, Karl Wilhelm Ramler and Daniel Chodowiecki, all of whom are commemorated with a wall plaque. Between 1905 and 1935 the building housed a museum devoted to Gotthold Ephraim Lessing. Today the rear wing features a fine staircase from the Weydinger-Haus, demolished in 1935. Installed in the Nicolai-Haus in the late 1970s, the staircase previously stood in the nearby Ermeler Haus *(see p84)*.

East German fashion now on show in the Märkisches Museum *(see p84)*

Galgenhaus ⓳

GALLOWS HOUSE

Brüderstrasse 10. **Map** 7 B4, 16 F4.
Tel 206 1329. Ⓤ *Spittelmarkt.*
🚌 147, 248, 347, M48. ⓞ *Only during special events.*

Local legend has it that an innocent girl was once hanged in front of this building, which dates from 1700. It was originally built as the presbytery of the now vanished church of St Peter. Redesigned in the Neo-Classical style in 1805, the front portal and one of the rooms on the ground floor are all that remain of the original Baroque structure.

Today the Galgenhaus houses an archive of historic photographs. These reveal the ways in which Berlin has developed over the years through changes in its buildings and monuments.

CÖLLN

An ancient settlement in the area called Fischerinsel at the southern end of Museum Island, the village of Cölln has now been razed almost to the ground. Not even a trace remains of the medieval St Peter's parish church. Until 1939, however, this working-class area with its tangle of narrow streets maintained a historic character and unique identity of its own. This vanished completely in the 1960s when most of the buildings were demolished, to be replaced with prefabricated tower blocks. A few historic houses, including Ermeler-Haus *(see p84)*, were reconstructed elsewhere, but the atmosphere of this part of town has changed forever.

An engraving of old Cölln

EAST OF THE CENTRE

This part of Berlin, belonging to the Mitte district, is the historic centre. A settlement called Berlin was first established on the eastern bank of the Spree river in the 13th century. Together with its twin settlement, Cölln, it grew into a town. This district contains traces of Berlin's earliest history, including the oldest surviving church (Marienkirche). In later centuries, it became a trade and residential district, but the Old Town (the Nikolaiviertel)

The organ-grinder at Gerichtslaube

survived until World War II. The GDR regime replaced the huge apartment buildings and department stores just to the north with a square, Marx-Engels-Forum, and built the Fernsehturm (television tower). Their redevelopment of the Nikolaiviertel was controversial – buildings were faithfully rebuilt but were grouped rather than being placed in their original locations. The area still offers cosy mews and alleys, which are surrounded by postwar high-rise blocks.

SIGHTS AT A GLANCE

Churches
Franziskaner Klosterkirche **16**
Heiliggeistkapelle **10**
Marienkirche **12**
Nikolaikirche **3**
Parochialkirche **18**

Fernsehturm p93 **13**
Marx-Engels-Forum **8**
Neptunbrunnen **11**
Nikolaiviertel **2**

Historic Buildings
Ephraim-Palais **6**
Gaststätte "Zur letzten
   Instanz" **19**
Gerichtslaube **7**
Knoblauchhaus **4**
Palais Podewils **17**
Palais Schwerin and Münze **5**
Rotes Rathaus **1**
Stadtgericht **15**
Stadtmauer **20**

Others
Alexanderplatz **14**
DDR Museum **9**

KEY
Street-by-Street map
See pp88–9

R Railway station

S S-Bahn station

U U-Bahn station

GETTING THERE
This area is served by S-Bahn 3, 5, 7 and 75, with stations at Hackescher Markt, Jannowitzbrücke and Alexanderplatz, which is the interchange for U-Bahn 2, 5 and 8, and for trams M2, M4, M5, M6 and M8. Buses 100, 200, 248 and TXL serve Karl-Liebknecht-Strasse; buses 248 and M48 serve Grunerstrasse.

◁ **Detail from the Neptunbrunnen (Neptune Fountain)**

Street-by-Street: Nikolaiviertel

St Nicholas' Quarter, or the Nikolaiviertel, owes its name to the parish church whose spires rise above the small buildings in this part of town. The Nikolaiviertel is full of narrow alleys crammed with popular restaurants, tiny souvenir shops and small museums. The district was once inhabited by artists and writers, but now it is usually filled with tourists looking for a place to rest after an exhausting day of sightseeing –

Bear on façade of the Rathaus

particularly in the summer. Almost every other house is occupied by a restaurant, inn, pub or café, so the area is quite lively until late at night.

Nikolaikirche
The church is now a museum, with its original furnishings incorporated into the exhibition ❸

Gerichtslaube
The replica arcades and medieval court-house now contain restaurants ❼

POSTSTRASSE

SPREEUFER

St George Slaying the Dragon
This statue once graced a courtyard of the Stadtschloss.

0 metres   75
0 yards   75

Knoblauchhaus
This Biedermeier-style room is on the first floor of the building, which is one of the few to survive World War II damage ❹

★ Ephraim-Palais
A feature of this palace is the elegant façade. Inside there is also an impressive spiral staircase and balustrade ❻

★ **Rotes Rathaus**
This monumental town hall, which once stood in a densely built-up area, now rises from an empty square ❶

LOCATOR MAP
See Street Finder, maps 7 & 8

NORTH OF THE CENTRE

EAST OF THE CENTRE

MUSEUM ISLAND

The Stadthaus, built in 1911 by Ludwig Hoffmann, now houses some of the departments of the Town Hall.

★ **Nikolaiviertel**
The narrow alleys of this district were a source of inspiration for Gotthold Ephraim Lessing, who lived here from 1752 to 1755 ❷

The Hemp Museum
is a small museum specializing in all aspects of the hemp plant.

SPANDAUER STRASSE

MÜHLENDAMM

JÜDENSTRASSE

MOLKEN MARKT

STRALAUER STRASSE

ROLANDUFER

Palais Schwerin and Münze
The palace façade is decorated with a Neo-Classical frieze by Johann Gottfried Schadow, depicting the development of metal processing and coin minting ❺

STAR SIGHTS

★ Ephraim-Palais

★ Rotes Rathaus

★ Nikolaiviertel

KEY

– – – Suggested route

Canal locks on the Spree

Red-brick walls giving the Red Town Hall its name

Rotes Rathaus ❶

RED TOWN HALL

Rathausstr. 15. **Map** 7 C3. **Tel** 90 26 0. **U** Klosterstrasse. **U** & **S** Alexanderplatz. 100, 200, 248, M48, TXL. ◯ 9am–6pm Mon–Fri.

This impressive structure is Berlin's main town hall. Its predecessor was a much more modest structure and by the end of the 19th century, it was insufficient to the needs of the growing metropolis.

The present building was designed by Hermann Friedrich Waesemann, and the construction went on from 1861 until 1869. The architect took his main inspiration from Italian Renaissance municipal buildings, but the tower is reminiscent of Laon cathedral in France. The walls are made from red brick and it was this, rather than the political orientation of the mayors, that gave the town hall its name. The building has a continuous frieze known as the "stone chronicle", which was added in 1879. It features scenes and figures from the city's history and the development of its economy and science.

The Rotes Rathaus was badly damaged during World War II and, following its reconstruction (1951–8), it became the seat of the East Berlin authorities. The West Berlin magistrate was housed in the Schöneberg town hall (see p177). After the reunification of Germany, the Rotes Rathaus became the centre of authority, housing the offices of the mayor, the magistrates' offices and state rooms. The forecourt sculptures were added in 1958. These are by Fritz Kremer and depict Berliners helping to rebuild the city.

Nikolaiviertel ❷

Map 7 C3, C4. **U** & **S** Alexanderplatz. **U** Klosterstrasse. 100, 200, 248, M48, TXL.

This small area on the bank of the Spree, known as the Nikolaiviertel (St Nicholas Quarter), is a favourite place for strolling, for both Berliners and tourists. Some of Berlin's oldest houses stood here until they were destroyed in World War II. The redevelopment of the whole area, carried out by the GDR government between 1979 and 1987, was an interesting, if somewhat controversial, attempt at recreating a medieval village. With the exception of one or two restored buildings, the Nikolaiviertel consists of replicas of historic buildings.

The narrow streets of the Nikolaiviertel tempt the visitor with their small shops, as well as many cafés, bars and restaurants. One of the most popular is Zum Nussbaum, a historical inn that was once located on Fischer Island. The original building, dating from 1507, was destroyed but was subsequently reconstructed at the junction of Am Nussbaum and Propststrasse.

The interior of the Nikolaikirche, one of Berlin's oldest churches

Nikolaikirche ❸

Nikolaikirchplatz. **Map** 7 C3. **Tel** 24 00 21 62. **U** & **S** Alexanderplatz. **U** Klosterstrasse. 100, 147, 200, 248, M48, TXL. ◯ 10am–6pm daily. ♿

The Nikolaikirche is the oldest sacred building of historic Berlin. The original structure erected on this site was started probably around 1230, when the town was granted its municipal rights. What remains now of this stone building is the massive base of the two-tower façade of the present church, which dates from c.1300. The presbytery was completed around 1402, but the construction of the main building went on until the mid-15th century. The result was a magnificent Gothic brick hall-church, featuring a chancel with an

Riverside buildings of the Nikolaiviertel

ambulatory and a row of low chapels. In 1877 Hermann Blankenstein, who conducted the church restoration works, removed most of its Baroque modifications and reconstructed the front towers.

Destroyed by bombing in 1945, the Nikolaikirche was eventually rebuilt in 1987 and shows a permanent exhibit on Berlin's history. The west wall of the southern nave contains Andreas Schlüter's monument to the goldsmith Daniel Männlich and his wife, which features a gilded relief portrait of the couple above a mock doorway.

A fine example of German Baroque architecture, the Ephraim-Palais

Knoblauchhaus ❹

Poststr. 23. **Map** 7 C3. **Tel** 24 00 21 62. Ⓤ & Ⓢ Alexanderplatz, Ⓤ Klosterstrasse. 100, 147, 200, 347, TXL. ☐ 10am–6pm Tue & Thu–Sun, noon–8pm Wed.

This small townhouse in Poststrasse is the only Baroque building in Nikolaiviertel that escaped damage during World War II. It was built in 1759 for the Knoblauch family which includes the famous architect, Eduard Knoblauch. His works include, among others, the Neue Synagoge (see p102).

The current appearance of the building is the result of work carried out in 1835, when the façade was given a Neo-Classical look. The ground floor houses a popular wine bar, while the upper floors belong to a museum. On the first floor it is possible to see the interior of an early 19th-century middle-class home, including a beautiful Biedermeier-style room.

Palais Schwerin and Münze ❺

Molkenmarkt 1–3. **Map** 7 C4. Ⓤ & Ⓢ Alexanderplatz. Ⓤ Klosterstrasse. 100, 147, 200, 347, TXL.

These two adjoining houses have quite different histories. The older one, at Molkenmarkt No. 2, is Palais

Schwerin, which was built by Jean de Bodt in 1704 for a government minister, Otto von Schwerin. Despite subsequent remodelling, the palace kept its beautiful sculptured window cornices, the interior wooden staircase, and the magnificent cartouche featuring the von Schwerin family crest.

The adjoining house is the mint which was built in 1936. Its façade is decorated with a copy of the frieze that once adorned the previous Neo-Classical mint building in Werderscher Markt. The antique style of the frieze was designed by Friedrich Gilly and produced in the workshop of JG Schadow.

Ephraim-Palais ❻

Poststr. 16. **Map** 7 C3. **Tel** 24 00 21 62. Ⓤ & Ⓢ Alexanderplatz. Ⓤ Klosterstrasse. 100, 147, 200, 347, TXL. ☐ 10am–6pm Tue & Thu–Sun, noon–8pm Wed.

The corner entrance of the Ephraim-Palais, standing at the junction of Poststrasse and Mühlendamm, used to be called "die schönste Ecke

Berlins", meaning "Berlin's most beautiful corner". This Baroque palace was built by Friedrich Wilhelm Diterichs in 1766 for Nathan Veitel Heinrich Ephraim, Frederick the Great's mint master and court jeweller.

During the widening of the Mühlendamm bridge in 1935 the palace was demolished, which may have been due in some part to the Jewish origin of its owner. Parts of the façade, saved from demolition, were stored in a warehouse in the western part of the city. In 1983 they were sent to East Berlin and used in the reconstruction of the palace, which was erected a few metres from its original site. One of the first floor rooms features a restored Baroque ceiling, designed by Andreas Schlüter. The ceiling previously adorned Palais Wartenberg, which was dismantled in 1889.

Currently Ephraim-Palais houses a branch of the Stadtmuseum Berlin (Berlin City Museum). It shows a series of temporary exhibitions on Berlin's local artistic and cultural history.

Frieze from the façade of the Münze (the Mint)

Gerichtslaube ❼

Poststrasse. 28. **Map** 7 C3. **Tel** 241
56 97. Ⓤ & Ⓢ *Alexanderplatz.*
Ⓤ *Klosterstrasse.* 🚌 *100, 200,
248, M48, TXL.*

This small building, with its
sharply angled arcades, has
had a turbulent history.
It was built around 1280
as part of Berlin's old town
hall in Spandauer Strasse. The
original building was a single
storey arcaded construction
with vaults supported by a
central pillar. It was open on
three sides and adjoined the
shorter wall of the town hall.
A further storey was added in
1485 to provide a hall to
which the magnificent lattice
vaults were added a few
decades later, in 1555.

In 1692, Johann Arnold
Nering refurbished the town
hall in a Baroque style but left
the arcades unaltered. Then,
in 1868, the whole structure
was dismantled to provide
space for the new town hall,
the Rotes Rathaus *(see p90).*
The Baroque part was lost
forever, but the Gothic
arcades and the first floor hall
were moved to the palace
gardens in Babelsberg, where
they were reassembled as a
building in their own right
(see pp210–11). When the
Nikolaiviertel was undergoing
restoration it was decided
to restore the court of justice
as well. The present building
in Poststrasse is a copy of
a part of the former town
hall, erected on a different
site from the original one.
Inside is a restaurant serving
local cuisine.

Marx-Engels-Forum ❽

Map 7 C3, 16 F2. Ⓢ *Hackescher
Markt or Alexanderplatz.*
🚌 *100, 200, 248, M48, TXL.*

This vast, eerily empty
square, stretching from the
Neptune river to the Spree
river in the west, was given
the inappropriate name
Marx-Engels-Forum (it is not
really a forum). Devoid of
any surroundings, the only

**Statue of Karl Marx and Friedrich
Engels in Marx-Engels-Forum**

features in this square are
the statues of Karl Marx and
Friedrich Engels. The statues,
added in 1986, are by Ludwig
Engelhart. Due to the
extension of an underground
line which started in 2010,
the statues will be moved into
a corner and the square will
be inaccessible for several
years. Berlin plans to build
up the area after completing
the underground works,
rather than restore the
uninspiring square.

DDR Museum ❾

Karl-Liebknecht-Strasse 1.
Map 7 B3, 16 F2. Ⓢ *Hackescher
Markt.* 🚌 *100, 200.*
www.ddr-museum.de

This hands-on museum on
the Spree embankment
opposite the Berlin cathedral,
gives an insight into the
daily lives of East Germans
and demonstrates how the
secret police kept a watchful
eye on the city's people.
Exhibits include the replica
of a typical living room and
a shiny Trabant car.

Heiliggeistkapelle ❿

CHAPEL OF THE HOLY SPIRIT

Spandauer Strasse 1. **Map** 7 B2,
16 F2. Ⓢ *Hackescher Markt.*
🚌 *100, 200, 248, M48, TXL.* 🚊
M4, M5, M6.

This modest Gothic structure is
the only surviving hospital
chapel in Berlin. It was built
as part of a hospital complex
in the second half of the 13th
century, but was subsequently
rebuilt in the 15th century. The
hospital was demolished in
1825, but the chapel was
retained. In 1906, it was made

into a newly erected College
of Trade, designed by Cremer
and Wolffenstein.

The chapel is a fine example
of Gothic brick construction.
Its modest interior features a
15th century star-shaped vault.
The supports under the vault
are decorated with half-statues
of prophets and saints.

Neptunbrunnen ⓫

NEPTUNE FOUNTAIN

Spandauer Str. (Rathausvorplatz).
Map 7 C3. Ⓢ & Ⓤ *Alexanderplatz.*
Ⓢ *Hackescher Markt.* 🚌 *100, 200,
248, M48, TXL.*

This magnificent, Neo-
Baroque style fountain,
sparkling with cascades of
running water, provides a
splendid feature on the main
axis of the town hall building.
It was created in 1886 by
Reinhold Begas, to stand in
front of the southern wall of
the former Stadtschloss
(Berlin Castle). It was moved
to its present site in 1969.

The statue of Neptune, in
a dynamic pose and in the
centre of the fountain, is
surrounded by four figures
representing Germany's
greatest rivers of the time:
the Rhine, the Vistula, the
Oder and the Elbe. The
naturalism of the composition
and the attention to detail,
such as the beautiful bronze
fish, crayfish, snails and
fishing nets, are noteworthy.

**Neptune surrounded by goddesses
personifying Germany's rivers**

Marienkirche ⓬

See pp94–95.

Fernsehturm ⑬

The television tower, called by the locals *Telespargel*, or toothpick, remains to this day the city's tallest structure at 365 m (1,197 ft), and one of the tallest structures in Europe. The tower was built in 1969 to a design by a team of architects including Fritz Dieter and Günter Franke, with the help of Swedish engineering experts. However, the idea for such a colossal tower in Berlin originated much earlier from Hermann Henselmann (creator of the Karl-Marx-Allee development) in the Socialist-Realist style.

VISITORS' CHECKLIST

Panoramastrasse. **Map** 7 C2. *Tel* 242 33 33. Ⓢ & Ⓤ Alexanderplatz. 🚌 100, 200, M48, TXL. 🚊 M2, M4, M5, M6. ⬜ Mar–Oct: 9am–midnight daily; Nov–Feb: 10am–midnight daily.

The television antenna is visible all over Berlin.

Viewing Platform
Situated inside a steel-clad giant sphere, the viewing platform is 203 m (666 ft) above the ground.

Transmitter aerials

Concrete structure rising to 250 m (820 ft)

Television Tower
The slim silhouette of the Fernsehturm is visible from almost any point in Berlin. The ticket office and elevator entrance are located at the base of the tower.

The metal sphere is covered with steel cladding.

The concrete shaft contains two elevators that carry passengers to the café and viewing platform.

The elevators are small, resulting in long queues at the base of the tower.

Tele-Café
One of the attractions of the tower is the revolving café. A full rotation takes about half an hour, so it is possible to get a bird's-eye-view of the whole city while sipping a cup of coffee.

View from the Tower
On a clear day the viewing platform offers a full view of Berlin. Visibility can reach up to 40 km (25 miles).

Marienkirche ⑫

St Mary's Church, or the Marienkirche, was first established as a parish church in the second half of the 13th century. Construction started around 1280 and was completed early in the 14th century. During reconstruction works in 1380, following a fire, the church was altered slightly but its overall shape changed only in the 15th century when it acquired the front tower. In 1790, the tower was crowned with a dome designed by Carl Gotthard Langhans. The church was once hemmed in by buildings, but today it stands alone in the shadow of the Fernsehturm (Television Tower). The early-Gothic hall design and the lavish decorative touches make this church one of the most interesting in Berlin.

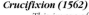

The Tower
The dome that crowns the tower includes both Baroque and Neo-Gothic elements.

Crucifixion (1562)
This image of Christ, flanked by Moses and St John the Baptist, was painted in the Mannerist style by Michael Ribestein.

Totentanz, meaning "dance of death", is the name of a 22-m (72-ft) long Gothic wall fresco, dating from 1485.

Retable
The central part of the Gothic altar, dating from 1510, features figures of three unknown monks.

STAR FEATURES

★ Pulpit

★ Baptismal Font

Main entrance

★ Pulpit

Carved from alabaster, this masterpiece by Andreas Schlüter, completed in 1703, is placed by the fourth pillar. The pulpit is decorated with bas-reliefs of St John the Baptist and the personifications of the Virtues.

VISITORS' CHECKLIST

Karl-Liebknecht-Str 8. **Map** 7 C2. **Tel** *242 44 67.* (S) & (U) *Alexanderplatz.* 🚌 *100, 200, 248, TXL, M48.* 🚋 *M4, M5, M6.* 🔲 *Oct–Mar: 10am–10pm; Apr–Sep: 10am–9pm daily.*

Von Röbel Family Tomb

This richly decorated Mannerist-Baroque tomb of Ehrentreich and Anna von Röbel was probably built after 1630.

Main Altar

The Baroque altar was designed by Andreas Krüger c.1762. The paintings, including Deposition from the Cross *in the centre;* Christ on the Mount of Olives *and* Doubting Thomas *on the sides, are the works of Christian Bernhard Rode.*

★ Baptismal Font

This Gothic font dating from 1437 is supported by three black dragons and decorated with the figures of Jesus Christ, Mary and the Apostles.

The magnificent interior of the Stadtgericht

Alexanderplatz ⓮

Map 8 D2. Ⓤ & Ⓢ *Alexanderplatz.*
🚌 *100, 200, 248, M48, TXL.*
🚋 *M5, M6, M8.*

Alexanderplatz, or "Alex" as it is locally called, has a long history, although it would be difficult now to find any visible traces of the past. Once called Ochsenmarkt (oxen market), it was the site of a cattle and wool market. It was later renamed after Tsar Alexander I, who visited Berlin in 1805. At the time, the square boasted a magnificent monumental colonnade designed by Carl von Gontard *(see p176)*.

With the passage of time, many houses and shops sprang up around the square, and a market hall and an urban train line were built nearby. "Alex" had become one of the town's busiest spots. Its frenzied atmosphere was captured by Alfred Döblin (1878-1957) in his novel, *Berlin Alexanderplatz*.

In 1929, attempts were made to develop the square, though only two office buildings were added – the Alexanderhaus and the Berolinahaus. These two, both by Peter Behrens, are still standing today.

World War II erased most of the square's buildings. It is now surrounded by characterless 1960s edifices, including the Park Inn (formerly Hotel Stadt Berlin) and the Fernsehturm *(see p93)*. Alexanderplatz awaits its next transformation, which might happen soon: a winning design has been chosen from a competition for the square's redevelopment.

Stadtgericht ⓯

COURTS OF JUSTICE

Littenstrasse 13–17. **Map** 8 D3.
Ⓤ & Ⓢ *Alexanderplatz or* Ⓤ
Klosterstrasse. 🚌 *100, 248.* 🚋 *M2.*

This gigantic building, situated on a long stretch of Littenstrasse, does not seem particularly inviting, but its interior hides a true master-piece of the Viennese Secession style of architecture.

At the time of its construction, the building was the largest in Berlin after the Stadtschloss *(see p74)*. The Neo-Baroque structure, built between 1896 and 1905, was designed by Paul Thomer and Rudolf Mönnich, but its final shape is the work of Otto Schmalz. This maze-like complex, with its 11 inner courtyards, was partly demol-ished in 1969. What remains, however, is still worth seeing, especially the magnificent staircase in the form of overlying ellipses. The staircase is an example of Secession architecture at its boldest. The slim Neo-Gothic pillars and the Neo-Baroque balustrades further enhance the fairytale interior.

Franziskaner Klosterkirche ⓰

FRANCISCAN FRIARY CHURCH

Klosterstrasse 74. **Map** 8 D3.
Ⓤ *Klosterstrasse.* 🚌 *248.*

These picturesque ruins surrounded by greenery are the remains of an early-Gothic Franciscan church. The Franciscan friars settled in Berlin in the early 13th century. Between 1250 and 1265 they built a church and a friary, which survived almost unchanged until 1945. The church was a triple-nave basilica with an elongated presbytery, widening into a heptagonal section that was added to the structure in c.1300. Protestants took over the church after the Reform-ation and the friary became a famous grammar school, whose graduates included Otto von Bismarck and Karl Friedrich Schinkel.

The friary was so damaged in World War II that it was subsequently demolished, while the church is gradually

Ruins of the Franziskaner Kloster-kirche (Franciscan Friary Church)

being reconstructed. The giant Corinthian capitals, emerging from the grass near the church ruins, are from a portal from the Stadtschloss (Berlin Castle) *(see p74)*.

Façade of the twice-restored Palais Podewils

Palais Podewils ⓱

PODEWILS PALACE

Klosterstrasse 68–70. **Map** 8 D3.
U *Klosterstrasse.* 248.

This charming Baroque palace, set back from the street, was built between 1701 and 1704 for the Royal Court's counsellor, Caspar Jean de Bodt. Its owes its present name to its subsequent owner, a minister of state called von Podewils, who bought the palace in 1732.

After World War II, the palace was restored twice: in 1954 and then again in 1966 after it had been damaged by fire. The carefully reconstructed building did not lose much of its austere beauty, but the interior completely changed to suit its current needs. Until the mid-2000s, it served as a cultural centre that organized concerts and theatre performances, including ballet.

Parochialkirche ⓲

PARISH CHURCH

Klosterstr. 67. **Map** 8 D3. *Tel* 247
59 510. **U** *Klosterstrasse.* 248.
◯ *10am–4pm Mon–Fri.*

This building was, at one time, one of most beautiful Baroque churches in Berlin. Johann Arnold

Nering prepared the initial design, with four chapels framing a central tower. Unfortunately, Nering died as construction started in 1695. The work was continued by Martin Grünberg, but the collapse of the nearly completed vaults forced a change in the design. Instead of the intended tower over the main structure, a vestibule with a front tower was built. The church was completed in 1703, but then, in 1714, its tower was enlarged by Jean de Bodt in order to accommodate a carillon.

World War II had a devastating effect on the Parochialkirche. The interior was completely destroyed, and the tower collapsed. Following stabilization of the main structure, the façade has been restored, with some reproduced historic elements set within a plain interior. During the summer, mass is held in the church.

Medallion from a headstone in the Parochialkirche

Gaststätte Zur letzten Instanz ⓳

INN OF THE LAST INSTANCE

Waisenstrasse 14–16. **Map** 8 D3.
U *Klosterstrasse.* 248.

The small street at the rear of the Parochialkirche leads directly to one of the oldest inns in Berlin, Zur letzten Instanz, which translates as the Inn of the Last Instance. The inn occupies one of the four picturesque houses on Waisenstrasse – the only survivors of the whole row of houses that

once adjoined the town wall. Their history goes back to medieval times, but their present form dates from the 18th century. The houses are actually the result of an almost total reconstruction carried out after World War II. This was when one of the houses acquired its spiral Rococo staircase, which came from a dismantled house on the Fischerinsel.

The Zur letzten Instanz was first established in 1621 and initially specialized in serving alcoholic beverages. Interestingly, it was frequently patronized by lawyers. Today, however, the Zur letzten Instanz is one of Berlin's finest historic pub-restaurants frequented by all types of people, not just lawyers *(see p237)*. Its interior is full of old memorabilia.

Stadtmauer ⓴

TOWN WALL

Waisenstrasse **Map** 8 D3.
U & **S** *Alexanderplatz or*
U *Klosterstrasse.* 248.

The town wall that once surrounded the settlements of Berlin and Cölln was erected in the second half of the 13th century. The ring of fortifications, built from fieldstone and brick, was made taller in the 14th century. Having finally lost its military significance by the 17th century, the wall was almost entirely dismantled. Today, some small sections survive around Waisenstrasse, because they were incorporated into other buildings.

Remains of the Berlin's Stadtmauer (old town wall)

NORTH OF THE CENTRE

The area northwest of Alexanderplatz, bounded by Friedrichstrasse and Karl-Liebknecht-Strasse, is the former Spandauer Vorstadt, so called because one of its main streets, Oranienburger Strasse, led to Spandau. The eastern part of the area is known as Scheunenviertel (Barn Quarter). In 1672, the Great Elector moved the hay barns – a fire hazard – out of the city limits. From that time it became a refuge for Jews fleeing Russia and Eastern Europe, and by the 19th century it had become the well-established centre for Berlin's Jewish community. The area also

Detail from Postfuhramt

attracted artists, writers and political activists in the 1920s. Shops, hospitals, small factories and narrow streets of houses inhabited by workers and merchants gave the district its unique, lively character. After World War II the area gradually fell into decay. However, it has recently become fashionable again. Today, its newly restored houses, grand buildings and trendy restaurants stand side by side with dilapidated tenement blocks, shabby courtyards and buildings engulfed in scaffolding. The area is popular with tourists and Berliners alike, especially in the evenings.

SIGHTS AT A GLANCE

Streets and Parks
Alte and Neue
  Schönhauser Strasse **10**
Monbijoupark **4**
Oranienburger Strasse **3**
Sophienstrasse **9**

Churches and Synagogues
Neue Synagoge **1**
Sophienkirche **8**

Theatres
Berliner Ensemble **13**
Deutsches Theater **14**
Friedrichstadtpalast **12**
Volksbühne **11**

Museums
Brecht-Weigel-Gedenkstätte **17**
Centrum Judaicum **2**

*Hamburger Bahnhof
pp110–11* **19**
Museum für Naturkunde **18**

Cemeteries
Alter Jüdischer Friedhof **7**
*Dorotheenstädtischer Friedhof
pp106–7* **16**

Others
Charité **15**
Gedenkstätte Grosse
  Hamburger Strasse **6**
Hackesche Höfe **5**

GETTING THERE
S-Bahn lines 3, 5, 7 and 9 run along the south of the area, with stops at Hauptbahnhof, Friedrichstrasse and Hackescher Markt. S-Bahn lines 1 and 2 stop at Oranienburger Strasse. U-Bahn line 6 goes to Oranienburger Tor station, line 8 to Weinmeisterstrasse and line 2 to Rosa-Luxemburg-Platz.

KEY

Street-by-Street map
See pp100–1

U U-Bahn station

S S-Bahn station

Tram stop

Bus stop

Railway station

Tourist information

0 metres   600
0 yards   600

◁ **The first courtyard in Hackesche Höfe**

Street-by-Street: Scheunenviertel

Until World War II Scheunenviertel lay at
the heart of Berlin's large Jewish district.
During the 19th century the community
flourished, its prosperity reflected in grand
buildings such as the Neue Synagoge, which
opened in 1866 in the presence of Chancellor
Otto von Bismarck. Left to crumble for
nearly 50 years after the double devastations
of the Nazis and Allied bombing, the district
has enjoyed a huge revival since the fall
of the Wall. Cafés and bars have opened
and visitors can expect to find some of
the liveliest nightlife in East Berlin.

**★ Neue
Synagoge**
*Sparkling with
gold, the
restored New
Synagogue is
now used again
for services* ❶

The Postfuhramt
was used originally as
stables for the horses
that delivered the
post. Its ceramic-clad
façade resembles
a palace more than
a post office.

Centrum Judaicum
*Standing next to the
Neue Synagoge, the
Jewish Centre houses
documents relating
to the history and
cultural heritage
of the Berlin
Jews* ❷

Heckmann-Höfe
*Today these lavishly restored
yards, the most elegant in Berlin,
attract visitors with a restaurant
and fashionable clothes shops.*

KEY

– – – Suggested route

STAR SIGHTS

★ Neue Synagoge

★ Hackesche Höfe

S-Bahn
line

Sophienkirche
This small Protestant church was founded in 1712 by Queen Sophie Luisa **8**

LOCATOR MAP
See Street Finder maps 1 & 6

Gedenkstätte Grosse Hamburger Strasse
This modest memorial to the Berlin Jews stands on the site of the city's first Jewish old people's home **6**

Dorotheen-
städtischerfriedhof

G
R
O
S
S
E

H
A
M
B
U
R
G
E
R

S
T
R
A
S
S
E

★ Hackesche Höfe
This attractive series of interconnected courtyards is home to many popular entertainment venues **5**

0 metres	50
0 yards	50

Alter Jüdischer Friedhof
Now a tree-filled park, the city's oldest Jewish cemetery was systematically destroyed by the Gestapo in 1943 **7**

HACKESCHER MARKT

→ **Fernsehturm (television tower)**

Monbijoupark
Once the grounds of a royal palace, this small park contains a marble bust of the poet Adelbert von Chamisso **4**

Neue Synagoge ❶

NEW SYNAGOGUE

Oranienburger Strasse 30. **Map** 7 A1.
Tel 880 28 316. Ⓢ *Oranienburger
Strasse.* ▥ 240. ▤ M1, M6, 12.
◯ *Mar–Oct: 10am–8pm Sun–Mon,
10am–6pm Tue–Thu, 10am–2pm Fri
(to 5pm Fri from Apr–Sep); Nov–Feb:
10am–6pm Sun–Mon.* ▨
◗ *Jewish festivals.* ⬛

The building of the New
Synagogue was started in 1859
by architect Eduard Knoblauch,
and completed in 1866. The
design, a highly sophisticated
response to the asymmetrical
shape of the plot of land, used
a narrow façade flanked by a
pair of towers and crowned
with a dome containing a
round vestibule. Small rooms
opened off the vestibule,
including an anteroom and
two prayer rooms – one large
and one small. The two towers
opened onto a staircase leading
to the galleries, and the main
hall had space for around 3,000
worshippers. An innovative
use of iron in the construction
of the roof and galleries put the
synagogue at the forefront of
19th-century civil engineering.

This fascinating structure
was Berlin's largest synagogue,
until 9 November 1938, when it
was partially destroyed during
the infamous *"Kristallnacht"*
(see pp28–9). The building
was damaged further by Allied
bombing in 1943 and was
finally demolished in 1958 by
government authorities.

Reconstruction started in
1988 and was completed with
due ceremony in 1995. The
front of the building is used
for public exhibitions by the
Centrum Judaicum.

The Centrum Judaicum, centre for research into Jewish heritage

Centrum Judaicum ❷

JEWISH CENTRE

Oranienburger Strasse 28–30. **Map** 7
A1. *Tel* 880 28 316. Ⓢ *Oranienburger
Strasse.* ▥ 240. ▤ M1, M6, 12.
◯ *Mar–Oct: 10am–8pm Sun–Mon,
10am–6pm Tue–Thu, 10am–2pm Fri
(to 5pm Fri from Apr–Sep); Nov–Feb:
10am–6pm Sun–Mon.* ▨
◗ *Jewish festivals.* ⬛

The entrance to the Jewish
Centre is easy to recognize
thanks to the policemen
permanently stationed here.
All visitors must undergo a
strict security check involving
the use of a metal detector:
the guards are polite but firm.
The Centrum Judaicum occupies the former premises of
the Jewish community council,
and contains a library, archives
and a research centre devoted
to the history and cultural
heritage of the Berlin Jews.
Next door to the Centrum, the
restored rooms of the Neue
Synagogue are used to exhibit
material relating to the local
Jewish community, including

one of the greatest of all Jewish
thinkers and social activists,
Moses Mendelssohn. Next to
the Centrum is the well-known
Oren restaurant, which serves
Jewish and Middle Eastern
cuisine *(see p238).*

Oranienburger Strasse ❸

Map 6 F1, 7 A1 & 7 B2. Ⓢ
*Oranienburger Strasse or Hackescher
Markt.* ▥ 240. ▤ M1, M6, 12.

Oranienburger Strasse is
home to many of Berlin's
most popular nightspots.
People of all ages flock here,
spending pleasant hours in
the area's numerous cafés,
restaurants and bars. The
district has traditionally been
a centre for alternative
culture, home to the famous
state-sponsored Tacheles
centre for the arts. The life
of the Tacheles centre may
now be coming to an end,
but many good art galleries
remain in this area. As you
stroll around the district it is
worth looking out for a

The Neue Synagoge with its
splendidly reconstructed dome

MOSES MENDELSSOHN (1729–1786)

One of the greatest German philosophers
of the 18th century, Moses Mendelssohn
arrived in Berlin in 1743 and was a
central figure in the Jewish struggle
for citizenship rights. About 50 years
later the first Jewish family was
granted full civic rights, however, it
wasn't until the Emancipation Edict of
1812 that Jewish men finally became full citizens. The
grandfather of composer Felix Mendelssohn-Bartholdy, he
is immortalized in the drama *Nathan der Weise* (Nathan
the Wise) by his friend Gotthold Ephraim Lessing.

number of interesting buildings, such as the one at
Oranienburger Strasse No.
71–2, which was built by
Christian Friedrich Becherer
in 1789 for the Great National
Masonic Lodge of Germany.

Monbijoupark ➍

MONBIJOU PARK

Oranienburger Strasse. **Map** 7 B2.
Ⓢ *Oranienburger Strasse or
Hackescher Markt.* 🚌 *240.*
🚊 *M1, M6, 12.*

This small park, situated
between Oranienburger
Strasse and the Spree river,
was once the grounds of the
Monbijou Palace. Damaged
by bombing during World
War II, the ruined palace was
dismantled in 1960. A rare
green space in this part of the
city, the well-kept park is a
pleasant place to spend time
relaxing. It features a marble
bust of the poet Adelbert von
Chamisso, and there is also a
swimming pool for children.

Hackesche Höfe ➎

Rosenthaler Strasse 40–41. **Map** 7
B1 7 B2. Ⓢ *Hackescher Markt.*
🚊 *M1, M6, 12.*

Running from Oranien-
burger Strasse and Rosen-
thaler up as far as Sophienstrasse, the Hackesche Höfe
(*Höfe* means yards) is a huge,
early 20th-century complex. It
is made up of an intricate
series of nine interconnecting

**One of the striking inner courtyards
at the Hackesche Höfe**

courtyards surrounded by tall
and beautifully proportioned
buildings. The development
dates from 1906, and was
designed by Kurt Berendt and
August Endell, both of whom
were outstanding exponents
of the German Secession style.
  Damaged during World War
II, Hackesche Höfe has been
restored recently to its original splendour. The first
courtyard is especially attractive, featuring glazed facings
with geometric designs
decorated in fabulous colours.
A whole range of restaurants,
bars, art galleries, shops and
restaurants can be found
here, as well as offices and
apartments on the upper
floors. The complex also has
its own theatre, the Hackesche
Hoftheater, specializing in
mime. For many Berliners the
Hackesche Höfe has became
something of a cult spot, and
for visitors it is definitely a
sight not to be missed.

Gedenkstätte
Grosse Hamburger
Strasse ➏

GROSSE HAMBURGER STRASSE
MEMORIAL

Grosse Hamburger Strasse. **Map** 7 B1.
Ⓢ *Hackescher Markt.* 🚊 *M1, M4,
M5, M6, 12.*

Until the years leading up
to World War II, Grosse
Hamburger Strasse was one
of the main streets of Berlin's
Jewish quarter. It was home
to several Jewish schools, an
old people's home and the
city's oldest Jewish cemetery,
established in 1672. The home
was used during World War II
as a detention centre for many
thousands of Berlin Jews condemned to death in the camps
at Auschwitz and Theresien-
stadt. The building was later
destroyed, and in its place
now stands a small monument
representing a group of Jews
being led to their deaths. A
modest commemorative
plaque is displayed nearby.
  Nearby, at Grosse Ham-
burger Strasse No. 27, stands
a Jewish school founded in
1778 by Moses Mendelssohn.
Rebuilt in 1906, the building
was reopened as a Jewish
secondary school in 1993. The
empty space once occupied
by house No. 15–16, which
was destroyed by World War
II bombing, is now an installation, *"The Missing House"* by
Christian Boltanski, with
plaques recording the names
and professions of the former
inhabitants of the house.

The Gedenkstätte Grosse Hamburger Strasse commemorating Berlin Jews murdered in the Holocaust

Alter Jüdischer Friedhof ⓐ

OLD JEWISH CEMETERY

Grosse Hamburger Strasse. **Map** 7 B2. Ⓢ *Hackescher Markt.* 🚊 *M1.*

The Old Jewish Cemetery was established in 1672 and, until 1827 when it was finally declared full, it provided the resting place for over 12,000 Berliners. After this date Jews were buried in cemeteries in Schönhauser Allee and in Herbert-Baum-Strasse. The Alter Jüdischer Friedhof was destroyed by the Nazis in 1943, and in 1945 the site was turned into a park. Embedded in the original cemetery wall, a handful of Baroque *masebas* (or tombstones) continue to provide a poignant reminder of the past. A *maseba* stands on the grave of the philosopher Moses Mendelssohn *(see p102)*, erected in 1990 by members of the Jewish community.

Tombstone of Moses Mendelssohn

Sophienkirche ⓑ

Grosse Hamburger Str. 29. **Map** 7 B1. **Tel** 308 79 20. Ⓢ *Hackescher Markt.* Ⓤ *Weinmeisterstrasse.* 🚊 *M1, M4, M5, M6.* ☐ *May–Sep: 3–6pm Wed, 3–5pm Sat.* ✝ *10am Sun.*

A narrow passageway and a picturesque gate take you through to this small Baroque church. Founded in 1712 by

Eighteenth-century buildings along Sophienstrasse

Queen Sophie Luisa, this was the first parish church of the newly developed Spandauer Vorstadt area *(see p99)*. Johann Friedrich Grael designed the tower which was built between 1729 and 1735.

In 1892 the building was extended to include a presbytery, though the church still retains its original Baroque character. A modest, rectangular structure, Sophienkirche is typical of its period, with the tower adjoining the narrower side elevation. The interior still contains a number of its original 18th-century furnishings, including the pulpit and the font.

Several gravestones, some from the 18th century, have survived in the small cemetery surrounding the church.

Sophienstrasse ⓒ

Map 7 B1. **Sammlung Hoffmann** Sophienstrasse 21. **Tel** 284 99 121. Ⓢ *Hackescher Markt.* Ⓤ *Weinmeisterstrasse.* 🚊 *M1, M4, M5, M6.* ☐ *11am–4pm Sat, by appointment.* 🎟

The area around Sophienstrasse and Gipsstrasse was first settled at the end of the 17th century. In fact, Sophienstrasse was once the main street of Spandauer Vorstadt. The area underwent extensive restoration during

the 1980s. It was one of the first parts of East Berlin in which renovation was chosen in favour of large-scale demolition and redevelopment. Now these modest but charming 18th-century Neo-Classical buildings are home to a number of different arts and crafts workshops, cosy bars, unusual boutiques and interesting art galleries.

One building with a particularly eventful history is Sophienstrasse No. 18. The house was erected in 1852, although its striking and picturesque, terracotta double doorway dates from the time of its extensive restoration, undertaken in 1904 by Joseph Franckel and Theodor Kampfmeyer on behalf of the Crafts Society. Founded in 1844, the Crafts Society moved its headquarters to Sophienstrasse in 1905. On 14 November 1918 the very same house was used as the venue for the first meeting of the Spartacus League *(see p132)*, which was later to become the Communist Party of Germany.

The main door of the house at Sophienstrasse No. 21 leads into a long row of interior courtyards running up as far as Gipsstrasse. In one of these courtyards is a private modern art gallery, the **Sammlung Hoffmann**, which can be reached by passing through a brightly-lit tunnel.

Interior of the Sophienkirche with its original 18th-century pulpit

Alte and Neue Schönhauser Strasse ❿

Map 7 B1, 7 C1. Ⓢ *Hackescher Markt.* Ⓤ *Weinmeisterstrasse.* 🚊 *M1.*

Alte Schönhauser Strasse is one of the oldest streets in the Spandauer Vorstadt district, running from the centre of Berlin to Pankow and Schönhausen. In the 18th and 19th centuries this was a popular residential area among wealthy merchants. The proximity of the neighbouring slum area of the Scheunenviertel *(see pp100–3)* to the west, however, lowered the tone of the neighbourhood quite considerably.

For a long time, bars, small factories, workshops and retail shops were the hallmark of the neighbourhood around Alte Schönhauser Strasse. Small private shops survived longer here than in most other parts of Berlin, and until recently the largely original houses maintained much of their pre-1939 atmosphere.

Much has changed, however, since the fall of the Berlin Wall. Some of the houses have now been restored, and many old businesses have been replaced by fashionable new shops, restaurants and bars. Throughout the district, the old and the new now stand side by side. One

One of the Neo-Renaissance buildings on Neue Schönhauser Strasse

poignant example is at Neue Schönhauser Strasse No. 14. This interesting old house in the German Neo-Renaissance style was built in 1891 to a design by Alfred Messel. The first-floor rooms were home to the first public reading-room in Berlin, while on the ground floor was a *Volkskaffeehaus*, a soup-kitchen with separate rooms for men and women. Here the poor of the neighbourhood could get a free bowl of soup and a cup of ersatz (imitation) coffee.

Ironically, in the 1990s, the building became home to one of Berlin's most fashionable restaurants.

Volksbühne ⓫

PEOPLE'S THEATRE

Rosa-Luxemburg-Platz. **Map** 8 D1. **Tel** 24 06 55. Ⓤ *Rosa-Luxemburg-Platz.* 🚌 *100, 200, 240, TXL.* 🚊 *M2, M8.*

Founded during the early years of the 20th century, this theatre owes its existence to the efforts of the 100,000 members of the Freie Volksbühne (Free People's Theatre Society). The original theatre was built to a design by Oskar Kaufmann in 1913, a time when the Scheunenviertel district was undergoing rapid redevelopment. During the 1920s the theatre became famous thanks to the director Erwin Piscator (1893–1966), who later achieved great acclaim at the Metropol-Theater on Nollendorfplatz.

Destroyed during World War II, the theatre was eventually rebuilt during the early 1950s to a design by Hans Richter.

The eye-catching façade of the Friedrichstadtpalast theatre complex

Friedrichstadt-palast ⓬

FRIEDRICHSTADT PALACE

Friedrichstrasse 107. **Map** 6 F2. **Tel** 23 26 23 26. Ⓤ *Oranienburger Tor.* Ⓢ *Oranienburger Strasse or Friedrichstrasse.* 🚌 *147.* 🚊 *M1, 12.*

Multi-coloured glass tiles and a pink, plume-shaped neon sign make up the gaudy but eye-catching façade of the Friedrichstadtpalast. Built in the early 1980s, this gigantic theatre complex specializes in revues and variety shows. Nearly 2,000 seats are arranged around a huge podium, used by turns as a circus arena, a swimming pool and an ice-rink. In addition, a further huge stage is equipped with every technical facility. There is also a small cabaret theatre with seats for 240 spectators.

The original and much-loved Friedrichstadtpalast suffered bomb damage during World War II, and was later condemned and replaced with the existing version. Built as a market hall, the earlier building was later used as a circus ring. In 1918 it became the Grosse Schauspielhaus, or Grand Playhouse, opening on 28 November 1919 with a memorable production of Aeschylus' *The Oresteia* directed by the extraordinary Max Reinhardt *(see p108)*.

The building itself was legendary, its central dome supported by a forest of columns and topped with an Expressionist, stalactite-like decoration. An equally fantastical interior provided seating for 5,000 spectators.

Dorotheenstädtischer Friedhof ⓰

This small cemetery, established in 1763, is the final resting place of many famous Berlin citizens. It was enlarged between 1814 and 1826, but in 1899, following the extension of Hannoversche Strasse, the southern section of the cemetery was sold and its graves moved. Many of the monuments are outstanding works of art, coming from the workshops of some of the most prominent Berlin architects, including Karl Friedrich Schinkel (see p187) and Johann Gottfried Schadow. A tranquil, tree-filled oasis, the cemetery is reached via a narrow path, leading from the street, between the wall of the French Cemetery and the Brecht-Weigel-Gedenkstätte house (see p109).

Copy of Schadow's Martin Luther

★ **Johann Gottfried Schadow** (1764–1850)
Schadow created the famous Quadriga, *which adorns the Brandenburg Gate.*

Friedrich August Stüler (1800–1865)
Damaged during World War II, the grave of this famous architect was rebuilt in a colourful, post-modernist style.

Heinrich Mann (1871–1950)
This famous German novelist died in California but was buried in Berlin. The portrait is the work of Gustav Seitz.

Bertolt Brecht (1898–1956)
The grave of this famous playwright is marked with a rough stone. Beside him rests his wife, the actress Helene Weigel.

Hermann Wentzel (1820–1889)
This architect designed his own tombstone; the bust was carved by Fritz Schaper.

Main entrance

BIRKENALLEE

BRECHTWEG

Friedrich Hoffmann
(1818–1900)
The tomb of this engineer, best known as the inventor of the circular brick-firing kiln, takes the form of a colonnade faced with glazed bricks.

VISITORS' CHECKLIST

Chausseestrasse 126. **Map** 6 F1.
Tel 461 72 79. 832 51 01.
Naturkundemuseum or Oranienburger Tor. 240, 245.
M6, 12. May–Aug: 8am–8pm; Sep–Apr: 8am–4pm.

★ Karl Friedrich Schinkel
(1781–1841)
Schinkel was the most prominent German architect of his time, and the creator of many of Berlin's best-loved buildings.

Georg Wilhelm Friedrich Hegel
(1770–1831)
Probably the greatest German philosopher of the Enlightenment era, Hegel worked for many years as a professor at Berlin University.

BIRKENALLEE

Luther's statue
is a copy of the monument designed by JG Schadow.

Chapel

Johann Gottlieb Fichte
(1762–1814)
A well-known philosopher of the Enlightenment era, Fichte was also the first Rector of Berlin University.

STAR FEATURES

★ JG Schadow

★ KF Schinkel

| 0 metres | 20 |
| 0 yards | 20 |

Bertolt Brecht's monument in front of the Berliner Ensemble

Berliner Ensemble ⓭

Bertolt-Brecht-Platz 1. **Map** 6 F2.
Tel *28 40 81 55.* Ⓢ *&* Ⓤ
Friedrichstrasse. 🚌 *147.* 🚋 *M1, 12.*

Designed by Heinrich Seeling in the Neo-Baroque style and built from 1891 to 1892, this theatre has been witness to many changes in Berlin's cultural life. First known as the Neues Theater am Schiffbauerdamm, it soon became famous for staging important premieres. In 1895 it put on the first performance of *The Weavers*, by Gerhart Hauptmann. Later on, the theatre was acclaimed for its memorable productions by Max Reinhardt. These included Shakespeare's *A Midsummer Night's Dream* in 1905 which, for the first time, used a revolving stage and real trees as part of the set. In 1928 the theatre presented the world premiere of Bertolt

Brecht's *The Threepenny Opera*. The building was destroyed during World War II and subsequently restored with a much simpler exterior, but its Neo-Baroque interior, including Ernst Westphal's decorations, survived intact. After 1954 the theatre returned to prominence with the arrival of the Berliner Ensemble under the directorship of Bertolt Brecht and his wife, the actress Helene Weigel. The move from its former home, the Deutsches Theater, to the new venue was celebrated in November 1954, by staging the world premiere of *The Caucasian Chalk Circle*, written by Brecht in 1947. After Brecht's death his wife took over running the theatre, maintaining its innovative tradition.

Deutsches Theater ⓮

Schumannstrasse 13A. **Map** 6 E2.
Tel *28 44 12 25.* **Kammerspiele**
Ⓤ *Oranienburger Tor.* 🚌 *147.*
🚋 *M1, 12.*

The theatre building was designed by Eduard Titz and built between 1849 and 1850 to house the Friedrich-Wilhelm Städtisches Theater. In 1883, following substantial reconstruction, it was renamed Deutsches Theater and opened with Friedrich Schiller's *Intrigue and Love*. The theatre became famous under its next director, Otto Brahm, and it was here that Max Reinhardt began his career as an actor,

before eventually becoming director from 1905 until 1933. On Reinhardt's initiative the theatre's façade was altered and in 1906 the adjacent casino was converted into a compact theatre – the Kammerspiele. At the time, the first-floor auditorium was decorated with a frieze by Edvard Munch (now in the Neue Nationalgalerie).

Another famous figure associated with the Deutsches Theater was Bertolt Brecht who, until 1933, wrote plays for it; after World War II he became the director of the Berliner Ensemble, whose first venue was the Deutsches Theater. Brecht's debut as director was his play, *Mother Courage and Her Children*.

Elegant 19th-century façade of the Deutsches Theater

Charité ⓯

Schumannstrasse 20–21. **Map** 6 E1, E2.
Tel *450 53 61 56.* Ⓤ *Oranienburger Tor.*
🚌 *147.* 🚋 *M1, 12.* ◯ *10am–5pm Tue, Thu–Sun, 10am–7pm Wed.*

This huge building complex near Luisenstrasse contains the Charité hospital. Germany's oldest teaching hospital, it was first established in 1726 and has been attached to the Humboldt University *(see p60)* since its foundation in 1810. The oldest buildings of the current complex date back to the 1830s. Over the years, Charité has been associated with many famous German doctors and scientists who worked here, including Rudolf Virchow and Robert Koch.

In 1899 Virchow founded the Museum of Pathology, which occupied purpose-built premises next to the Institute of Pathology. Its collection consisted of some 23,000 specimens, which were also available for public viewing.

MAX REINHARDT (1873–1943)

This actor and director became famous as one of the 20th century's greatest theatre reformers. He worked in Berlin, first as an actor in the Deutsches Theater, and then from 1905 as its director. As well as setting up the Kammerspiele, he produced plays for the Neues Theater am Schiffbauerdamm (renamed the Berliner Ensemble) and the Schumann Circus (later to become the Friedrichstadtpalast), which was converted specially for him by Hans Poelzig. His experimental productions of classic and modern works brought him world-wide fame. Forced to emigrate because of his Jewish origins, he left Germany in 1933 and settled in the United States, where he died in 1943.

Although many artifacts were destroyed in World War II, the museum itself has survived and reopened in 1999.

Dorotheenstädtischer Friedhof

See pp106–107.

Brecht-Weigel-Gedenkstätte

BRECHT-WEIGEL MEMORIAL

Chausseestrasse 125. *Tel* 200 571 844. **Map** 6 E1. *Naturkundemuseum or Oranienburger Tor.* 147, 245. M6, 12. 10–11:30am, 2–3:30pm Tue, 10–11:30am Wed & Fri, 10–11:30am, 5–6:30pm Thu, 10am–3:30pm Sat, 11am–6pm Sun. compulsory. Every half hour (every hour on Sun). Mon, public hols.

Bertolt Brecht, one of the greatest playwrights of the 20th century, was associated with Berlin from 1920, but emigrated in 1933. After the war, his left-wing views made him an attractive potential resident of the newly created German socialist state. Lured by the promise of his own theatre he returned to Berlin in 1948, with his wife, actress Helene Weigel. He directed the Berliner Ensemble until his death, concentrating mainly on the production of his plays.

He lived in a first-floor apartment at Chausseestrasse 125 from 1953 until his death in 1956. He is buried in Dorotheenstädtischer Friedhof

(see pp106–7). His wife lived in the second-floor apartment, and after Brecht's death moved to the ground floor. She also founded an archive of Brecht's works which is located on the second floor of the building.

Museum für Naturkunde

NATURAL HISTORY MUSEUM

Invalidenstrasse 43. **Map** 6 E1. *Tel* 20 93 85 91. *Naturkundemuseum.* 147, 245. 8:30am–6pm Tue–Fri, 10am–6pm Sat, Sun, public hols.

One of the biggest natural history museums in the world, the collection here contains over 60 million exhibits.

Occupying a purpose-built Neo-Renaissance building, constructed between 1883 and 1889, the museum has been operating for over a century, and despite several periods of renovation, has maintained its unique old-fashioned atmosphere.

The highlight of the museum is the world's largest original dinosaur skeleton which is housed in the glass-covered courtyard. This colossal 23-m (75-ft) long and 12-m (39-ft) high brachiosaurus was discovered in Tanzania in 1909 by a German fossil-hunting expedition. Six other smaller reconstructed dinosaur skeletons and a replica of the fossilized remains of an archaeopteryx, thought to be the prehistoric link between reptiles and birds, complete this fascinating display.

The adjacent rooms feature extensive collections of colourful shells and butterflies, as well as stuffed birds and mammals. Particularly popular are the dioramas – scenes of stuffed animals set against the background of their natural habitat. A favourite with young children is Bobby the Gorilla, who was brought to Berlin Zoo in 1928 as a 2-year old and lived there until 1935. The museum also boasts an impressive collection of minerals and meteorites.

Brachiosaurus skeleton in the Museum für Naturkunde

Bertolt Brecht's study in his former apartment

Hamburger Bahnhof ⑲

This museum is situated in a specially adapted Neo-Classical building that was built in 1847 as a railway station. Following extensive refurbishment by Josef Paul Kleihues, it was opened to the public in 1996. The neon installation surrounding the façade is the work of Dan Flavin. The museum has works by Joseph Beuys, contemporary art donated by the Neue Nationalgalerie and a continually changing selection from the world-renowned Flick Collection of art from the second half of the 20th century as well as from the Marx and Marenza collections. The result is one of the best modern art museums in Europe, which features film, video, music and design alongside painting and sculpture.

★ **Richtkräfte** (1974–77)
Joseph Beuys' work – often a record of his thoughts – created an archive of the artist's vision.

Untitled (1983)
This is a fine example of Anselm Kiefer's work, which often attempts to come to terms with Germany's past.

GALLERY GUIDE
The gallery has over 12,000 sq m (129,000 sq ft) of exhibition space. The west wing contains works by Beuys and the main hall is used for special installations. The Rieckhallen shows selected works from the Flick Collection in rotation.

First floor

Rieckhallen

Ground floor

Genova (1980)
In this painting, Sandro Chia contrasts a finely-drawn Renaissance palace with a colourful sky full of movement and two mysteriously floating figures.

Main entrance

Untitled (1983)
Keith Haring uses a simple means of expression, one that is reminiscent of graffiti, comic book art and woodblock prints.

Untitled (1990)
This painting is a fine example of Cy Twombly's distinctive style, characterized by apparently random scrawls and scribbles, rejecting traditional composition.

VISITORS' CHECKLIST

Invalidenstrasse 50/51. **Map** 6
D1. Ⓢ & Ⓤ *Hauptbahnhof.*
120, 123, 147, 240, 245,
TXL. *Tel* 266 424 242.
🕙 10am–6pm Tue–Fri,
11am–8pm Sat, 11am–6pm Sun.
⬤ 1 Jan, 24, 25 & 31 Dec.
🍴 🅿 ♿ 🚻 📷 ✗ 🛒
www.hamburgerbahnhof.de

Bourgeois Bust – Jeff and Ilona (1991)
The Rococo-style marble bust by Jeff Koons depicts himself with his wife at the time, Ilona, better known as La Cicciolina. The sculpture is deliberately pretentious and tawdry.

Second floor

Not Wanting to Say Anything About Marcel (1969)
John Cage created this work after the death of his friend, the famous artist Marcel Duchamp.

★ **Mao** (1973)
This well-known portrait by Andy Warhol initially elevated the Chinese communist leader to the rank of pop icon.

First Time Painting (1961)
This work by American artist Robert Rauschenberg was created while he worked with John Cage at Black Mountain College.

KEY

☐ Exhibitions

☐ Flick Collection

STAR EXHIBITS

★ Mao

★ Richtkräfte

TIERGARTEN

Once a royal hunting estate, the Tiergarten became a park in the 18th century. In the 19th century a series of buildings, mostly department stores and banks, was erected at Potsdamer Platz. During World War II many of these buildings were destroyed. The division of Berlin changed the character of the area. The Tiergarten area ended up on the west side of the Wall, and later regained its glory with the creation of the Kulturforum and the Hansaviertel. The area around Potsdamer Platz fell in East Berlin, and became a wasteland. Since reunification, however, this area has witnessed exciting development. Together with the new government offices near the Reichstag, this ensures that the Tiergarten area is at the centre of Berlin's political and financial district.

The Caller, on Strasse des 17 Juni

SIGHTS AT A GLANCE

Museums and Galleries
Bauhaus-Archiv ⓮
Bendlerblock (Gedenkstätte
  Deutscher Widerstand) ⓬
Gemäldegalerie pp122–5 �
Kunstbibliothek ⓺
*Kunstgewerbemuseum
  pp118–21* ❹
Kupferstichkabinett ❺
Musikinstrumenten-Museum ❷
Neue Nationalgalerie ❾

Districts, Squares and Parks
Diplomatenviertel ⓯
Grosser Stern ⓱
Hansaviertel ⓳

Potsdamer Platz pp128–31 ❿
Regierungsviertel ㉒
Tiergarten ⓰

Historic Buildings
Haus der Kulturen der Welt ㉑

Philharmonie und
  Kammermusiksaal ❸
Reichstag ㉓
Shell-Haus ⓫
Schloss Bellevue ⓴
Staatsbibliothek ❶
St-Matthäus-Kirche ❼
Villa von der Heydt ⓭

Monuments
Siegessäule ⓲
Sowjetisches Ehrenmal ㉔

KEY

▨	Street-by-Street map *See pp114–15*
Ⓤ	U-Bahn station
Ⓢ	S-Bahn station
▥	Bus stop

0 metres   600
0 yards   600

◁ **One of the many charming stretches of water in the Tiergarten**

Street-by-Street: Around the Kulturforum

Sculpture by Henry Moore

The idea of creating a new cultural centre in West Berlin was first mooted in 1956. The first building to go up was the Berlin Philharmonic concert hall, built to an innovative design by Hans Scharoun in 1961. Most of the plans for the various other components of the Kulturforum were realized between 1961 and 1987, and came from such famous architects as Ludwig Mies van der Rohe. The area is now a major cultural centre which attracts millions of visitors every year.

★ **Kunstgewerbe-museum**
Among the collection at the Museum of Arts and Crafts you can see this intricately carved silver and ivory tankard, made in an Augsburg workshop in around 1640 ❹

Kupferstichkabinett
The large collection of prints and drawings owned by this gallery includes this portrait of Albrecht Dürer's mother ❺

★ **Gemäldegalerie**
Among the most important works of the Old Masters exhibited in this gallery of fine art is this Madonna in Church *by Jan van Eyck (circa 1425)* ❽

Kunstbibliothek
The Art Library boasts a rich collection of books, graphic art and drawings, many of which are displayed in its exhibition halls ❻

REICHPIETSCHUFER

LANDWEHRKANAL

STAR SIGHTS

★ Gemäldegalerie
★ Kunstgewerbe-museum
★ Philharmonie

KEY
‒ ‒ ‒ Suggested route

Neue Nationalgalerie
Sculptures by Henry Moore and Alexander Calder stand outside this streamlined building, designed by Ludwig Mies van der Rohe ❾

★ **Philharmonie**
Its outside covered in a layer of golden aluminium, the Berlin Philharmonic concert hall is known all over the world for its superb acoustics **3**

LOCATOR MAP
See Street Finder maps 4, 5 & 6

TIERGARTEN

AROUND KURFÜRSTEN-DAMM

KREUZBERG

Musikinstrumenten-Museum
This harpsichord is part of a collection of musical instruments dating from the 16th to 20th centuries **2**

St-Matthäus-Kirche
This picturesque 19th-century church stands out among the modern buildings of the Kultur-forum **7**

SCHAROUNSTRÄSSE

POTSDAMER STRASSE

MATTHÄI-KIRCH PLATZ

MUNDSTRASSE

POTSDAMER STRASSE

0 metres 50

0 yards 50

Staatsbibliothek
Hans Scharoun designed this public lending and research library built in 1978 **1**

The main reading room in the Staatsbibliothek

Staatsbibliothek ❶

STATE LIBRARY

Potsdamer Strasse 33. **Map** 6 D5.
Tel 266 23 03. Ⓢ & Ⓤ *Potsdamer
Platz.* 🚌 *147, 200, M29, M48.*
◯ *9am–9pm Mon–Fri, 9am–7pm Sat.*

An unusual-shaped building
with an east facing gilded
dome, the Staatsbibliothek is
home to one of the largest
collections of books and
manuscripts in Europe and is
fondly referred to by Berliners
as the Stabi. After World War
II, East and West Berlin each
inherited part of the pre-war
state library collection and
the Staatsbibliothek was built
to house the part belonging
to West Berlin. The building
itself was designed by
Hans Scharoun and Edgar
Wisniewski and constructed
between 1967 and 1978.

It is a building where the
disciplines of function and
efficiency took precedence to
that of form. The storerooms
hold about five million
volumes; the hall of the vast
reading room is open plan,
with an irregular arrangement
of partitions and floor levels;
general noise and the sound
of footsteps is muffled by

fitted carpets, making the
interior a very quiet and cosy
place in which to work.

The library itself houses
more than four million
books, and an excellent
collection of manuscripts.
The Staatsbibliothek has been
formally linked to the Staatsbibliothek on Unter den
Linden *(see p61).*

Musikinstrumen-
ten-Museum ❷

MUSEUM OF MUSICAL
INSTRUMENTS

Tiergartenstrasse 1. **Map** 6 D5.
Tel 25 48 11 78. Ⓢ & Ⓤ *Potsdamer
Platz or* Ⓤ *Mendelssohn-Bartholdy-
Park.* 🚌 *200, 347.* ◯ *9am–5pm
Tue–Fri (10pm Thu), 10am–5pm
Sat–Sun.* **Wurlitzer Organ
demonstration** *noon Sat.*
📷 ♿ 🚻 🛬

Hidden behind the Phil-
harmonie, in a small
building designed by Edgar
Wisniewski and Hans Scharoun
between 1979 and 1984, the
fascinating Museum of Musical
Instruments houses over 750
exhibits in a collection dating

from 1888. Intriguing displays
enable you to trace each
instrument's development from
the 16th century to the present
day. You can marvel at the
harpsichord of Jean Marius,
once owned by Frederick the
Great, and the violins made
by Amati and Stradivarius.

Most spectacular of all is the
silent-film era cinema organ, a
working Wurlitzer dating from
1929. With a range of sounds
that extends even to locomotive impressions, the
Saturday demonstrations of its
powers attract enthusiastic
crowds. However, during the
the week the sounds of exhibited instruments can be heard
on tapes. The museum also
has an excellent archive and
library open to the public.

Philharmonie
und Kammer-
musiksaal ❸

PHILHARMONIC AND CHAMBER
MUSIC HALL

Herbert-von-Karajan-Str. 1. **Map** 6 D5.
Tel 25 48 81 32. Ⓢ & Ⓤ *Potsdamer
Platz or* Ⓤ *Mendelssohn-Bartholdy-
Park.* 🚌 *200, 347.*

Home to one of the most
renowned orchestras in
Europe, this unusual building
is among the finest postwar
architectural achievements in
Europe. The Philharmonie,
built between 1960 and 1963
to a design by Hans Scharoun,
pioneered a new concept for
concert hall interiors. The
orchestra's podium occupies
the central section of the
pentagonal-shaped hall,
around which are galleries
for the public, designed to
blend into the perspective
of the five corners.

The tent-like gilded exterior of the Philharmonie and Kammermusiksaal

The exterior reflects the interior and is reminiscent of a circus tent. The gilded exterior was added between 1978 and 1981.

The Berlin orchestra was founded in 1882, and has been directed by such luminaries as Hans von Bülow, Wilhelm Furtwängler, the controversial Herbert von Karajan, who led the orchestra from 1954 until his death in 1989, and Claudio Abbado. The current director is Sir Simon Rattle. The orchestra attained renown not only for the quality of its concerts but also through its prolific symphony recordings.

Between the years 1984 to 1987 the Kammermusiksaal, which was designed by Edgar Wisniewski on the basis of sketches by Scharoun, was added to the Philharmonie. This building consolidates the aesthetics of the earlier structure by featuring a central multi-sided space covered by a fanciful tent-like roof.

Kunstgewerbe-museum ❹

MUSEUM OF ARTS AND CRAFTS

See pp118–121.

Kupferstich-kabinett ❺

PRINT GALLERY

Matthäikirchplatz 8. **Map** 5 C5. **Tel** 266 29 51. Ⓢ & Ⓤ *Potsdamer Platz or* Ⓤ *Mendelssohn-Bartholdy-Park.* 🚌 200, 347. **Exhibitions** *10am–6pm Tue–Fri, 11am–6pm Sat–Sun.* 🖼 ♿ ♨ 📷 🎦 🚻 ⌀

The print collections of galleries in the former East and West Berlin were united in 1994 in this building located in the Kulturforum. These displays originate from a collection started by the Great Elector in 1652, which has been open to the public since 1831. Despite wartime losses it has an imposing breadth and can boast around 2,000 engraver's plates, over 520,000 prints and at least 80,000 drawings and watercolours.

Edvard Munch's *Girl on a Beach*, a coloured lithograph

Unfortunately, only a small fraction of these delicate treasures can be even briefly exposed to daylight. Therefore the museum does not have a permanent exhibition, only galleries with temporary displays of selected works. For those with a special interest, items in storage can be viewed in the studio gallery by prior arrangement.

The collection includes work from every renowned artist from the Middle Ages to contemporary times. Well represented is the work of Botticelli (including illustrations for Dante's *Divine Comedy*), Dürer, Rembrandt and the Dutch Masters, Watteau, Goya, Daumier, and painters of the Brücke art movement.

Kunstbibliothek ❻

ART LIBRARY

Matthäikirchplatz 6. **Map** 5 C5. **Tel** 266 29 51. Ⓢ & Ⓤ *Potsdamer Platz or* Ⓤ *Mendelssohn-Bartholdy-Park.* 🚌 200, 347. **Exhibits** *10am–6pm Tue–Fri, 11am–6pm Sat, Sun.* **Library** *2–8pm Mon, 9am–4pm Tue–Fri.* 🎦

The Kunstbibliothek is not only a library with a wide range of publications about the arts, it is also a museum with a huge collection of posters, advertisements and an array of other forms of design. Worth seeing is a display on the history of fashion, as well as a vast collection of items of architectural interest. The

latter includes around 30,000 original plans and drawings by architects such as Johann Balthasar Neumann, Erich Mendelssohn and Paul Wallot.

The exhibitions can be seen in the reading and studio rooms, although parts of the collection are also exhibited in the library's own galleries.

St-Matthäus-Kirche ❼

ST MATTHEW'S CHURCH

Matthäikirchplatz. **Map** 5 C5. **Tel** 262 12 02. Ⓢ & Ⓤ *Potsdamer Platz or* Ⓤ *Mendelssohn-Bartholdy-Park.* 🚌 200, 347. 🕐 *noon–6pm Tue–Sun, and for services.*

St Matthew's Church once stood in the centre of a small square surrounded by buildings. After bomb damage in World War II, the structure was restored, making it the focal point of the Kulturforum. The church was originally built between 1844 and 1846 to a design by Friedrich August Stüler and Hermann Wentzel in a style based on Italian Romanesque temples.

Each of the three naves is covered by a separate two-tier roof, while the eastern end of the church is closed by a semi-circular apse. The exterior of the church is covered in a two-tone brick façade arranged in yellow and red lines. Ironically, this picturesque church with its slender tower now creates quite an exotic element among the many ultramodern and sometimes extravagant buildings of the Kulturforum complex.

The colourful exterior of the St-Matthäus-Kirche

Kunstgewerbemuseum ₄

Meissen porcelain figure

The Museum of Decorative Arts embraces many genres of craft and decorative art, from the early Middle Ages to the modern day. Goldwork is especially well represented. Among the most valuable exhibits is a collection of medieval goldwork from the church treasuries of Enger near Herford, and the Guelph treasury from Brunswick. The museum also takes great pride in its collection of late-Gothic and Renaissance silver from the town of Lüneberg's civic treasury. There are also fine examples of Italian majolica, and 18th- and 19th-century German, French and Italian glass, porcelain and furniture. While the museum is closed for renovations, until summer 2012, the medieval collection will be on display at the Bodemuseum.

★ Domed Reliquary (1175–80)
From the Guelph treasury in Brunswick, the figures in this temple-shaped reliquary are made from walrus ivory.

Main entrance

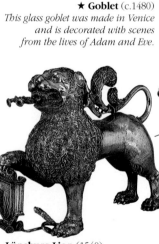

Minneteppich (c.1430)
The theme of this famous tapestry is courtly love. Amorous couples, accompanied by mythical creatures, converse on topics such as infidelity, their words extending along the banners they hold.

★ Goblet (c.1480)
This glass goblet was made in Venice and is decorated with scenes from the lives of Adam and Eve.

Lüneburg Lion (1540)
From the civic treasury in Lüneburg, this gold-plated silver jug in the form of a lion was crafted in the workshop of Joachim Worm.

Basement

VISITORS' CHECKLIST

Herbert Von Karajan Strasse 10.
Map 5 C5. **Tel** 266 424 242.
Ⓢ *Potsdamer Platz.*
Ⓤ *Potsdamer Platz or
Mendelssohn-Bartholdy-Park.*
200, 347, M29, M48, M85.
⬤ *for renovation until summer
2012. Medieval collection on
display at the Bodemuseum,
see p79.*

Candelabra (1900)
*This striking Art
Nouveau candelabra
made from silver,
ivory and onyx is the
work of Belgian artists
Egide Rombaux and
Frans Hoosemans.*

Wedding Dress (c.1780)
*Made from brocade, with a lace
collar and cuffs, this Rococo
wedding dress belonged to
Eleonor Schuster from
Breslau (now Wrocław).*

★ **Harlequin Group** (c.1740)
*These highly decorative, comic
porcelain characters from
Meißen are just one of the
treasures from the cabinets
of curiosities and Baroque
collections to be found
on the second floor.*

Second floor

First floor

Ground floor

KEY

- ☐ Middle Ages
- ☐ Renaissance
- ☐ Baroque
- ☐ Neo-Classical, Art Nouveau
- ☐ 20th-century
- ☐ Temporary exhibitions

GALLERY GUIDE
*The entrance to the museum
is on the first floor, where
there is also an information
gallery. In the basement is an
exhibition of contemporary
design, on the ground floor are
exhibits from the Middle Ages
and the Renaissance, and on
the second floor are handi-
crafts from the Renaissance
through to Art Nouveau.*

STAR EXHIBITS

★ Domed
Reliquary

★ Goblet

★ Harlequin Group

Exploring the Kunstgewerbemuseum

Opened in 1867, the Museum of Decorative Arts was the first of its kind in Germany. It was housed initially in the Martin-Gropius-Bau *(see p140)*, then from 1919 to 1939 occupied the Stadtschloss *(see p74)*. In 1940 it was moved to Schloss Charlottenburg *(see pp160–61)*. The current building, completed in 1985, is closed for renovations until summer 2012. The medieval collection is on display at the Bodemuseum, and another collection is on show in the Schloss Köpenick *(see p175)*.

Pendant of the suffering of Christ

MIDDLE AGES

A large part of this collection is devoted to sacred art, much of it originating from church treasuries. A fine 8th-century reliquary in the shape of a burse (the container used in the Roman Catholic mass to hold the white linen cloth on which the bread and the wine are placed), comes from the treasury of a church in Enger in Westphalia. More reliquaries, many in the form of crosses, date from the 11th and 12th centuries. Two of the most interesting are the Heinrichskreuz, a gift to the cathedral in Basel from the Roman Emperor Heinrich II, and the Welfenkreuz, which comes from the Guelph treasury in Brunswick. Also from the latter comes a beautiful domed reliquary in the form of a small temple, and a portable altarpiece decorated with enamelwork, produced around 1150 by the craftsman Eilbertus of Cologne.

Exhibits from the Gothic period (12th to 16th centuries) include the stunning reliquary of St George of Elbing, made around 1480. Also fascinating are examples of secular art from this period, including caskets, vessels, a mirror, a knight's amulet and the renowned Minnetroppich. This tapestry depicts a number of love scenes, and is designed to hang on the wall above a seat as a decorative means of keeping out draughts.

RENAISSANCE

The arts and crafts of the Renaissance period are well represented here. Especially valuable is a collection of Italian majolica, a type of pottery glazed in bright metallic oxides, imported into Tuscany from Majorca in the 15th century. Majolica workshops flourished during the 16th century, and many, including those of Faenza, Cafaggiolo and Urbino, are on show here. Other interesting exhibits in this section are the 15th- and 16th-century Venetian glass, porcelain decorated with enamel work from Limoges in central France, and fine furniture and tapestry collections.

The highlight of the collection is a set of 32 magnificent, richly decorated goblets, bowls and jugs from the civic treasury at Lüneburg in

11th-century reliquary cross

northern Germany, acquired by the museum in 1874. Made of gold-plated silver, the set is the work of the skilled metal-workers of the town; some take the form of lions. Also notable are the works of the Nürnberg master craftsmen, above all the renowned Wenzel Jamnitzer and his nephew Christoph Jamnitzer.

As a result of the 16th-century fashion for *Kunstkammern*, or curiosity cabinets, the collection also includes rare examples of naturalistic and exotic creations from other cultures, as well as some unusual technical equipment. Look out for a few pieces from the Pommersche Kunstschrank (curio cabinet), made for a 16th-century Pomeranian prince, Phillip II, as well as a display of 17th-century clocks and scientific instruments.

BAROQUE

Treasures from the Baroque period include an exquisite collection of German and Bohemian glass. A few of the pieces are made from so-called "ruby glass", a technique that was pioneered by Johann Kunckel in the second half of the 17th century.

A varied and rich collection of 18th-century ceramics includes some German faïence work, with amusingly decorated jugs and tankards. The porcelain display begins with a series of Böttger ceramics, the result of some of the very first European

16th-century tapestry entitled *The Triumph of Love*

Desk-board (c.1610–17) from the Pommersche Kunstschrank

experiments in porcelain production, undertaken by Johann Friedrich Böttger with the assistance of Ehrenfried Walther von Tschirnhaus.

Among some of the finest works from a variety of European factories, the porcelain from the Meißen factory is particularly well represented, with several pieces by one of the most famous Meißen modellers and designers, Johann Joachim Kändler.

Also on show is a fascinating selection of artifacts from the Königliche Porzellan-Manufaktur (Royal Porcelain Factory) in Berli *(see p133)* which is well-known for its porcelain pieces depicting views of the city.

The collection of porcelain is complemented by a display of silver dishes produced in European work-shops at the same period.

NEO-CLASSICAL REVIVAL AND ART NOUVEAU

A comprehensive collection of late-18th and early-19th century Neo-Classical artifacts includes porcelain from some of the most famous European and Russian factories, French and German silver, as well as comprehensive exhibitions of glassware and furniture.

The Revival movement in central European art and crafts took place during the second half of the 19th century and is well represented here. A high standard of craftsmanship is seen in the sophisticated Viennese glass and jewellery. The collection also includes furniture made from papier-mâché. This interesting technique was first applied to furniture in England around 1850 and involves a wooden or wire frame which is covered in layers of paste and paper. Decorative techniques include painting and inlaying with mother-of-pearl.

The Secessionist and Art Nouveau movements of the 1890s and 1900s are represented by various artists including Henri van der Velde and Eugène Gaillard. Many pieces were acquired at the

Baroque clock by Johann Gottlieb Graupner (1739)

various World Fairs that occurred at this time. Of note are the frosted glass vases by French artist Emile Gallé, and pieces by the American Louis Comfort Tiffany, creator of the Favrile style of iridescent stained glass. Also displayed are pieces by the legendary René Lalique, including jewellery and glassware.

An interesting diversion is offered by two entertaining pieces of furniture, both dating from 1885, by the Italian designer, Carlo Bugatti. Taking inspiration from Native American, Islamic and Far Eastern art, Bugatti made unique and spectacular use of rare woods and delicate inlays.

THE 20TH CENTURY

The years between the two World Wars were a time of mixed trends in the decorative arts. On the one hand the traditions of the 19th-century Historical movement were continued, while on the other many artists were developing a completely new perspective on both form and decoration.

Art Nouveau vase, Emile Gallé (1900)

This part of the museum includes pieces that embody both approaches, but the strongest emphasis is placed on the innovative Art Deco style. Notable examples include a small porcelain tea service by Gertrud Kant, and a silver coffee set decorated with inlaid ebony, designed by Jean Puiforcat.

The museum's unique 20th-century collection has been continually updated since 1945, aiming to document developments in 20th- and 21st-century decorative arts. On display are a wide range of ceramics, furniture by well-known designers, and a variety of items in daily use.

Gemäldegalerie ⑧

Woman in a Bonnet by Rogier van der Weyden

The Gemäldegalerie collection is exceptional in the consistently high quality of its paintings. Unlike those in many other collections, they were chosen by specialists who, from the beginning of the 19th century, systematically acquired pictures to ensure that all the major European schools of painting were represented. Originally part of the Altes Museum collection (see p75), the paintings achieved independent status in 1904 when they were moved to what is now the Bodemuseum (see p79). After the division of Berlin in 1945, part of the collection was kept in the Bodemuseum, while the majority ended up in the Dahlem Museums (see pp178–9). Following reunification, with the building of a new home as part of the Kulturforum development, this unique set of paintings was united again.

★ **Cupid Victorious** (1602)
Inspired by Virgil's Omnia vincit Amor, *Caravaggio depicted a playful god, trampling over the symbols of Culture, Fame, Knowledge and Power.*

Madonna with Child (c.1477)
A frequent subject of Sandro Botticelli, the Madonna and Child depicted here are surrounded by singing angels holding lilies, symbolizing purity.

Circular lobby leading to the galleries

Birth of Christ (c.1480)
This beautiful religious painting is one of the few surviving paintings on panels by Martin Schongauer.

Portrait of Hieronymus Holzschuher (1529)
Albrecht Dürer painted this affectionate portrait of his friend, who was the mayor of Nuremberg.

Main entrance

The Glass of Wine
(c.1658–61)
Jan Vermeer's carefully composed picture of a young woman drinking wine with a young man gently hints at the relationship developing between them.

VISITORS' CHECKLIST

Matthäikirchplatz 4–6.
Map 5 C5. **Tel** 266 2951.
Ⓢ & Ⓤ Potsdamer Platz.
Ⓤ Mendelssohn-Bartholdy-Park.
🚌 129, 148, 200, 348.
🕙 10am–6pm Tue–Sun (to 10pm Thu). ⬤ first Tue after Easter and Whitsun, 1 May, 24, 25 & 31 Dec. 📷 🍽 🌲 ♿ 🚻 ⬇ 🚫 🛗

Love in the French Theatre
This picture has a companion piece called Love in the Italian Theatre (see p23). *Both are the work of French painter, Jean-Antoine Watteau.*

★ Portrait of Hendrickje Stoffels (1656–7)
This portrait of Rembrandt's lover, Hendrickje Stoffels, is typical in that the painter focuses on the subject and ignores the background.

KEY

▨	13th–16th-century German painting
▨	14th–16th-century Dutch and French painting
☐	17th-century Flemish and Dutch painting
☐	18th-century French, English and German painting
☐	17th–18th-century Italian painting, 17th-century German, French and Spanish painting
☐	13th–16th-century Italian painting
▨	16th–18th-century miniatures
☐	Digital gallery
▨	Non-exhibition space

GALLERY GUIDE
The main gallery contains over 900 masterpieces grouped according to their country of origin and period. The educational gallery on the lower floor houses 13th–18th-century European paintings and another digital gallery.

STAR EXHIBITS

★ Cupid Victorious

★ Portrait of Hendrickje Stoffels

★ Dutch Proverbs

★ Dutch Proverbs (1559)
Pieter Bruegel managed to illustrate more than 100 proverbs in this painting.

Visiting the Gemäldegalerie

The Gemäldegalerie's Modern building was designed by Heinz Hilmer and Christoph Sattler and its exhibition space offers a superb environment in which to view the paintings. The pictures are gently lit by the diffused daylight that streams in from above, while the walls are covered in light-absorbing fabric. The vast hall which occupies the centre of the building allows the visitor to take a break from sightseeing at any time. The hall, with a futuristic sculpture by Walter de Maria set in a water-filled pool, provides an ideal setting for a few moments of quiet contemplation and rest.

Frans Hals' portrait, *Malle Babbe* or *Crazy Babette* (c.1629–30)

Hans Holbein's *Portrait of Georg Gisze* (1532)

GERMAN PAINTING

German paintings are exhibited in several areas of the gallery. The first group comprises art from the 13th–16th centuries. A fine body of religious paintings and altarpieces contains a historic 13th-century rectangular altarpiece from Westphalia. Other religious artifacts include the side panels of the 15th-century *Wurzach Altar*, ascribed to Hans Multscher, which vividly depict the torment of Christ and the life of the Virgin Mary. A real rarity is the *Nativity* by Martin Schongauer. Often thought of primarily as an engraver, he was one of the most significant painters of the late 15th century but few of his paintings have survived.

Another artist known for his engravings as well as paintings, Albrecht Dürer was a major figure in Renaissance art in northern Europe. His works displayed here include *Madonna with the Siskin*, painted in 1506 while he was visiting Italy, and two later portraits of Nürnberg patriarchs. There are also exhibits by Hans Süss von Kulmbach, Hans Baldung Grien and Albrecht Altdorfer. Among the many works by Lucas Cranach the Elder is the delightful *Fountain of Youth*, from which old women emerge young and beautiful, while men regain their youth through amorous liaisons with the women. Another excellent painting in this collection is a portrait of the Danzig merchant Georg Gisze, painted by Hans Holbein the Younger at a time when both men were living in London. 17th- and 18th-century paintings, including the works of Adam Elsheimer and Johann Heinrich Tischbein, are on show elsewhere.

DUTCH AND FLEMISH PAINTING

The gallery with Dutch and Flemish paintings begins with the captivating canvases of Jan van Eyck. In addition to his precise portraits, you can see here the celebrated *Madonna in a Church*. The high quality of paintings is maintained with the works of Petrus Christus and Rogier van der Weyden. Among the pictures by Hugo van der Goes, the most prized is *The Adoration of the Magi*, once the centre panel of a triptych.

The collection has four paintings by Hans Memling, and also the small *Madonna with Child* painted by one of his pupils, Michel Sittow. There is a large group of paintings by Gerard David, Jan Gossaert and Joos van Cleve. Try to keep an eye out for a modest picture by Hieronymus Bosch called *St John on Patmos*. One of the most outstanding paintings of the collection is Pieter Bruegel the Elder's *Dutch Proverbs*. However, in order to fully appreciate the mastery and humour in this work, make sure you use the accompanying board which explains all the one hundred or so proverbs illustrated here.

Within the large collection of excellent Flemish paintings you can marvel at the Baroque vitality and texture evident in the canvases of friends and

Salomon van Ruysdael's *Riders and Cattle* (1656)

sometime collaborators Petrus Paulus Rubens, Jacob Jordaens, Jan Brueghel the Elder and Frans Snyders. The exceptional portraits of Anton van Dyck, who painted complex, psychologically revealing studies, are indicative of the artist at the height of his powers.

The gallery of 17th-century Dutch paintings probably holds the richest collection in the museum. Included among these are the portraits by Frans Hals, which perfectly illustrate his enormous artistic talents. Excellent examples of his varied work are the vigorous *Malle Babbe* (*c.1629–30*) – a portrait of the "crazy Babette" of Haarlem.

In fact, all the most famous Dutch painters are represented here but, of course, the works of Jan Vermeer and the master, Rembrandt, attract the greatest amount of interest. The works of Rembrandt include the paintings *Samson and Delilah, Susanna and the Two Elders,* and *Joseph and the Wife of Potiphar*. It is also worth taking time to view the *Man in the Golden Helmet*, a sad yet noble painting originally attributed to Rembrandt. Carbon dating has shown it to be the work of members of his studio. It is a magnificent tribute to his skill as a teacher.

Jean Baptiste Siméon Chardin's *The Draughtsman* (1737)

FRENCH, ENGLISH AND SPANISH PAINTING

The collection of French art can be found in various parts of the gallery. Paintings of the 15th and 16th century are exhibited alongside Dutch paintings of that era. The oldest works date from the

Titian's *Venus with the Organ Player* (1550–52)

beginning of the 15th century, and the *Madonna with Child*, dating from c.1410, is one of the oldest preserved works of art painted on a canvas. One of the most valuable French works is by Jean Fouquet, entitled *Étienne Chevalier with Saint Stephen*. Comprising half of the *Diptych of Melun* this is one of Fouquet's few non-miniature paintings.

Nicolas Poussin, the mainspring of the French Classical tradition, and Claude Lorrain, famous for his idealized landscapes, represent 17th-century French painting. Eighteenth-century painting is strongly represented by the canvases of Jean-Antoine Watteau, Jean Baptiste Siméon Chardin and François Boucher.

Two areas in which this collection is less complete are Spanish and English painting. Nevertheless, there is a portrait by Diego Velázquez which is worth seeing, while the English pictures include good portraits by rivals Sir Joshua Reynolds and Thomas Gainsborough.

Sir Joshua Reynolds' *Portrait of Lady Sunderlin* (1786)

ITALIAN PAINTING

The collection of Italian paintings is fairly comprehensive. There are exemplary works by 14th-century masters, including *Laying the Body to Rest in the Grave* by Giotto and parts of *Scenes from the Life of St Humilitas* by Pietro Lorenzetti. Paintings by Piero della Francesca, Fra Angelico, Masaccio, Andrea del Verrocchio, Sandro Botticelli, and Antonio del Pollaiuolo all represent the 15th century. In this collection you will also find later works by Raphael, including the *Madonna di Casa Colonna*, and the *Madonna di Terranuova*, painted after Raphael's arrival in Florence around 1505. There is also a collection of works by the Venetian Renaissance painter, Giovanni Bellini.

Indeed, the Venetian school in general is well represented: *Portrait of a Young Man* by Giorgione is a vibrant and colourful study; there is also Titian's *Venus and the Organ Player* and Tintoretto's *Virgin and the Child Adored by Saints Mark and Luke*. It is worth comparing Caravaggio's *Cupid Victorious*, whose provocative and distinctly human sexuality contrasts with the spiritual orthodoxy of *Heavenly and Earthly Love,* by Giovanni Baglione. Similar in style, the two paintings convey opposing ideologies. Cardinal Giustiani, whose brother owned Caravaggio's controversial canvas, commissioned the latter painting. Works by Giovanni Battista Tiepolo, Francesco Guardi and Antonio Canaletto represent the art of 18th-century Venice.

Karl Schmidt-Rottluff's *Farm in Daugart* (1910), Neue Nationalgalerie

Neue Nationalgalerie ❾

NEW NATIONAL GALLERY

Potsdamer Strasse 50. **Map** 5 C5.
Tel 266 424 510. 🇺 & 🇸
Potsdamer Platz or 🇺 *Mendelssohn-*
Bartholdy-Park. 🚌 *100, 347, M28.*
⭕ *10am–6pm Tue–Fri (to 10pm*
Thu), 11am–6pm Sat & Sun. 📷 ♿

The magnificent collection
of modern art housed in the
Neue Nationalgalerie has a
troubled history. The core of
the collection consisted of 262
paintings that belonged to
banker JHW Wagener. In the
late 1860s, when Wagener
died, he bequeathed them to
Crown Prince William, who
housed them in the Nationalgalerie on Museum Island.
    However, in 1937, a Nazi
programme of cultural
cleansing meant that many
of the works in the collection,
which had grown to include
paintings by Monet, Manet
and Renoir, were confiscated.
    After World War II the
Berlin municipal authority
decided to rebuild the
collection and authorized
the construction of a suitable
building in West Berlin to
house it. A commission was
given to the elder statesman
of modern architecture, the
75-year-old Mies van der
Rohe. The result was the
first museum in what would
later become known as the
Kulturforum. The national

gallery is a striking, minimalist
building with a flat steel roof
over a glass hall, which
appears to float in mid-air
supported only by six slender
interior struts. The permanent
collection is in the basement
of the museum, while the
spacious ground-level glass
hall plays host to temporary
exhibitions.
    The collection of the Neue
Nationalgalerie comprises
largely 20th-century art, but
begins with artists of the
late 19th century, such as
Edvard Munch, Ferdinand
Hodler and Oskar Kokoschka.
German movements, such
as Die Brücke, are well
represented, with pieces
by Ernst Ludwig Kirchner
(notably his *Potsdamer Platz)*
and Karl Schmidt-Rottluff.
    As well as the Bauhaus
movement, represented by
Paul Klee and Wassily

Kandinsky, the gallery shows
works by exponents of a
crass realism, such as Otto
Dix and Georg Grosz. The
most celebrated artists of
other European countries
are also included in the
collection – Pablo Picasso,
Ferdinand Léger, and the
Surrealists Giorgio de Chirico,
Salvador Dalí, René Magritte
and Max Ernst. Post-World
War II art is represented by
the works of Barnett Newman
and Frank Stella, among
many others. The sculpture
garden houses a variety
of important works, both
figurative and abstract.
    Following reunification, a
number of new works have
been added to the collection.
The most recent of these are
displayed in the Hamburg
Bahnhof branch *(see*
pp110–11) of the museum.

Potsdamer Platz ❿

See pp128–131.

Shell-Haus ⓫

Reichpietschufer 60. **Map** 11 C1.
🇺 *Mendelssohn-Bartholdy-Park.*
🚌 *200, M29.*

This is undoubtedly a
gem for lovers of the
architecture developed
during the period between
World Wars I and II. This
modernist office block was
designed by Emil Fahren-
kamp. Built from 1930 to
1931, it was one of the first
buildings in Berlin to use a
steel-frame construction.
    The most eye-catching wing
extends along Landwehrkanal
with a zig-zag elevation; from
a height of five storeys it climbs
upwards in a series of steps,
finishing up ten storeys high.
    Damaged during World
War II, Shell-Haus went
through several stages of
restoration and several
incarnations, including as
headquarters of the German
navy and as a military hospital.
Beautiful proportions and
original design place the
structure among the finest of
Berlin's buildings of its era.

**The impressive exterior of the
Shell-Haus office building**

The German State Naval Office, now part of the Bendlerblock complex

Bendlerblock (Gedenkstätte Deutscher Widerstand) ⑫

Stauffenbergstrasse 13–14. **Map** 5 B5, 5 C5. **Tel** 26 99 50 00. Ⓤ *Mendelssohn-Bartholdy-Park.* 🚌 *200, 347, M29.* ⭘ *9am–6pm Mon–Fri (to 8pm Thu), 10am–6pm Sat & Sun.* ⬤ *1 Jan, 24, 25 & 31 Dec.* 🖼

The collection of buildings known as the Bendlerblock was originally built during the Third Reich as an extension to the German State Naval Offices. During World War II these buildings were the headquarters of the Wehrmacht (German Army). It was here that a group of officers planned their famous and ultimately unsuccessful assassination attempt on Hitler on 20 July 1944. When the attempt led by Claus Schenk von Stauffenberg failed, he and his fellow conspirators were quickly rounded up and arrested. The death sentences on these men were passed at the Plötzensee prison

(see p186). General Ludwig Beck was forced to commit suicide, while Stauffenberg, Friedrich Olbricht, Werner von Haeften and Ritter Mertz von Quirnheim were shot in the Bendlerblock courtyard.

A monument commemorating this event, designed by Richard Scheibe in 1953, stands where the executions were carried out. On the upper floor of the building there is an exhibition documenting the history of the German anti-Nazi movements.

Villa von der Heydt ⑬

Von-der-Heydt-Strasse 18. **Map** 11 B1. Ⓤ *Nollendorfplatz.* 🚌 *200, 347, M29.*

This fine villa, built in a late-Neo-Classical style, is one of the few surviving reminders that the southern side of the Tiergarten was one of the most expensive and beautiful residential areas of Berlin.

Designed by Hermann Ende and GA Linke, the villa was built from 1860 to 1862. The neatly manicured gardens and railings around the villa are adorned with busts of Christian Daniel Rauch and Alexander von Humboldt. The statues, by Reinhold Begas, originally lined the Avenue of Triumph in the Tiergarten before being moved here. After restoration in 1967, the villa became the headquarters of one of the most influential cultural bodies, the Stiftung Preussischer Kulturbesitz (Foundation of Prussian Cultural Heritage).

The captivating, streamlined buildings of the Bauhaus-Archiv

Bauhaus-Archiv ⑭

Klingelhöferstrasse 14. **Map** 11 A1. **Tel** 254 00 20. Ⓤ *Nollendorfplatz.* 🚌 *100, 106, 187, M29.* ⭘ *10am–5pm Wed–Mon.* 🖼♿🚻🛍🎦

The Bauhaus school of art, started by Walter Gropius in 1919, was one of the most influential art institutions of the 20th century. The belief of the Bauhaus group was that art and technology should combine in harmonious unity.

Originally based in Weimar, and from 1925 in Dessau, this school provided inspiration for numerous artists and architects. Staff and students included Mies van der Rohe, Paul Klee, Wassily Kandinsky, Theo van Doesburg and László Moholy-Nagy. The school moved to Berlin in 1932, but was closed down by the Nazis in 1933.

After the war, the Bauhaus-Archiv was relocated to Darmstadt. In 1964 Walter Gropius designed a building to house the collection, but it was never realized. The archive was moved to Berlin in 1971 and the design had to be adapted to the new site. Because the maestro was no longer alive, the project was taken over by Alexander Cvijanovic. The gleaming white building with its distinctive glass-panelled gables was built between 1976 and 1979 and houses the archive, library and exhibition halls for temporary displays.

Neo-Classical façade of the elegant Villa von der Heydt

Potsdamer Platz ⑩

To experience the vibrant energy of the new Berlin, there is no better place to visit than Potsdamer Platz. During the Roaring Twenties it was Europe's busiest plaza and a bustling entertainment centre, but during World War II it was bombed into a mountain of rubble. After the war, the square was left as a derelict wide open space, a no-man's-land beside the Berlin Wall. With reunification, the square was redeveloped by various international business concerns, such as DaimlerChrysler and Sony, who subsequently sold the properties. This building project is Berlin's largest to date. Berlin's old hub is once again a dynamic centre, a jewel of modern architecture created by architects such as Renzo Piano, Helmut Jahn and Arata Isozaki.

View of modern-day Potsdamer Platz

Beisheim Center

Lenné-, Bellevue- and Ebertstrasse

Otto Beisheim, the founder and owner of the Metro retail chain, and one of Europe's wealthiest entrepreneurs, has created a glass and steel monument on Potsdamer Platz – the Beisheim Center. The two elegant high-rise towers on the northern edge of the square encompass several de luxe apartments. The largest was sold for around $5 million, to an American émigrée returning to her home city, and is probably Berlin's most expensive apartment. The center also incorporates a luxurious Ritz-Carlton and an elegant Marriott hotel.

The building was designed by the Berlin architectural team Hilmer, Sattler & Albrecht, although parts of the building were also created by architect David Chipperfield. The sandstone appearance of the small 19-floor skyscrapers, with receding façades on the upper levels, is meant to be a modern reinterpretation of New York's Rockefeller Center.

Filmmuseum Berlin

Potsdamer Strasse 2 (at Sony Center). **Tel** 30 09 030. ☐ 10am–6pm Tue–Sun, 10am–8pm Thu. 📷 🚫 🎦

In a city once famous for its world-class film industry, the new film museum takes visitors backstage to Hollywood and the historic UFA (Universal Film AG) film studios.

Located in the Sony Center and run by the Freunde der Deutschen Kinemathek, a non-profit-making association for film-lovers, the museum chronicles the development of cinema from the first silent movie hits to the latest science-fiction productions. However, the main focus is on German films from the glorious UFA days in the 1920s, when Germany's leading film company produced one smash hit after another at the Babelsberg studios *(see p205)*. Films such as *The Cabinet of Dr Caligari*, directed by Friedrich Wilhelm Murnau (1888–1931), or *M* and *Metropolis* by Fritz Lang (1890–1976) are presented with costumes, set sketches, original scripts, models and photos. The Nazi era, when film making became a propaganda machine, is particularly interesting, and the museum documents the life and work of the actor Kurt Gerron, who died in Auschwitz, as well as other exhibits relating to the uses of propaganda in film.

One of the treasure-troves of the museum is the collection of personal effects of the Berlin-born diva Marlene Dietrich (1901–1992). The exhibition presents her gowns, personal correspondence and complete luggage set. A unique item is a minute cigarette case, given to her as a gift by the director Josef von Sternberg (1894–1969), bearing the inscription: "To Marlene Dietrich, woman, mother and actress as there never was one before". Also on display are personal possessions from German film and television stars such as Heinz Rühmann (1902–1994) and Hans Albers (1891–1960).

The museum features a range of exhibitions with changing themes and special film programmes.

Façade of the Filmmuseum Berlin

Arkaden, one of Berlin's favourite shopping centres

Potsdamer Platz Arkaden

Alte Potsdamer Str. 7. *Tel* 25 59 270.
◯ 10am–9pm Mon–Sat.
CinemaxX Potsdamer Str. 5. *Tel*
Programme info: 25 92 21 11; reservations: (0180) 524 63 62 99. ✉

This entertainment and shopping complex is hugely popular with visitors. Spread over three floors, the building includes around 140 shops, restaurants and boutiques. The basement houses a food court with many budget eateries offering regional specialities from all over Germany, as well as several grocery shops.

Berlin's largest cinema, the **CinemaxX**, is nearby. With 19 screens it can accommodate up to 3,500 filmgoers.

Theater am Potsdamer Platz

Marlene-Dietrich-Platz 1. *Tel* (018 0)
544 44. ◯ 8am–8pm daily. ✉
Spielbank Berlin Marlene-Dietrich-Platz 1. *Tel* 25 59 90.
◯ 3pm–3am daily. ✉

Situated in a square dedicated to the famous actress Marlene Dietrich, Berlin's largest musical stage is housed in the modern Theater am Potsdamer Platz, designed by Renzo

Piano as part of the Daimler Quartier *(see pp130–1)*. It stages German versions of Broadway hit musicals and shows such as *Beauty and the Beast*.

The exclusive Adagio nightclub is located in the basement of this building and Berlin's most popular casino, **Spielbank Berlin**, can also be found here.

A large blue, bubble-like sculpture – *Balloon Flower* by the American artist Jeff Koons – adorns the square at the front of the building.

The theatre complex is also the main forum for the Berlinale, Berlin's world-renowned film festival. It is Berlin's largest cultural event and is held throughout the city each February *(see p51)*.

Bluemax Theater, the Blue Man Group's Berlin location, is found on the opposite side of Marlene-Dietrich-Platz. The famous mute performers hold seven shows a week.

Balloon Flower by Jeff Koons

HISTORIC POTSDAMER PLATZ

Potsdamer Platz first evolved from a green park in 1831 and was named after one of the city's gates, the Potsdamer Tor, located to the east of today's square. Thanks to a new railway station of the same name, where the city's first ever train made its maiden journey in 1838, the square developed into a major traffic hub at the intersection of Potsdamer Strasse and other thoroughfares. Later an underground train line, along with a total of 31 tram and bus lines, added to the traffic chaos here. At the beginning of the 20th century it became the centre of Berlin's celebrated nightlife, with legendary, huge entertainment venues such as Haus Vaterland and the Café Josty (a meeting place for famous artists including author Theodor Fontane

and painter Adolph von Menzel), as well as several luxury hotels. Germany's first radio transmission was broadcast in 1923 at the Vox Haus. The square was almost destroyed by Allied bombardments during the final Battle of Berlin in April 1945. It became a vast open space in the shadow of the Berlin Wall where Western tourists, standing on high observation platforms, could peek over the wall. The empty square featured in Wim Wenders' 1987 hit film, *Wings of Desire*.

Development commenced in 1992, and Potsdamer Platz rose to become Europe's largest construction site where a total of $25 billion has been invested.

Bustling Potsdamer Platz in the 1930s

Sony Center

Potsdamer Strasse 2. ☐ *24 hrs.*

The Sony Center, designed by the German-American architect Helmut Jahn, is Berlin's most exciting new architectural complex. Built between 1996 and 2000, the glitzy steel and glass construction covers a breathtaking 4,013 sq m (43,195 sq ft).

The piazza at the heart of the Center has become one of Berlin's most popular attractions. Set under a soaring tent-like roof, it is dominated by a pool with constantly changing fountains where the water sprays high above the pool, then falls back to rise again in a different location. The light and airy piazza is surrounded by the offices of Sony's European headquarters, as well as apartment complexes, several restaurants, cafés and shops including the Sony style store. There is also the Cinestar *(see pp264–5)*, a huge multiplex cinema with eight different screens, in addition to the Filmmuseum Berlin *(see p128)*. At the rear of the building is the blue-domed IMAX cinema which shows nature and science films on imposing 360° screens.

Inside the Sony Center is the small but magnificent **Kaisersaal**, a historic architectural gem that is set behind a glass façade. This dining hall, one of the city's finest but private function locations, was once part of the Grand Hotel Esplanade. The epitome of luxury in pre-war Berlin, it was almost

Interior of the cupola of the Sony Center, designed by Helmut Jahn

destroyed during World War II. When the site was sold to Sony by the City of Berlin in the early 1990s, the Berlin magistrate stipulated that the Kaisersaal, stairways, bathrooms and several other smaller rooms should be restored and integrated into the Sony Center. The historic ensemble originally stood some 46 m (150 ft) away and was carefully moved on air cushions to its present location in 1996. The fully restored Kaisersaal is dominated by a portrait of Kaiser Wilhelm II, the last German emperor, whose frequent visits to the original hotel gave this hall its name, although he never actually dined in this particular room.

Replica traffic lights, DaimlerChrysler Quartier

Daimler Quartier

Around Alte Potsdamer Strasse. **Panorama Punkt observation platform** Potsdamer Platz 1. *Tel* 25 29 43 72. ☐ *11am–8pm daily.* 📷

This vast complex was built between 1993 and 1998 and comprises 19 modern buildings, all designed in different styles according to an overall plan by architects Renzo Piano and Christoph Kohlbecker. The buildings form a long, narrow column of modern architectural jewels leading south from Potsdamer Platz all the way down to the Landwehr Canal.

Standing on either side of Alte Potsdamer Strasse, the red-brick high-rise block and its sister building opposite mark the entrance to this city quarter, and were designed by Berlin architect Werner Kollhoff. The western skyscraper is topped by a 96-m (315-ft) high observation platform called **Panorama Punkt** (Panorama Point). It offers a breathtaking view which can be reached via Europe's fastest elevator.

The green traffic-light tower in front of the Daimler Quartier is a replica of the first automatic traffic light in Berlin, which was erected on the same spot in 1924. In

The glass façade of the Kaisersaal, part of the Sony Center

prewar days, Potsdamer Platz was an intricate crossing of several major streets and avenues, making it Europe's busiest traffic junction at the time.

At the southern end of this complex is yet another high-rise tower block, the **Debis-Haus** (formerly the Daimler-Chrysler software subsidiary). This 90-m (295-ft) high, 22 floor, yellow and green skyscraper is topped by a striking green cube and was designed by Renzo Piano and Hans Kollhoff *(see p45)*. A captivating sculpture by Jean Tinguely, entitled *Meta-Maxi*, adorns its soaring atrium. The sculpture is powered by 16 engines and symbolizes the constant movement of time.

Various works of art were commissioned for this complex and these can be seen throughout the public areas.

The red-brick office block of Daimler House

Leipziger Platz

Leipziger Platz, a small square just east of Potsdamer Platz, was partially reconstructed, but development has stalled, leaving large parts of the octagon empty and unfinished. The original octagonal but rather bland square was created between 1732 and 1734 and later renamed Leipziger Platz in commemoration of the Battle of Leipzig in 1813 (the first decisive defeat of Napoleon). In the 19th century, the architects Karl-Friedrich Schinkel (1781–1841) and Peter Joseph Lenné (1789–1866) transformed the square into an architectural gem with beautifully landscaped gardens, surrounded by some of the most elegant city palaces and mansions in the whole of Berlin.

At the beginning of the 20th century the modern buildings,

most notably the Kaufhaus Wertheim by Alfred Messel (1853–1909) built in 1905, made Leipziger Platz one of the major, and more fashionable, shopping districts in pre-war Berlin.

Unfortunately, there are no historic remnants left. The current buildings have a modern look but are restricted to a maximum height of only 35 m (115 ft), the same height as the original buildings. They house various shops and restaurants, the Canadian Embassy and further international company headquarters.

Haus Huth

Alte Potsdamer Strasse 5. *Tel 25 94 14 20.* ☐ *11am–6pm daily.* **Sammlung DaimlerChrysler Contemporary** ☐ *as Weinhaus Huth.* ☐ *6pm daily.*

The only historic building on Potsdamer Platz to escape destruction in World War II was the grey limestone building of the Haus Huth. Originally a restaurant and wine shop, it was one of the first buildings in Berlin to be erected with a steel frame, intended to support the weight of the wine. It was designed by architects Conrad Heidenreich and Paul Michel in 1912. After the war, it stood alone on the vast

Rauschenberg's sculpture *Riding Bikes*, with Weinhaus Huth in the background

eroded square. Today however, the offices of the famous car manufacturers DaimlerChrysler are located here, along with the Diekmann im Haus Huth restaurant, a small café and Hardy's, an upmarket wine shop.

Haus Huth is also home to the **Sammlung DaimlerChrysler Contemporary**, a small exhibition featuring the latest additions to the corporation's collection of 20th-century art, which mostly consists of abstract and geometric paintings by German and international artists.

The best view of the building is from its south side where a jubilant, bright light installation by Robert Rauschenberg called *Riding Bikes* can be found.

The historic Haus Huth on Leipziger Platz

Diplomaten-viertel ⑮

DIPLOMATIC QUARTER

Map 4 F5, 5 A5, B5, C5.
Ⓤ *Nollendorfplatz.* 🚌 *100, 106, 187.*

Although a number of consulates existed in the Tiergarten area as early as 1918, the establishment of a diplomatic district along the southern edge of the Tiergarten, between Stauffenberg-strasse and Lichtensteinallee, did not take place until the period of Hitler's Third Reich between 1933 and 1945. During the years 1938 to 1943 large embassies representing the Axis Powers, Italy and Japan, were built here.

Despite the fact that these monumental buildings were designed by a number of different architects, the Fascist interpretation of Neo-Classicism and the influence of Albert Speer as head architect meant that the group was homogenous, if bleak. Many of the buildings did not survive World War II bombing.

A diplomatic area has now emerged along Tiergarten-strasse. The Austrian embassy designed by Hans Hollein stands at the junction of Stauffenbergstrasse, next door to the embassies of Turkey and the Republic of South Africa. At Tiergartenstrasse Nos. 21–3 the pre-World War II Italian embassy still stands, while next door is a copy of the first Japanese embassy. Between Klingel-höferstrasse and Rauchstrasse stands an imposing complex of five embassies. Completed in 1999, these represent Norway, Sweden, Denmark, Finland and Iceland.

Tiergarten ⑯

Map 4 E4, 5 A3, 6 D3. Ⓢ *Tiergarten or Bellevue.* 🚌 *100, 106, 187, 200.*

This is the largest park in Berlin. Situated at the geographical centre of the city it occupies a surface area of more than 200 ha (495 acres). Once a forest used as

One of many tranquil areas within the Tiergarten

the Elector's hunting reserve, it was transformed into a landscaped park by Peter Joseph Lenné in the 1830s. A half-kilometre Triumphal Avenue was built in the eastern section of the park at the end of the 19th century, lined with statues of the country's rulers and statesmen.

World War II inflicted huge damage on the Tiergarten, including the destruction of the Triumphal Avenue, many of whose surviving monuments can now be seen in the Lapidarium (*see p144*). Replanting, however, has now restored the Tiergarten which is a favourite meeting place for Berliners. Its avenues are now lined with statues of figures such as Johann Wolfgang von Goethe and Richard Wagner.

By the lake known as Neuer See and the Landwehrkanal are memorials to the murdered leaders of the Spartacus move-ment, Karl Liebknecht and Rosa Luxemburg (*see p28*). Also worth finding is a collection of gas lamps, displayed near the Tiergarten S-Bahn station.

Grosser Stern ⑰

GREAT STAR

Map 5 A4. Ⓢ *Bellevue.* Ⓤ *Hansaplatz.* 🚌 *100, 106, 187.*

This vast roundabout at the centre of the Tiergarten has five large roads leading off it in the shape of a star. At its centre is the enormous Siegessäule (Triumphal Column). Surrounding it are various monuments brought over from the nearby Reichstag

building (*see pp134–5*) during the late 1930s. At the same period the Strasse des 17 Juni was widened to twice its size, the square surrounding the roundabout was enlarged and much of the existing statuary removed.

In the northern section of the square stands a vast bronze monument to the first German Chancellor, Otto von Bismarck (1815–98). Around it stand allegorical figures, the work of late-19th-century sculptor Reinhold Begas. Other statues represent various national heroes including Field Marshal Helmuth von Moltke (1800–91), chief of the Prussian general staff between the years 1858 and 1888, who won the Franco-German war.

Monument to Otto von Bismarck at the Grosser Stern

Siegessäule ⑱

TRIUMPHAL COLUMN

Grosser Stern. **Map** 5 A4. **Tel** *391 29 61.* Ⓢ *Bellevue.* Ⓤ *Hansaplatz.* 🚌 *100, 106, 187.* ⏰ *Apr–Oct: 9:30am–6:30pm daily; Nov–Mar: 9:30am–5:30pm daily.* 📷

The triumphal column is based on a design by Johann

Heinrich Strack, and was built
to commemorate victory in the
Prusso-Danish war of 1864.
After further Prussian victories
in wars against Austria (1866)
and France (1871), "Goldelse",
a gilded figure by Friedrich
Drake representing Victory,
was added to the top. The
monument stood in front of
the Reichstag building until the
Nazi government moved it to
its present location in 1938.
The base is decorated with bas-
reliefs commemorating battles.
Higher up the column a mosaic
frieze by Anton von Werner
depicts the 1871 founding of
the German Empire. An observation terrace at the top offers
magnificent vistas over Berlin.
The monument is undergoing
renovation until May 2011.

KÖNIGLICHE PORZELLAN-MANUFAKTUR

Established in 1763, the Königliche
Porzellan-Manufaktur (Royal Porcelain
Factory) was soon producing items of the
highest artistic quality, competing with
the products of the older Meissen
factory in Saxony. The Berlin factory
is particularly renowned for its Neo-
Classical urns and plates decorated with
views of the city. Large collections of
porcelain with the markings KPM can be
seen at the Ephraim-Palais (see
p 91), in the Kunstgewerbemuseum (see
pp118–21) and at the Belvedere within the
grounds of Schloss Charlottenburg (see
pp160–61). It is also worth visiting the
factory, located at Wegelystrasse 1, which is
still producing porcelain, and includes
a sales gallery and exhibition hall.

**Neo-Classical vase
with a view of the
Gendarmenmarkt**

Siegessäule (Triumphal Column)

Hansaviertel ⓳

Map 4 E3, E4, F3. Ⓢ Bellevue. 🚌
100, 106, 187. **Akademie der
Künste** Hanseatenweg 10. **Tel** 20 05
72 00 0. ◯ 11am–8pm Tue–Sun. 🖼

This area to the west of
Schloss Bellevue is home to
some of the most interesting

modern architecture in Berlin,
built for the 1957 Internationale
Bauausstellung (International
Architectural Exhibition).
Taking on a World War II
bomb site, prominent architects from around the world
designed 45 projects, of which
36 were realized, to create a
varied residential development
set in an environment of lush
greenery. The list of distinguished architects involved in
the project included Walter
Gropius (Händelallee Nos.
3–9), Alvar Aalto (Klopstock-
strasse Nos. 30–32) and Oskar
Niemeyer (Altonaer Strasse
Nos. 4–14). The development
also includes a school, a
commercial services building
and two churches.
In 1960, a new headquarters
for the **Akademie der Künste**
(Academy of Arts) was built
at Hanseatenweg No. 10.
Designed by Werner Dütt-
mann, the academy has a
concert hall, an exhibition
area, archives and a library. In
front of the main entrance is a
magnificent piece, *Reclining
Figure*, by eminent British
sculptor Henry Moore.

Schloss Bellevue ⓴

BELLEVUE PALACE

Spreeweg 1. **Map** 5 A3. Ⓢ Bellevue.
🚌 100, 187. ◉ to the public.

This captivating palace with
its dazzlingly white Neo-
Classical façade is now the
official residence of the
German Federal President.
Built in 1786 to a design by
Philipp Daniel Boumann for
the Prussian Prince August
Ferdinand, the palace served
as a royal residence until 1861.
In 1935 it was refurbished to
house a Museum of German
Ethnology. Refurbished again
in 1938, it became a hotel for
guests of the Nazi government.
Following bomb damage
during World War II, the
palace was carefully restored
to its former glory, with the
oval ballroom rebuilt to a
design by Carl Gotthard
Langhans. The palace is set
within an attractive park laid
out to the original late-18th-
century design, though
unfortunately the picturesque
garden pavilions did not
survive World War II.

Imposing façade of Schloss Bellevue, now the official Berlin residence of the German President

Haus der Kulturen der Welt or "pregnant oyster" as it is also known

Haus der Kulturen der Welt ㉑

HOUSE OF WORLD CULTURE

John-Foster-Dulles-Allee 10. **Map** 5 C3. **Tel** 39 78 70. Ⓢ & Ⓤ *Hauptbahnhof & Bundestag.* 🚌 100. ⬜ **Exhibitions** 10am–6pm Tue, Wed, noon–8pm Thu–Sun. 🅰

This former congress hall's squat structure and parabolic roof has given rise to its affectionate nickname "the pregnant oyster". Built between 1956 and 1957 to a design by the American architect Hugh Stubbins, it was intended as the American entry in the international architecture competition "Interbau 1957", (from which the Hansaviertel apartment blocks originated). It soon became a symbol of freedom and modernity in West Berlin during the Cold War, particularly when compared to the GDR-era monumental buildings of Karl-Marx-Allee in East Berlin *(see pp172–3)*. However, its roof failed to withstand the test of time and the building partially collapsed in 1980.

After reconstruction it was re-opened in 1989, with a change of purpose. It is now used to bring world cultures to a wider German audience, and stages various events and performances to this effect. It is known for its jazz festivals in particular *(see pp48–51)*.

Standing nearby is the black tower of the Carillon built in 1987 to commemorate the 750th anniversary of Berlin. Suspended in the tower is the largest carillon in Europe, comprising 67 bells. Daily at noon and 6pm, the bells give a brief computer-controlled concert.

Regierungsviertel ㉒

GOVERNMENT DISTRICT

Map 6 D2, E2. Ⓢ *Unter den Linden.* 🚌 100, 248.

This bold concept for a government district in keeping with a 21st-century capital was the winning design in a competition held in 1992. Construction of the complex began in 1997 and was completed in 2003. Axel Schultes and Charlotte Frank's grand design proposed a rectangular site cutting across the meander of the Spree river just north of the Reichstag.

While many of the buildings have been designed by other architects, their plans fitting within the overall concept, Schultes and Frank designed the Bundeskanzleramt, situated opposite the Reichstag, which is the official residence of the German Chancellor.

The offices – Alsenblock and Luisenblock – are the work of Stephan Braunfels, as is the office Dorotheenblöcke, built by a consortium of five architects. The whole project will be complemented by an ultra-modern, integrated transport system which will include a road tunnel under the Tiergarten and a vast subterranean railway station – Berlin Hauptbahnhof. The architects responsible for the station project are Mainhard von Gerkan, Oswald Mathias Ungers and Max Dudler.

Reichstag ㉓

Platz der Republik. **Map** 6 D3, E3. Ⓤ *Bundestag.* 🚌 100, 248. **Tel** 227 32 152. **Dome** ⬜ 8am–midnight daily (last admission 10pm). **Assembly Hall** ⬜ by appointment only. 🕐 10:30am, 1:30, 3:30 & 6:30pm daily when parliament is not sitting. 🔲 1 Jan, 24–26 & 31 Dec.

Built to house the German Parliament, the Reichstag was intended as a symbol of national unity and the aspirations of the new German Empire, declared in 1871. The Neo-Renaissance design by Paul Wallot captured the prevailing spirit of German optimism. Constructed between the years 1884 and 1894, it was funded by money paid by the French as wartime reparations.

On 23 December 1916, the inscription *"Dem Deutschen Volke"* ("To the German People") was added to the façade. The Reichstag became a potent symbol that would be exploited in the years to come.

In 1918 Philipp Scheidemann declared the formation of the

The Bundeskanzleramt, the official residence of the Federal Chancellor

The Reichstag crowned by a dome designed by Sir Norman Foster

Weimar Republic from the building. The next time the world heard about the Reichstag was on the night of 28 February 1933, when a fire destroyed the main hall. The Communists were blamed, accelerating a political witch-hunt driven by the Nazis, who subsequently came to power.

With the onset of World War II, the building was not rebuilt. Yet its significance resonated beyond Germany, as shown by the photograph of the Soviet flag flying from the Reichstag in May 1945, which became a symbol of the German defeat.

Between 1957 and 1972, the dome and most of the ornamentation was removed. As well as providing a meeting-place for the lower house of the German Bundestag (Parliament), the Reichstag also made a spectacular back-drop for huge festivals and rock concerts, much to the annoyance of the East German authorities.

On 2 December 1990, the Reichstag was the first meeting-place of a newly-elected Bundestag following German reunification. On 23 June 1995 the artist Christo and his wife Jeanne-Claude wrapped the Reichstag in glistening fabric – an artistic statement that lasted for two weeks.

The latest phase of rebuilding, between 1995 and 1999 to a design by Sir Norman Foster, transformed the Reichstag into a modern meeting hall beneath an elliptical dome. Visits to the cupola's viewing gallery are free and the views are breath-taking. The first parliamentary meeting in the new building took place on 19 April 1999.

Sowjetisches Ehrenmal 24

MONUMENT TO SOVIET SOLDIERS

Strasse des 17 Juni. **Map** 6 D3. Ⓢ & Ⓤ Brandenburger Tor. 🚌 100, 248.

This huge monument near the Brandenburg Gate was unveiled on 7 November 1945, on the anniversary of the start of the October Revolution in Russia. Flanked by the first two tanks into the city, the monument commemorates over 300,000 Soviet soldiers who perished in the battle for Berlin at the end of World War II. The vast column was made from marble taken from the headquarters of the Chancellor of the Third Reich, when it was being dismantled. The column was designed by Nicolai Sergiejev, while the imposing figure on top, a soldier cast in bronze, is the work of Lew Kerbel. This monument is also a cemetery for around 2,500 Soviet casualties. Following the partition of Berlin, the site ended up in the British sector, but formed a kind of non-territorial enclave to which Soviet soldiers posted to East Berlin had access.

The sculpture of a Soviet soldier atop the Sowjetisches Ehrenmal

BERLIN'S BRIDGES

Despite wartime damage, Berlin's bridges are still well worth seeing. The Spree river and the city's canals have some exemplary architecture on their banks, while many of the bridges were designed and decorated by famous architects and sculptors. Probably the most renowned bridge is the Schlossbrücke designed by Karl Friedrich Schinkel (see p74). Further south along the Kupfergrabenkanal, the Schleusenbrücke dates from c.1914, and is decorated with reliefs of the early history of the city's bridges and sluices. The next bridge, heading south, is the Jungfernbrücke dating from 1798, which is the last drawbridge in Berlin. The next bridge along is the Gertraudenbrücke (see p85). Where Friedrichstrasse crosses the Spree river is the Weiden-dammer Brücke, originally built in 1695-7 and subsequently rebuilt in 1923, with an eagle motif decorating its balustrade. On the Spree near the Regierungsviertel is the magnificent Moltkebrücke (1886–91). The bridge is guarded by a huge griffin wielding a shield adorned with the Prussian eagle, while cherubs dressed in a military fashion hold up lamps. On the arches of the bridges are portraits of leaders designed by Karl Begas.

Ornamental feature of a bear on the Liebknechtbrücke

KREUZBERG

The area covered in this chapter is only a part of the suburb of the same name. The evolution of Kreuzberg began in the late 19th century when it was a working-class area. After World War II unrepaired buildings were abandoned by those who could afford to move, leaving a population of artists, foreigners, the unemployed and members of a variety of sub-cultures.

Detail from the Martin-Gropius-Bau façade

Kreuzberg is now an area of contrasts, with luxury apartments next to dilapidated buildings. Some parts of Kreuzberg are mainly Turkish, while others are inhabited by affluent young professionals. The district's attractions are its wealth of restaurants and Turkish bazaars, as well as an interesting selection of nightclubs, cinemas, theatres and galleries.

SIGHTS AT A GLANCE

Museums
Berlinische Galerie ❺
Checkpoint Charlie ❹
Deutsches Technikmuseum
  Berlin ❾
Jüdisches Museum ❻
Lapidarium ❽
Martin-Gropius-Bau ❷
Topographie des Terrors ❸

Historic Buildings
Anhalter Bahnhof ❶
Flughafen
  Tempelhof ⓭
Riehmers
  Hofgarten ⑪

Squares, Parks and Cemeteries
Friedhöfe vor dem
  Halleschen Tor ❿
Mehringplatz ❼
Viktoriapark ⑫

| 0 metres | 800 |
| 0 yards | 800 |

GETTING THERE
U-Bahn line 6, with stations at Kochstrasse, Hallesches Tor, Mehringdamm and Platz der Luftbrücke, crosses the area from north to south, while U-Bahn lines 1 and 7 run east to west.

KEY

    Street-by-Street map
    See pp138–9

U U-Bahn station

S S-Bahn station

🚌 Bus stop

◁ The magnificent 24-metre waterfall in Viktoriapark, Kreuzberg

Street-by-Street: Mehringplatz and Friedrichstrasse

The areas north of Mehringplatz are the oldest sections of Kreuzberg. Mehringplatz, initially called Rondell, together with the Oktogon (Leipziger Platz) and the Quarré (Pariser Platz), were laid out in 1734 as part of the enlargement of Friedrichstadt. World War II totally changed the character of this area. It is now full of modern developments such as the Friedrichstadt Passagen – a huge complex of shops, apartments, offices, galleries and restaurants. Only a few buildings recall the earlier splendour of this district.

★ Checkpoint Charlie
This small hut marks the place of the notorious border crossing between East and West Berlin ❹

Topographie des Terrors
A shocking exhibition detailing Nazi crimes is housed within the former Gestapo and SS headquarters ❸

Martin-Gropius-Bau
This interesting, multi-coloured Neo-Renaissance building was once home to the Kunstgewerbemuseum (see pp118–21) ❷

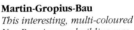

Deutsches
Technikmuseum ◄

| 0 metres | 150 |
| 0 yards | 150 |

STAR SIGHTS

★ Checkpoint Charlie

★ Jüdisches Museum

Haus am Checkpoint Charlie
Butterflies on a piece of the Berlin Wall mark the entrance to this museum.

Springerhaus
This shopping and restaurant complex is located next to the Axel-Springer-Hochhaus, a 1960s highrise built adjacent to the Berlin Wall as a highly-visible political statement.

LOCATOR MAP
See Street Finder maps 12 & 13

AROUND UNTER DEN LINDEN

TIERGARTEN

KREUZBERG

Märkisches Museum

RUDI-DUTSCHKE STRASSE

CHARLOTTENSTRASSE

MARKGRAFENSTRASSE

SSELSTRASSE

STRASSE

Z-KLUHS-STRASSE

★ **Jüdisches Museum**
Windows made to resemble cracks create a striking effect in the metallic facing of this building by architect Daniel Libeskind **6**

Mehringplatz
The former Rondell was known for many years as Belle-Alliance-Platz. Completely destroyed during World War II, it was rebuilt by Hans Scharoun, who followed the original design **7**

KEY

– – – Suggested route

Anhalter Bahnhof ❶

Askanischer Platz 6–7. **Map** 12 E1.
Ⓤ *Mendelssohn-Bartholdy-Park.*
🚌 *200, 347, M29, M41.*

Only a tiny fragment now remains of Anhalter Bahnhof, which was named after the Saxon Royal Family. It was once Berlin's largest and Europe's second largest railway station.

The hugely ambitious structure was designed by Franz Schwechten and constructed in 1880. The station was intended to be the largest and most elegant in Europe in order to impress official visitors to the capital of the German Empire. Some of the most famous people to alight at Anhalter Bahnhof were the Italian king Umberto, who was welcomed by Kaiser Wilhelm II himself, and the Russian tsar Nicholas. The station was taken out of public use in 1943 after its roof was destroyed by Allied bombing. Only the front portico remains, crowned by still-damaged sculptures and the hole that housed a large electric clock, as well as fragments of its once glorious façade. On the vast grounds behind it is the tent-like entertainment venue Tempodrom *(see p269).*

Martin-Gropius-Bau ❷

Niederkirchnerstrasse 7 (corner of Stresemannstrasse). **Map** 12 E1. *Tel* 25 48 60. ⬜ *10am–8pm Wed–Mon.* Ⓢ & Ⓤ *Potsdamer Platz.* 🚌 *200, 347, M29, M41.* 🖼

The innovative Martin-Gropius-Bau was originally built to fulfil the requirements of an arts and crafts museum. It was designed by Martin Gropius with the participation of Heino Schmieden and constructed in 1881. The building is in a style reminiscent of an Italian Renaissance palace, with a magnificent glazed interior courtyard, an impressive atrium and unusual, richly decorated elevations. Located between the windows are the crests of German cities, and within the friezes are reliefs illustrating the different arts and crafts. In the plaques between the windows of the top storey are beautiful mosaics containing allegorical figures representing the cultures of different eras and countries.

From 1922 Martin-Gropius-Bau accommodated the Museum of Ethnology, but after World War II the building was abandoned and left in ruins. Although plans for an inner-city motorway threatened it until the 1970s, a reconstruction programme eventually commenced in 1981, led by architects Winnetou Kampmann and Ute Westroem. This was followed in 1999 by a further refurbishment, and since then the building has housed a changing series of exhibitions on art, photography and architecture.

Exhibition documenting Nazi crimes at the Topographie des Terrors

Topographie des Terrors ❸

Stresemannstrasse 110 (entrance on Niederkirchnerstrasse). **Map** 6 F5, 12 F1. *Tel* 25 45 09 50. Ⓢ & Ⓤ *Potsdamer Platz.* 🚌 *200, M29, M41.* ⬜ *May–Sep: 10am–8pm daily; Oct–Apr: 10am–6pm daily.* 🖼

During the Third Reich Prinz-Albrecht-Strasse was probably the most frightening address in Berlin. In 1934, three of the most terrifying Nazi political departments had their headquarters in a block between Stresemann-, Wilhelm-, Anhalter-, and Prinz-Albrecht-Strasse (now Niederkirchner Strasse), making this area the government district of National Socialist Germany.

The Neo-Classical Prinz-Albrecht palace at Wilhelmstrasse No. 102 became the headquarters of Reinhard Heydrich and the Third Reich's security service (SD). The arts and crafts school at Prinz-Albrecht-Strasse No. 8 was occupied by the head of the Gestapo, Heinrich Müller, while the Hotel Prinz Albrecht at No. 9 became the headquarters of the Schutzstaffel or SS, with Heinrich Himmler in command. It was from the buildings in this area of the city that decisions about the Germanization of the occupied territories were made, as well as plans on the genocide of European

Allegorical mosaic on display in the Martin-Gropius-Bau

Jews. After World War II, the buildings were pulled down. In 1987, however, in some surviving cellars that were once torture cells, an exhibition was mounted that documented Nazi crimes.

A preserved section of the Berlin wall runs alongside the grounds of the Topographie des Terrors at Niederkirchner Strasse.

Checkpoint Charlie ❹

Friedrichstrasse 43–45. **Map** 7 A5. *Tel* 253 72 50. **U** *Kochstrasse.* 🚌 *M29.* **Haus am Checkpoint Charlie** ⏰ *9am–10pm daily.* 🖼

A Alpha, B Bravo, C Charlie. Not many people remember that the name of this notorious border crossing between the American and Soviet sectors stemmed from the word that signifies the letter C in the international phonetic alphabet.

Between 1961 and 1990, Checkpoint Charlie was the only crossing point for foreigners between East and West Berlin. During that time, it represented a symbol of both freedom and separation for the many East Germans trying to escape from the DDR's Communist regime.

Little remains of the former crossing point, which was witness to a number of dramatic events during the Cold War, including a tense two-day standoff between Russian and American tanks in 1961.

In 1990, the checkpoint was formally closed with an official ceremony attended by the foreign ministers of the four occupying powers: the US, Great Britain, France and the Soviet Union.

Today, there are no longer any gates, barriers or barbed wire to be seen; instead there is a replica checkpoint booth, complete with sand bags and the famous, huge sign on the old Western side that reads "You are leaving the American Sector".

Also on Friedrichstrasse are two large photographs of an

The replica booth at the former Checkpoint Charlie

American and a Russian soldier, that form part of a well-known series by the Berlin photographer Frank Thiel. His portraits of four Allied soldiers commemorate the departure of the Allies.

One of the original watchtowers is worth visiting at the museum nearby – **Haus am Checkpoint Charlie**. The museum's rich collection details Cold War border conflicts, and the construction of the Berlin Wall. Of special interest are the exhibits connected with the escape attempts of East Germans to the West. The ingenuity and bravery of these escapees is astonishing, using devices such as secret compartments built into cars, and specially constructed suitcases.

A separate exhibition illustrates the peaceful campaigns carried out in the name of democracy in a number of totalitarian countries.

Berlinische Galerie ❺

Alte Jakobstrasse 124–28. **Map** 7 C5. *Tel* 78 90 26 00. **U** *Kochstrasse.* 🚌 *248, M29.* ⏰ *10am–6pm Wed–Mon.* 🖼

The city's museum for modern art, design and architecture is one of the finest regional museums in the country. Themed exhibitions, which are regularly changed, draw upon its huge collection of German, East European and Russian paintings, photographs, graphics and architectural artefacts.

One of the highlights is the 5,000-strong painting collection, which covers all the major art movements from the late 19th century until today. It includes works by Max Liebermann, Otto Dix, Georg Baselitz, Alexander Rodtschenko, Iwan Puni and Via Lewandowsky.

The museum's collection of sketches, prints and posters encompasses the Berlin Dadaists George Grosz, Hanna Höch and Werner Heldt, as well as works by Ernst Ludwig Kirchner and Hanns Schimansky.

Amongst the architectural items held by the Galerie are drawings and models for buildings that were never built, offering fascinating glimpses into how the city might have looked. A fine example is the shell-like Expressionist Sternkirche (Star Church), designed by Otto Bartning in 1922.

Kühn Malvessi's *Letter Field* in front of the Berlinische Galerie

Jüdisches Museum Berlin ⑥

The Jewish Museum designed by Daniel Libeskind, a Polish-Jewish architect based in the United States, is an exciting and imaginative example of late 20th-century architecture. The plan, shape, style, and interior and exterior arrangement of the building are part of a complicated philosophical programme to illustrate the history and culture of Germany's Jewish community, and the repercussions of the Holocaust. The exhibition has gathered together many artifacts, such as books and photographs, to bring the memories and stories of Jewish life alive. The long, narrow galleries with slanting floors and sharp zig-zagging turns are designed to evoke the feeling of loss and dislocation. These are interspersed by "voids" that represent the vacuum left behind by the destruction of Jewish life.

★ Moses Mendelssohn's Glasses
These glasses are on show in the section entitled "Moses Mendelssohn and the Enlightenment", which details the philosopher's fight for religious tolerance in a time when Jews possessed no civil rights.

"Darwinian" (1904)
This caricature, published in the magazine Schlemiel, *shows the evolution of a Jewish Hanukkah light into a Christian Christmas tree, implying that the wish of many Jews was to assimilate with Germans.*

Rural Jews and Court Jews

At the Heart of the Family

German and Jewish at the Same Time

STAR SIGHTS

- ★ Moses Mendelssohn's Glasses
- ★ Daniel Libeskind's Design
- ★ Garden of Exile

MUSEUM GUIDE

Entrance to the museum is via an underground path from the former Berlin Museum next door. Stairs lead up to the start of the exhibition which is divided into 14 sections, taking visitors through German Jewish history and culture from early history, through the Middle Ages and up to the present day.

VISITORS' CHECKLIST

Lindenstrasse 9–14. **Map** 13 A2.
Tel 25 99 33 00. **U** Hallesches
Tor or Kochstrasse. M29, M41,
248. 10am–10pm Mon,
10am–8pm Tue–Sun. Jewish
hols and 24 Dec. Audio
guides are available.
www.jmberlin.de

Entrance to exhibition via underground tunnel

World War I and Weimar Republic

Persecution – Resistance – Extermination

Exit

★ Daniel Libeskind's Design

The extraordinary zinc-clad, jagged structure of the museum is likened to a deconstructed Star of David, and attracted over 350,000 visitors to the museum in the two years before the exhibitions were installed.

Electric Iron AEG

An iron made by one of Germany's largest electrical companies, founded by Emil Rathenau, forms part of the collection celebrating the dominant position of Jews in trade and industry in Berlin throughout the late 19th and early 20th centuries.

...st and ...est

KEY

▨	Beginnings
▨	Middle Ages
▨	1500–1800
☐	Tradition and Change
▨	1850–1933
▨	Modern Judaism and Urban Life
☐	1914–1933
☐	1933–1945
▨	The Present
▨	Non-exhibition space
– –	Suggested Route

★ Garden of Exile

Comprising 49 tilted pillars to represent the foundation of the state of Israel in 1948 plus one for Berlin, the garden also symbolizes the forced exile of Germany's Jews.

A representation of Peace, by Albert Wolff, in Mehringplatz

Mehringplatz 7

Map 13 A2. U Hallesches Tor.
248, M41.

Mehringplatz was planned
in the 1830s, when the
boundaries of the city were
extended. Its original name
was Rondell, meaning roundabout. This was an appropriate
name as Wilhelmstrasse,
Friedrichstrasse and Lindenstrasse all converged here.

Mehringplatz was the work
of Philipp Gerlach then, in the
1840s, Peter Joseph Lenné
designed the decoration of
the square. At the centre is the
Column of Peace, designed by
Christian Gottlieb Cantian,
commemorating the Wars of
Liberation in 1815. The column
is crowned by the figure of
Victory by Christian Daniel
Rauch. Two sculptures were
added in the 1870s: *Peace* by
Albert Wolff; and *Clio* (the
Muse of History) by Ferdinand
Hartzer. In the 19th and early
20th centuries the area was
fashionable and populated
with politicians, diplomats
and aristocrats. The current
buildings date from the 1970s.

Lapidarium 8

Hallesches Ufer 78. Map 12 E2.
U Mendelssohn-Bartholdy-Park.

This interesting building,
decorated with an enchanting
Oriental-style chimney, was
once Berlin's pumping
station. It was built from
1873 to 1876 and designed
by Hermann Blankenstein.
The original steam pumps
have survived to this day. The

Lapidarium once contained
numerous sculptures, including
virtually all the sculptures that
once decorated the Avenue of
Victory in the Tiergarten,
known as "Puppenallee".
These majestic statues of
celebrated warriors and rulers
stood side by side in their
robes and weapons, only
slightly diminished by the loss
of many heads, arms and
other body parts. In 2009 the
Lapidarium was sold, and all
the statues were transferred to
the Zittadelle Spandau.

Deutsches Technikmuseum Berlin 9

Trebbiner Strasse 9. Map 12 E2.
Tel 90 25 40. U Gleisdreieck.
M29, M41. 9am–5:30pm
Tue–Fri, 10am–6pm Sat–Sun.

The Technical Museum was
first established in 1982 with
the intention of grouping more
than 100 smaller, specialized
collections under one roof.
The current collection is
arranged on the site of the
former trade hall, the size of
which allows many of the
museum's exhibits, such as
locomotives, aircraft, boats,
water towers and storerooms,
to be displayed full-size and
in their original condition.

Of particular interest in the
collection are the dozens of
locomotives and railway
carriages from different eras
as well as the vintage cars.
There are also exhibitions
dedicated to flying, the history
of paper manufacture, printing,
weaving, electro-technology

and computer technology.
There are also two windmills,
a brewery and an old forge.
The section called Spectrum
is especially popular with
children as it allows them
to conduct "hands-on"
experiments.

Friedhöfe vor dem Halleschen Tor 10

Mehringdamm, Blücher-, Baruther
& Zossener Strasse. Map 13 A3. Tel
691 6138. U Hallesches Tor. 140,
248, M41. Dec & Jan: 8am–4pm
daily; Feb & Nov: 8am–5pm daily;
Mar & Oct: 8am–6pm; Apr & Sep:
8am–7pm; May–Aug: 8am–8pm.

Beyond the city walls, next to
the Hallesches Tor, are four
cemeteries established in 1735.
Among the beautiful gravestones are great Berlin artists
including the composer Felix
Mendelssohn-Bartholdy,
architects Georg Wenzeslaus
von Knobelsdorff, David Gilly
and Carl Ferdinand Langhans,
and the writer, artist and
composer ETA Hoffmann.

Riehmers Hofgarten 11

Yorckstr. 83–86, Grossbeerenstr. 56–57
& Hagelberger Strasse 9–12.
Map 12 F4. U Mehringdamm.
140, 248, M19.

Riehmers Hofgarten is the
name given to the 20 or so
exquisite houses arranged
around a picturesque garden
in the area bordered by the

**Headstone in the picturesque
Friedhöfe vor dem Halleschen Tor**

Renaissance-style façade in Riehmers Hofgarten

streets Yorck-, Hagelberger and Grossbeerenstrasse. These houses were built between 1881 and 1892 to the detailed designs of Wilhelm Riehmer and Otto Mrosk, respected architects who not only designed intricate, Renaissance-style façades but also gave equal splendour to the elevations overlooking the courtyard garden. The streets of Riehmers Hofgarten have been carefully restored and Yorckstrasse also has quite a few cafés. Next to Riehmers Hofgarten is the church of St Bonifaz, which was designed by Max Hasak. Adjacent to the church is a similar complex of houses built in an impressive Neo-Gothic style.

To experience the authentic atmosphere of old Kreuzberg, you need to go no further than Bergmannstrasse. Here, entire districts of 19th-century houses have been restored to their original state. The atmosphere is further enhanced by antique street-lamps, a pedestrianized street, and bars and galleries. This is also true for Marheinekeplatz, where there is a lively covered market.

Viktoriapark ⑫

Map 12 E4, E5, F5. **U** Platz der Luftbrücke. 🚌 104, 140.

This rambling park, with several artificial waterfalls, short trails and a small hill, was designed by Hermann Machtig and built between 1884 and 1894. The Neo-Gothic Memorial to the Wars of Liberation at the summit of the hill is the work of Karl Friedrich Schinkel, created

between 1817 and 1821. The monument commemorates the Prussian victory against Napoleon's army in the Wars of Liberation. The cast-iron tower is well ornamented. In the niches of the lower section are 12 allegorical figures by Christian Daniel Rauch, Friedrich Tieck and Ludwig Wichmann. Each figure symbolizes a battle and is linked to a historic figure – either a military leader or a member of the royal family.

Flughafen Tempelhof ⑬

Platz der Luftbrücke. **Plan** 12 F5. **U** Platz der Luftbrücke. 🚌 104, 248.

Situated beyond Kreuzberg, Tempelhof airport was once Germany's largest. Built in 1923, it was enlarged during the Third Reich. The building is typical of Third Reich architecture, even though the eagles that decorate the buildings predate the Nazis. The additions to the original structure were designed by Ernst Sagebiel in 1939.

In 1951, a monument was added in front of the airport. Designed by Edward Ludwig, it commemorates the airlifts of the Berlin Blockade. The three spikes on the top symbolize the air corridors used by Allied planes. Following heated political debate, the airport was permanently closed in late 2008.

THE BERLIN BLOCKADE (1948–9)

On 24 June 1948, as a result of rising tensions between East Germany and West Berlin, Soviet authorities blockaded all the roads leading to West Berlin. In order to ensure food and fuel for the residents, US General Lucius Clay ordered that provisions be flown into the city. British and American planes made a total of 212,612 flights, transporting almost 2.3 million tons of goods, among which were parts of a power station. In April 1949, at the height of the airlifts, planes were landing every 63 seconds. The blockade ended in May, 1949. Although the airlifts were successful, there were casualties: 70 airmen and 8 ground crew lost their lives.

Allied plane bringing supplies during the Berlin Airlift

AROUND KURFÜRSTENDAMM

The eastern area of the Charlottenburg region, around the boulevard known as Kurfürstendamm, was developed in the 19th century. Luxurious buildings were constructed along Kurfürstendamm (the Ku'damm), while the areas of Breitscheidplatz and Wittenbergplatz became replete with hotels and department stores. After World War II, with the old centre (Mitte) situated in East Berlin,

Sculpture from the Jüdisches Gemeindehaus

Charlottenburg became the centre of West Berlin. Traces of wartime destruction were removed very quickly and this area was transformed into the heart of West Berlin, and dozens of new company headquarters and trade centres were built. The situation changed after the reunification of Berlin, and although many tourists concentrate on Mitte, the heart of the city continues to beat around Kurfürstendamm.

SIGHTS AT A GLANCE

Museums
Käthe-Kollwitz-Museum ❿
Newton-Sammlung ❻

Streets and Squares
Fasanenstrasse ❾
Kurfürstendamm ❹
Savignyplatz ⓫
Tauentzien-
strasse ⓮

Parks
Zoologischer
Garten ❶

Historic Buildings
Europa-Center ❷
Jüdisches Gemeindehaus ❽
KaDeWe ⓯
*Kaiser-Wilhelm-Gedächtnis-
Kirche pp152–3* ❸
Ludwig-Erhard-Haus ❺
Technische Universität ⓭
Theater des Westens ❼
Universität der Künste ⓬

KEY

▦	Street-by-Street map *pp148–9*
🚉	Railway station
Ⓢ	S-Bahn station
Ⓤ	U-Bahn station
🚌	Bus station
ℹ	Tourist information

GETTING THERE
S-Bahn lines 3, 5, 7, 9 and 75 go to Savigny-platz and Zoologischer Garten. U-Bahn lines 1, 2, 9 and 15 also traverse the area. Next to Zoo station is a large bus terminal.

0 metres 400
0 metres 400

◁ Mosaic depicting a standard-bearer inside the Kaiser-Wilhelm-Gedächtnis-Kirche

Street-by-Street: Breitscheidplatz and Ku'damm

The area surrounding the eastern end of the Ku'damm, especially Tauentzienstrasse and Breitscheidplatz, is the centre of the former West Berlin. Thirty years ago this ultramodern district, full of department stores and office blocks, attracted visitors from all over the world. Today, although the area still retains its unique atmosphere, it is becoming overshadowed by Potsdamer Platz and the arcades of Friedrich-strasse. However, nowhere else in Berlin is there a place so full of life as Breitscheidplatz, a department store with such style as KaDeWe, or streets as refined as Fasanenstrasse.

Kant-Dreieck
This building, containing only right angles, was designed by Josef Paul Kleihues. The "sail" on the roof makes it instantly recognizable.

Jüdisches Gemeindehaus
Some of the remaining fragments of the old synagogue have been incorporated into the façade of this building ⑧

Literaturhaus
contains a charming café and a good bookshop.

Käthe-Kollwitz-Museum
The museum is housed in one of the charming villas on Fasanenstrasse ⑩

Fasanenstrasse
This tranquil street features some of the most expensive shops in Berlin ⑨

STAR SIGHTS

★ Kaiser-Wilhelm-Gedächtniskirche

★ Zoologischer Garten

Ku'damm
A stroll along the Ku'damm is a stroll into the heart of Berlin, and an essential part of any visit to the city ④

KEY

- - - Suggested route

Ludwig-Erhard-Haus
The structure of the new Berlin Stock Exchange is based on parabolic arches ❺

LOCATOR MAP
See Street Finder maps 4, 9, 10 & 11.

Theater des Westens
The façade of this musical theatre is fittingly decorated with dancing women ❼

Bahnhof Zoo

Europa-Center
One of the attractions of the Europa-Centre is a glazed courtyard containing a fountain with moving parts ❷

★ Zoologischer Garten
The Oriental-style Elephant Gate is one of two entrances to the Zoological Gardens ❶

★ Kaiser-Wilhelm-Gedächtnis-Kirche
The mosaics on the wall of the sacristy, by Hermann Schaper, survived World War II undamaged ❸

0 metres	400
0 yards	400

Bao-Bao, one of the star attractions at the Zoo Berlin

Zoo Berlin ❶

ZOOLOGICAL GARDEN

Hardenbergplatz 8 or Budapester Strasse 34. **Map** 4 E5, 10 E1. **Tel** 25 40 10. Ⓢ & Ⓤ *Zoologischer Garten.* 🚌 *100, 109, 110, 200, 204, 245, 249, M45, M46, M49, X9, X10, X34.* ◻ *21 Mar–14 Sep: 9am–7pm daily; 15 Sep–25 Oct: 9am–6pm daily; 26 Oct–20 Mar: 9am–5pm daily.* 🎦

Zoo Berlin is one of Berlin's greatest attractions. Many animal "stars" are to be found here, including world-famous polar bear "Knut". It is part of the Tiergarten and dates from 1844, which makes this zoo one of the oldest in Germany. You can enter from Hardenbergplatz through the Lion's Gate, and from Budapester Strasse through the decorative Oriental-style Elephant Gate.

The zoo offers a number of attractions, including the monkey house, which contains a family of gorillas, and a darkened pavilion for nocturnal animals. The hippopotamus pool has a glazed wall that enables visitors to observe these enormous animals underwater. The aquarium, one of the largest in Europe, contains sharks, piranhas and unusual animals from coral reefs. There is also a huge terrarium with an over-grown jungle that is home to a group of crocodiles.

Europa-Center ❷

Breitscheidplatz. **Map** 10 E1. Ⓢ & Ⓤ *Zoologischer Garten.* 🚌 *100, 109, 146, 200, X9.*

The Europa-Center stands on the site of the legendary Romanisches Café, a famous meeting place for Dada artists in the 1920s. The current building was estab-lished in 1965, and since that time it has been one of the largest complexes of its type in the whole of Germany. Designed by Helmut Hentrich and Hubert Petschnigg, the Europa-Center is a group of low-rise buildings housing a trade centre, numerous restaurants and pubs. The uninspiring edifice of the deluxe Hotel Palace Berlin *(see p226)* has been incorporated into the centre, as well as a 22-storey office block.

Around the Center are dotted some amusing fountains, including the "Flow of Time Clock", designed by Bernard Gitton. Seconds, minutes and hours are measured in vials and spheres of green liquid. The Europa-Center also houses the political cabaret *Die Stachelschweine.*

Kaiser-Wilhelm-Ge-dächtnis-Kirche ❸

See pp152–3.

Kurfürstendamm ❹

Map 9 A2, B2, C3, 10 D1. Ⓤ *Kurfürstendamm.* 🚌 *109, 110, M19, M29.*

This is undoubtedly one of the most elegant streets in Berlin. The wide avenue was established in the 1880s on the site of a former track that led to the Grunewald forest. It was quickly populated with imposing buildings and grand hotels. In the 20 years between World Wars I and II, the Ku'damm (as it is popularly called) was renowned for its great cafés, visited by famous writers, directors and painters.

After World War II, the damaged houses were replaced with modern buildings, but this did not change the essential character of this fine street. During the Cold War years it became a symbol of free-market consumerism and the main shopping street in West Berlin. Today, elegant shops and cafés with pretty summer gardens continue to attract a chic crowd.

Ludwig-Erhard-Haus ❺

Fasanenstrasse 83–84. **Map** 4 D5. Ⓢ & Ⓤ *Zoologischer Garten.* 🚌 *245, M45, M49, X34.*

The distinctive curve of this innovative new building houses the headquarters of the Berlin stock exchange as well as a trade and industry centre. Completed in 1998, Ludwig-Erhard-Haus is the creation of British architect Nicholas Grimshaw and has been compared to the skin of an armadillo, a giant skeleton and the ribbing of a shell.

The main structure of the building is composed of 15 elliptical arches, which extend above the roof and down through the glass walls on each side of the building.

A fountain representing Earth, outside the Europa-Center

Newton-Sammlung ❻

Jebensstrasse 2. **Map** 4 D5. **Tel** 31 86 48 25. Ⓢ & Ⓤ Zoologischer Garten. ☐ 10am–6pm Tue–Wed Fri–Sun, 10am–10pm Thu. 📷

After his death in 2004, the society and art photographer Helmut Newton (1931–2004) bequeathed his life's work to the city of Berlin. Newton, who was born and received his first training as a photographer in Berlin, became one of the 20th-century's most well-known photographers with his images of nudes and por-traits of the rich and famous.

The museum is constantly extending its collections so as to serve as the city's muse-um of photography. Currently, it exhibits selections of Newton's work, including his early fashion and nude pho-tography as well as self-portraits and landscapes.

The façade of the Theater des Westens on Kantstrasse

Theater des Westens ❼

Kantstrasse 9–12. **Map** 10 D1. **Tel** (0180) 544 44. Ⓢ & Ⓤ Zoologischer Garten. 🚌 M49, X34.

The Theater des Westens, one of the most picturesque of all Berlin's theatres, was built in 1896 to a design by Bernhard Sehring. The composition of its façade links Neo-Classical elements with Palladian and Art Nouveau details. The interior of the theatre has been designed in a splendid Neo-Baroque style, while the back and the sections that houses the stage have been rebuilt

within a Neo-Gothic structure, incorporating the decorative elements of a chess set.

From its very beginning the theatre catered for lighter forms of musical entertainment. Operettas and vaudeville were staged here, followed by musicals such as *Les Miserables*. Some of the world's greatest stars have appeared on the stage here, including Joseph-ine Baker, who performed her famous banana dance in 1926. Near the theatre is the renowned Delphi cinema and popular jazz club Quasimodo.

Jüdisches Gemeindehaus ❽

JEWISH COMMUNITY HOUSE

Fasanenstrasse 79/80. **Map** 10 D1. Ⓤ Uhlandstrasse or Kurfürstendamm. 🚌 109, 110, M49, X10, X34.

The Jewish community has its headquarters in this building, constructed on the site of a synagogue that was burned down during *Kristallnacht* on 9 November 1938 *(see p29)*. The original synagogue was designed by Ehenfried Hessel in a Romanesque-Byzantine style and built in 1912. The ruins of the synagogue were removed only in the mid-1950s. The new building,

The entrance of the Jüdisches Gemeindehaus

designed by Dieter Knoblauch and Heinz Heise, was con-structed in 1959. The only reminders of the splendour of the former synagogue are the portal at the entrance to the building and some decorative fragments on the façade.

Inside there are offices, a school, a kosher restaurant called Arche Noah and a prayer room covered by three glazed domes. At the rear there is a courtyard with a place of remembrance. There is also an emotive statue at the front of the building, depicting a broken scroll of the Torah (the holy book of Jewish Law).

GERMAN CINEMA

The 1920s were a boom time for the arts, and German cinema gained prominence throughout the world with the rise of Expressionism. The opening of the UFA film studios in 1919 in Babelsberg *(see p205)* was a milestone in the development of German cinema. The studios became the heart of the film industry and rivalled Hollywood as a centre for innovation. Many famous films were produced

Marlene Dietrich in the well-known film *The Blue Angel*

here, including the Expressionist masterpiece *The Cabinet of Dr Caligari* (1920) by Robert Wiene, Ernst Lubitsch's *Madame Dubarry* (1919) with Pola Negri and *Nosferatu* (1922) by Friedrich Murnau. Other films released by the studios were Fritz Lang's *Doctor Mabuse* (1922) and his futuristic film *Metropolis* (1927). In April 1930, the studios premiered Josef von Sternberg's *The Blue Angel* featuring the young Marlene Dietrich in the lead role. After Hitler came to power many directors and actors left Germany.

Kaiser-Wilhelm-Gedächtnis-Kirche ❸

This church-monument is one of Berlin's most famous landmarks, surrounded by a lively crowd of street traders, buskers and beggars. The vast Neo-Romanesque church was designed by Franz Schwechten. It was consecrated in 1895 but was destroyed by bombs in 1943. After World War II the ruins were removed, leaving only the massive front tower at the base of which the Gedenkhalle (Memorial Hall) is situated. This hall documents the history of the church and contains some of the original ceiling mosaics, marble reliefs and liturgical objects from the church. In 1961, Egon Eiermann designed an octagonal church in blue glass and a new freestanding bell tower.

Kaiser's Mosaic
Kaiser Heinrich I is depicted here in this elaborate mosaic, sitting on his throne.

Mosaic Decoration
Original mosaics remain on the arches and the walls near the staircase. These feature the Dukes of Prussia among the other decorative elements.

Bell Tower
The new hexagonal bell tower stands on the site of the former main nave of the destroyed church.

Rose window

Walls of reinforced concrete and blue-coloured glass form a dense grid.

Main Altar
The vast figure of Christ on the Cross is the work of Karl Hemmeter.

Tower Ruins
The damaged roof of the former church has become one of the best-known symbols of Berlin.

VISITORS' CHECKLIST

Breitscheidplatz. **Map** 10 D1.
Tel *218 50 23.* Ⓢ *&* Ⓤ
Zoologischer Garten or
Ⓤ *Kurfürstendamm.*
🚌 *100, 109, 110, 200, 204,*
219, 245, X9. ⬜ **Church**
9am–7pm daily. **Gedenkhalle**
10am–6pm Mon–Sat.
🔼 *noon–5:30pm Sun.* 📷

Tower Clock
The tower is decorated with a clock based on a Classical design.

★ Mosaic of the Hohenzollerns
The mosaic of the Hohenzollerns is in the vestibule. The family is led by Queen Luise and the centre is dominated by Kaiser Wilhelm I.

Orthodox Cross
This cross was a gift from the Russian Orthodox bishops from Volokolamsk and Yuryev, given in memory of the victims of Nazism.

Figure of Christ
This vast sculpture by Hermann Schaper once decorated the church altar. It survived World War II damage.

Main entrance

★ Coventry Crucifix
This modest cross was fashioned from nails found in the ashes of Coventry Cathedral, England. The Cathedral was destroyed during German bombing raids in 1940.

STAR SIGHTS

★ Mosaic of the Hohenzollerns

★ Coventry Crucifix

Fasanenstrasse – one of the most elegant streets in Berlin

Fasanenstrasse ⑨

Map 9 C2, 10 D1, 10 D3.
Ⓤ *Uhlandstrasse.* 🚌 *109, 110, M49, X10, X34.*

The discreet charm of Fasanenstrasse, particularly between Lietzenburger Strasse and Kurfürstendamm, has attracted the most exclusive designer shops in the world. Well maintained buildings, *fin-de-siècle* villas set in tranquil gardens and elegant shop windows of jewellers, art galleries and fashion shops will all entice you to take an afternoon stroll along this street.

It is worth seeing the villas at No. 23–5, which are called the Wintergarten-Ensemble. The first one, No. 23, dates from 1889. Tucked away in a garden, the villa is home to the Literaturhaus, which organizes interesting exhibitions and readings. It has an excellent café that extends into a conservatory. At No. 24 is the Käthe-Kollwitz museum, and No. 25, built in 1892 by Hans Grisebach, accommodates an auction house and art gallery.

Käthe-Kollwitz-Museum ⑩

Fasanenstrasse 24. **Map** 9 C2.
Tel *882 52 10.* Ⓤ *Uhlandstrasse or Kurfürstendamm.* 🚌 *109, 110, 204, 249, X10.* ◻ *11am–6pm daily.* 📷 🔲

This small private museum provides a unique opportunity to become acquainted with the work of Käthe Kollwitz (1867–1945). Born in

Königsberg, the artist settled in Berlin where she married a doctor who worked in Prenzlauer Berg, a working-class district *(see p170)*. Her drawings and sculptures portrayed the social problems of the poor, as well as human tragedy and suffering. She frequently took up the theme of motherhood and war after losing a son and grandson in World Wars I and II.

The museum exhibits her work, including sculptures, posters and drawings, as well as letters and photographs.

Mother and Child, from the Käthe-Kollwitz-Museum

Savignyplatz ⑪

Map 9 C1. Ⓢ *Savignyplatz.* 🚌 *M49, X34.*

Savignyplatz is enclosed on the south side by the arcade of a railway viaduct, which appears in the film *Cabaret* by Bob Fosse. During the day the square does not look interesting – there are no

remarkable buildings, only carefully tended greenery and flower beds. However, the area around the square truly comes alive at night. The dozens of cafés and restaurants fill up, while in summer the entire edge of the square and neighbouring streets turn into one big garden filled with tables and umbrellas. People come from outlying districts to visit popular restaurants and cafés such as Zwiebelfisch, Dicke Wirtin, or XII Apostel *(see p240)*. The arcades in the viaduct contain many cafés and bars, and one section has been taken up by the Bücherbogen bookshop *(see p254)*.

Universität der Künste ⑫

UNIVERSITY OF THE ARTS

Hardenbergstrasse 32–33 and Fasanenstrasse 1b. **Map** 4 D5. Ⓢ *Zoologischer Garten or* Ⓤ *Ernst-Reuter-Platz.* 🚌 *245, M45, X9.*

The Universität der Künste was originally called Preussische Akademie der Künste, which was established in 1696. It continued a long tradition of teaching artists in Berlin and has been headed by well-known figures including Johann Gottfried Schadow and Anton von Werner. As a result of a number of reforms between 1875 and 1882, the Academy was divided into two separate colleges. A complex of buildings was erected for them on Hardenbergstrasse and Fasanenstrasse. The Neo-Baroque buildings were constructed between 1897 and 1902 to a design by Heinrich Keyser and Karl von Grossheim.

After World War II, only two large buildings, both with decorative façades, survived. On the Hardenbergstrasse side was the Hochschule für Bildende Künste (College for Fine Art), while on the Fasanenstrasse side was the Hochschule für Musik und Darstellende Kunst (College for Music and Performing Arts). Unfortunately, the concert hall did not survive. A new one was built in 1955, designed by Paul Baumgarten.

Bas-relief sculpture on the façade of the Hochschule der Künste

A small *fin-de-siècle* building that looks like a castle, at Hardenbergstrasse No. 36, is a college for religious music which belongs to this group of college buildings.

Technische Universität ⑬

TECHNICAL UNIVERSITY

Strasse des 17 Juni 135.
Map 3 C4. 🚇 *Ernst-Reuter-Platz.*
🚌 245, M45, X9.

The vast area that lies to the east of Ernst-Reuter-Platz along the Strasse des 17 Juni is occupied by the buildings of the Technische Universität. Officially called Technische Hochschule Berlin (TUB), it was established in 1879 after the unification of the School of Crafts and the renowned Bauakademie. From its inception the Technische Universität had five different departments, which were all housed, from 1884, in a Neo-Renaissance building designed by Richard Lucae, Friedrich Hitzig and Julius Raschdorff. After World War II, the ruined front wing was rebuilt as a flat block without any divisions, while the rear wings and three internal courtyards retained their original appearance.

It is worth continuing along Strasse des 17 Juni towards the colonnade of the Charlottenburger Tor (or gate), dating from 1908. The colonnade is ornamented with the figures of Friedrich and Sophie Charlotte holding a model of Schloss Charlottenburg *(see pp160–1)* in their hands. Beyond the gate and to the right, on the island, is an unusual green building with a gigantic pink pipe. This is the centre that monitors water currents and caters to the needs of seagoing vessels.

Tauentzienstrasse ⑭

Map 10 E1. 🚇 *Wittenbergplatz.*
🚌 M19, M29, M46.

This is one of the most important streets for trade and commerce in this part of Berlin. The shops are not as expensive or as elegant as on Kurfürstendamm – but they attract more visitors for this reason. One of the highlights of the street is the unusual façade of the department store Peek & Clopenburg. Designed by Gottfried Böhm, the walls of the building are covered with transparent, gently slanting and undulating "aprons".

Other highlights include the central bed of colourful flowers as well as an interesting sculpture entitled *Berlin*. Created by Brigitte and Martin Matschinsky-Denninghoff, the sculpture was erected near Marburger Strasse in 1987 on the occasion of the 750th anniversary of Berlin.

KaDeWe ⑮

Tauentzienstrasse 21–24. **Map** 10 E2.
Tel 21 21 00. 🚇 *Wittenbergplatz.*
🚌 M19, M29, M46. 🕐 10am–
8pm Mon–Thu, 10am–9pm Fri,
9:30am–8pm Sat.

Kaufhaus des Westens, or KaDeWe, as it is popularly known, is the largest department store in Europe. It was built in 1907 to a design by Emil Schaudt, but it has been extended several times from the original building. From the very beginning KaDeWe was Berlin's most exclusive department store with a comprehensive collection of goods for sale and with a slogan that ran "In our shop a customer is a king, and the King is a customer".

After World War II, KaDeWe effectively became the symbol of the economic success of West Berlin. You can buy everything here, however, the main attraction must be the gourmet's paradise, with the largest collection of foodstuffs in the whole of Europe. Here there are exotic fruits and vegetables, live fish and seafood, 100 varieties of tea, more than 2,400 wines and a host of other gastronomic delights. KaDeWe also has a restaurant, the Wintergarten.

The sculpture *Berlin*, symbolizing the former divided Berlin

AROUND SCHLOSS CHARLOTTENBURG

The area surrounding Schloss Charlottenburg is one of the most enchanting regions of the city, full of greenery and attractive buildings dating from the end of the 19th century. Originally a small settlement called Lützow, it was only when Elector Friedrich III (later King Friedrich I) built his wife's summer retreat here at the end of the 17th century *(see p21)* that this town attained significance. Initially called Schloss Lietzenburg, the palace was renamed Schloss Charlottenburg after the death of Queen Sophie Charlotte. By the 18th century Charlottenburg had become a town, and was for many years an independent administration, inhabited by wealthy people living in elegant villas. It became officially part of Berlin in 1920, and despite World War II and the ensuing division of the city, the central section of this area has kept its historic character.

Urn at Schloss Charlottenburg

SIGHTS AT A GLANCE

Museums
Bröhan-Museum ⓫
Gipsformerei Berlin ❻
Museum Berggruen ❿
Museum Scharf-
 Gerstenberg ❾
Neuer Flügel ❸

Historic Buildings
Belvedere ❽
Luisenkirche ⓭
Mausoleum ❼

Neuer Pavillon
 (Schinkel-Pavillon) ❹
*Schloss Charlottenburg
 pp160–61* ❶
Schlossstrasse Villas ⓬

Parks and Gardens
Schlosspark ❺

GETTING THERE
The best routes to the palace are bus 109, 110, 309, M45 and X21; U-Bahn 7 to Richard-Wagner-Platz, U-Bahn 2 to Sophie-Charlotte-Platz or S-Bahn 41, 42 or 46 to West-end station.

Monuments
Reiterdenkmal des Grossen
 Kurfürsten ❷

KEY

▨	Street-by-Street map *pp158–9*
Ⓤ	U-Bahn station
Ⓢ	S-Bahn station
🚌	Bus terminus

0 metres   600

0 yards   600

Street-by Street: Around the Schloss

The park surrounding the former royal summer residence in Charlottenburg is one of the most picturesque places in Berlin. Visitors are drawn here by the meticulous post-war rebuilding of this luxury Baroque complex and outlying structures, whose marvellous interiors were once home to Prussian nobles. The wings of the palace and its pavilions house interesting exhibitions. After a stroll in the beautiful park, you can take refreshment in the Kleine Orangerie.

Detail from the main gate

★ **Schloss Charlottenburg**
The central section of the palace is called Nering-Eosanderbau, in honour of the architects who designed the building ❶

Museum für Vor- und Frühgeschichte
The museum is housed in a pavilion which served formerly as the court theatre, designed by Carl Gotthard Langhans ❺

Monument to the Great Elector
The momument to the Great Elector was funded by his son King Friedrich I and designed by Andreas Schlüter ❷

Kleine Orangerie

Neuer Flügel
The palace's new wing was once home to the royal art collection. Today the building houses changing art and history exhibits ❸

KEY

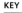 – – – Suggested route

Mausoleum
In the Neo-Classical mausoleum built for Queen Luise, members of the royal family are laid to rest **7**

LOCATOR MAP
See Street Finder map 2.

AROUND SCHLOSS CHARLOTTENBURG

Belvedere
In 1960 Karl Bobeck created the group of statues that surmount the Belvedere, in imitation of the original figures which were designed by Johann Eckstein **8**

Palace Park
A French-style park, laid-out in a geometric pattern, extends behind the palace **6**

★ Neuer Pavillon
In front of the western elevation of this pavilion are two granite columns (1840), topped by statues of Victory, the work of Christian Daniel Rauch **4**

STAR SIGHTS

★ Schloss Charlottenburg

★ Neuer Pavillon

0 metres   150

0 yards   150

Schloss Charlottenburg ❶

The palace in Charlottenburg was intended as a summer home for Sophie Charlotte, Elector Friedrich III's wife. Construction began in 1695 to a design by Johann Arnold Nering. Between 1701 and 1713 Johann Friedrich Eosander enlarged the palace, crowning it with a cupola and adding the orangery wing. Subsequent extensions were undertaken by Frederick the Great (Friedrich II), who added the Neuer Flügel, designed by Georg Wenzeslaus von Knobelsdorff, between 1740 and 1746. Restored to its former elegance following World War II, its collection of richly decorated interiors is unequalled in Berlin.

GALLERY GUIDE

Both the Altes Schloss and the Neuer Flügel can be visited by guided tour or by using audio guides, which are available in German, English, French, Spanish, Italian and Japanese.

First floor

Ground floor

★ Porzellankabinett

This exquisite mirrored gallery has walls lined from top to bottom with a fine display of Japanese and Chinese porcelain.

Schlosskapelle

Only parts of the pulpit in the court chapel are original to the palace. All the other furniture and fittings, including the royal box, are reconstructions.

Main entrance

Façade

The central section of the palace is the oldest part of the building, and is the work of Johann Arnold Nering.

Cupola

The palace's tall, Baroque cupola completes the perspective from Schlossstrasse.

Fortuna
A sculpture by Richard Scheibe crowns the palace, replacing the original statue destroyed during World War II.

Goldene Galerie
This garden ballroom dating from 1746 is one of the most creative examples of Prussian Rococo interior design.

Weisser Saal

Entrance to Neuer Flügel

VISITORS' CHECKLIST

Luisenplatz. **Map** 2 E2.
Altes Schloss (Nering-Eosanderbau) *Tel* (0331) 96 94 198/199. Ⓤ *Richard-Wagner-Platz & Sophie-Charlotte- Platz.* Ⓢ *Westend.* 🚌 *109, 145, 210, X21.* 🕐 *9am–5pm Tue–Sun.* 📷 *compulsory on ground floor only.* 📷 **Neuer Flügel (Knobelsdorff-Flügel)** *Tel* (0331) 96 94 198/199. 🕐 *Apr–Oct: 10am–6pm Wed–Mon; Nov–Mar: 10am–5pm Wed–Mon.* 📷 **www**.spsg.de

KEY

🔲	Official reception rooms
🔲	Apartments of Sophie-Charlotte
🔲	Neuer Flügel or Knobelsdorff-Flügel exhibition space
🔲	Friedrich Wilhelm II's summer apartments
🔲	Mecklenburg apartments
🔲	Apartments of Friedrich Wilhelm IV
🔲	Friedrich Wilhelm II's winter apartments
🔲	Frederick the Great's apartments

Neuer Flügel
The new wing holds the elegant apartments and exquisite furniture of Frederick Wilhelm III.

★ Gersaint's Shop Sign (1720)
An avid collector of French painting, Frederick the Great bought this and other fine canvases by Antoine Watteau for his collection.

The Monument to the Great Elector standing in front of Schloss Charlottenburg

Reiterdenkmal des Grossen Kurfürsten ②

MONUMENT TO THE GREAT ELECTOR

Luisenplatz. **Map** 2 E2. Ⓤ Richard-Wagner-Platz & Sophie-Charlotte-Platz. Ⓢ Westend. 🚌 109, 309, M45, X9.

The statue of the Great Elector (Friedrich Wilhelm) is the finest in Berlin and was paid for by his son, Elector Friedrich III (later King Friedrich I). Designed by Andreas Schlüter to be cast in one piece, the statue was started in 1696 but not finished until 1703. It was initially erected near the former Berlin palace, by Lange Brücke (now called Rathausbrücke). The statue was moved to safety during World War II but ironically, on the return journey, the barge transporting the monument sank in the port of Tegel.

In 1949 the statue was retrieved intact from the water and erected in the courtyard of Schloss Charlottenburg. However, it lacked the original base which was left behind in East Berlin, so a copy was commissioned. The original base finally ended up in the Bodemuseum topped with a replica of the statue.

The statue portrays the Great Elector as a warrior in ancient armour (albeit wearing a 17th-century wig) mounted on horse-back, triumphant over the figures of prisoners of war around the base. The base itself is decorated with patriotic reliefs of allegorical scenes. One scene depicts the kingdom surrounded by figures representing History, Peace and the Spree river; another shows the kingdom protected by embodiments of Faith, Bravery (in the form of Mucius Scaevola) and Strength (represented by the figure of Hercules).

Neuer Flügel ③

Luisenplatz (Schloss Charlottenburg–Neuer Flügel). **Map** 2 E2. **Tel** (0331) 969 420. Ⓤ Richard-Wagner-Platz & Sophie-Charlotte-Platz. Ⓢ Westend. 🚌 109, 309, M45, X9. ◷ Apr–Oct: 10am–6pm Wed–Mon; Nov–Mar: 10am–5pm Wed–Mon.

Built between 1740 and 1746, the new wing of Schloss Charlottenburg used to house the popular Galerie der Romantik. The main part of this collection of Romantic paintings has now been returned to the Alte Nationalgalerie (see p78). The rest

have been moved to the Neuer Pavillon. In its place, the new wing houses Frederick the Great's private quarters. Items on display include paintings he acquired and curiosities, such as his collection of snuff boxes. The wing also hosts temporary art and history exhibitions.

Neuer Pavillon (Schinkel-Pavillon) ④

Luisenplatz (Schlosspark Charlottenburg). **Map** 2 F2. **Tel** 208 6444. Ⓤ Richard-Wagner-Platz & Sophie-Charlotte-Platz. Ⓢ Westend. 🚌 309, 309, M45, X9. ◷ noon–6pm Thu–Sun. 📷

This charming Neo-Classical pavilion, with its clean lines and first-floor balcony, was built for Friedrich Wilhelm III and his second wife, Princess Auguste von Liegnitz. During a visit to Naples, the king stayed in the Villa Reale del Chiamonte and was so impressed that he commissioned Karl Friedrich Schinkel to build him something similar. The pavilion was finished for the king's birthday on 3 August 1825. Schinkel designed a two-storey structure with a central staircase and ranged the rooms around it in perfect symmetry. Pillared galleries, on the first floor, added variety to the eastern and western elevations. A cast iron balcony runs around the entire structure. Like many other Schloss Charlottenburg buildings, the pavilion burned down completely in World War II and

The Neuer Pavillon which was modelled on a Neapolitan villa

French-style garden in the Schloss Charlottenburg park

was rebuilt in 1960. Current renovation works will be completed in 2012.

The display inside the pavilion reveals the original splendour and atmosphere of the aristocratic interiors, enhanced with pictures and sculptures of the period. The prize picture is a renowned panorama of Berlin dated 1834, painted by Eduard Gärtner from the roof of the Friedrichswerdersche Kirche *(see p63)*. You can also admire paintings by Karl Friedrich Schinkel, who was not only a great architect but also a fine painter of fabulous architectural fantasies.

Schlosspark **5**

PALACE PARK

Luisenplatz (Schloss Charlottenburg). **Map** 2 D1. Ⓤ *Richard-Wagner-Platz & Sophie-Charlotte-Platz.* Ⓢ *Westend.* 🚌 *109, 309, M45, X9.*

This extensive royal park surrounding Schloss Charlottenburg *(see pp160–61)*, criss-crossed with tidy gravel paths, is a favourite place for Berliners to stroll at the weekend. The park is largely the result of reconstruction work carried out after World War II, when 18th-century prints were used to help reconstruct the varied layout of the original grounds. Immediately behind Schloss Charlottenburg is a French-style Baroque garden, made to a strict geometrical design with a vibrant patchwork of flower beds, carefully trimmed shrubs

and ornate fountains adorned with replicas of antique sculptures. Further away from the palace, beyond the curved carp lake, is a less formal English-style landscaped park, the original layout of which was created between 1819 and 1828 under the direction of the renowned royal gardener, Peter Joseph Lenné. The lakes and waterways of the park are the habitat of various water fowl including herons. A bike path stretches along the Spree river from the palace park to the Grosses Tiergarten and beyond.

Gipsformerei Berlin **6**

REPLICA WORKSHOP

Sophie-Charlotten-Strasse 17–18. **Map** 2 D3. **Tel** 326 769 0. Ⓤ *Sophie-Charlotte-Platz.* Ⓢ *Westend.* 🚌 *309, M45.* ⏰ *9am–4pm Mon–Fri, 9am–6pm Wed.*

Founded by Friedrich Wilhelm III in 1819, the Gipsformerei produces original-size replicas from items in Berlin museums and other collections. The first head of the workshop that also repairs damaged sculptures was renowned sculptor Christian Daniel Rauch.

Visitors are welcome to this modest brick building west of Schloss Charlottenburg and can purchase items on the spot or choose from catalogues to have them made to order and shipped home. Sculptures are generally copied in white plaster or painted

true to the original. Most moulds originate from the Middle Ages, the Renaissance and the 19th century.

Mausoleum **7**

Luisenplatz (Schlosspark Charlottenburg). **Map** 2 D2. **Tel** 32 09 14 46. Ⓤ *Richard-Wagner-Platz & Sophie-Charlotte-Platz.* Ⓢ *Westend.* 🚌 *109, 309, M45, X9.* ⏰ *Apr–Oct: 10am–6pm Tue–Sun; Nov–Mar: noon–4pm Tue–Sun.* 📷

Queen Luise, the beloved wife of Friedrich Wilhelm III, was laid to rest in this dignified, modest building, set among the trees in Schlosspark. The mausoleum was designed by Karl Friedrich Schinkel, in the style of a Doric portico-fronted temple.

In the original design, the queen's sarcophagus was housed in the crypt while the tombstone (actually a cenotaph sculpted by Christian Daniel Rauch) stood in the centre of the mausoleum. After the death of Friedrich Wilhelm in 1840, the mausoleum was refurbished; an apse added and the queen's tomb moved to one side, leaving room for her husband's tomb, also designed by Rauch. The second wife of the king, Princess Auguste von Liegnitz, was also buried in the crypt of the mausoleum, but without a tombstone.

Between the years 1890 and 1894, the tombs of Kaiser Wilhelm I and his wife, Auguste von Sachsen-Weimar, were added to the crypt. Both monuments are the work of Erdmann Encke.

The Schinkel-designed Mausoleum, final resting place of German royalty

The Belvedere's Baroque flourishes and clean Neo-Classical lines

Belvedere ●

Spandauer Damm (Schlosspark
Charlottenburg). **Map** 2 E1.
Tel 32 09 14 45. **U** Richard-
Wagner-Platz & Sophie-Charlotte-
Platz. **S** Westend. 108, 309,
M45, X9. Apr–Oct: 10am–
6pm Tue–Sun; Nov–Mar: 10am–
4pm Tue–Sun.

The Belvedere is a summer-
house in the Schlosspark
which served as a tea pavilion
for Friedrich Wilhelm II and,
in times of war, as a watchtower. It dates from 1788 and
was designed by Carl Gotthard
Langhans. The architect mixed
Baroque and Neo-Classical
elements, giving the building
an oval central structure with
four straight-sided annexes.
The building is crowned by
a low dome topped with a
sculpture of three cherubs
dragging a basket of flowers.
Ruined during World War II,
the summer-house was reconstructed between 1956 and
1960 and adapted to serve as
exhibition space. The exhibition is a large collection of
porcelain from the Berlin Königliche Porzellan-Manufaktur
(Royal Porcelain Workshop),
which has pieces from the
Rococo period up to late
Biedermeier, including some
outstanding individual items.

Museum Scharf-Gerstenberg ●

Schlossstrasse 70. **Map** 2 E3.
Tel 34 35 73 15. **U** Richard-
Wagner-Platz & Sophie-Charlotte-
Platz. **S** Westend. 309, M45,
X9. 10am–6pm Tue–Sun.

The two pavilions on either
side of Schlossstrasse were
intended as officers' barracks
for the King's Guard du
Corps. Built between the
years 1851 and 1859 by
Friedrich August Stüler,
they were inspired by a
design by King Friedrich
Wilhelm IV. The eastern

Odilon Redon's work in pastel,
Museum Scharf-Gerstenberg

pavilion joins the stable block
and once housed the
Ägyptisches Museum
(Egyptian Museum), which
has now moved to Museum
Island (see p75) before it
returns to its original historic
location, the Neues Museum.
Since the departure of the
Egyptian Museum, the Marstall
(stable block) has housed the
Museum Scharf-Gerstenberg.
Titled "Surreal World", the
museum presents paintings,
sculptures and works on
paper by Surrealist artists such
as Goya, Piranesi and Redon,
but also modern works by
Dalí, Magritte, Max Ernst
and Dubuffet. More than 250
objects are presented over
three floors, explaining the
history of surreal art, with
pieces from almost all the
leading Surrealists. A film
programme features classic
Surrealist films by Luis Buñuel
and Salvador Dalí.

Museum Berggruen ●

Schlossstrasse 1. **Map** 2 E3.
Tel 34 35 73 15. **U** Richard-
Wagner-Platz & Sophie-Charlotte-
Platz. **S** Westend. 109, 309,
M45. 10am–6pm Tue–Sun.

Heinz Berggruen assembled
this tasteful collection of art
dating from the late 19th and
first half of the 20th century.
Born and educated in Berlin,
he emigrated to the US in
1936, spent most of his life in
Paris, but finally entrusted his
collection to the city of his
birth. The museum opened
in what was once the west
pavilion of the barracks using
space freed up by moving
the Antikensammlung to
Museum Island (see p75).
The exhibition halls were
modified according to the
designs of Hilmer and Sattler,
who also designed the layout
of the Gemäldegalerie. The
Museum Berggruen is particularly well-known for its large
collection of quality paintings,
drawings and gouaches by
Pablo Picasso. The collection
begins with a drawing from
his student days in 1897 and
ends with works he painted

Pablo Picasso's *Woman in a Hat* (1939), Museum Berggruen

in 1972, one year before his death. In addition to these, the museum displays more than 60 works by Swiss artist Paul Klee and more than 20 works by Henri Matisse. The museum also houses paintings by other major artists, such as Van Gogh, Braque and Cézanne. The collection is supplemented by some excellent sculptures, particularly those of Henri Laurens and Alberto Giacometti.

Bröhan-Museum ⓫

Schlossstrasse 1a. **Map** 2 E3.
Tel 32 69 06 00. Ⓤ *Richard-Wagner-Platz & Sophie-Charlotte-Platz.* Ⓢ *Westend.* 🚌 *109, 309, M45.* ⭘ *10am–6pm Tue–Sun.* ⬛ *24 & 31 Dec.*

Located in a late-Neo-Classical building which, like the Museum Berggruen, was formerly used as army barracks, is this small but interesting museum. The collection of decorative arts was amassed by Karl H Bröhan, who from 1966 collected works of art from the Art Nouveau (Jugendstil or Secessionist) and Art Deco styles. The paintings of the artists particularly connected with the Berlin Secessionist movement, such as Karl Hagermeister and Hans Baluschek, are especially well represented. Alongside the paintings there are fine examples of other media and crafts: furniture, ceramics, glassware, silverwork and

Art Deco vase, Brohan-Museum

textiles. Each of the main halls features an individual artist, but often using an array of artistic media. There is also a display of furniture by Hector Guimard, Eugène Gaillard, Henri van de Velde and Joseph Hoffmann, glasswork by Emile Gallé, and porcelain from the best European manufacturers.

Schlossstrasse Villas ⓬

Schlossstrasse 65–67. **Map** 2 E3.
Ⓤ *Sophie-Charlotte-Platz.* 🚌 *309.*

Most of the historic villas and buildings that once graced Schlossstrasse no longer exist. However, careful restoration of a few villas enables the visitor to get a feel for what the atmosphere must have been like at the end of the 19th century. It is worth taking a stroll down Schlossstrasse to look at three of the renovated villas – No. 65, No. 66 and especially No. 67. The latter villa was built in 1873, in a Neo-Classical style to a design by G Töbelmann. After World War II, the building was refurbished to return it to its former splendour. The front garden, however, a characteristic of the area, was only returned to its original state in 1986, when several villas had their

gardens restored. If you continue the walk down the nearby Schustehrusstrasse, there is an interesting school building at No. 39–43 linked to the Villa Oppenheim since the end of the 19th century.

Luisenkirche ⓭

LUISE CHURCH

Giekerplatz 4. **Map** 2 F3. *Tel* 341 90 61. Ⓤ *Richard-Wagner-Platz & Sophie-Charlotte-Platz.* 🚌 *109, M45, X9.* ⭘ *9am–7pm Mon–Tue & Thu–Fri, 2–6pm Wed, & during Sunday service (10 & 11:30am).*

This small church has undergone a series of re-designs and refurbishments in its lifetime. The original plans by Philipp Gerlach were first adapted by Martin Böhme, before the church was built (1713–16). Its Baroque styling was removed in the next course of rebuilding, undertaken by Karl Friedrich Schinkel from 1823 to 1826, when the church was renamed in memory of Queen Luise, who died in 1810. The latest refurbishment took place after the church suffered major damage during World War II.

The shape of the church is based on a traditional Greek cross, with a tower at the front. The interior fixtures and fittings are not the originals, and the elegant stained-glass windows were only made in 1956.

FURTHER AFIELD

Coat of Arms on the Oberbaumbrücke

Berlin is an extensive city with a totally unique character, shaped by its history. Up until 1920 the actual city of Berlin consisted only of the districts which now comprise mainly Mitte, Tiergarten, Wedding, Prenzlauer Berg, Friedrichshain and Kreuzberg. It was surrounded by satellite towns and villages, which for many years had been evolving independently. Each of these had its own administrative centre, parish church, and individual architecture.

In 1920, as part of great administrative reforms, seven towns were incorporated into Berlin, along with 59 communes, and 27 country estates. This reform effected the creation of an entirely new city occupying around 900 sq km (348 sq miles), with a population that had expanded to 3.8 million.

In this way the range of the metropolis extended to small towns with medieval origins, such as Spandau.

Private estates and palaces, such as Britz and Niederschönhausen, were absorbed into Berlin. So were many old villages, such as Marienfelde with its 13th-century church. Suburban housing developments full of luxury villas were also incorporated.

Over the last hundred years the faces of many of these places have changed. Modern housing developments have arisen together with industrial centres, although the character of individual areas has remained intact. Thanks to this diversity, a stay in Berlin is like visiting many cities simultaneously. A short journey by S-Bahn enables you to travel from a metropolitan city centre of the 21st century to the vast forests of the Grunewald or the beach at Wannsee. You can explore everything from Dahlem's tranquil streets lined with villas to Spandau with its Renaissance citadel and vast Gothic church of St Nicholas.

MAP OF GREATER BERLIN

See pp186–7

0 kilometres 3

0 miles 3

See pp168–9

See pp184–5

See pp170–71

See pp172–3

See pp182–3

See pp178–9

See pp176–7

See pp174–5

See pp180–81

KEY

▨ Central Berlin	▥▥ Motorway under construction	═ Minor road
▨ Outskirts of Berlin	═ Autobahn (motorway)	▬ Railway line
✈ Airport	▬ Main road	

◁ **The tranquil Botanischer Garten in Southwest Berlin** *(see p177)*

Northeast Berlin

At Bernauer Strasse in the northeast of Berlin, but still within the Mitte district, a Wall documentation centre – complete with a stretch of wall and an observation tower – reminds of the city's division. Further east extends Prenzlauer Berg *(see pp170–71)*, a now-gentrified former working class and bohemian district. In southern Pankow is the Baroque palace of Schönhausen. From here it is also worth visiting the Weissensee district, which has one of the largest Jewish cemeteries in Europe.

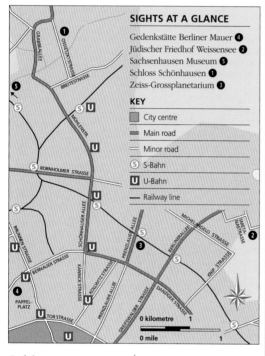

SIGHTS AT A GLANCE

Gedenkstätte Berliner Mauer ❹
Jüdischer Friedhof Weissensee ❷
Sachsenhausen Museum ❺
Schloss Schönhausen ❶
Zeiss-Grossplanetarium ❸

KEY

▨	City centre
▬	Main road
—	Minor road
Ⓢ	S-Bahn
Ⓤ	U-Bahn
—	Railway line

0 kilometre 1

0 mile 1

Schloss Schönhausen ❶

Tschaikowskistrasse. **Tel** (0331) 96 94 20. Ⓢ & Ⓤ Pankow. ▦ 107, 150, 250, X33. ▦ M1. ◯ Apr–Oct: 10am–6pm Thu–Sun; Nov–Mar: 10am–5pm Sat, Sun & hols.

This palace, located in an extensive and picturesque park, belonged to the von Dohna family during the 17th century. Ownership of the estate passed to the Elector Friedrich III in 1691, for whom Johann Arnold Nering designed the palace. In 1704 it was extended to a design by Johann Friedrich Eosander von Göthe, who added side wings. The palace

was home to Queen Christine, estranged wife of Frederick the Great, between 1740 and 1797. In 1763 further extensive refurbishment was undertaken by architect Johann Boumann.

A section of the garden elevation of Schloss Niederschönhausen

The property remained in the hands of the Prussian royal family for the next hundred years. Among those who resided here were Princess Auguste von Liegnitz, following the death of her husband, King Friedrich Wilhelm III.

After World War II the rebuilt palace was occupied by the president of the German Democratic Republic, Wilhelm Pieck. In 1990 Round Table discussions were held here and the treaty to reunify Germany was signed here on 3 October that year.

Make time for a stroll through the vast park, which has kept the character bestowed by Peter Joseph Lenné in the 1820s.

Jüdischer Friedhof Weissensee ❷

Herbert-Baum-Strasse 45. **Tel** 925 33 30. ◯ Apr–Sep: 7:30am–5pm Mon–Thu, 7:30am–2:30pm Fri & 8am–5pm Sun; Oct–Mar: 7:30am–4pm Mon–Thu, 7:30am–2:30pm Fri & 8am–4pm Sun. ▨ Sat & public hols. Ⓢ Greifswalder Strasse, then ▦ 12, M4, M13. ▦ 156, 200.

This extensive Jewish cemetery, established in 1880 according to a design by Hugo Licht, is the final resting place for more than 115,000 Berliners, many of whom were victims of Nazi persecution.

By the main entrance is a place of remembrance for the victims of the Holocaust, with plaques bearing the names of the concentration camps. Buried here are renowned figures from Berlin's Jewish cultural and commercial past. Among others here rest the publisher Samuel Fischer and the restaurateur Berthold Kempinski.

Some tombstones are outstanding works of art, such as that of the Panowsky family, designed by Ludwig Hoffmann, or the Cubist tombstone of Albert Mendel, designed by Walter Gropius.

In 1999 Weissensee cemetery was desecrated in an act of anti-Semitic vandalism. More than 100 headstones were kicked over and some were smeared with swastikas.

Silvery dome of the Zeiss-Grossplanetarium

Zeiss-Gross-planetarium ❸

Prenzlauer Allee 80 (Ernst-Thälmann-Park). *Tel* 42 18 45 12 *(reservations).*
Ⓢ *Prenzlauer Allee, then* 🚊 *1, M2.*
🕐 *call for details.* ♿

The silvery dome visible from afar is the huge planetarium, built in the grounds of a park dedicated to the memory of the inter-war communist leader Ernst Thälmann, who died at Buchenwald concentration camp. The foyer of the planetarium houses an exhibition of optical equipment and various accessories produced by the renowned factory of Carl-Zeiss-Jena.

Gedenkstätte Berliner Mauer ❹

Bernauer Strasse 111. Ⓢ *Nordbahn-hof.* Ⓤ *Bernauer Strasse.* 🚌 *147, 245.* **Wall Documentation Center**
Tel 467 98 36 66. 🕐 *Apr–Oct: 9:30am–7pm Tue–Sun; Nov–Mar: 9:30am–6pm Tue–Sun.* 📷 *call ahead.*

On the night between 12 and 13 August 1961 the East German authorities decided to close the border around the western sectors of Berlin. Initially the Berlin Wall *(die Mauer)* consisted simply of rolls of barbed wire. However, these were soon replaced by a 4-m (13-ft) wall safeguarded by a second wall made from reinforced concrete. This second wall was topped with a thick pipe to prevent people from reaching the top of the Wall with their fingers. Along the Wall ran what was known as a "death zone", an area controlled by guards with dogs. Where the border passed close to houses, the inhabitants were relocated, while windows on to the "western" street were bricked up. Along the border with West Berlin there were 293 watch towers along with 57 bunkers and, later on, alarms.

On 9 November 1989, with the help of Soviet leader Mikhail Gorbachev, the Berlin Wall was finally breached. Dismantling it took much longer, however, with more than a million tons of rubble to be removed.

Only small fragments of the Wall have survived. One of these, along Bernauer Strasse between Acker- and Berg-strasse, is now an official place of remembrance.

During the Wall's 28-year existence, about 5,000 people managed to escape into West Berlin; a total of 192 people were killed by the Eastern border guards while attempting to do so.

Sachsenhausen Museum ❺

Strasse der Nationen 22, Oranienburg. *Tel* 03301/2000.
Ⓢ *Oranienburg, then* 🚌 *804.*
🕐 *Mid-Mar–mid-Oct: 8:30am–6pm Tue–Sun; mid-Oct–mid-Mar: 8:30am–4:30pm Tue–Sun.* 📷
www.stiftung-bg.de

Built by the Nazis in 1936, the concentration camp at Sachsenhausen was liberated in 1945 by the Russians. Up to 200,000 people were incarcerated in this camp during its nine-year existence. However, when the Soviet Army entered Sachsenhausen, there were only 3,000 inmates in the camp, mostly women and sick people.

The iron gate at the entrance bears a sign that reads *"Arbeit macht frei"* ("Work will set you free"), and indeed, many early prisoners were released upon demonstrating that they had learned how to be "good German citizens". By 1939, however, fewer prisoners were being released. It is estimated that over 30,000 people died in the camp, killed by hunger, disease or mass extermination.

Sachsenhausen is now a museum. Each area of the camp hosts a relevant exhibit – for example, the one in the former infirmary focuses on medicine and racism under the Nazi regime. Other exhibits illustrate the daily life of the prisoners, or the way Sachsenhausen worked as a Soviet Special Camp between 1945 and 1950, when it housed Nazi functionaries and political undesirables.

Former entrance to the Sachsenhausen Prison Camp

Prenzlauer Berg

Once one of the most impoverished and densely populated working-class districts of Berlin, Prenzlauer Berg and its beautifully renovated 19th-century tenement houses are now occupied by a bourgeois bohemia from all over the world. During communist times, this area was known for its independent art and nightlife scene which still thrives today in former factories and breweries, while the area around Kollwitzplatz, with its bustling street cafés and trendy shops, has an almost Parisian flair.

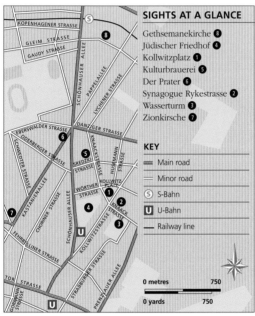

SIGHTS AT A GLANCE

Gethsemanekirche ❽
Jüdischer Friedhof ❹
Kollwitzplatz ❶
Kulturbrauerei ❺
Der Prater ❻
Synagogue Rykestrasse ❷
Wasserturm ❸
Zionkirsche ❼

KEY

▬▬	Main road
──	Minor road
Ⓢ	S-Bahn
Ⓤ	U-Bahn
──	Railway line

0 metres   750
0 yards   750

Kollwitzplatz ❶

Ⓤ *Senefelderplatz.*

This green square is named after the German painter and sculptress Käthe Kollwitz (1867–1945), who once lived nearby. It was here that the socially engaged artist observed and painted the daily hardships of the working-class people living in overcrowded tenements. One of her sculptures stands on the square which is now the socializing hub of the district, with a Saturday organic farmers' market, trendy bars, restaurants and shops that extend into the surrounding streets. Käthe Kollwitz's work can be seen at the Käthe-Kollwitz-Museum *(see p154)*.

Synagogue Rykestrasse ❷

Rykestrasse 53. **Tel** *88 02 80 316.*
◯ *Apr–Oct: 2–6pm Thu, 1–5pm Sun. Open services 9:30am Sat.*
Ⓤ *Senefelderplatz.*

This synagogue, which was restored to its historic splendor in 2007, is one of the few reminders of old Jewish life in Berlin, and one of the few in Germany left almost intact during the Nazi terror regime. Built in 1904, the red-brick synagogue has a basilica-like nave with three aisles and certain Moorish features. Thanks to the fact that it was built inside a huge tenement area, Nazi SA troops did not set it on fire during the *"Kristallnacht"* pogrom on 9 November 1938, when hundreds of other synagogues were razed to the ground. The synagogue welcomes visitors to its public services.

Wasserturm ❸

Knaackstrasse/Belforter Strasse.
Ⓤ *Senefelderplatz.*

The unofficial symbol of the district is a 30 m (98 ft) high water tower, standing high on the former mill hill in the heart of Prenzlauer Berg. It was here that some of the windmills, once typical in Prenzlauer Berg, turned and ground grain, providing flour for the city's population. The distinctive brick water tower was built in 1874 by Wilhelm Vollhering and served as a water reservoir for the country's first running water system. Later, the tower was transformed into an apartment complex. In the 1930s, the basement served as a *wildes Konzentrationslager*, a make-shift jail, where Nazi SA troops held and tortured Communist opponents. This dark period is commemorated by a plaque.

The giant Wasserturm looming high in Knaackstrasse

Jüdischer Friedhof ❹

Schönhauser Allee 22–25. **Tel** *441 98 24.* Ⓤ *Senefelderplatz.* ◯ *Apr–Sep: 7:30am–5pm Mon–Thu, 7:30am–2:30pm Fri, 8am–5pm Sun; Oct–Mar: 7:30am–4pm Mon–Thu, 7:30am–2:30pm Fri, 8am–4pm Sun.* ⬤ *Sat, public hols.*

This small Jewish cemetery is hidden behind thick walls on Schönhauser Allee, but the

Gravestones in the peaceful Jüdischer Friedhof

serene atmosphere, with tall trees and thick undergrowth between the gravestones, is a welcome oasis. The cemetery was laid out in 1827, though the oldest gravestone dates back to the 14th century. It served as Berlin's second largest Jewish cemetery after the Jüdischer Friedhof Weissensee *(see p168)*. Among the many prominent Berliners resting here are the painter Max Liebermann (1847–1935); the composer and musical director of the Staatsoper Unter den Linden, Giacomo Meyerbeer (1791–1864); and the author David Friedländer (1750–1834).

Kulturbrauerei ❺

Schönhauser Allee 36–39. **Tel** 44 31 51 00. Ⓤ Eberswalder Strasse. 🚊 20, 50, 53. **Sammlung Industrielle Gestaltung** 🕐 Varies for each exhibition. Telephone to check.

This vast Neo-Gothic, industrial red and yellow brick building was once Berlin's most famous brewery, Schultheiss, built by Franz Schwechten in 1889–92. Now housing the Kulturbrauerei, the vast complex with several courtyards has been revived as a cultural and entertainment centre with concert venues, restaurants and cafés, a cinema, as well as artists' ateliers. Inside the Kulturbrauerei, the **Sammlung Industrielle Gestaltung** (Collection of Industrial Design) features changing exhibitions on East German industrial product designs.

Der Prater ❻

Kastanienallee 7–9. **Tel** 448 56 88. Ⓤ Eberswalder Strasse. 🚊 50, 53.

Der Prater has been one of Berlin's best known entertainment institutions for more than a century. The building, along with its quiet courtyard, was constructed in the 1840s and later became the city's oldest and largest beer garden *(see p249)*. It now not only houses a restaurant, serving Berlin specialities, but also stages a wide variety of pop, rock and folk concerts.

Zionskirche ❼

Zionskirchplatz. **Tel** 88 70 98 70. Ⓤ Senefelderplatz, Rosenthaler Platz. 🚊 M1, 12. 🕐 noon–4pm Sun, 8am–10pm Mon, 10am–7pm Thu.

Located in the square of the same name, Zionsplatz, this Protestant church was built between 1866 and 1873 – a tranquil oasis in the middle of this lively district. Both the square and the church have always been centres of political opposition. During the Third Reich, resistance groups against the Nazi regime congregated at the church, and when the communists were in power in East Germany the alternative "environment library" (an information and documentation centre) was established here. Church and other opposition groups active here played a decisive role in the transformation of East Germany in 1989–90.

Kulturbrauerei tower

Gethsemanekirche ❽

Stargader Strasse 77. **Tel** 44 57 745. Ⓤ & Ⓢ Schönhauser Allee. 🔔 11am Sun.

The quaint little area surrounding this Neo-Gothic red-brick church is one of the most intact original communities to be found anywhere in Berlin. The neighbourhood is dominated by the Protestant Gethsemanekirche, which dates back to 1890. The church was one of several built on the order of Emperor Wilhelm II, who wanted to increase religious worship among the mostly Social Democratic working-classes living in Prenzlauer Berg and other areas. The building was designed by August Orth (1828–1911), one of the period's most important architects of churches and railway stations.

The Protestant community here is proud to have pioneered civil rights movements, and hosted political Anti-Nazi rallies from 1933–45. The congregation also questioned the socialist regime after World War II, while the church itself served as an assembly hall for peaceful opponents in October 1989. On 2 October that year, the praying crowd was brutally attacked by the East German secret service police, marking the start of the Communist regime's demise.

Today, the square is surrounded by beautiful restored buildings, housing many sidewalk restaurants, cafés and quaint little shops.

Entrance to the red-brick Gethsemanekirche

Friedrichshain and Treptow

Both these districts are situated to the southeast of Mitte and provide excellent opportunities for walks amid some spectacular remnants of Berlin's recent history. Visitors can see the official face of the German Democratic Republic, as shown in the Socialist Realist architecture of Karl-Marx-Allee, and of Soviet patriotism, in the huge monument to the Red Army in Treptower Park. Beside stark reminders of the past – the Berlin Wall, the East Side Gallery and the grim watchtower on the border – Friedrichshain attracts visitors with its nightlife.

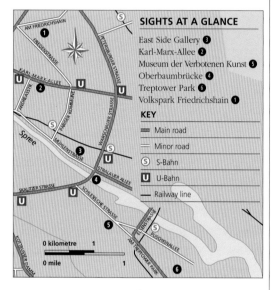

SIGHTS AT A GLANCE

East Side Gallery ❸
Karl-Marx-Allee ❷
Museum der Verbotenen Kunst ❺
Oberbaumbrücke ❹
Treptower Park ❻
Volkspark Friedrichshain ❶

KEY

▬▬	Main road
──	Minor road
Ⓢ	S-Bahn
Ⓤ	U-Bahn
──	Railway line

0 kilometre 1
0 mile 1

by the Brothers Grimm. The park's frequent redesigns included, during World War II, the construction of two large bunkers. After the war, the site was covered with a mound of earth.

Between the years 1969 and 1973 a sports and games area was established in the park, although there is still plenty of room for leisurely strolls.

Fragment of Socialist Realist decoration from Karl-Marx-Allee

Karl-Marx-Allee ❷

Map 8 F3. Ⓤ *Strausberger Platz, Frankfurter Tor or Weberwiese.*
🚊 *M10.*

The section of Karl-Marx-Allee between Strausberger Platz and Frankfurter Tor is effectively a huge open-air museum of Socialist Realist architecture. The route leading east to Poland and Moscow, was named Stalinallee in 1949 and chosen as the site for the construction showpiece of the new German Democratic Republic. The avenue was widened to 90 m (300 ft) and in the course of the next ten years, huge residential tower blocks and a row of shops were built on it. The designers, led by Hermann Henselmann, succeeded in combining three sets of architectural guidelines. They used the style known in the Soviet Union as "pastry chef" according to the precept "nationalistic in form but socialist in content", and linked the whole work to Berlin's own traditions. Hence there are motifs taken from famous Berlin architects Schinkel and Gontard, as well as from the renowned Meissen porcelain.

The buildings on this street, renamed Karl-Marx-Allee in 1961, are now considered historic monuments. The buildings have been cleaned up and the crumbling details are gradually being restored.

Volkspark Friedrichshain ❶

Am Friedrichshain/Friedenstrasse.
Map 8 F1. 🚌 *200, 240, M5, M6, M8.*

This extensive park complex of Friedrichshain, with its picturesque nooks and crannies, was one of Berlin's first public parks. It was laid out in the 1840s on the basis of a design by Peter Joseph Lenné, with the idea of creating an alternative Tiergarten for the inhabitants of the eastern districts of the city.

The greatest attraction of the park is the Fountain of Fairy Tales – Märchenbrunnen by Ludwig Hoffmann, built from 1902 until 1913. It is a spectacular feature, in a Neo-Baroque style with fountain pools made from Tivoli stone, decorated

with small statues of turtles and other animals. The fountain is surrounded by well-known characters from the fairy tales

Neo-Baroque Märchenbrunnen in Volkspark Friedrichshain

East Side Gallery **3**

Mühlenstrasse. Ⓢ & Ⓤ *Warschauer Strasse.* Ⓢ *Ostbahnhof.* 🚌 *140, 240.* 🚊 *M10.*

Since 1990, this 1300-m (1 mile) section of the Berlin Wall along Mühlenstrasse between Hauptbahnhof and Oberbaumbrücke has been known as the East Side Gallery. A huge collection of graffiti on display here, the work of 118 different artists from 21 countries, organized by the Scottish artist Chris MacLean, was restored in 2009 to mark the 20th anniversary of the fall of the Wall.

Oberbaumbrücke **4**

Ⓢ & Ⓤ *Warschauer Strasse* Ⓤ *Schlesisches Tor.* 🚌 *347.* 🚊 *M10.*

This pretty bridge crossing the Spree river was built from 1894 to 1896 to a design by Otto Stahn. It is made from reinforced concrete, but the arches are covered with red brick. The central arch is marked by a pair of crenellated Neo-Gothic towers. The most decorative element of the bridge, a Neo-Gothic arcade, supports a line of the U-Bahn.

The bridge was not open to traffic for 12 or so years prior to reunification, as it linked districts from opposing sides of the Berlin Wall. Only pedestrians with the relevant documents were able to use this bridge. After reunification and renovation, it was returned to full working order.

The picturesque Neo-Gothic archway of Oberbaumbrücke

Museum der Verbotenen Kunst **5**

MUSEUM OF FORBIDDEN ARTS

Im Schlesischen Busch (Puschkinallee/ Schlesische Strasse). Ⓢ *Schlesisches Tor. Treptower Park. 265. Park* **Tel** *229 287. Apr–Oct: noon–6pm Sat, Sun.*

In a neglected park near the former Berlin Wall stands one of the last remaining watchtowers in the border control system that divided East and West Berlin.

The upper floor has been preserved as it was during the Cold War years, when it was used by border guards to monitor the Wall. While it is possible to visit the park, you will need to telephone ahead to find out when the tower is open to the public.

Museum der Verbotenen Kunst in one of the last remaining watchtowers

Treptower Park **6**

Archenhold-Sternwarte, Alt-Treptow 1. Ⓢ *Treptower Park.* 🚌 *166, 167, 265.* **Archenhold Sternwarte** *Tel 536 06 37 19.* 🕐 *2–4:30pm Wed–Sun.* 📷 *8pm Thu, 3pm Sat & Sun.*

The vast park in Treptow was laid out in the 1860s on the initiative and design of Johann Gustav Meyer. In 1919 it was where revolutionaries Karl Liebknecht, Wilhelm Pieck and Rosa Luxemburg assembled 150,000-strong group of striking workers.

The park, however, is best known for the colossal monument to the Red Army. Built between 1946 and 1949, it

Gigantic wreath commemorating the Red Army in Treptower Park

stands on the grave of 5,000 Soviet soldiers killed in the battle for Berlin in 1945. The gateway is marked by a vast granite sculpture of a grieving Russian Motherland surrounded by statues of Red Army soldiers. This leads to the mausoleum, topped by an 11-m (35-ft) high figure of a soldier rescuing a child and resting his mighty sword on a smashed swastika. The whole scheme was the work of architect Jakow Biełopolski and sculptor Jewgien Wuczeticz.

In the farthest section of the park it is worth going to see the astronomical observatory, **Archenhold Sternwarte**, built for a decorative arts exhibition held here in 1896. Given a permanent site here in 1909, the observatory was used by Albert Einstein for a lecture on the Theory of Relativity in 1915. It is also home to the longest refracting telescope in the world (21-m or 70-ft), and a small planetarium.

Beyond Treptower Park lies another park, Plänterwald, while the Spree river provides an ideal place for a riverside stroll or maybe a trip in one of the rowing or pedal boats.

At the beginning of the 19th century, Berliners flocked to the banks of the Spree to enjoy themselves at the weekend. However, from the many dance halls and restaurants, only one historic building has remained – Zenner. This can trace its history back as far as the 17th century.

The small Insel der Jugend can be reached via the Abteibrücke, an ornamental bridge built by French prisoners of war in 1916. The island was once home to an abbey.

Southeast Berlin

An expedition to Berlin's furthest corners, Lichtenberg and Hohenschönhausen, provides an occasion to visit shocking museums documenting the work of the German Democratic Republic's security services (Stasi). However, you can just as easily stroll through the zoological garden in the park at the Baroque Schloss Friedrichsfelde or enjoy a leisurely break in Köpenick, which has retained the atmosphere of a small town.

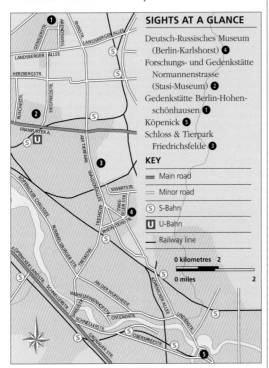

SIGHTS AT A GLANCE

Deutsch-Russisches Museum
(Berlin-Karlshorst) **4**
Forschungs- und Gedenkstätte
Normannenstrasse
(Stasi-Museum) **2**
Gedenkstätte Berlin-Hohen-
schönhausen **1**
Köpenick **5**
Schloss & Tierpark
Friedrichsfelde **3**

KEY

▬▬	Main road
▬▬	Minor road
Ⓢ	S-Bahn
Ⓤ	U-Bahn
▬▬	Railway line

0 kilometres 2

0 miles 2

Gedenkstätte Berlin-Hohen schönhausen **1**

Genslerstrasse 66. **Tel** 9860 82 30.
Ⓢ Landsberger Allee, then 🚋 16,
27, M5, M6, M17. 🚌 256. ◯
9am–6pm daily. 📷 obligatory, (in
German) 11am, 1pm daily (also
3pm Sat & Sun); (in English)
2:30pm Wed, 2pm Sat.

This museum was established in 1995 in the former custody building of the Stasi – the dreaded security service of the GDR. The custody building was part of a huge complex built in 1938. In May 1945 the occupying Russian authorities created a special transit camp

here, in which they interned war criminals subsequently transported to Siberia. Shortly thereafter they started to bring anyone under political suspicion to the camp. During this time more than 20,000 people passed through here.

From 1946 this group of buildings was refashioned into the custody area for the KGB (Soviet Secret Service), and in 1951 it was given over for the use of the Stasi.

During a visit you can see prisoners' cells and interrogation rooms, two of which have no windows and are lined with rubber. Housed in the cellars was the "submarine" – a series of cells without daylight for the most "dangerous" suspects.

Forschungs- und Gedenkstätte Normannenstrasse (Stasi-Museum) **2**

Ruschestrasse 103 (Haus 1).
Tel 553 68 54. Ⓤ Magdalenen-
strasse. ◯ 11am–6pm Mon–Fri,
2–6pm Sat & Sun. 📷

Under the German Democratic Republic, this huge complex of buildings at Ruschestrasse housed the Ministry of the Interior. It was here that the infamous Stasi (GDR secret service) had its headquarters. The Stasi's "achievements" in infiltrating its own community were without equal in the Eastern bloc.

Since 1990 one of the buildings has housed a museum that displays photographs and documents depicting the activities of the Stasi. You can see a model of the headquarters, and equipment used for bugging and spying on citizens suspected of holding an unfavourable view of the political regime. You can also walk around the office of infamous Stasi chief Erich Mielke. A "big-brother"-like figure, Mielke's legacy of suffering still lives on in the memory of millions of German citizens.

Stasi chief Erich Mielke's office at the Stasi Museum

Schloss & Tierpark Friedrichsfelde **3**

Am Tierpark 125. Ⓤ Tierpark. **Tel** 66
63 50 35. 🚌 296, 396. **Schloss** 📷
obligatory, (in German) 11am, noon,
1pm, 2pm Tue–Sun. **Park Tel** 51
53 10. ◯ mid-Mar–mid-Sep: 9am–
7pm daily; mid-Sep–Oct: 9am–6pm
daily; Nov–mid-Mar: 9am–5pm daily. 📷

This charming Baroque palace was built for the Dutchman Benjamin von

The façade of Schloss Friedrichsfelde

Raule around 1695, to a design by Johann Arnold Nering. Under successive owners, it underwent major renovations. It was redesigned in 1719 by Martin Heinrich Böhme, and again in 1786, by Peter Biron. It was this renovation which gave the residence its current appearance.

The well-balanced structure, typical of the style during the transition from Baroque to Neo-Classical, was extensively restored in the 1970s. It now houses a museum of interiors, and is chiefly furnished with 18th- and 19th-century pieces. The palace's park was redesigned into the zoological garden of East Berlin in 1957.

Deutsch-Russisches Museum (Berlin-Karlshorst) ❹

Zwieseler Strasse 4/Rheinsteinstrasse *Tel* 50 15 08 10. Ⓢ *Karlshorst.* 27, 37, M17. 296, 396. 10am–6pm Tue–Sun.

This building was erected in the 1930s as the casino of the Wehrmacht (armed services of the Third Reich). It was here on the night of 8 May 1945 that Hitler's successor Grossadmiral Karl Dönitz, Field Marshal Wilhelm Keitel, Admiral Hans Georg von Friedeburg and General Hans-Jürgen Stumpff signed the unconditional surrender of Germany's armed forces. You can visit the renowned hall in which the surrender was signed, the office of Marshal Zhukov, and see an exhibition documenting the history of World War II.

Köpenick ❺

Kunstgewerbemuseum *Tel* 65 66 170. Ⓢ *Spindlersfeld, then* 167, or Ⓢ *Köpenick, then* 269, X69. 60, 61, 62, 63, 68. 10am–5pm Thu–Sun.

Köpenick is much older than Berlin. Already in the 9th century AD this island contained a fortified settlement called Kopanica. It was inhabited by Slavs from the Łaba river region, which in the 12th century was ruled by Duke Jaksa, who was waging a war against the Ascanian Albrecht the Bear over Brandenburg *(see p19)*. From the late 12th century Köpenick belonged to the Margrave of Brandenburg, also an Ascanian. In about 1240 a castle was built, around which a town began to evolve, though over the years it lost out in importance to Berlin. Craftsmen settled here, and after 1685 a large colony of Huguenots also settled here. In

Part of the town hall's Neo-Gothic façade

A reconstructed drawing room dating from 1548 in Köpenick's Kunstgewerbemuseum

the 19th century Köpenick recreated itself as an industrial town. Despite wartime devastation it has retained its historic character. There are no longer any 13th-century churches, which in the years 1838 to 1841 were replaced by buildings in the style of Schinkel, nevertheless it is worth strolling around the old town. By the old market square and the neighbouring streets, such as Alt Köpenick and Grünstrasse, modest houses have survived which recall the 18th century, next to buildings from the end of the 19th century.

At Alt Köpenick No. 21 is a vast brick town hall built in the style of the Brandenburg Neo-Renaissance between the years 1901 and 1904 by Hans Schütte and Hugo Kinzer. It was here on 16 October 1906 that a famous swindle took place. Wilhelm Voigt dressed himself in a Prussian officer's uniform and proceeded to arrest the mayor and then fraudulently empty everything from the city treasury. This incident inspired a comedy, *The Captain from Köpenick* by Carl Zuckmayer, which is still popular.

Köpenick's greatest attraction is a magnificent palace on the island in the southern part of town. It was built between 1677 and 1681 for the heir to the throne Friedrich (later King Friedrich I), to a design by the Dutch architect Rutger van Langfeld. The three-storey Baroque building that resulted was extended to a design by Johann Arnold Nering, but until 1693 only part of the extension was completed: the chapel, entrance gate and a small gallery wing.

In 2004 the **Kunstgewerbemuseum** *(see pp118–21)* opened a series of Renaissance and Baroque rooms in the Köpenick palace. This collection also includes some examples of magnificent furniture.

Southwest Berlin

An excursion to Britz provides a chance to visit one of the few surviving manor houses in the suburbs of Berlin, Schloss Britz. In Schöneberg you can see the town hall from which President Kennedy gave his famous speech, and visit the grave of Berlin-born actress and singer, Marlene Dietrich. The Botanical Gardens are great for those who enjoy a stroll through cultivated and wild gardens, but you should allow at least half a day.

Neo-Classical Königskolonnaden, gateway to the Kleistpark

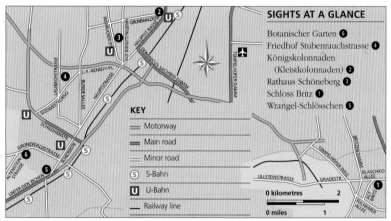

SIGHTS AT A GLANCE

Botanischer Garten **6**
Friedhof Stubenrauchstrasse **4**
Königskolonnaden (Kleistkolonnaden) **2**
Rathaus Schöneberg **3**
Schloss Britz **1**
Wrangel-Schlösschen **5**

KEY

▬▬	Motorway
▬▬	Main road
▬▬	Minor road
Ⓢ	S-Bahn
Ⓤ	U-Bahn
▬▬	Railway line

0 kilometres   2
0 miles   1

Schloss Britz **1**

Alt-Britz 73. **Tel** 60 97 92 30.
Ⓤ Parchimer Allee. ▦ 144, 174, 181.
☐ 10am–4pm Tue–Fri, 11am–6pm Sat & Sun. 📷 compulsory.

Originally a small manor house built in 1706 for Sigismund von Erlach, Schloss Britz was extended to its current size between 1880 and 1883 to a design by Carl Busse. It is a one-storey palace with a modest Neo-Classical aspect adorned with Baroque statues at the front and a tower on the garden side. As well as housing a permanent museum, the building is often used as a venue for concerts and temporary exhibitions. The palace displays furnishings from the *Gründerzeit* – the years after the founding of the German Empire in 1871. The 19th-century interiors are excellent but it is also worth strolling through the park, where there is a bust of one of the former owners, Rüdiger von Ilgen, which once stood in the Tiergarten.

Next to the palace is a housing estate called Hufeisensiedlung (Horseshoe Colony), built in the late 1920s to a design by Bruno Taut and Bruno Schneidereit. The architects' aim was to create spacious and affordable housing for Berliners.

Königskolonnaden (Kleistkolonnaden) **2**

Potsdamer Strasse **Map** 11 B4.
Ⓤ Kleistpark. ▦ 148, 187, 348.

A short walk north of U-Bahn Kleistpark, the unremarkable architecture of Potsdamer Strasse suddenly transforms dramatically. Leading to the park, the elegant sandstone Königskolonnaden captivates the passer-by with its Baroque ornamental sculptures. The royal colonnade, designed by Carl von Gontard and built between 1777 and 1780, once graced the route from Königsstrasse to Alexanderplatz. In 1910, to protect it from traffic, it was moved to this new site.

The huge Kammergericht at the far boundary of the park was built between 1909 and 1913 to a design by Carl Vohl, Rudolf Mönnich and Paul Thömer. The site of the notorious Nazi Volksgericht or "People's Court", it was also used to try members of the failed July 1944 Bomb Plot against Hitler (*see p127*).

Schloss Britz's Neo-Classical façade

Rathaus Schöneberg ❸

SCHONEBERG TOWN HALL

John-F-Kennedy-Platz.
U *Rathaus Schöneberg.*

The gigantic building with a tower is the Schöneberg town hall, built between 1911 and 1914. From 1948 to 1990 it was used as the main town hall of West Berlin. Here, on 26 June 1963, the US President John FKennedy gave his famous speech. More than 300,000 Berliners assembled to hear the young president say *"Ich bin ein Berliner"* – "I am a Berliner", intended as an expression of solidarity from the democratic world to a city defending its right to freedom.

While Kennedy's meaning was undoubtedly clear, pedants were quick to point out that, strictly speaking, he said "I am a small doughnut".

Rathaus Schöneberg – the site of President Kennedy's speech

Friedhof Stubenrauchstrasse ❹

STUBERAUCHSTRASSE CEMETERY

Stubenrauchstrasse/Südwestkorso.
S & **U** *Bundesplatz.* 348.

This small cemetery in the shadow of a motorway achieved renown in 1993 as the burial place of Marlene Dietrich, who died on 6 May. Born Maria Magdalena von Losch in 1901, she grew up at Leberstrasse No. 65 in Schöneberg. For a few years she struggled to make a career as an actress, playing small parts.

The pleasantly cultivated spaces of the Botanischer Garten

In 1929 she was discovered in Berlin by Hollywood director Josef von Sternberg who was filming *The Blue Angel*, based on Heinrich Mann's novel *Professor Unrat*. The ensuing role of Lola took Marlene to the height of fame. She sang only once more in Berlin, giving a concert at the Titania-Palast in 1960. Although she died in Paris, she was laid to rest in the city of her birth.

Wrangel-Schlösschen ❺

Schlossstrasse 48. **Tel** 902 99 39 24.
U *Rathaus Steglitz.* M48, 170, 185, 277, 280, 283, 285.

This compact Neo-Classical palace derives its name from Field Marshal Wrangel, the building's mid-19th century owner. However, the house was built much earlier, in 1804, following a design by Heinrich Gentz. The simplicity and clarity of its details make it a prime example of early Neo-Classical architecture. It currently houses the cultural centre for the district of Steglitz.

Botanischer Garten ❻

BOTANICAL GARDEN

Unter den Eichen 5–10 & Königin-Luise-Strasse 6–8. **Tel** 83 85 01 00.
U *Dahlem-Dorf.* **S** *Botanischer Garten.* M48, X83. daily; Nov–Jan: 9am–4pm; Feb: 9am–5pm; Mar & Oct: 9am–6pm; Apr & Aug: 9am–8pm; May–Jul: 9am–9pm; Sep: 9am–7pm. **Museum** 10am–6pm daily.

The Botanical Garden is one of the most beautiful places in Berlin. The expansive park was created towards the end of the 19th century and has a romantic character with gentle hills and picturesque lakes. Of particular interest is the 19th-century palm house, designed by Alfred Koerner. The new greenhouses were built from 1984 to 1987 to a design by Engelbert Kremser. The most popular plants are the exotic species such as the orchids and cacti. By the entrance on the Königin-Luise-Platz side is the Botanisches Museum, home to an excellent collection of plant specimens.

COUNTRY CHURCHES

The establishment of Greater Berlin in 1920 swallowed up nearly 60 villages, some of which were older than the city itself. Now they have evolved into large residential estates, and many of the parish churches (more than 50) have survived. The most treasured, dating from the 13th century, can be seen in the south of Berlin, for instance in Britz by Backbergstrasse, Buckow (Alt-Buckow) or in Mariendorf (Alt Mariendorf). The oldest church, dating from the 13th century, has survived in Marienfelde (Alt Marienfelde).

St Anna's in Dahlem

Wittenau

Marienfelde

Dahlem

Dahlem is first mentioned in 1275 and it remained a small village surrounded by private estates until the 19th century. Retaining its Gothic parish church and its manor house, Dahlem was transformed into an affluent, tranquil city suburb with grand villas and a clutch of museums, designed by Bruno Paul, at the beginning of the 20th century. The district was confirmed as a major cultural and educational centre after World War II with the establishment of the Freie Universität and the completion of the museum complex. The Botanischer Garten also sits on the borders of Dahlem (*see p177*).

SIGHTS AT A GLANCE

Brücke-Museum ❺
Domäne Dahlem ❸
Freie Universität ❻
Museen Dahlem ❶
Museum Europäischer Kulturen ❷
St-Annen-Kirche ❹

KEY

━━ Main road
─── Minor road
Ⓢ S-Bahn
Ⓤ U-Bahn
━━ Railway line

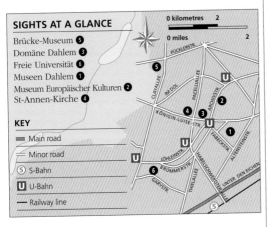

Museen Dahlem ❶

Museum für Asiatische Kunst, Ethnologisches Museum (*formerly Museum für Völkerkunde*), **Museum Europäischer Kulturen**
Lansstrasse 8. *Tel 266 424 242.*
Ⓤ *Dahlem Dorf.* 🚌 *110, X11, X83.*
◯ *10am–6pm Tue–Fri, 11am–6pm Sat & Sun.* ● *Mon, Dec 24 & 31.* 📷

Dahlem's first museums were built between 1914 and 1923. After World War II, with many of Berlin's collections fragmented, a large miscellany of art and artifacts was put on display here. In the 1960s the museums were extended considerably: the Museen was created to rival East Berlin's Museum Island. Reunification in 1990 meant the collections could be reunited and reorganized. Paintings were moved to the Kulturforum (*see pp122–5*), and sculptures to the Bodemuseum (*see p79*). Three museums are now housed at Dahlem:

the Ethnologisches Museum (Museum of Ethnology); the Museum für Europäischer Kulturen (Museum of European Culture) and the Museum für Asiatische Kunst (Museum of Asian Art). The Museum of Asian Art assembles the formerly separate East Asian and Indian collections. It now

Japanese woodcut from the Museum für Ostasiatische Kunst

shows the world's most important art collections from that area from 4000BC onwards and pays special homage to the art along the Silk route and early Indian sculptures. Among the many exquisite pieces is a collection of Japanese paintings and East Asian lacquered art. Other highlights include gold Inca jewellery at the Museum of Ethnology. When the Humboldt Forum re-opens in 2010 (*see p74*), these collections will move from Dahlem to Mitte, putting Asian art in the centre of cosmopolitan Berlin.

An East Prussian carpet from the Museum Europäischer Kulturen

Museum Europäischer Kulturen ❷

MUSEUM OF EUROPEAN CULTURE

Arnimallee 25. *Tel 266 424 242.*
Ⓤ *Dahlem Dorf.* 🚌 *110, 183, X11, X83.* ◯ *10am–6pm Tue–Fri, 11am–6pm Sat & Sun.* ● *Mon, Dec 24 & 31.* 📷

This ethnographic museum specializes in European folk art and culture, documenting the daily life of its inhabitants. It hosts long-running but temporary exhibitions, often in conjunction with museums from other European countries. Among the exhibits you can expect to see are earthenware items, costumes, jewellery, toys and tools.

Domäne Dahlem ❸

DAHLEM CITY FARM

Königin-Luise-Str. 49. *Tel 66 63 000.*
Ⓤ *Dahlem Dorf.* 🚌 *110, X11, X83.*
◯ *10am–6pm Wed–Mon.* 📷
(*museum only*).

Domäne Dahlem, a manor house and farming estate, is a rare oasis of country life in the Berlin suburbs. The Baroque house was built for

The combined museum and working farm of Domäne Dahlem

The church was built initially with a plain roof. The chancel was completed in the 15th century, the vaulting in the 17th century and the tower was added in the 18th century.

Inside the church, 14th-century wall paintings depict scenes from the life of St Anna, alongside items of ecclesiastical furnishings. These include a 15th-century painting called *The Crucifixion* and 11 late-Gothic figures of saints.

Brücke-Museum **⑤**

Bussardsteig 9. **Tel** 831 20 29. 🚌 115. ◯ 11am–5pm Wed–Mon.

One of the more interesting museums dedicated to 20th-century art is hidden away on a leafy, tranquil street lined with picturesque villas. The elegant Functionalist building was built by Werner Düttmann in 1966 to 1967. The museum houses a collection of German Expressionist painting linked to the artistic group known as Die Brücke, which originated in Dresden in 1905 and was based in Berlin from 1910. The members of this group included Karl Schmidt-Rottluff, Emil Nolde, Max Pechstein, Ernst Ludwig Kirchner and Erich Heckel. The collection is based on almost 80 works by Schmidt-Rottluff bequeathed to the town in 1964. The collection quickly grew, thanks to donations and acquisitions. In addition to displaying other works of art contemporary to Die Brücke (which was disbanded in 1913), there are also some paintings from the later creative periods of these artists, as well as works of other closely associated artists.

Nearby, at Käuzchensteig No. 8, lie the foundation's headquarters, established in the former studio of the sculptor Bernhard Heliger. The garden, which borders the Brücke-Museum, has a display of his metal sculptures.

A Bernhard Heliger sculpture outside the Brücke-Museum

Freie Universität **⑥**

Henry-Ford-Bau Garystrasse 35–39. Ⓤ Thielplatz. 🚌 110.

The Free University was established on 4 December 1948 on the initiative of a group of academics and activists, led by Ernst Reuter. This was a reaction to the restrictions introduced at the Humboldt-Universität in the Soviet sector and further evidence of the competition between the two halves of the city. The new university was initially located in rented buildings. It was only thanks to the American Ford Foundation that the university's Henry-Ford-Bau, housing the rector's office, the auditorium and the library, was built. Designed by Franz Heinrich Sobotka and Gustav Müller, and built from 1951 to 1954, the building is distinguished by its fine proportions.

Gothic St-Annen-Kirche dating back to the 14th century

St-Annen-Kirche **④**

Königin-Luise-Strasse 55. **Tel** 841 70 50. Ⓤ Dahlem Dorf. 🚌 110, X11, X83. ◯ 11am–1pm Sat–Sun.

At the centre of a small leafy cemetery stands the Gothic 14th-century St-Annen-Kirche.

Cuno Johann von Wilmersdorff around 1680 and still retains its original character. Part of the Stadtmuseum Berlin (Museum of the City of Berlin), the manor house boasts period interiors, while the 19th-century farm buildings hold a collection of agricultural tools. Also on show is a large and varied collection of beehives.

Domäne Dahlem is a farm and a museum with a garden, workshops and farm animals. Festivals and markets held here demonstrate rural crafts and skills – you can learn how to shoe a horse or milk a cow, or, if you prefer, you can just relax with a glass of cold beer.

Henry-Ford-Bau, the rector's office and library at the Freie Universität

Zehlendorf

With nearly half of Zehlendorf covered by forests, lakes and rivers, the region has a quiet, rustic atmosphere that belies the fact that it is a mere 20 minutes away from the hustle and bustle of a huge metropolis. The area is dotted with picture-postcard villas and small settlements where life carries on at an unchanging, slow pace. It is worth taking a walk *(see pp208–211)* to see the stunning lakeside summer residences and royal parks, Pfaueninsel and Klein Glienicke, which are located in the furthest corner of this district.

Reconstructed medieval settlement at the Museumdorf Düppel

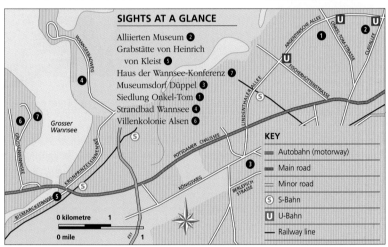

SIGHTS AT A GLANCE

Alliierten Museum ❷
Grabstätte von Heinrich
  von Kleist ❺
Haus der Wannsee-Konferenz ❼
Museumsdorf Düppel ❸
Siedlung Onkel-Tom ❶
Strandbad Wannsee ❹
Villenkolonie Alsen ❻

KEY

▬▬▬	Autobahn (motorway)
▬▬▬	Main road
▬▬▬	Minor road
Ⓢ	S-Bahn
🅄	U-Bahn
▬▬▬	Railway line

0 kilometre   1
0 mile   1

Siedlung Onkel-Tom ❶

Riemeister Strasse/Argentinische Allee. 🅄 *Onkel-Toms-Hütte.*

This housing estate, known as "Uncle Tom's Estate", represents one of the most interesting urban architectural achievements of the Weimar Republic. It was built from 1926 to 1932, to a design by

The Siedlung (estate) Onkel-Tom, built between 1926 and 1932

Bruno Taut, Hugo Häring and Otto Rudolf Salvisberg. Their primary intention was to solve the city's housing shortage by building large developments that were both pleasant to live in and fairly inexpensive. This project in Zehlendorf was the realization of the English concept of garden cities. The result is an enormous housing estate comprising single- and multiple-family houses. It is set in lush greenery on the borders of Grunewald and accommodates nearly 15,000 people.

Alliierten-museum ❷

Clayallee 135. **Tel** *818 19 90.*
Ⓢ *Zehlendorf, then* 🚌 *115.*
🅄 *Oskar-Helene-Heim.* ◻ *10am–6pm Thu-Tue.* 📷 *by appointment.*

In the heart of the former US military sector of Berlin is the Allied Museum, which combines exhibition space with open-air grounds.

A fascinating exhibition of everyday objects, military memorabilia, photographs and films explains life during the Cold War and the story of Berlin and its inhabitants between 1945 and 1994.

Museumsdorf Düppel ❸

Clauerstrasse 11. **Tel** *802 66 71.*
Ⓢ *Mexikoplatz or* 🅄 *Krumme Lanke,* then 🚌 *629.* ◻ *late Mar–early Oct: 3–7pm Thu, 10am–5pm Sun.* 📷

A visit to the Museumsdorf Düppel takes the visitor on a trip back in time. A reconstruction of a medieval village has been made on the site of a 13th-century settlement, discovered in the 1940s. It is a living village surrounded by still cultivated gardens and fields, where traditional breeds of pigs and sheep are raised in the sheds and pigsties.

On Sundays the village puts on displays of traditional

crafts. Here you can see how primitive saucepans and tools were fashioned; how wool was spun, dyed and woven; and how baskets were made.

Strandbad Wannsee ❹

Wannseebadweg 2s. ⑤ Nikolassee. 🚌 218.

The vast picturesque lake of Wannsee, situated on the edge of Grunewald, is a principal destination for Berliners who are looking for some kind of recreation. Here you can take part in water sports, enjoy a lake cruise, bathe, or simply enjoy relaxing on the shore. The most developed part is the southeastern corner of the lake. Here, near S-Bahn Wannsee, there are yachting marinas and harbours, while further north is one of the largest inland beaches in Europe – Strandbad Wannsee. It has been in use since the beginning of the 20th century, and was developed between 1929 and 1930 by the construction of a complex of changing rooms, shops and cafés on top of man-made terraces.

On sunny summer days, sun-worshippers completely cover the sandy shore, while the lake is filled with yachts and windsurfers. It is also quite pleasant to take a walk around Schwanenwerder island. It has many elegant villas, one of which, Inselstrasse No. 24/26, was built for Axel Springer, the German newspaper publisher.

Grabstätte von Heinrich von Kleist ❺

GRAVE OF HEINRICH VON KLEIST

Bismarckstrasse (near No. 3). ⑤ Wannsee. 🚌 114, 316, 318.

A narrow street running from Königstrasse at the viaduct of the S-Bahn Wannsee leads to the spot where the playwright Heinrich von Kleist committed suicide. On 21 November 1811 he shot his companion Henriette Vogel and then turned the pistol on himself. They are both buried here. A stone marks their grave, on which flowers are left by well-wishers.

Villenkolonie Alsen ❻

Am Grossen Wannsee. ⑤ Wannsee, then 🚌 114.

This clutch of villas forms a delightful holiday resort – the oldest of its kind in Berlin. The villas are thought to be the most beautiful, not just because of their picturesque lakeside location, but also because of the quality of their architecture.

Strolling along Am Grossen Wannsee, it is worth looking at the villa at No. 39/41, known as Haus Springer. It was designed by Alfred Messel in 1901 and is covered with shingles which reflect contemporary American designs. At No. 42 stands a villa that

The exterior of Haus der Wannsee-Konferenz

was designed by Paul Baumgarten in 1909 for the painter Max Liebermann, who spent many summers here painting.

Haus der Wannsee-Konferenz ❼

Am Grossen Wannsee 56/58. Tel 805 00 10. ⑤ Wannsee, then 🚌 114. ⏰ 10am–6pm daily.

This is one of the most beautiful of the luxury Alsen holiday villas, and yet the most abhorrent. Designed by Paul Baumgarten between 1914 and 1915, it is in the style of a small Neo-Baroque palace with an elegant portico. In 1940 the villa was sold to the Nazi SS. On 20 January 1942, a meeting took place between Richard Heydrich and 14 other officers from the secret service and the SS, among them Adolf Eichmann. It was then that the decision was taken about "the final solution on the question of Jews". Their plans for the outright extermination of 11 million Jews embraced the whole of Europe, including Great Britain and neutral countries.

Since 1992 this has been a museum and place of remembrance. An exhibition depicts the history of the Holocaust with some shocking documents and photographs from the ghettos and extermination camps. For security reasons, the gate to the villa is always locked, and to enter the park you have to announce yourself through the intercom.

Boarding point for lake cruises on the Wannsee

Western Berlin

West of Charlottenburg, beyond the city ring road, stretches an area notable for its striking Funkturm (Radio Tower) and Internationales Congress Centrum, as well as a number of large exhibition centres. After World War II, a residential estate of villas was built here, one of which belonged to the sculptor Georg Kolbe and now houses a museum of his works. A radio station has its recording studios in a very large building nearby; its plain, almost boring looking façade hides one of Berlin's most beautiful art deco interiors.

The futuristic exterior of the Internationales Congress Centrum

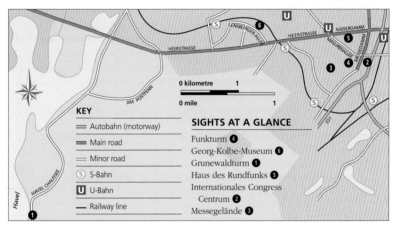

KEY

═══ Autobahn (motorway)

▬▬▬ Main road

▬▬▬ Minor road

Ⓢ S-Bahn

Ⓤ U-Bahn

─── Railway line

SIGHTS AT A GLANCE

Funkturm ❹

Georg-Kolbe-Museum ❻

Grunewaldturm ❶

Haus des Rundfunks ❺

Internationales Congress
  Centrum ❷

Messegelände ❸

Grunewaldturm ❶

Havelchaussee 61. 🚌 218.

The neo-gothic tower built on a hill at the edge of the Havel river is one of the most prominent features of the area. This type of tower became popular in Germany during the 19th century as a way of commemorating important events or people. The Grune-waldturm was built in 1899 on the centenary of the birth of Wilhelm I. After 1871, he was the first Emperor of the Second Reich, and the tower was initially named "Kaiser-Wilhelm-Turm". The 56-m (185-ft) tower was designed by Franz Schwechten and is made of red brick with plaster details. The tower is made all the more striking by the green background provided by the surrounding leafy trees.

Currently used as an observation tower, the view from the top of this structure is well worth climbing the 204 steps for. There is a popular restaurant in the base of the tower and above, in the domed hall, is a marble statue of the Emperor that was designed by Ludwig Mansel.

The impressive red-brick Neo-Gothic Grunewaldturm

Internationales Congress Centrum ❷

Messedamm 19. Ⓢ Messe Nord/ICC. Ⓤ Kaiserdamm. 🚌 104, 218, X34, X49.

This silver futuristic structure stands on a peninsula of land, surrounded on two sides by a continuous stream of fast moving cars. The Internationales Congress Centrum (ICC) marked yet another stage in the rivalry between East and West Berlin – it was built in reply to the East's Palast der Republik.

Constructed between 1973 and 1979, to a design by Ralf Schüler and Ursulina Schüler-Witte, the building is a mass of angular aluminium shapes that disguise its well thought-out construction. The conference area is separate from the concert halls, for good sound-proofing. One of the most modern buildings of its type in the world, it has a state-of-the-art electronic security system and an advanced means of co-ordinating and directing the several thousand people who come here to attend various meetings and conferences. More than 80 rooms and halls enable the venue to host a variety of events, from rock concerts for up to 5,000 spectators to a small artistic workshop or seminar. The building also has a roof garden, where you can rest during intervals. In front of the main entrance stands *Alexander the Great in front of Ekbatana*, by French sculptor Jean Ipoustéguy (born 1920).

Monumental façade of the Ehrenhalle part of the Messegelände

Messegelände ❸

Hammarskjöldplatz. Ⓢ *Messe Nord/ICC.* Ⓤ *Kaiserdamm.* 🚌 *104, 139, 349, X34.*

The pavilions of the vast exhibition and trade halls which lie south of Hammarskjöldplatz cover more than 160,000 sq m (1,700,000 sq ft). Many of the international events organized here, including the food and agricultural fair Grüne Woche, are among the largest events of their kind in Europe. Even so, the exhibition areas are constantly enlarged and updated.

The original exhibition halls on this site were built before World War I, but nothing of these buildings remains. The oldest part is the Funkturm and the group of pavilions which surround it. The huge building at the front – Ehrenhalle – was built in 1936 to a design by Richard Ermisch, and is one of the few surviving buildings in Berlin designed in a Fascist architectural style.

The straight motorway that lies at the rear of the halls, in the direction of Nikolassee, is the famous Avus, the first German autobahn, built in 1921. It was adapted for motor racing, and became Germany's first car-racing track. It was here that the world speed record was broken before World War II. Now it forms part of the autobahn system.

Funkturm ❹

Hammarskjöldplatz. **Tel** *30 38 19 05.* Ⓢ *Messe Nord/ICC.* Ⓤ *Kaiserdamm.* 🚌 *104, 139, 149, 218, X34.* **Observation Terrace** ⏱ *10am–8pm Mon, 10am–11pm Tue–Sun.*

The radio tower, resembling Paris' Eiffel tower, has become one of Berlin's most recognizable landmarks. Built in 1924 to a design by Heinrich Straumer, it rises 150 m (500 ft) into the air. It now operates as both an air-traffic control tower and a radio mast. Visitors can enjoy views on the observation terrace at 125 m (400 ft), or dine at the Funkturm's lofty restaurant at 55 m (180 ft).

Haus des Rundfunks ❺

Masurenallee 8–14. Ⓢ *Messe Nord/ICC.* Ⓤ *Theodor-Heuss-Platz.* 🚌 *104, 218, X34, X49.*

This building's depressing, flat, brick-covered façade hides an interior of startling beauty. The huge edifice was constructed as a radio station between 1929 and 1931 to a design by Hans Poelzig. The building has a triangular shape, with three studio wings radiating from the central five-storey hall. The impressive Art Deco interiors, which are spectacularly lit from above, are enhanced by geometrically-patterned rows of balconies and large, pendulous,

Clean, geometric shapes in the Art Deco lobby, Haus des Rundfunks

octagonal lamps. They represent one of the finest architectural achievements of this era in Berlin.

From the studio concert hall, concerts are often broadcast on radio SFB.

Fountain in the garden of the sculptor Georg Kolbe's villa

Georg-Kolbe-Museum ❻

Sensburger Allee 25. **Tel** *304 21 44.* Ⓢ *Heerstrasse.* 🚌 *218, X34, X49.* ⏱ *10am–6pm Tue–Sun.*

One of the most renowned German sculptors, Georg Kolbe (1877–1947) bequeathed the house in which he lived and worked almost his entire life to the city of Berlin. The villa was built by the Swiss architect, Ernst Reutsch, between 1928 and 1929 in a Functionalist style. Extended a few years later by the architect Paul Lindner, it was given an old-fashioned styling with rooms that open onto a large hall. Kolbe also left the city 180 of his sculptures, as well as his own art collection, which includes works by the Expressionist painter Ernst Ludwig Kirchner and the sculptor Wilhelm Lehmbruck. Visiting here is not only a rare chance to get to know Kolbe's works but also an opportunity to see his house and workshop, which display the tools and various devices for lifting a heavy or large sculpture.

Northwest Berlin

A visit to this part of the city provides a chance to see the grandeur of the Olympiastadion, which was inspired by the monumental architecture of ancient Rome. Nearby stands the monolithic Le Corbusier Haus, once regarded as the model for future housing. The historic town of Spandau has some pretty medieval streets and a well-preserved Renaissance citadel. A number of original timber-framed houses remain and are well worth seeing, along with the Gothic St-Nikolai-Kirche.

500 two-storey apartments with integral services, such as a post office, shops, a sports hall and nursery school. The structure fell short of Le Corbusier's aspirations as financial pressure meant the estate lacked some service elements; in addition, structural alterations changed the building's proportions from the original plans.

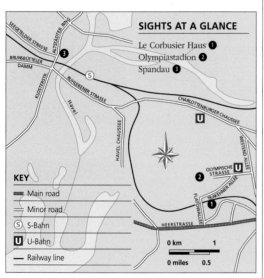

SIGHTS AT A GLANCE

Le Corbusier Haus ❶
Olympiastadion ❷
Spandau ❸

KEY

- 🚋🚋🚋 Main road
- === Minor road
- Ⓢ S-Bahn
- Ⓤ U-Bahn
- — Railway line

0 km   1
0 miles   0.5

Two sculptures of athletes decorating the Olympiastadion

Olympiastadion ❷

Olympischer Platz. **Tel** 25 00 23 22. Ⓢ & Ⓤ Olympiastadion. 🚌 218. 🕐 for tours: mid-Mar–Oct: 9am–7pm daily (until 8pm Jun–mid-Sep); Nov–mid-Mar: 9am–4pm daily.

The Olympiastadion, or Reichssportfeld, as it was originally known, was built for the 1936 Olympic Games in Berlin. It was designed by Werner March in the Nazi architectural style and was inspired by the architecture of ancient Rome. The Olympia-stadion was immortalized in the final scenes of István Szabó's classic film *Mephisto*. To the west lie the Maifeld and the Waldbühne. The former is an enormous assembly-ground surrounded by grandstands and fronted by the Glocken-turm, a 77-m (250-ft) tower, while the latter is an open-air amphitheatre. To the north are swimming pools and sports grounds.

Following a 236-million euro refurbishment, including a seemingly free-floating roof, the stadium was re-opened in 2004 as a high-tech arena.

Le Corbusier Haus ❶

Flatowallee 16. Ⓢ Olympiastadion. 🚌 218.

This apartment building by Le Corbusier, on a hill near the site of the Olympiastadion, was this architect's entry to the 1957 Interbau Exhibition (*see p133*). Following World War II,

there was a housing shortage all over Europe, especially in the bomb-damaged cities. Le Corbusier's innovative design for what he called a *Unité d'Habitation* was his attempt to create fully self-sufficient housing estates in answer to this problem. He built three of these complexes, the most famous being in Marseilles. For his Berlin design, Le Corbusier wanted to build over

Le Corbusier Haus, by the renowned French architect

Interior of the Gothic St-Nikolai-Kirche in Spandau

Spandau ③

Zitadelle Spandau Am Juliusturm.
Tel 354 94 40. Ⓤ *Zitadelle.*
🕐 *10am–5pm daily.* 🈂

Spandau is one of the oldest towns within the area of greater Berlin, and it has managed to retain a distinct character for itself. Evidence of the earliest settlement dates back to the 8th century, although the town of Spandau was only granted a charter in 1232. The area was spared the worst of the World War II bombing, so there are still some interesting sights to visit. The heart of the town is a network of medieval streets with a picturesque market square and a number of original timber-framed houses; in the north of Spandau sections of town wall still stand, dating from the 15th century. In the centre of town is the magnificent Gothic St-Nikolai-Kirche dating from the 15th century. The church holds many valuable ecclesiastical furnishings, such as a splendid Renaissance stone altar from the end of the 16th century, a Baroque pulpit from around 1700 which came from a royal palace in Potsdam, a Gothic baptismal font and many epitaphs.

Crowned black Prussian eagle

A castle was first built on the site of the Zitadelle Spandau (citadel) in the 12th century, but today only the 36-m (120-ft) Juliusturm (tower) remains. In 1560 the building of a fort was begun here, to a design by Francesco Chiaramella da Gandino. It took 30 years to bring to completion, however, and most of the work was supervised by architect Rochus Guerrini, Graf zu Lynar. Though the citadel had a jail, Rudolf Hess, Spandau's most infamous resident, was incarcerated a short distance away in a military prison after the 1946 Nuremberg trials. In 1987 the former deputy leader of the Nazi party died, and the prison was torn down.

The Hohenzollern coat of arms above the main gate of the citadel

ZITADELLE SPANDAU

This magnificent and perfectly proportioned 16th-century citadel stands at the confluence of the Spree and Havel rivers. Both the main citadel and its various 19th-century additions are still in excellent condition. The "Iron Chancellor", Otto von Bismarck *(see p24)*, moved the gold treasure of the Reichskriegsschatz (Imperial War Fund) here in 1874, where it remained until 1919. The citadel now holds museums of local history, and an observation terrace on the crenellated Juliusturm (tower).

KEY

Bastion Kronprinz ①
Bastion Brandenburg ②
Palace ③
Main gate ④

Bastion König ⑤
Bastion Königin ⑥
Juliusturm ⑦
Ravelin Schweinekopf ⑧

Northern Berlin

Beyond the Tiergarten lie the AEG-Turbinenhalle, designed by Peter Behrens, and the Gedenkstätte Plötzensee, a sombre memorial to those executed for their supposed crimes against the Third Reich. Further north past the airport, the Tegel area contains the picturesque Schloss Tegel and the IBA-Viertel, an unusually colourful, modern housing estate designed by a team of architects. It is worth taking a cruise boat to Tegel and linking together sight-seeing in this area and a visit to Spandau with a relaxing voyage along the Havel river.

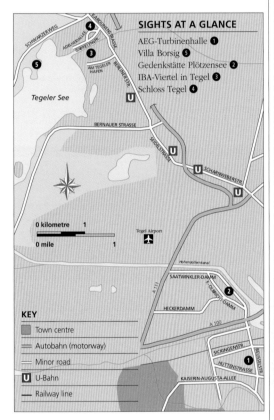

SIGHTS AT A GLANCE

AEG-Turbinenhalle ❶
Villa Borsig ❺
Gedenkstätte Plötzensee ❷
IBA-Viertel in Tegel ❸
Schloss Tegel ❹

Tegeler See

Tegel Airport

KEY

- ▨ Town centre
- ▤ Autobahn (motorway)
- — Minor road
- Ⓤ U-Bahn
- — Railway line

0 kilometre 1
0 mile 1

AEG-Turbinen-halle ❶

Huttenstrasse 12–16.
Ⓤ *Turmstrasse, then* 🚌 *M27.*

This building is one of the most important textbook examples of modern architecture dating from the beginning of the 20th century. It was commissioned by the electronics company, AEG, in 1909 and designed by Peter Behrens in conjunction with Karl Bernhardt. It was among the earliest structures not to incorporate any element, decorative or otherwise, that reflected previous architectural styles. A huge hangar of a building, it has enormous windows and stretches 123 m (400 ft) down Berlichingenstrasse. The principal design imperative for this structure was to maintain a streamlined profile, while making no effort to disguise the materials used in its construction.

Gedenkstätte Plötzensee ❷

PLOTZENSEE MEMORIAL

Hüttigpfad. ***Tel** 344 32 26.*
Ⓢ *Beuselstrasse, then* 🚌 *123.*
🕐 *Mar–Oct: 9am–5pm; Nov–Feb: 9am–4pm.*

A narrow street leads from Saatwinkler Damm to the site where nearly 2,500 people convicted of crimes against the Third Reich were hanged. The Gedenkstätte Plötzensee is a simple memorial in a brick hut, which still has the iron hooks from which the victims were suspended. The main figures in the unsuccessful assassination attempt against Hitler, on July 20 1944, were executed in Bendlerblock *(see p127)*, although the remainder of the conspirators were killed here. Count Helmut James von Moltke, one of the leaders of the German resistance movement, was also executed here. The count organized the Kreisauer Kreis – a political movement which gathered together and united German opposition to Hitler and the Third Reich.

Memorial to concentration camp victims at Gedenkstätte Plötzensee

IBA-Viertel in Tegel ❸

Karolinenstrasse & Am Tegeler Hafen. Ⓤ *Alt Tegel.*

The development around the southern edge of the port of Tegel is an essential stop for lovers of modern, and

The elegant Neo-Classical façade of Schloss Tegel

particularly post-modern, architecture. This complex developed out of the IBA (Internationale Baustellung) building exhibition in 1987. Over 30 architects were involved in this project, although the main designers were Charles Moore, John Ruble and Buzz Yudell. Within this complex stands the Humboldt-Bibliothek, which draws on Neo-Classical themes. In 1997 a monument was established to the eminent scientists Wilhelm and Alexander von Humboldt in front of this library.

Running the length of Am Tegeler Hafen street is a large housing estate where each unit has been designed by a different architect. For instance, at No. 8, the house by Stanley Tigerman recalls a style popular in Hanseatic architecture, while the red house at No. 10, designed by Paolo Portoghesi, looks as though it has been cracked lengthwise in two.

To the north, the IBA-Viertel estate borders another modern building, the Hotel Sorat, carefully built around the remaining section of an old windmill that was once part of the Humboldt estate.

Schloss Tegel ❹

Adelheidallee 19–21. **Tel** 434 31 56. Ⓤ *Alt Tegel.* 🚌 *124, 133, 222.* 🚫 *the palace is currently closed for renovations. Call for possible re-opening date and for opening times of grounds during renovations.*

Schloss Tegel is one of the most interesting palace complexes in Berlin. In the

16th century there was already a manor house on this site, which in the second half of the 17th century was rebuilt into a hunting lodge for the Elector Friedrich Wilhelm. In 1766 the ownership of the property passed to the Humboldt family, and between the years 1820 and 1824, Karl Friedrich Schinkel thoroughly rebuilt the palace, giving it its current style.

There are tiled bas-reliefs decorating the elevations on the top floor of the towers. These were designed by Christian Daniel Rauch and depict the ancient wind gods. Some of Schinkel's marvellous interiors have survived, along with several items from what was once a large collection of antique sculptures. The palace is still privately owned by descendants of the Humboldt family, but guided tours are offered when the palace is

open. It is also worth visiting the park. On its western limits lies the Humboldt family tomb designed by Schinkel and decorated with a copy of a splendid sculpture by Bertel Thorwaldsen; the original piece stands inside the palace.

Villa Borsig ❺

Reiherwerder. Ⓤ *Alt Tegel.* 🚌 *124, 133, 222, 224,* then a 15-minute walk.

This villa sits on a peninsula which cuts into the Tegeler See and is reminiscent of Schloss Sanssouci in Potsdam. It was built much later, however, between 1911 and 1913. It was designed by Alfred Salinger and Eugen Schmohl, for the Borsig family, one of the wealthiest industrialist families in Berlin. This villa is particularly picturesque when observed from the lake, so it is worth looking out for it while cruising in a boat.

The Villa Borsig façade viewed from the garden

KARL FRIEDRICH SCHINKEL (1781–1841)

Schinkel was one of the most renowned German architects; even today his work forms an essential element of the architectural landscape of Berlin. He graduated from the Berlin Bauakademie, and for many years held a high-profile position in the Prussian Building Ministry. He was equally skilled in producing both Neo-Classical and Neo-Gothic designs. In Berlin and Potsdam he designed a few dozen buildings – palaces, civic buildings and churches, many of which still stand today. He also excelled at painting and even designed scenery for the opera house on Unter den Linden, among others. You can admire his paintings in the Galerie der Romantik in Schloss Charlottenburg. Schinkel's creativity had a truly enormous influence on the next generation of architects working in Prussia.

Terraced vineyard approach to Schloss Sanssouci ▷

GREATER
BERLIN

POTSDAM

Potsdam is an independent city bordering Berlin. It is also the capital of Brandenburg, with almost 140,000 inhabitants. The first historical reference to Potsdam dates from AD 993. The town blossomed in the 1600s, during the era of the Great Elector *(see p20)*, and then again during the 18th century. Potsdam suffered very badly during World War II, particularly on the nights of 14 and 15 April 1945, when the Allies bombed the town's centre. Today, despite its

Sculpture from Park Sanssouci

wartime losses, Potsdam is one of the most interesting cities in Germany. Tourists flock to see the royal Park Sanssouci and palaces such as the Marmorpalais and Schloss Cecilienhof. It is also worth strolling around Neuer Garten and the historic area around the Rathaus. The Russian colony of Alexandrowka, the Holländisches Viertel, the film studios of Babelsberg and Babelsberg park *(see pp210–211)* also rate among the attractions of Potsdam.

SIGHTS AT A GLANCE

Historic Buildings
Altes Rathaus ㉑
Bildergalerie ⑪
Chinesisches Teehaus ⑥
Communs ③
Historische Mühle ⑫
Marmorpalais ⑯
Neue Kammern ⑨
Neues Palais pp194–5 ❶
Orangerie ⑦
Römische Bäder ⑤
Schloss Cecilienhof ⑮
Schloss Charlottenhof ④
Schloss Sanssouci pp200–1 ⑩

Wasserwerk Sanssouci ㉔

Historic Areas
Alexandrowka ⑬
Holländisches Viertel ⑰

Churches
Französische Kirche ⑲
Friedenskirche ⑧
Nikolaikirche ⑳
Peter und Paul Kirche ⑱

Parks and Theme Parks
Filmpark Babelsberg ㉖

Neuer Garten ⑭
Park Sanssouci ②
Telegrafenberg ㉕

Museums
Marstall (Filmmuseum) ㉒
Potsdam-Museum ㉓

KEY

	Street-by-Street map *pp192–3*
🚉	Railway station
Ⓢ	Bahn Station

0 metres   750
0 yards   750

GETTING THERE
S-Bahn 7 goes to Potsdam from Berlin. From Potsdam station, bus 606 goes to Neues Palais and trams 94, 96 and X-98 go to the centre of town. Bus 695 travels between Park Sanssouci and Neuer Garten.

◁ **Colonnaded cloister at the Friedenskirche**

Street-by-Street: Park Sanssouci

Flower-filled urn, Park Sanssouci

The enormous Park Sanssouci, covering an area of 287 hectares, is among the most beautiful palace complexes in Europe. The first building to be constructed was Schloss Sanssouci, the summer palace of Frederick the Great. It was built between 1745 and 1747 on the site of an orchard. Over the years, Park Sanssouci was expanded and enriched by the addition of other palaces and pavilions. Allow yourself at least a whole day to enjoy the park fully.

Communs
This house for the palace staff has an unusually elegant character, and is situated next to a pretty courtyard **3**

★ Neues Palais
This monumental building of the New Palace, constructed between 1763 and 1769, is crowned by a massive dome **1**

Römische Bäder
The Roman baths include a mock-Renaissance villa and a suite of Roman-style rooms **5**

| 0 metres | 200 |
| 0 yards | 200 |

STAR SIGHTS

★ Neues Palais

★ Schloss Sanssouci

Schloss Charlottenhof
This Neo-Classical palace gained its name from Charlotte von Gentzkow, the former owner of the land on which the palace was built **4**

Park Sanssouci
The extensive parkland is made up of several gardens. The one near the Orangerie is called the Botanischergarten (botanical garden) ❷

Orangerie
This Neo-Renaissance palace, the largest in the park, was built in the mid-19th century to house foreign royalty and guests ❼

Neue Kammern
This Rococo pavilion was once the orangerie of the Sanssouci Palace, but was rebuilt as a guest house ❾

★ Schloss Sanssouci
A beautifully terraced vineyard creates a grand approach to Schloss Sanssouci, the oldest building in the complex ❿

Bildergalerie
Built between 1755 and 1764, this pavilion houses an art gallery. It is Germany's oldest purpose-built museum building ⓫

Chinesisches Teehaus
The small Rococo-style Chinese Teahouse features an exhibition of exquisite Oriental porcelain ❻

Friedenskirche
The Neo-Romanesque Church of Peace is modelled on the Basilica of San Clemente in Rome ❽

Neues Palais ●

This imposing Baroque palace, on the main avenue in Park Sanssouci, was built at the request of Frederick the Great. The initial plans were prepared in 1750 by Georg Wenzeslaus von Knobelsdorff. However, construction only began in 1763, after the Seven Years' War (see p21), to a design by Johann Gottfried Büring, Jean Laurent Le Geay and Carl von Gontard. The result was a vast two-storey building, decorated with hundreds of sculptures and more than 200 richly adorned rooms, which together make up one of Germany's most beautiful palaces.

Cabinet from the study

Façade
The entrance to the Neues Palais is through the gate on the western façade. The imposing gate is flanked by stone sentry boxes.

The Schlosstheater was completed in 1768, and designed by JC Hoppenhaupt.

Study
This Rococo-style study was part of Frederick the Great's personal apartment.

Upper Gallery
The Rococo interior, with a beautiful inlaid floor, is decorated with Italian paintings.

STAR FEATURES

★ Marmorsaal

★ Grottensaal

Bas-reliefs
on the triangular
tympanum depict
figures from
Greek mytho-
logy, including
Minerva, the
Muses and
Pegasus.

Figures on the Dome
*The Neues Palais is
crowned by a dome
with a gilded royal
crown. The crown is
carried by a sculpture
of three nymphs.*

VISITORS' CHECKLIST

Am Neuen Palais.
Tel (0331) 96 94 198/199.
605, 606, 695. Apr–Oct:
10am–5pm Wed–Mon; Nov–
Mar: 10am–4pm Sat–Thu.
only. **www**.spsg.de

★ Marmorsaal
*This vast ballroom
features walls inlaid
with marble and a
beautiful painting on
the ceiling. The gallery
was used by the
orchestra.*

Main entrance

Commode
*This Rococo commode was
designed by JF Spindler in
c.1765. It is located in the Red
Room in the Duke's Apartments.*

★ Grottensaal
*The walls of this
unusual grotto-
style room are
lined with semi-
precious stones,
coral and shells
as well as man-
made stalactites.*

Upper Vestibule
*This elegant room was designed by
Carl von Gontard. The walls are
covered with Silesian marble and the
ceiling depicts Venus and the Graces.*

Park Sanssouci ❷

Schopenhauerstrasse/ Zur Historischen Mühle. 🚌 *612, 614, 695.*

This vast park, covering some 287 ha (700 acres), was established in 1725 on the site of an orchard. However, it was only transformed into an enormous landscaped park when construction work began on Schloss Sanssouci (*see pp200–1*). Today, the park is made up of smaller gardens dating from different eras, each of which has been maintained in the original style. At the foot of Schloss Sanssouci is the oldest section of the park, containing the Dutch garden, a number of fountains and the French-style Lustgarten (pleasure garden), with a symmetrical layout and lovely rose beds. Surrounding Friedenskirche is the Marly-garten, created in the mid-19th century by Ludwig Persius.

The eastern part of the park is called the Rehgarten, a beautifully landscaped park in the English style, designed by Peter Joseph Lenné, and established on the site of former hunting grounds. This park extends right up to the Neues Palais. To the south, surrounding the small palace,

extends the Charlottenhof Park, also designed by Lenné. In the northern section of the park, next to the Orangerie, is the Nordischer Garten and the Paradiesgarten.

The range of different garden styles makes a simple stroll through this park particularly pleasant. There are also a large number of sculptures, columns, obelisks and grottoes for the visitor to explore. The perspectives that suddenly open up across the park, and the picturesque groupings of trees, are also beautiful.

Communs ❸

Am Neuen Palais. 🚌 *606, 695.*

This area of the park consists of a pair of two-storey pavilions linked by a semi-circular colonnade. They are unusually elegant buildings considering they were used for servants' quarters and the palace kitchens. However, they also served to screen from view the cultivated fields that extended past the park from the palace.

The Communs were built between 1766 and 1769 by Carl von Gontard, to a design by Jean Laurent Le Geay. The

Elegant façade of the Communs, the servants' quarters

buildings are enclosed by an elegant courtyard reflected in the style of the buildings. The kitchen was in the south pavilion, linked to the palace by an underground passage-way, and the north pavilion accommodated the servants of the king's guests. Today, the rectors' offices of the University of Potsdam are located here in the Communs.

Schloss Charlottenhof ❹

CHARLOTTENHOF PALACE

Geschwister-Scholl-Strasse (Park Charlottenhof). **Tel** *(0331) 969 42 28.* 🚌 *605, 606, 610.* 🚋 *91, 94, 96.* ◯ *1 May–31 Oct: 10am–5pm Tue–Sun.*

This small Neo-Classical palace is located in the southern extension of Park Sanssouci, Park Charlottenhof. It was designed by Karl Friedrich Schinkel in 1829 for the heir to the throne, later King Friedrich Wilhelm IV. This small one-storey building was built in the style of a Roman villa. The rear of the palace has a portico that opens out onto the garden terrace.

Some of the wall paintings which were made in the so-called Pompeiian style, designed by Schinkel, are still in place. The most interesting part of the interior is the blue-and-white-striped Humboldt Room, also called the Tent Room due to its resemblance to a tent. The palace is sur-rounded by a picturesque landscaped park designed by Peter Joseph Lenné.

One of the many sculptures on display in Park Sanssouci

Römische Bäder ❺
ROMAN BATHS

Lenné-Strasse (Park Charlottenhof).
Tel *(0331) 969 42 25.* 🚌 *605, 606.*
🚃 *94, 96.* ⏰ *May–Oct:*
10am–6pm Tue–Sun.

This picturesque group of pavilions, situated by the edge of a lake, forms the Roman Baths, which actually served as accommodation for the king's guests. It was designed by Karl Friedrich Schinkel, with the involvement of Ludwig Persius, between 1829 and 1840. At the front is the gardener's house, which is adjacent to an asymmetrical low tower in the style of an Italian Renaissance villa. In the background, to the left, extends the former bathing pavilion, which is currently used for temporary exhibitions. All of the pavilions are arranged around an internal garden planted with a multi-coloured carpet of shrubs. A closer look will reveal that many of these colourful plants are actually vegetables.

Spring of water, Römische Bäder

Chinesisches Teehaus ❻
CHINESE TEAHOUSE

Ökonomieweg (Rehgarten).
Tel *(0331) 969 42 25.* 🚌 *606.*
🚃 *94, 96.* ⏰ *May–Oct:*
10am–6pm Tue–Sun.

The lustrous, gilded pavilion that can be seen glistening from a distance is the Chinese Teahouse. Chinese art was

The Chinesisches Teehaus, now housing a collection of porcelain

popular during the Rococo period – people wore Chinese silk, rooms were wallpapered with Chinese designs, furniture was lacquered, drinks were served in Chinese porcelain, and Chinese pavilions were built in gardens.

The Chinesisches Teehaus was built in Park Sanssouci between 1754 and 1756 to a design by Johann Gottfried Büring. It is circular in shape with a centrally located main hall surrounded by three studies. Between each of these are pretty *trompe l'oeil* porticos. Ornaments, together with gilded figures of Chinese gentlemen and ladies, surround the pavilion. Originally the Chinesisches Teehaus served as a tea room and a summer dining room. Today, it houses a collection of porcelain.

Orangerie ❼

Maulbeerallee (Nordischer Garten).
Tel *(0331) 96 94 280.* 🚌 *695.*
⏰ *Apr: 10am–6pm Sat, Sun, hols;*
May–Oct: 10am–6pm Tue–Sun.
Observation terrace
⏰ *Apr: 10am–6pm Sat, Sun, hols;*
May–Oct: 10am–6pm Tue–Sun.

Towering above the park is the Orangerie, designed in the Italian Renaissance style and crowned by a colonnade. The Orangerie was built to house guests, not plants. It was constructed between 1851 and 1860 by Friedrich August Stüler, on the initiative and direction of Friedrich Wilhelm IV. The final design was partly based on the plans of Ludwig Persius. It served as a guest residence for the

king's sister and her husband Tsar Nicholas I. The rooms were grouped around the Raphael Hall, which was based on the Regia Hall in the Vatican and decorated with copies of the works of Italian artist Raphael. It is also worth climbing up to the observation terrace, from where the view extends over Potsdam.

Friedenskirche ❽

Allee nach Sanssouci (Marlygarten).
Tel *(0331) 97 40 09.* 🚌 *695.* 🚃 *91,*
94. ⏰ *May–Oct: 10am–6pm daily;*
Nov–Apr: 11am–4pm Sat,
11:30am–4pm Sun.

Close to Schloss Sanssouci is Friedenskirche, or the Church of Peace. The foundation stone was laid by King Friedrich Wilhelm IV in 1845 and the church was completed in 1848. Designed by Ludwig Persius, Friedrich August Stüler and Ludwig Hesse, the church is based on San Clemente in Rome.

Inside, the vaulted ceiling of the apse is almost completely covered by an enchanting 12th-century mosaic depicting the figure of Christ as a judge. This Byzantine mosaic was originally located in the church of San Capriano on the island of Murano in Venice, Italy. Next to the church is a colonnaded atrium and a mausoleum containing the tombs of Friedrich Wilhelm I, Friedrich Wilhelm IV and Kaiser Friedrich III.

Long flight of stairs leading to the Renaissance-style Orangerie

Neue Kammern ❾

NEW CHAMBERS

Zur Historischen Mühle (Lustgarten). *Tel* (0331) 969 42 06. 612, 614, 695, X15. Apr: 10am–6pm Sat–Sun; May–Oct: 10am–6pm Tue–Sun.

The Neue Kammern contains residential apartments. It is the mirror image of the Bildergalerie and was originally built as an orangery in 1747 to a design by Georg Wenzeslaus von Knobelsdorff. In 1777 Frederick the Great (Friedrich II) ordered the building to be remodelled as guest accommodation. The architect, Georg Christian Unger, left the elegant Baroque exterior of the orangery largely untouched and instead concentrated on converting the interior. As well as the sumptuous guest suites, the new design included four elegant halls. The best of these is the Ovidsaal, with its rich reliefs and marble floors. The interior décor has been maintained in Frederick's Rococo style. The building also houses a collection of Meissen figurines.

Schloss Sanssouci ❿

See pp200–201.

Detail of Caravaggio's *Doubting Thomas*, in the Bildergalerie

Bildergalerie ⓫

Zur Historischen Mühle. *Tel* (0331) 969 42 02. 695. May–Oct: 10am–6pm Tue–Sun.

The picture gallery housed in the building adjacent to Schloss Sanssouci is the first purpose-built gallery in Germany. It was constructed between 1755 and 1764 to a design by JG Büring. The garden elevation reveals an allegorical tableau representing Art, Education and Crafts, while busts of renowned artists have been placed in the windows.

The gallery contains an exhibition of Baroque paintings once owned by Frederick the Great, although part of the collection can be found in the Gemäldegalerie *(see pp122–5)*. Highlights include Caravaggio's *Doubting Thomas* and Guido Reni's *Cleopatra's Death*, as well as a number of canvases by Rubens and van Dyck.

Historische Mühle ⓬

HISTORIC WINDMILL

Mauelbeerallee 5. *Tel* (0331) 550 68 51. 695. Apr–Oct: 10am–6pm daily; Nov, Jan–Mar: 10am–4pm Sat–Sun.

A mill has been located here since the early 18th century, although this is actually a reconstruction, dating from 1993. According to local legend, the original windmill was so noisy that Frederick the Great ordered it to be dismantled. However, a court upheld the miller's cause and the mill stayed. In 1790 a new windmill was built in its place, which lasted until 1945. The mill currently houses a museum of mechanical windmills.

Alexandrowka ⓭

Russische Kolonie Allee/ Puschkinallee. 92, 96. 604, 609, 692, 697.

A trip to Alexandrowka takes the visitor into the world of Pushkin's stories. Wooden houses made from logs, decorated with carved

A Russian-style wooden house in the settlement of Alexandrowka

motifs and set in their own gardens, create a very pretty residential estate. Although they appear to be picture-book, traditional Russian houses, they were constructed in 1826 under the direction of a German military architect called Captain Snethlage. What is interesting is that the estate was created for the singers of a Russian choir. The choir was set up in 1812 to entertain the troops and was recruited from over 500 Russian prisoners of war, who had fought with Napoleon. In 1815, when the Prussians and the Russians joined forces, the choir was retained by Friedrich Wilhelm III.

Peter Joseph Lenné was responsible for the overall appearance of the estate, and it was named Alexandrowka after the Tsarina, the Prussian Princess Charlotte. It is based on the shape of the cross of St Andrew inscribed within an oval. In all, 12 houses were built here, as well as an out-house which now contains a small museum. Some of the dwellings are still owned by the descendants of the choir. To the north of this estate stands the Russian Orthodox church of Alexander Nevski (1829).

Orange growing in the Neuer Garten's Marmorpalais

Neuer Garten ⑭

NEW GARDEN

Am Neuen Garten. 🚌 692.

Running along the edge of Heiliger See, on what was once the site of palace vine-yards, is a park laid out between 1787 and 1791. It was landscaped originally by Johann August Eyserbeck on the instructions of Friedrich Wilhelm II, while the current

Schloss Cecilienhof, summer residence of the Hohenzollern family

layout was created by Peter Joseph Lenné in 1816. It is a Romantic park ornamented with numerous pavilions and sculptures. The charming Marmorpalais stands beside the lake, while the northern section contains the early 20th-century Schloss Cecilienhof. Elsewhere you can see the red and green gardeners' houses, the pyramid-shaped ice house and a Neo-Gothic library pavilion completed in 1794.

Schloss Cecilienhof ⑮

Am Neuen Garten. **Tel** (0331) 969 42 00. 🚌 692. 🔲 Apr–Oct: 10am–6pm Tue–Sun; Nov–Mar: 10am–5pm Tue–Sun.

The Cecilienhof residence played a brief but important part in history because the 1945 Potsdam Conference took place here. Built between 1914 and 1917, the palace is the most recent of the Hohenzollern dynasty buildings and was designed by Paul Schultze-Naumburg in the style of an English country manor. It is a sprawling, asymmetrical building with wooden beams making a pretty herringbone pattern on its walls. The gate-house passageways leading to the courtyards are decorated with Baroque reliefs.

The palace was the Hohenzollern family residence after they lost the crown; the family remained in Potsdam until February 1945. It now functions as a first-class hotel and restaurant, where history lovers can relax amid care-fully tended shrubbery. Most of the historic furnishings used during the famous Potsdam conference are on display.

THE POTSDAM CONFERENCE OF 1945

On 17 July 1945 the heads of government for Great Britain (Winston Churchill, later represented by Clement Attlee), the United States (Harry Truman) and the Soviet Union (Joseph Stalin) met in Schloss Cecilienhof to confirm the decisions made earlier that year at Yalta. The aim of both conferences was to resolve the problems arising at the end of World War II. They decided to abolish the Nazi Party, to limit the size of the German militia and monitor it indef-initely, and also to punish war criminals and establish reparations. They also revised the German borders and arranged the resettlement of Germans from Poland. The con-ference played a major part in estab-lishing the political balance of power in Europe, which continued for the next 45 years.

Attlee, Truman and Stalin at Cecilienhof

Schloss Sanssouci ⑩

The name Sanssouci is French for "without a care" and gives a good indication of the flamboyant character of this enchanting Rococo palace, built in 1745. The original sketches, made by Friedrich II (Frederick the Great) himself, were finalized by Georg Wenzeslaus von Knobelsdorff. The glorious interiors were designed by Knobelsdorff and Johann August Nahl. The king clearly loved this palace, as his final wishes were that he should be buried here, near the tomb of his Italian greyhounds. He was actually interred in the Garnisonkirche, Potsdam, but his final wishes were carried out in 1991.

Bacchanalian Figures
The carved male and female bacchanalian figures on the pilasters are the work of Friedrich Christian Glume.

The colonnade frames the view of the artificial ruins on the hill.

The wings were added to the building between 1841 and 1842.

Voltaire Room
This room is decorated with naturalistic carvings of birds, flowers and fruit.

Domed Roof
The oxidized green dome covers the Marmorsaal. It is decorated with Baroque sculptures.

Marmorsaal
The imposing marble hall is decorated with pairs of columns made from Carrara marble. Frederick the Great wanted this room to be loosely based on the Pantheon in Rome.

STAR SIGHTS

★ Fêtes Galantes by Antoine Watteau

★ Konzertzimmer

Arbour
The palace design is completed by picturesque arbours and pergolas decorated with sun motifs.

VISITORS' CHECKLIST

Park Sanssouci.
Tel *(0331) 96 94 198/199.*
🚌 *612, 614, 650, 695.* 🚃 *91, 94, X98.* ⏰ *1 Apr–31 Oct: 9am–5pm Tue–Sun; Nov, Jan–31 Mar: 9am–4pm Tue–Sun.* **Damenflügel** *May–Oct: 10am–6pm Sat–Sun.* 📷 ✔ *compulsory.* **www.spsg.de**

★ Fêtes Galantes (c. 1715)
The real jewels in the palace are the enchanting paintings by Antoine Watteau. He was one of Frederick the Great's favourite artists.

Weimar Urn (1785)
This Neo-Classical urn from the Berlin company KPM (see p133) is a copy of the original urn, which was presented to the Duchess of Weimar.

★ Konzertzimmer
The walls of the salon are decorated with paintings by Antoine Pesne, based on Greek mythology.

Bibliothek
The library of Frederick the Great contains about 2,100 books. The walls are lined with cedar panelling to create a contemplative atmosphere.

Marmorpalais

MARBLE PALACE

Am Ufer des Heiligen Sees (Neuer Garten). *Tel (0331) 969 45 50.* 📟 *692, 695.* 🔲 *May–Oct: 10am–6pm Tue–Sun; Nov–Apr: 10am–4pm Sat–Sun, hols.*

The Marmorpalais is situated on the edge of the lake in Neuer Garten *(see p199)*, a park northeast of the centre of Potsdam. This small palace is a beautiful example of early Neo-Classical architecture. The palace owes its name to its façade, which is lined with Silesian marble.

The square main body of the palace was the initiative of King Friedrich Wilhelm II. The original building was completed in 1791 to a design by Carl von Gontard, under the direction of Carl Gotthard Langhans. The single-storey building had small rooms around a central staircase, but this turned out to be too small, and in 1797 it was extended. An extra floor and two projecting wings were added. This gave the Marmorpalais the character of a Palladian villa.

The main part of the palace contains Neo-Classical furnishings from the late 1700s, including furniture from the workshops of Roentgen and porcelain from Wedgwood, the English firm. The interiors of the wings date from slightly later, from the 1840s. The concert hall in the right hand wing is particularly beautiful. King Friedrich Wilhelm II died in this palace in 1797.

Neo-Classical Marmorpalais, with its inlaid marble façade

The historic Dutch district known as the Holländisches Viertel

Holländisches Viertel

DUTCH QUARTER

Friedrich-Ebert-/Kurfürsten-/Hebbel-/ Gutenbergstr. 📟 *604, 638, 639, 692, 695.* 🚋 *92, 93, 94, 96, 99.*

Just as amazing as the Russian district of Alexandrowka *(see pp198–9)* is this Dutch district. The area is popular with tourists, with numerous shops, galleries, cafés and beer cellars, especially along the central Mittelstrasse.

Dutch workers, invited by Friedrich Wilhelm I, arrived in Potsdam at the beginning of the 18th century. Between 1733 and 1742 a settlement was built for them, comprising 134 gabled houses arranged in four groups, according to plans by Johann Boumann the Elder. They were built from small red bricks, and finished with stone and plaster details. These houses are typically three-storey, with picturesque roofs and gables.

Peter und Paul Kirche

Bassinplatz. *Tel (0331) 230 79 90.* 📟 *604, 606, 609, 612, 638.* 🚋 *90, 92, 93, 96, X98.* 🔲 *10am–4pm daily.* ✝ *10am Sun.*

This 19th-century church was the first large Catholic church built in Potsdam, at the initiative of Friedrich Wilhelm IV. The first designs came from Friedrich August Stüler, but the final version is the work of Wilhelm Salzenberg. The church was built in 1870, in the shape of a

Neo-Romanesque cross. Its slender tower is a copy of the campanile of San Zeno Maggiore in Verona, Italy. Inside are three beautiful paintings by Antoine Pesne.

The colonnaded portico of the Französische Kirche

Französische Kirche

FRENCH CHURCH

Bassinplatz. *Tel (0331) 29 12 19.* 📟 *604, 606, 609, 612, 638.* 🚋 *90, 92, 93, 96, X98.* 🔲 *Mar–Oct 1:30–5pm daily.*

This church, reminiscent of the Pantheon in Rome, was built especially for the Hugenots in 1752. Following their expulsion from France, they were given the option of settling in Prussia in 1685 *(see p21)*. Those who settled in Potsdam initially benefited from the hospitality of other churches, then eventually the Französische Kirche was built for them. It was designed by Johann Boumann the Elder in the shape of an ellipse. The front elevation is supported by a grand columned portico. The side niches, which are the entrances of the church, are decorated with the allegorical figures of Faith and Knowledge. The interior dates from the 1830s and is based on designs by Karl Friedrich Schinkel.

Nikolaikirche ⑳

Am Alten Markt. *Tel (0331) 270 86 02.* 604, 605, 609, 610, 695. 91, 92, 93, 94, 96, 99, X98. 10am–5pm daily.

This imposing church, built in a late Neo-Classical style, is the most beautiful church in Potsdam. It was designed in 1830 by Karl Friedrich Schinkel and the building work was overseen by Ludwig Persius. The main body of the church is based on a square cross, with a semicircular presbytery.

It was decided only in the 1840s to crown the church with a vast dome, supported on a colonnaded tambour (wall supporting a dome). Schinkel had envisaged this from the beginning of the project, but it was not included in the orders of the king. Initially it was thought that the dome would be supported by a wooden structure, though ultimately it was built using iron between 1843 and 1848, according to a design by Persius and Friedrich August Stüler. The interior decoration and the furnishings of the church date back to the 1850s, and in the main area of the church they were based on the earlier designs by Schinkel.

In front of the church stands an obelisk built between 1753 and 1755 to a design by

Nikolaikirche's imposing exterior, with its green, weathered dome

Prussian architect Georg Wenzeslaus von Knobelsdorff. Initially it was decorated by medallions depicting the portraits of Prussian rulers, but during the post-World War II restorations, they were replaced with portraits of renowned Prussian architects.

Altes Rathaus ㉑

OLD TOWN HALL

Am Alten Markt. 604, 609, 692, 694. 90, 92, 93, 96, X98.

This elegant, colonnaded building, located on the eastern side of Alter Markt, is the old town hall. Designed by Johann Boumann the Elder, it was built in 1753 on the site of an earlier building that served a similar purpose. The uppermost storey, which features an ornamental attic roof, is decorated with the crest of Potsdam and allegorical sculptures. At the summit of the small tower are two gilded figures

Atlas at Altes Rathaus

of Atlas, each carrying a globe of the earth. The Altes Rathaus is currently used as a cultural centre. The interior of the neighbouring mid-18th century building was also refurbished, and a glassed-in passageway was built, linking the two buildings.

The Potsdam Royal Palace was located at one time on the west side of Alter Markt. It was a massive two-storey building with three wings. There was also an elegant courtyard and a superb gateway crowned by a tower. The palace was built in 1662 on the site of a former castle, on the initiative of the Great Elector. Over the following years the palace was greatly enlarged and modernized for members of the royal family, including Frederick the Great (Friedrich II). After a bombing raid in 1945 the palace remained in ruins for many years, but the East German Government decided finally to pull down the remains in 1960. A temporary theatre now occupies the site.

POTSDAM TOWN GATES

The city of Potsdam was enclosed by a wall in 1722. This wall did not serve a defensive purpose – it was supposed to contain criminals and stop soldiers deserting. When the borders of the town were extended in 1733, new districts were also enclosed by the wall. There was a total of five city gates, of which three have survived. Jägertor has survived in its original condition and dates from 1733. Featuring solid, wide pillars, the gate is crowned with a group of sculptures depicting hunting dogs attacking a deer. Nauener Tor was redesigned in 1755 by Johann Gottfried Büring and, interestingly, it is one of the earliest examples of Neo-Gothic design occurring outside Great Britain. The most imposing of the gates is the Brandenburger Tor. It was rebuilt in 1770 in a Neo-Classical style to commemorate victory in the Seven Years' War (see p21). The designers, Gontard and Unger, gave it the appearance of an ancient triumphal arch. At the very top is a number of different groups of sculptures. These include figures from Greek mythology, such as Hercules and Mars.

Nauener Tor

Jägertor

Brandenburger Tor

Stately building of the Marstall (Filmmuseum)

Marstall (Filmmuseum) 22

Breite Str 1A. *Tel* (0331) 27 18 10.
⬭ 10am–6pm daily. 🎫 🚌 695.

This Baroque pavilion, once used as a royal stables, hence the name Marstall, is the only remaining building of a former royal residence. It was first established in 1714 by refashioning the orangery built by Johann Nering in 1685. In 1746 it was extended and refashioned once more, according to a design by the architect GW von Knobelsdorff. It suffered extensive damage in World War II and in 1977, after major restoration, it was converted to a film museum. As well as temporary exhibitions, this museum documents the history and work of the Babelsberg studios, Germany's earliest film studios. Exhibits include old projectors, cameras and other equipment as well as props used in some of the most famous German films.

Potsdam-Museum 23

Benkert Strasse 3. *Tel* (0331) 289 68 03. ⬭ 10am–6pm Tue–Sun. 🎫 🚌 609, 692. 🚋 92, 96.

The Potsdam-Museum's collection embraces natural science and historical exhibits equally, including a display illustrating the geography and nature of the Havel river basin. In the main building, the history of Potsdam is documented up until 1900 and the exhibition continues in two smaller buildings, called the Hiller-Brandt's Häuser (houses). These were built in

1769 by Georg Christian Unger and were a deliberate copy of Inigo Jones's Banqueting House on Whitehall, London.

Cherubs decorating the façade of the Potsdam-Museum

Wasserwerk Sanssouci 24

Breite Strasse. *Tel* (0331) 969 42 02. ⬭ 15 May–11 October: 10am–6pm Sat–Sun. 🚌 605, 606. 🚋 91, 94, X98. 🎫

Although Potsdam once boasted a Russian and a Dutch community, the remarkable mosque (also called Dampfmaschinenhaus) was not built to serve the needs of an Islamic community, but to hide the special steam pump that serviced the fountains in Park Sanssouci. This Moorish-style building, with its minaret and Oriental dome, was designed by Ludwig Persius in 1842. The dome does not serve any useful purpose, although within the minaret there is a huge chimney. While visiting you can see the preserved steam-powered machinery made by the Borsig company.

Telegrafenberg 25

Albert-Einstein-Strasse. Ⓢ *Potsdam Hauptbahnhof.* **Einsteinturm**
🏢 (0331) 29 17 41. ⬭ by appointment only. 🎫 compulsory.

The buildings on the Telegrafenberg are considered to be some of the best 20th-century structures in the world and attract many admirers of modern architecture. The hill received its current name in 1832, when an optical telegraph station linking Berlin and Koblenz was built here. In the late 19th century, various educational institutes were located here, including the Institute of Astrophysics, for which the complex of buildings in yellow brick was built.

The meandering avenues lead to a picturesque clearing where the small Einsteinturm (Einstein's Tower) breaks through the surrounding trees. Specially designed to observe the solar system, the tower was intended to provide information that would support Einstein's Theory of Relativity. It was built in 1920 by Erich Mendelsohn and is regarded as one of the finest architectural examples of German Expressionism. Its fantastical appearance was intended to show what could be achieved with reinforced concrete. However, the costs of the complicated form limited the use of concrete, and above the first storey the building is made from brickwork covered in plaster.

Moorish Wasserwerk Sanssouci, complete with minaret

Filmpark Babelsberg ㉖

This amazing theme park was laid out on the site of the film studios where Germany's first films were produced in 1912. From 1917 the studio belonged to Universum-Film-AG (UFA), which produced some of the most renowned films of the silent era, such as *Metropolis (see p151)*. Nazi propaganda films were also made here. The studio is still operational today, although part of the complex is open to visitors. Expect to see the sets from old films, special effects at work and stuntmen in action.

VISITORS' CHECKLIST

August-Bebel Strasse 26–53 (enter at Grossbeeren Strasse). **Tel** (0331) 721 27 50. 🚌 690, 696. Ⓢ *Griebnitzsee.* ⬜ Apr–Oct: 10am–6pm daily. ⬤ most Mon. 📷 **www**.filmpark-babelsberg.de

Sandmann
Sandmann is a character from an animated television series. Sandmann has entertained children in East Germany from 1959 to the present day.

World of Horrors
You can take a spine-chilling stroll through a world of haunted houses, eerie graveyards and ghostly figures.

Simulator ride

Submarine (U-Boot "Boomer")

Panama – Janosch's Dreamland
A short boat trip will take you through the enchanting world of the children's illustrator Janosch in the company of Little Tiger and Little Bear.

Adventure Restaurant
This is in a medieval castle made for the film Prinz Eisenherz (Prince Valiant).

Main entrance

Stuntshow
at the Vulkan gives the Babelsberg stunt crew the chance to impress and thrill in a spectacular daily show.

THREE GUIDED WALKS

Berlin is full of enchanting parks, gardens, lakes and interesting monuments, and one of the best ways to enjoy them is by going on a guided walk. The three walks suggested in this chapter provide for relaxation far from the hustle and bustle of the city centre. The first takes you onto the picturesque Pfaueninsel (Peacock Island), which at the end of the 18th century was refashioned into a romantic English-style park with garden pavilions and an enchanting little palace. After visiting the island you can pay a short visit to Nikolskoe – a Russian-style *dacha* (country house) built for the future Tsar Nicholas I and his wife, the daughter of King Friedrich Wilhelm III. The second walk begins in Berlin and takes you first through the grounds of the Klein

Statue at Klein Glienicke

Glienicke Park, which was laid out in the 1820s for Prince Karl of Prussia. This route continues across the former border between East and West Germany, in an area which is now part of Potsdam. There you can visit the Romantic-era park of Babelsberg, and the Neo-Gothic palace designed for Prince Wilhelm by Karl Friedrich Schinkel. The third walk, around the forest called Grunewald, takes you initially through a deluxe villa resort of the late 19th century, and then along forest paths to the Grunewaldsee. On the shores of this lake stands an enchanting hunting lodge. From there you can continue walking to the Brücke-Museum. Because each of these three walks leads you across unpaved paths, remember to wear comfortable shoes.

GREATER BERLIN

2/5

2

A 100

Grunewald
(see pp212–13)

A 115

Havel

Pfaueninsel
and Nikolskoe
(see pp208–9)

UNTER DEN EICHEN

Grosser
Wannsee

POTSDAMER CHAUSEE

KÖNIGSTRASSE   1

Klein Glienicke
and Babelsberg
(see pp210–11)

KEY

···· Walking route

▬▬ Autobahn (motorway)

▬▬ Major road

═══ Minor road

─── Railway line

0 kilometres   2

0 miles   2

◁ **A picturesque corner of the Neo-Gothic Babelsberg palace**

Pfaueninsel and Nikolskoe

Statue at the small palace

This walk takes you around Pfaueninsel (Peacock Island). This picturesque park, now a nature reserve, was laid out in 1795 according to a design by Johann August Eyserbeck. Its final form, which you see today, is the work of the renowned landscape architect Peter Joseph Lenné. This pleasant, relaxing walk allows you to explore several interesting sights, and to encounter the peacocks for which the island is named. Afterwards you can have refreshments at the lakeside, or head straight to Nikolskoe, the location of one of Berlin's finest restaurants.

James's Well, deliberately built to resemble a picturesque ruin

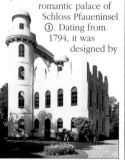

One of the colourful peacocks on Pfaueninsel (Peacock Island)

Around Pfaueninsel

At the jetty ① you board a small passenger ferry which takes you to the island in a few minutes. After disembarking, follow the path which leads to the left. It continues along the edge of the island, gently uphill to the Castellan's House ② and further on to the Swiss House, dating from 1830, in which the gardener lived. Continue along the path to the extensive clearing with a picturesque flower garden, beyond which is the small romantic palace of Schloss Pfaueninsel ③. Dating from 1794, it was designed by

Johann Gottlieb Brendel for Friedrich Wilhelm II and his mistress Wilhelmine Encke (the future Countess Lichtenau). The palace was built of wood, with a façade (hidden away) fashioned in the form of a ruined medieval castle. The façade was visible from Neuer Garten in Potsdam. The cast-iron bridge which links the towers was built in 1807. During the summer months you can go inside the palace to see its furnishings from the 18th and 19th centuries.

After leaving the palace follow the path that leads along the edge, passing by the kitchen pavilion ④ on the left, which is set amid greenery. At the next junction turn gently right into the depths of the island. You will pass by the James's Well ⑤ which was built to resemble an ancient ruin, and cross a meadow heading towards a small wood which contains the Kavalierhaus ⑥. This building was used to provide the

royal household with accommodation. At the front of the house, Karl Friedrich Schinkel installed an authentic façade from a late Gothic house brought over from Danzig (now Gdansk) in Poland. From here you proceed further in the same

PEAUENINSELCHAUSSEE

NIKOLSKOER WEG

| 0 metres | 200 |
| 0 yards | 200 |

KEY

••• Suggested route

– – Ferry route

⛴ Ferry boarding point

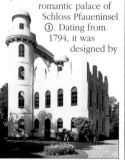

The Neo-Gothic Schloss Pfaueninsel designed by Johann Brendel

direction, and emerge again in a large clearing. To the left you can marvel at the Parschenkessel bay ⑦ in the distance, surrounded by dead trees on which cormorants nest. Take the path on the left to the Neo-Gothic Dairy ⑧

Guests on the terrace of the Blockhaus Nikolskoe in summer

mausoleum in Schlosspark Charlottenburg *(see p163)* in 1829. The path leads further along the edge of the lake, while on the right side among the trees you pass the stone commemorating Johannes Kunckel, an alchemist who lived on Pfaueninsel in the 17th century. In his quest to uncover how to make gold he, in fact, discovered a method of producing ruby-coloured glass. Carry on further through the forest, passing the Gothic Bridge ⑪, and then take the path to the right up towards the hill of the Aviary ⑫, home to multicoloured parrots and pheasants. From here you continue towards the tall column of a Fountain ⑬ designed by Martin Friedrich Rabe in 1824. Next, walk onward to the jetty, passing the market gardens with their hothouses on the way.

From the Jetty to Nikolskoe

Once you've taken the little ferry back to the mainland, head off to the right, going

Havel

and the Dutch House ⑨. This was a cow shed and dates from 1802, while the Dairy is an artificial ruin of a medieval abbey dating from 1795. From here take the path along the edge of the lake heading south; you can marvel at the wonderful views. To the right by the edge of the forest you can see Luisentempel ⑩ in the form of a Greek temple. Its sandstone portico at the front was moved to the island from the

TIPS FOR WALKERS

Beginning of the walk: the jetty for the ferry to Pfaueninsel.
Length: 4.4 km (2.7 miles).
Duration: 2.5–3 hours.
Getting there: Bus 216 or 316 from S-Bahn Wannsee; or ferry from Wannsee or Potsdam.
Stops: Pfaueninsel has no restaurants. "Wirtshaus zur Pfaueninsel" is by the jetty; "Blockhaus Nikolskoe" is in Nikolskoe.
Schloss Pfaueninsel
☐ Apr–Oct: 10am–5pm daily; Nov–Dec: 10am–5:30pm Sat–Sun, hols. **Tel** 805 86 830.

south. When you come to the fork take the left hand path leading gently uphill. This leads to the church of Saints Peter and Paul ⑭, which rises above a large terrace from where there are pretty views of Pfaueninsel. The church was built between the years 1834 and 1837, according to a design by Friedrich August Stüler. The small, orderly, body of the church is fronted by a tower crowned by an onion-shaped dome, which reflects Russian Orthodox sacral architecture. This links to the adjacent Blockhaus "Nikolskoe" ⑮, a Russian-style wooden *dacha* (country house), built in 1819 by the architect Snethlage, who created the Alexandrowka estate in Potsdam. The *dacha* was a present from King Friedrich Wilhelm III to his daughter and son-in-law, the future Tsar Nicholas I. Following a fire in 1985 the *dacha* was reconstructed, and it currently houses a restaurant. Nearby you will find a bus-stop where you can catch buses back to the S-Bahn Wannsee.

The little ferry on the Havel river which takes passengers to Pfaueninsel

Glienicke and Babelsberg

This guided walk takes you through an area covered by two interesting palace-park complexes – Glienicke and Babelsberg. They were built originally for members of the royal family during the mid-19th century. The buildings of Glienicke were designed by Schinkel, Persius and von Arnim in a Neo-Classical style. Peter Joseph Lenné created the charming park in which they are located. Babelsberg has a more romantic park that was completed by Hermann von Pückler-Muskau. It is maintained in a completely different style, with regal Neo-Gothic pavilions.

A griffin in Glienicke

Mosaic from the Klosterhof in the gardens of Klein Glienicke

Around Glienicke

The walk begins by the main gate leading into the park. The southern section of the park has the feel of an Italianate Arcadian garden. Soon on the left you will see the Stibadium ①, a roofed pavilion designed by Ludwig Persius. Nearby you can marvel at the imposing Fountain of Lions ②, decorated with gilded figures of these royal beasts. The fountain stands on the axis of the palace ③ which was built in 1825, according to a design

by Karl Friedrich Schinkel for Prince Carl of Prussia. During the summer, you can visit the palace between 10am and 6pm. Beyond the symmetrical, Neo-Classical building extends an irregular cluster of buildings, grouped around a courtyard with a veranda, which include a pergola and staff cottages. You pass by the palace and approach the Coach House ④, designed by Schinkel but refurbished several times. This now houses the Coach House restaurant (see p243).

Beyond the Coach House you can see the orangery and greenhouses built by Persius. A path leads in the direction of the lake, but on the way it is worth diverting to the right to the Klosterhof ⑥, a mock monastery with pavilions, also by Persius. In the walls of these buildings are numerous Byzantine and Romanesque architectural elements from Italy. Further to the north extends a second "wild" section of the park created to resemble an alpine and Carpathian landscape, with man-made waterfalls, planks

The reconstructed Gothic Gerichts-laube (arcaded courthouse)

for crossing the water, and hunting lodges. You can return in the direction of the lake and go up to the Casino ⑦, which once contained guest apartments. From here a path extending along the lake takes you to the Grosse Neugierde ⑧, a circular pavilion with a roof supported by Doric columns, based on the Athenian monument to Lysikrates from the 4th century BC. From here there are beautiful views across the Havel river and Glienicker Brücke ⑨, known paradoxically as the bridge of unity under the East German

contain original Roman and
Byzantine fragments.

From Glienicke to Babelsberg
On leaving the park you cross
to the other side of Potsdamer
Chaussee and proceed along
Mövenstrasse, passing the
massive building of the Jagdschloss Glienicke ⑪ on the
right. Located on the site of
an earlier hunting lodge,
its Neo-Mannerist appear-
ance is the result of a
massive rebuilding proc-
ess undertaken
in 1889 by Albert
Geyer, on behalf of
Prince Friedrich
Leopold. It now
houses an interna-
tional meeting centre
as well as an academy
of folk art. Passing the
Jagdschloss you turn
right into Waldmüller-
strasse, then right again
into Lankestrasse, which
leads you to the bridge linking Glienicke with
Babelsberg.

Around Schloss Babelsberg
From the bridge you head right
towards the engine house ⑫,
designed by Persius to look
like a medieval castle with a
tall tower covering the
chimney. From here you head
towards Schloss Babelsberg
⑬, designed by Karl Friedrich
Schinkel for the future Kaiser
Wilhelm I of Germany. The
palace was built between 1833
and 1835 in a Neo-Gothic
style and shows the influence
of English architecture on
Schinkel. This beautiful,
irregular building with many

regime. The
border with
West Berlin ran
across this bridge,
where the exchange
of spies was conduc-
ted during the Cold
War. You return via a
path along the wall of the
main gate, passing the Kleine
Neugierde ⑩, a pavilion
serving as a tea room. This
was built in the form of an
ancient temple, and its walls

Babelsberg's Neo-Gothic Flatow-turm dating from 1853 to 1856

towers and bay windows is
one of Schinkel's greatest
works. Visitors can go inside.
 From here, take the path
leading along the edge of the
Havel to the so-called Kleines
Schloss ⑭. Another Neo-
Gothic palace, although much
smaller in scale, this was where
ladies of the court once
resided. It now houses a café.
 From here you proceed
further to the edge of the
lake, taking the left branch to
the Neo-Gothic stable ⑮, and
further to the Gerichtslaube
(Gothic arcaded courthouse)
⑯ which was moved here
from Berlin. The final sight on
this walk is the Flatowturm ⑰,
a Neo-Gothic tower dating
from 1853 to 1856, from
which there are marvellous
views of the surrounding area.
From here follow the path to
the park exit at Grenzstrasse.
Turning left, you reach the
bus stop for the No. 694
which goes to S-Bahn
Babelsberg station.

TIPS FOR WALKERS
Beginning of the walk: *bus
stop at Glienicke.* ***Length:*** *4.2
km (2.6 miles).* ***Duration:*** *3
hours.* ***Getting there:*** *bus 116
from S-Bahn station Wannsee or
ferry from Wannsee or Potsdam.*
Stops: *Café at Park Babelsberg;
Coach House at Glienicke.*
Schloss Babelsberg
🚪 *Apr–Oct: 10am–6pm
Tue–Sun.* ***Tel*** *(0331) 969 42 50
for latest information.*

**The Neo-Gothic Schloss Babelsberg,
designed by KF Schinkel**

KEY
• • • Suggested route
⛴ Ferry boarding point

0 metres 300
0 yards 300

Grunewald

This walk leads initially through one of Berlin's most elegant residential areas, established in 1889. Once the haunt of politicians, wealthy industrialists, renowned artists and academics, some villas now serve as the headquarters of academic institutes. This walk continues through the forest to a small hunting lodge with an interesting art collection, and ends at the edge of the Grunewald in a residential estate of elegant villas, home of the Brücke-Museum.

The elegant villa at Winklerstrasse No. 11

From Bahnhof Grunewald to Hagenstrasse

From the S-Bahn Grunewald station follow the signs to "Grunewald (Ort)". Be sure to take a close look at the station itself ① – this picturesque wooden framed building was built in 1899. The station has a dark past, though, as Berlin's Jews were transported from here to the concentration camps. From the square in front of the station go along Winklerstrasse, which turns left. Along the way you will pass stunningly beautiful villas. The Neo-Classical house at No. 15, dating from 1899, was home to architect Ewald Becher ②. Not much further on the same side of the road, at No. 11, is a villa dating from 1906 ③. It was designed by Hermann Muthesius, who transplanted onto German soil the style of English rustic building. On the right at No. 12 is Villa Maren, dating from 1897, an example of a Neo-Renaissance building in the style of an Italian palazzo with *sgraffito* decorations ④. The villa at No. 8–10,

dating from 1902, boasts costly stone elevations, which fan out richly with decorations in the German Renaissance style ⑤. By this villa turn right into Hasensprung, which leads across the bridge decorated with running hares, dividing Diana-see from Königssee. You reach Königsallee and turn left before immediately turning right into Lassenstrasse, and then right again into Bismarckstrasse, which leads to a small square where you can marvel at the picturesque Neo-Gothic Grunewald-Kirche ⑥. From here go left into Furtwänglerstrasse, where it is worth looking at the villa at No. 15, a beautiful example of a southern German country house ⑦. Next turn right into Hubertusbader Strasse, where at No. 25 an interesting villa has survived with Neo-Classical motifs ⑧, which is the work of Arnold Hartmann dating from 1896. He is also responsible for the villa at No. 23

Rose window, Grunewald-Kirche

Seebergsteig, featuring fantastic elevations decorated with Secessionist motifs ⑨. From here continue along Hubertusbader Strasse to Hagenstrasse.

From Hagenstrasse to the Brücke-Museum

You cut through Hagenstrasse and continue further, straight into Wildpfad, where you turn left in Waldmeisterstrasse, which leads along the fence of the grounds of private clubs. Turn right into Eichhörnchensteig, which gradually becomes surrounded by forest and changes from being a

Königssee

Herthasee

Bismarckbrücke

Hubertussee

⑥

⑦   TONI, LESSLER STR.   JOSEPH-
⑧   JOACHIM-PLATZ
⑨

MORGENROTHSTRASSE

REHKITZSTEIG

FRISCHLINGSSTEIG

WILDENTENSTEIG

FISCHOTTERSTEIG

BIBERSTEIG

PÜCKLERSTR.

ücklerteich ⑫   BUSSARDSTEIG
               KÄUZCHENSTEIG

CLAYALLEE

0 metres   400

0 yards   400

KEY

• • • Suggested route

Ⓢ S-Bahn

road into a forest path. Once past the grounds of the private clubs, follow a road which goes gently to the right, and down to the edge of the picturesque Grunewaldsee. Turn left and continue along its edge to Jagdschloss Grunewald ⑩. This is one of the oldest civic buildings to survive in Berlin. It was built for the Elector Joachim II in 1542, and around 1700 it was rebuilt in a Baroque style. Through the gate you enter a courtyard enclosed on three sides with household buildings. In the small palace is Berlin's only surviving Renaissance hall. It houses a collection of paintings, with canvases by Rubens and van Dyck among others. In the east wing is the small Waldmuseum, with illustrations that depict forest life. Following a fire, which destroyed the roof and other parts of the building, the Jagdschloss underwent extensive renovation work and reopened in 2009.

From the palace you proceed further along the edge to Forsthaus Paulsborn ⑪. This picturesque building was constructed in 1905, according to a design by Friedrich Wilhelm Göhre *(see p243)*. The entire building is maintained in the style of a hunting lodge with decorations that reflect hunting themes. During the summer the garden is filled

The household buildings in the hunting lodge in Grunewald

with tables, where you can enjoy a tasty meal and have a rest, following the walk.

From Paulsborn you return to Jagdschloss Grunewald; at the crossroads you should take the central avenue sign-posted "Wilmersdorf". This leads through the forest and emerges on Pücklerstrasse. Passing modern deluxe villas you continue straight on, and then turn right into Fohlenweg, then turn right again into Bussardsteig, at the end of which is the Brücke-Museum *(see p179)* ⑫. It is also worth looking at the exhibition of sculptures by Bernhard Heliger arranged in the garden surrounding the villa at Käuzchensteig No. 8. From here you continue to Clayallee where buses on the No. 115 route operate.

Detail from Toni-Lessler-Strasse No. 23

TIPS FOR WALKERS

Beginning of the walk: *Grunewald S-Bahn station.*
Distance: *3 km (1.8 miles).*
Duration: *2.5–3 hours.*
Getting there: *S-Bahn line 3 or 7; U-Bahn Oskar-Helene-Heim; Bus 115.*
Museum: *Jagdschloss Grunewald.* ***Tel*** *813 35 97.*
🕐 *Apr–Oct: 10am–6pm Thu–Sun; Nov–Mar: guided tours only, 11am, 1pm, 3pm Sat–Sun & hols.*
Stops: *The Grunewald area has numerous cafés and restaurants, including Forsthaus Paulsborn near Jagdschloss Grunewald.*

Restaurant in the Forsthaus Paulsborn near Jagdschloss Grunewald

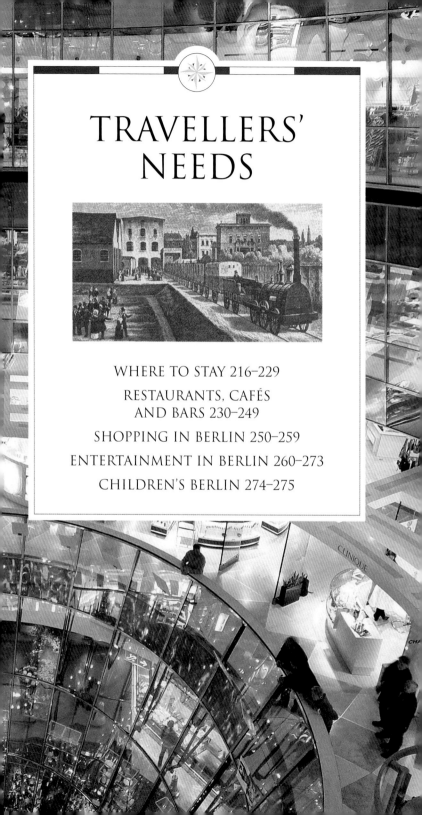

TRAVELLERS' NEEDS

WHERE TO STAY

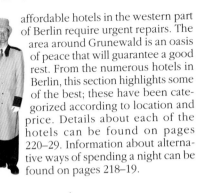

Berlin has a good selection of hotels to suit any budget. Many of the expensive hotels belong to well-known international chains, but you can also find reasonably priced rooms in and around the centre. There are good-quality mid-range hotels in eastern Berlin, where many new hotels have been built recently. There is no lack of luxurious hotels in eastern Berlin, either, particularly around Unter den Linden. Many of the more affordable hotels in the western part of Berlin require urgent repairs. The area around Grunewald is an oasis of peace that will guarantee a good rest. From the numerous hotels in Berlin, this section highlights some of the best; these have been categorized according to location and price. Details about each of the hotels can be found on pages 220–29. Information about alternative ways of spending a night can be found on pages 218–19.

The elegant lobby of the Hotel Adlon Kempinski (see p220)

WHERE TO LOOK

There are a few areas in Berlin with large concentrations of hotels. In each area there is usually at least one luxury hotel as well as several more affordable places. In Charlottenburg, around Kurfürstendamm and Tauentzienstrasse, are well-known hotels, such as the Kempinski, Savoy, Palace Berlin and the Steigenberger. Bear in mind that this part of Berlin was severely damaged during World War II and the majority of these hotels occupy modern buildings; hotels in old buildings, like the Brandenburger Hof, are a rarity. Inexpensive hotels and pensions can be found in the side streets off the main road, but ask to see the rooms before you decide. Good hotels are also situated in the east part of Tiergarten, around Lützowufer.

The most luxurious hotels can be found in Eastern Berlin, where many first-class hotels occupy lavishly restored historic landmark buildings or have been built in response to Berlin's growing appeal to tourists. The Adlon (now called Hotel Adlon Kempinski), Regent and Hotel de Rome, situated in the western part of Mitte around Unter den Linden, are the most luxurious. In the eastern part of this area, around Alexanderplatz, the hotels are more reasonably priced but still offer good-quality rooms.

Grunewald is an oasis of peace far from the bustle of Berlin. There is the luxurious Schlosshotel Berlin, as well as cosy pensions and little hotels, some of them in 19th-century villas and palaces.

If you want to be certain of finding a room and you don't mind staying outside the centre of Berlin, you should head for Neukölln. Here, close to Treptower Park, is the enormous Estrel – the largest hotel in Germany.

HOTEL PRICES

Hotel prices in Berlin do not alter much with the season. However, major events and trade fairs do push up prices. Many more luxurious hotels offer weekend discounts and often, if you just turn up without a reservation, you can find yourself a good deal. If you intend to stay for an extended period of time, try to negotiate a better rate. Many hotels offer discounts if you book ahead via their website.

HIDDEN EXTRAS

In Germany, taxes are included in hotel room rates, but you are expected to tip for any additional services, such as bringing luggage to the room or booking a theatre ticket. Hotels from the Dorint chain are an exception: they provide a range of services (such as free bicycle hire) at no additional cost.

Swimming pool at the Hotel de Rome (see p221)

◁ Galeries Lafayette, Friedrichstrasse

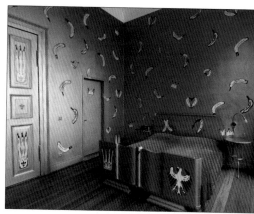

One of the artist-decorated rooms in the Arte Luise Kunsthotel *(see p222)*

There is no hard and fast rule about breakfast: it is best to ask if it is included in the price when making a reservation.

Most Berlin hotels have their own parking spaces, but rates are sometimes exorbitant. Ask about telephone charges before using the phone in your room and check the exchange rates and the commission for cashing travellers' cheques before using this service. Items from the minibar and paid-television channels can also turn out to be surprisingly costly. Wi-Fi is available at most hotels, however you may be charged for using the Internet.

FACILITIES

There is no standardized system of categorizing hotels by stars in Germany, although the price of a room usually reflects the quality. Small hotels usually include breakfast – typically rolls, jam, chocolate spread, cereal, cold meats, cheese and coffee – in the price of the room. They will probably not have a restaurant and their services are limited. Larger hotels tend to provide a full American buffet on top of the traditional German fare.

If you are staying for a longer period, consider an Aparthotel – an apartment, complete with a fully equipped kitchen. You can also find private apartments for short-term rent on websites such as www.craigslist.org/berlin. This is a good idea if you are travelling with a small group.

SAUNAS AND SPAS

Many of the more expensive hotels are equipped with spa and sauna facilities. These are usually unisex (though some spas have women's days) and it is very unusual for either sex to wear a swimsuit. Whilst a truly relaxing activity, guests should be prepared to only wear towels and for other sauna users to be in the nude. In fact, wearing swimsuits in sauna areas is often considered rude and unhygienic, particularly in Finnish or steam saunas, as well as in whirlpools. Spa etiquette usually also calls for silence in the room. In dry Finnish saunas, an "Aufguss", the repeated infusion of fresh herbs and heat is usually announced.

When entering a steam sauna, clean the seat before you sit down. There is usually

Conference room in the Villa Kastania *(see p229)*

a water hose at the entrance for this purpose. After 8–15 minutes in the sauna, shower or rinse off with ice-cold water (the cold-water bath is only suitable for the physically fit). Rest and then continue the cycle once or twice. Do not drink alcohol when visiting a sauna, and make sure you take in fluids and vitamins (usually offered in the form of water and lemon slices).

Many independently-owned spas and health clubs, such as Aspria, Ars Vitalis, and Le Méridien Spa, offer suberb services and larger facilities than most hotels. Among hotel spas, those at the Grand Hyatt, Hotel de Rome and Hotel Intercontinental are exceptional. In winter, try the Badeschiff Arena, a sauna and swimming pool complex built on pontoons on the Spree river *(see p272)*.

HOW TO BOOK

You can book a room in Berlin by mail, telephone, email or online. If you prefer, you can use the city's tourist service **Berlin Tourismus Marketing** *(see p219)*, www.visit-berlin.de. This company can make your booking in hotels throughout Berlin. When making a reservation, however, be prepared to give your credit card details.

If you are already in Berlin and would like to find a comfortable room, your best option is to go to one of the large tourist information bureaux. Some of the best of these are situated in the **Neues Kranzler-Eck**, at the **Brandenburg Gate**, and at **Hauptbahnhof** and **Alexanderplatz** *(see p219)*.

PRIVATE ROOMS

Bed & Breakfast-style accommodation is not particularly popular in Berlin, although this kind of service can be found in some of the residential districts far from the city centre. You can obtain information about them from tourist information bureaux and the other organizations whose numbers are listed in the Directory *(see p219)*.

The luxurious lounge at the Kempinski Hotel *(see p226)*

TRAVELLING WITH CHILDREN

Travelling with children in Berlin should not present a problem. A cot can be requested in most hotels, and there is usually no extra charge for having a small child in the room, although an extra bed for an older child may sometimes incur a cost. In better hotels, a reliable babysitter can be obtained at a few hours' notice. In hotel restaurants, high chairs for children are standard.

The elegant lobby area of the Marriott Hotel *(see p223)*

DISABLED TRAVELLERS

Nearly all top-quality and luxury hotels are able to accommodate disabled travellers – at least one entrance will have wheelchair access and some rooms will have specially-adapted bathrooms. Unfortunately, the situation in mid-range and lower standard hotels is not as promising; special equipment is a rarity

and in many cases these hotels are not situated on the ground floor. In very old buildings, there may not be an elevator. The **Hotel Mondial** *(see p226)*, located near Kurfürstendamm, is recommended for disabled travellers. It has many facilities for wheelchair users in all its public rooms and has as many as 22 bedrooms equipped for people with special needs.

DEPOSITS

In many Berlin hotels, a deposit may be requested either when reserving the room or upon checking in at the hotel. A credit card number is the most common way to secure a room over the telephone. If you do not have one, however, be prepared to use cash to pay about 20 to 40 per cent of the price for one night's stay. The amount you pay as a deposit should always be credited to the final bill. In some smaller hotels or pensions, don't be

surprised if you are asked to pay for your first night's accommodation in full when you arrive.

YOUTH HOSTELS

It is easy to find inexpensive accommodation in Berlin at a youth hostel. The **DJH (Landesverband Berlin-Brandenburg)**, an organization that belongs to the International Youth Hostels Association, gives discounts to all its members. Membership is usually inexpensive and you will have to join to stay at a hostel. The DJH has hostels in different locations throughout Berlin. There are also many independent youth hostels and hotels for students in Berlin that do not belong to any organization. You can find them at www.hostelworld.com.

The type of accommodation offered usually consists of dormitory-style rooms with bunk beds. There is often a communal bathroom on each floor and a kitchen is usually available for cooking your own meals. Most youth hostels have a dining room where breakfast and a hot evening meal are served. Some youth hostels are closed during the day, allowing no access to the rooms; confirm this in advance.

CAMPING

Camping is a popular pastime throughout Germany, and the **Deutscher Camping Club** has a lot of information about campsites in and around Berlin. This organization also

Illuminated façade of the Westin Grand *(see p220)*

provides information about other independently run campsites in Berlin.

Campsites are open usually from the beginning of April until the end of October. There are two exceptions: the Berlin-Kladow in Spandau and the Am Krossinsee in Köpenick, which are open year round. The majority of people that stay at campsites are young, particularly during the Oktoberfest *(see p50)* and in June, when the Christopher Street Day Parade takes place *(see p49)*. During these times some campsites can be very busy and noisy.

The spacious lobby of the Hotel Palace *(see p226)*

ORGANIZED YOUTH GROUPS

Berlin has a large base of accommodation for organized youth groups. Most of these consist of hostel-style accommodation,

situated on the outskirts of the city, often in green belt areas. They were established not only for the purpose of school trips to Berlin but also for children from West Berlin; until the unification of Germany in 1990, it was difficult for youth groups to

organize trips to the country-side so they had to opt for trips to the Grunewald instead. Information about availability and reservations is offered by **Berlin Tourismus Marketing** and by larger tourist information centres, such as the one at Neues Kranzler Eck.

DIRECTORY

INFORMATION AND BOOKING

Berlin Tourismus Marketing
Am Karlsbad 11, Berlin.
Map 12 D1.
Tel *25 00 25*.
www.visitberlin.de

Tourist Information
Neues Kranzler-Eck,
Kurfürstendamm 21.
Map 10 D1.
⏰ *10am–8pm Mon–Sat,
10am–6pm Sun.*

Alexanderplatz
in Alexa Shopping Centre,
near Alexanderplatz.
⏰ *10am–8pm Mon–Sat.*

Brandenburg Gate
Pariser Platz,
southern building.
Map 6 E3, 15 A3.
⏰ *10am–6pm daily.*

Hauptbahnhof
Europaplatz 1, level 0,
northern entrance.
Map 6 D1.
⏰ *8am–10pm daily.*

Potsdam Tourismus Service
Brandenburger Strasse 3.
Tel *(0331) 275 58 0.*
Fax *(0331) 275 58 29.*
www.potsdamtourismus.de

CAMPING

Deutscher Camping Club
Kladower Damm 213-17,
14089 Berlin. **Map** 10 E3,
10 F3. **Tel** *218 60 71.*
⏰ *10:30am–6pm Mon,
8am–4pm Wed,
8am–1pm Fri.*

DCC-Campingplatz Berlin-Kladow (Spandau)
Krampnitzer Weg 111–117
14089 Berlin.
Tel *365 27 97.*
Fax *365 12 45.*

YOUTH HOSTELS

DJH (Landes-verband Berlin-Brandenburg)
Schulstrasse 9, 14482
Berlin. **Tel** *264 95 20.*

Hostelworld
www.hostelworld.com

Jugendherberge Berlin International
Kluckstrasse 3
10785 Berlin.
Map 11 C1.
Tel *747 68 79 10.*
Fax *747 68 79 11.*

Jugendherberge Ernst Reuter
Hermsdorfer Damm 48
13467 Berlin.
Tel *(0331) 581 30.*
Fax *(0331) 581 34 44.*

Jugendherberge Berlin am Wannsee
Badeweg 1, 14129 Berlin.
Tel *803 20 34.*
Fax *803 59 08.*

DISABLED TRAVELLERS

Berliner Behinderten-verband
Jägerstrasse 63d
10117 Berlin-Mitte.
Tel *204 38 47.*

Behinderten-beauftragter des Landes Berlin
Oranienstrasse 106
10997 Berlin.
Tel *90 28 29 17.*

BED & BREAKFAST

Bed & Breakfast in Berlin
Tel *746 14 46.*
Fax *44 05 05 83.*
www.bed-and-breakfast-berlin.de

Coming Home
Tel *21 79 800.*
Fax *21 79 80 21*
www.coming-home.org

Erste Mitwohn-zentrale
Sybelstrasse 53.
10629 Berlin-
Charlottenburg.
Map 9 A2. **Tel** *324 30 31.*
Fax *324 99 77.*

Fine and mine
Neue Schönhauser Str. 20
10178 Berlin.
Map 7 C2. **Tel** *23 55 120.*
Fax *23 55 12 12.*
@ *office@fineandmine.de*

Wohnwitz
Holsteinische Strasse 55.
10717 Berlin-Wilmersdorf.
Map 9 C4, 9 C5.
Tel *861 82 22.*
Fax *861 82 72.*
www.wohnwitz.com

Choosing a Hotel

The choice of hotels selected in this guide is based on quality of accommodation and service as well as location. The list of hotels covers all the areas and price categories with additional information to help you choose a hotel that best meets your needs. Hotels within the same price category are listed alphabetically.

PRICE CATEGORIES
Listed below are the price ranges for a double room per night, including all taxes:

€ Under €80
€€ €81–130
€€€ €131–180
€€€€ €181–230
€€€€€ Over €230

AROUND UNTER DEN LINDEN

Arcotel John F.   €€
Werderscher Markt 11, 10117 **Tel** *405 046 0* **Fax** *405 046 100* **Rooms** *190*   **Map** *7 B4, 16 E3*

Located between Museum Island and Gendarmenmarkt, this hotel is an excellent, stylish and affordable starting point for exploring the city. Large, airy rooms furnished with much love for detail. Free Wi-Fi and a rocking chair (as a tribute to John F. Kennedy) in every room. The wellness area includes a steam bath and sauna. **www.arcotel.at**

Artist Riverside Hotel & Spa   €€€
Friedrichstrasse 106, 10117 **Tel** *284 900* **Fax** *284 90 49* **Rooms** *40*   **Map** *6 F3*

Proudly dubbing itself *tolles Hotel* (great hotel), this delightful place has late 19th-century, individual rooms stuffed with colourful Art-Nouveau antiques. When making a reservation, you might like to ask for the biggest and nicest room (Wedding), which even has a waterbed. **www.great-hotel.com**

Berlin Hilton   €€€
Mohrenstrasse 30, 10117 **Tel** *202 30* **Fax** *202 342 69* **Rooms** *591*   **Map** *7 A4, 16 D4*

This hotel is near the Gendarmenmarkt. There are spectacular views of the Konzerthaus and two churches from the rooms at the front of the building. The bedrooms are wonderfully furnished and spacious, and there are two splendid restaurants. **www.hilton.com**

Hotel Gendarm   €€€
Charlottenstrasse 61, 10117 **Tel** *206 06 60* **Fax** *206 066 66* **Rooms** *27*   **Map** *7 A4*

The Gendarm's reputation as one of the best and most popular smaller hotels in Berlin is more than justified. An excellent service, a great location off Gendarmenmarkt and historic, elegantly furnished rooms make this a serious competitor for the big five-star hotels nearby. **www.hotel-gendarm-berlin.de**

Mandala Suites   €€€
Friedrichstrasse 185-190, 10117 **Tel** *202 920* **Fax** *202 929 20* **Rooms** *81*   **Map** *6 F4, 15 C4*

Offering suites for a price depending on the size and the duration of stay, the Mandala provides services including car and bicycle rental, shopping, clothes repair and CD players in all rooms. Ideal for a week-long stay, though even on a per-night basis the prices are much lower than many other hotels. **www.themandala.de**

Maritim ProArte Hotel Berlin   €€€
Friedrichstrassse 151, 10117 **Tel** *203 35* **Fax** *203 334 090* **Rooms** *403*   **Map** *6 F3, 15 C2*

Although this hotel aims to attract mainly conference business, its central location and excellent facilities make it one of Berlin's most attractive hotels. An ultra-modern building with furnishings and art displays, it has lavish rooms in three categories with marble and granite bathrooms. **www.maritim.de**

Meliá Hotel Berlin   €€€
Friedrichstrasse 103, 10117 **Tel** *206 079 00* **Fax** *206 790 444* **Rooms** *364*   **Map** *6 F2*

Based in the heart of the entertainment district on Friedrichstrasse, this Spanish-owned hotel is a perfect base from which to visit Museum Island, Unter den Linden and Hackesche Markt. It offers bright, modern rooms, combined with first-class amenities. One of the restaurants serves Spanish dishes and tapas. **www.meliaberlin.com**

Westin Grand   €€€€
Friedrichstrasse 158-164, 10117 **Tel** *202 70* **Fax** *202 733 62* **Rooms** *358*   **Map** *6 F3, 15 C3*

A lavish hotel built at the end of the 19th century in Empire and Secessionist styles. The main hall is particularly impressive, with a huge atrium and a breathtaking staircase. Close to most historic sites as well as various good restaurants and cafés. **www.westin-grand.com**

Hotel Adlon Kempinski   €€€€€
Unter den Linden 77, 10117 **Tel** *226 10* **Fax** *226 122 22* **Rooms** *386*   **Map** *6 E3, 15 A3*

This deluxe hotel located near the Brandenburg Gate opened in 1997 and continues the traditions of its illustrious predecessor, which was bombed during World War II. Marble, leather and exotic woods line the interior. The hotel has a good service. Special rooms for people with allergies. **www.kempinski.com**

Key to Symbols *see back cover flap*

Hotel de Rome
☰ 🅿 🍴 ⚏ 🛠 🖵 🗐   €€€€€

Behrenstrasse 37, 10117 **Tel** *460 60 90* **Fax** *460 60 92 000* **Rooms** *146*   **Map** *7 A4*

The shining star among the city's first-class hotels is one of Sir Rocco Forte's luxurious, imaginative hotels. It is hidden behind the façade of a former bank, close to Unter den Linden, Friedrichstrasse and many other sights. Rooms are fairly large and some offer great views of historic Opernplatz. Service is impeccable. **www.hotelderome.com**

Regent Hotel
☰ 🅿 🍴 🛠 🖵 🗐   €€€€€

Charlottenstrasse 49, 10117 **Tel** *203 38* **Fax** *203 361 19* **Rooms** *195*   **Map** *7 A4, 16 D3*

Ranked as one of the best hotels in Berlin, the Regent Hotel near the Gendarmenmarkt has an impressive façade and opulent Neo-Baroque interiors. It offers luxurious rooms in three categories and an impeccable service. The restaurant here serves excellent light cuisine. **www.theregentberlin.com**

Sofitel Berlin Gendarmenmarkt
☰ 🅿 🍴 🛠 🖵 🗐   €€€€€

Charlottenstrasse 50-52, 10117 **Tel** *203 750* **Fax** *203 751 00* **Rooms** *92*   **Map** *7 A4, 16 D4*

This hotel offers well-furnished rooms and an excellent service. Conveniently located near the Gendarmenmarkt, not far from Unter den Linden. The Aigner restaurant, with its Viennese themed interior, specializes in modern Austrian cuisine. **www.accorhotels.com**

MUSEUM ISLAND

Art'otel Berlin Mitte
☰ 🅿 🍴 🛠   €€

Wallstrasse 70-73, 10179 **Tel** *240 620 22* **Fax** *240 622 22* **Rooms** *109*   **Map** *7 C4*

Overlooking the Spree river, this upmarket hotel is well-priced and one of the most popular places in Mitte. Inside, it is modern with simple and elegant furniture. In summer there is a café on a riverboat tied to the bank of the Spree. The hotel is popular with young, culture-oriented guests. **www.artotel.de**

Derag Hotel Grosser Kurfürst
☰ 🅿 🍴 🖵 🗐   €€

Neue Rossstrasse 11-12, 10179 **Tel** *246 000* **Fax** *246 003 00* **Rooms** *144*   **Map** *7 C4*

A good middle-range hotel, with modern facilities and a convenient location close to the U-Bahn station Märkisches Museum. The breathtaking lobby has a statue of the Great Elector. The hotel offers personal and impeccable services. The restaurant has a pretty patio beside the Spree. **www.deraghotels.de**

Derag Residenz Hotel Henriette
☰ 🅿 🍴 🖵   €€

Neue Rossstrasse 13, 10179 **Tel** *246 009 00* **Fax** *246 009 40* **Rooms** *54*   **Map** *8 C5*

The small and intimate Henriette is the nicest – and the most unknown – of the many Derag hotels in town. It exudes an incredibly elegant, historic flair, with oak furniture, precious carpets and beds. The hotel offers a great service. **www.deraghotels.de**

Hotel Luisenhof
☰ 🅿 🛠   €€€

Köpenicker Strasse 92, 10179 **Tel** *24 62810* **Fax** *24 28160* **Rooms** *27*   **Map** *8 D5*

Situated at the Märkisches Museum, this hotel occupies the oldest building (1882) in this part of Berlin. Extensive restoration has created a charming hotel with nice rooms and a delightful restaurant in the cellar. Given its size and decor, the Luisensuite is a great deal. **www.luisenhof.de**

Radisson Blu Hotel Berlin
☰ 🅿 🍴 ⚏ 🛠 🖵 🗐   €€€€

Karl-Liebknecht-Strasse 3, 10178 **Tel** *238 280* **Fax** *238 28 10* **Rooms** *427*   **Map** *16 F2, 7 B3*

The Radisson is one of the hotel group's stars. It is built around the AquaDom, a huge, cylindric aquarium in the lobby. Standard rooms face this atrium; superior rooms and suites overlook the neighbouring Berliner Dom and Alexanderplatz. All rooms are furnished with five-star amenities. **www.radissonblu.com**

EAST OF THE CENTRE

Citystay Hostel
🖵 🍴   €

Rosenstrasse 16, 10178 **Tel** *236 240 31* **Fax** *279 071 70* **Rooms** *55*   **Map** *7 C2*

Housed in an 1896 former department store building, this clean and safe hostel offers dorms and basic rooms, en suite or with shared facilities. Impeccably central and yet on a quiet street between Hackescher Markt and Alexanderplatz. Organic food and cocktails served at a little cafeteria. There's also a chill-out garden courtyard. **www.citystay.de**

Park Inn Berlin Alexanderplatz
☰ 🅿 🍴 🖵 🗐   €€

Alexanderplatz 8, 10178 **Tel** *238 90* **Fax** *238 943 05* **Rooms** *1012*   **Map** *8 D2*

This 37-storey building was constructed under the GDR and, despite modernization, has an ugly exterior. Completely refurbished, it has standard rooms with very comfortable beds and great views of central Berlin. A rooftop casino and various restaurants offer entertainment. **www.parkinn.de**

Lux 11   🏠 🅿 🍴 ♨ 📺 🖩   €€€

Rosa-Luxemburgstr 9-13, 10178 **Tel** *936 28 00* **Fax** *936 280 80* **Rooms** *120*

The sleek Lux 11 hotel located in the heart of the hip Mitte district offers a unique blend of bright and ultra-modern, sleek but minimalist designed rooms and apartments in a historic 19th century tenement house typical of Berlin. The chic Luchs Asian restaurant makes the hotel a perfect choice. **www.lux-eleven.com**

Alexander Plaza Berlin   🏠 🅿 🍴 📺 🖩   €€€€

Rosenstrasse 1, 10178 **Tel** *240 010* **Fax** *240 017 77* **Rooms** *92*   *Map 7 B2, 16 F1*

This top-quality hotel is located near the S-Bahn station Hackescher Markt. Rooms in the late 19th-century building, an intriguing mixture of stucco ceilings, glass and steel, are large, comfortable and full of light, with soundproof windows. Nice lobby bar and café. **www.alexander-plaza.de**

NORTH OF THE CENTRE

Hotel Garni am Scheunenviertel   €

Oranienburger Strasse 38, 10117 **Tel** *282 21 25* **Fax** *282 11 15* **Rooms** *18*   *Map 16 E1, 7 A1*

This small and privately-run hotel is right in the historic Jewish quarter near the renovated synagogue. An ideal starting point for exploring Mitte and Prenzlauer Berg, the hotel features small but clean standard rooms and mostly attracts international, art-oriented young guests. **www.hotelas.com**

Märkischer Hof   🅿   €

Linienstrasse 133, 10115 **Tel** *282 71 55* **Fax** *282 43 31* **Rooms** *20*   *Map 6 F1*

A small, snug hotel with a family atmosphere. The building dates from the 19th century, but the rooms have been redecorated. They are of a surprisingly high standard considering their low prices and all have a private bathroom and a TV set. Rooms with three beds are the best deal here. **www.maerkischer-hof-berlin.de**

The Circus Hotel   🏠 🍴 🏃   €€

Rosenthaler Strasse 1, 10119 **Tel** *200 039 39* **Fax** *28 39 14 84* **Rooms** *64*   *Map 7 B1*

The Circus has a hostel and a hotel part, catering to budget and more affluent guests. It puts an emphasis on sustainability, radiates hipness and is aptly located on the edge of Prenzlauer Berg. Excellent service. Bicycles, Segways and Smart cars for rent. Healthy German cuisine at the in-house Fabisch restaurant. **www.circus-berlin.de**

Flower's Boardinghouse Berlin   🏠 🅿   €€

Mulackstrasse 1, 10119 **Tel** *280 45306* **Fax** *280 45308* **Rooms** *21*   *Map 7 C1*

The Flower's Boardinghouse consists of stylish, bright apartments with all the modern amenities of a good standard hotel room. Breakfast is included in the tariff. There is also an attached kitchen which guests can use. Ideal for a longer stay. **www.flowersberlin.de**

Hotel Albrechtshof   🏠 🅿   €€

Albrechtstrasse 8, 10117 **Tel** *308 860* **Fax** *308 861 00* **Rooms** *100*   *Map 6 F2, 15 B1*

This charming hotel is situated near the Spree river, in a modernized, early 19th-century building. It offers not only a bar, restaurant and banqueting hall, but a chapel as well. Weekend discounts are available. Internet access in all spacious rooms and a warm, personal service. **www.hotel-albrechtshof.de**

MitArt Hotel & Cafe   🏠 🅿 🍴   €€

Linienstrasse 139, 10115 **Tel** *283 904 3 0* **Fax** *283 904 32* **Rooms** *30*   *Map 6 F1*

This trendy hotel near the alternative art centre, Tacheles, offers small, quiet rooms, all adorned by original paintings. It also has its own art gallery downstairs. Breakfast is a feast of natural-grown produce. The nightlife in Mitte is just around the corner. **www.mitart.de**

NH Berlin Friedrichstrasse   🏠 🅿 🍴 ♨ 🏃 🖩   €€

Friedrichstrasse 96, 10117 **Tel** *206 26 60* **Fax** *206 266 933* **Rooms** *262*   *Map 6 F3*

This delightful designer hotel lies at the northern end of the Friedrichstrasse, just steps away from the hip Hackescher Markt and Unter den Linden. Its fairly large rooms feature extremely comfortable beds. It also has a wellbeing centre with a Turkish bath and an Italian restaurant. **www.nh-hotels.de**

Arte Luise Kunsthotel   🅿 🏠   €€€

Luisenstrasse 19, 10117 **Tel** *284 480* **Fax** *284 484 48* **Rooms** *50*   *Map 6 E2*

An authentic Berlin artist's hotel, the Küenstlerheim (literally "home for artists") welcomes the artsy crowd into individually designed rooms, created by various German artists. The early 19th-century house is steps away from the Scheunenviertel and has a great personal service. **www.luise-berlin.com**

Hotel Hackescher Markt   🏠 🅿 🏃   €€€

Grosse Präsidentenstrasse 8, 10178 **Tel** *280 030* **Fax** *280 031 11* **Rooms** *32*   *Map 7 B2, 16 F1*

This charming hotel has an excellent location opposite Hackesche Höfe. The rooms are elegantly furnished and have stylish bathrooms with heated floors. Its restaurant, Mags, offers excellent French cuisine. The real highlight is a pretty courtyard where breakfast is served. **www.hotel-hackescher-markt.com**

Key to Price Guide *see p220* **Key to Symbols** *see back cover flap*

Casa Camper

🖥 🍴 €€€€

Weinmeisterstrasse 1, 10178 **Tel** *200 034 10* **Fax** *200 034 11* **Rooms** *51* **Map** *7 C1*

A modern design hotel in a vibrant location between Mitte and Prenzlauer Berg. Designers Fernando Amat und Jordi Tio created a "home away from home" atmosphere with hardwood floors and pleasant colours. Free Wi-Fi, business centre and library. At the 24-hour roof bar, snacks and drinks are free for hotel guests. **www.casacamper.com/berlin**

Honigmond

🖥 P 🍴 €€€€

Tieckstrasse 12, 10115 **Tel** *284 45 50* **Fax** *284 455 11* **Rooms** *60* **Map** *6 F1*

The Honigmond is great for exploring the Mitte and Prenzlauer Berg arts scenes. Originally a traditional tenement house, it has individually designed rooms, some of which feature four-poster beds and parquet floors. Other rooms, in a 19th-century house with a courtyard, will entice you with their summerhouse look. **www.honigmond-berlin.de**

TIERGARTEN

Grand Hotel Esplanade Berlin

🖥 P 🍴 ≋ 🎿 📺 🗐 €€

Lützowufer 15, 10785 **Tel** *254 780* **Fax** *254 788 222* **Rooms** *391* **Map** *11 A1*

A modern, lavish establishment overlooking the Landwehrkanal, the hotel has well-furnished rooms that attract prominent guests. Harry's New York Bar is famous and the Ellipse Lounge restaurant is one of the city's best. The hotel's boat offers trips along the rivers. **www.esplanade.de**

Pullman Berlin Schweizerhof

🖥 P 🍴 ≋ 🎿 📺 🗐 €€€

Budapester Strasse 25, 10787 **Tel** *269 60* **Fax** *296 610 00* **Rooms** *384* **Map** *10 F1*

This luxurious hotel sports an elegant, sand-finished façade and offers beautifully furnished rooms, two restaurants, a ballroom and a conference centre. The rooftop indoor pool and fitness area is one of the most beautiful to be found in Berlin. **www.pullmanhotels.com**

Berlin Marriott Hotel

🖥 P 🍴 ≋ 🎿 📺 🗐 €€€€

Inge-Beisheim-Platz 1, 10785 **Tel** *220 000* **Fax** *220 001 000* **Rooms** *379* **Map** *6 D5*

The Marriott at the Beisheim-Center near Potsdamer Platz is an elegant four-star hotel with a towering entrance atrium. Its spacious rooms offer lovely views of the green Tiergarten and the government district. You get the same facilities for less than half the rate of the adjacent Ritz-Carlton. **www.marriott.de**

Inter-Continental Berlin

🖥 P 🍴 ≋ 🎿 📺 🗐 €€€€

Budapester Strasse 2, 10787 **Tel** *2602* **Fax** *2602* **Rooms** *584* **Map** *10 F1*

This hotel is situated on the outskirts of the Zoologischer Garten. The massive building is hard to miss, with a glass dome covering the lobby. The hotel offers large rooms in several categories. A swimming pool and a salon provide the chance to relax. **www.interconti.com**

The Mandala Hotel

🖥 P 🍴 🎿 📺 🗐 €€€€

Potsdamer Strasse 3, 10785 **Tel** *590 050 000* **Fax** *590 050 500* **Rooms** *165* **Map** *6 D5*

This all-suite four-star hotel, adjacent to the Sony Centre, has a perfect location for touring both the Eastern and Western downtown areas. Elegantly furnished with modern desks, hi-tech audio and big-screen TV equipment, as well as full kitchenettes. Impeccable service. **www.themandala.de**

Grand Hyatt Berlin

🖥 P 🍴 ≋ 🎿 📺 🗐 €€€€€

Marlene-Dietrich-Platz 2, 10785 **Tel** *255 312 34* **Fax** *255 312 35* **Rooms** *342* **Map** *6 D5*

One of Berlin's most modern and splendid hotels, the Hyatt is close to the Potsdamer Platz and Kulturforum. It has a sushi bar inside its stylish VOX restaurant and a bistro with cocktail bar. In February, it serves as the official host to the Berlinale film festival, attracting stars and fans alike. **www.berlin.grand.hyatt.com**

The Ritz-Carlton Berlin

🖥 P 🍴 ≋ 📺 🗐 €€€€€

Potsdamer Platz 3, 10785 **Tel** *337 777* **Fax** *337 775 555* **Rooms** *302* **Map** *6 E5*

The ultra-luxurious Ritz-Carlton Berlin's modern façade is reminscent of the Rockefeller Centre. The hotel lobby with its marble columns and gold leaf is as stunning as the bar, The Curtain Club, and the brasserie Desbrosses. Rooms with Prussian Neo-Classicist designs are comfortably furnished. **www.ritzcarlton.com**

KREUZBERG

Hotel Transit

🖥 €

Hagelberger Strasse 53-54, 10965 **Tel** *789 04 70* **Fax** *789 047 77* **Rooms** *50* **Map** *12 E4*

The Berlin namesake of its famous Paris counterpart is a small Kreuzberg "sleep-in" resembling a private youth hostel, located in two lofts. Every room comes with an attached modern bathroom, though the best deals are shared-bed rooms. The large, bright singles are particularly nice. **www.hotel-transit.de**

Pension Kreuzberg 🖪 🅿 €

Grossbeerenstrasse 64, 10963 **Tel** *251 13 62* **Fax** *251 06 38* **Rooms** *12* **Map** *12 F3*

This tiny hotel is one of the few upscale Kreuzberg pensionen offering a warm and personal service – and tourist information – by owner Angelika Dehner. Breakfast is appetizing and hearty. The location is great, while the district's nightlife is just a short walk away. **www.pension-kreuzberg.de**

Hotel am Anhalter Bahnhof 🅿 €€

Stresemannstrasse 36, 10963 **Tel** *258 00 70* **Fax** *251 48 97* **Rooms** *42* **Map** *12 E1*

This small and friendly hotel is situated in an old apartment block. Its low prices only apply to rooms without bathrooms; expect to pay more for en suite bathrooms. The more expensive rooms face on to a courtyard. **www.hotel-anhalter-bahnhof.de**

Hotel Riehmers Hofgarten 🖪 🅿 🍴 €€

Yorckstrasse 83, 10965 **Tel** *780 988 00* **Fax** *780 988 08* **Rooms** *23* **Map** *12 F4*

Housed in a 19th-century Gothic red-brick complex, this is one of the most magnificent hotels in town. Though only sparsely furnished, its rooms are comfortable and elegant, and the best ones overlook the courtyard. Don't miss the German food served at its restaurant, E.T.A. Hoffman. **www.hotel-riehmers-hofgarten.de**

Mövenpick Hotel Berlin 🖪 🅿 🍴 🏋 🛗 🗐 €€€

Schöneberger Strasse 3, 10963 **Tel** *230 060* **Fax** *230 061 99* **Rooms** *243* **Map** *12 E1*

The Mövenpick is a surprisingly pleasant hotel located close to vibrant Potsdamer Platz. The spacious designer rooms all have modern office and entertainment amenities. The deluxe rooms under the roof are particularly cosy and recommended. **www.moevenpick-berlin.com**

Relexa Hotel Stuttgarter Hof 🖪 🅿 🍴 🏋 🛗 €€€€

Anhalter Strasse 9, 10963 **Tel** *264 830* **Fax** *264 839 00* **Rooms** *206* **Map** *12 F1*

This is a well-kept, top-quality hotel, dating back to 1907. Situated behind Potsdamer Platz, it has modern, good-sized rooms, a restaurant called Boulevard and a charming, green courtyard. The location is perfect for exploring both Kreuzberg and Mitte. **www.relexa-hotels.de**

AROUND KURFÜRSTENDAMM

A & O Hostel am Zoo 🛗 €

Joachimsthaler Strasse 1-3, 10623 **Tel** *809 475300* **Fax** *809 475390* **Rooms** *550* **Map** *10 D1*

Located in a former Aldi budget grocery store, this hostel is a favourite among budget travellers looking for a cheap night's sleep. Conveniently located opposite the Zoo railway station, it offers packages such as combined hostel and dancing club weekends, which appeal to the younger guests. **www.aohostels.com**

Hotel Berolina an der Gedächtniskirche 🛗 🅿 €

Rankestrasse 35, 10789 **Tel** *236 396 82* **Fax** *236 396 83* **Rooms** *42* **Map** *10 E1*

With an eye-catching bright-yellow façade, the Hotel Berolina is adjacent to the renowned Memorial Church. The comfortable, inexpensive rooms cater to young tourists from around the world. Double rooms are furnished with greater detail than the singles. **www.berolinahotels.de**

Hotel Boulevard 🛗 €

Kurfürstendamm 12, 10719 **Tel** *884 250* **Fax** *884 254 50* **Rooms** *57* **Map** *10 D1*

Centrally located on Kurfürstendamm, this bland hotel is an insider's choice for travellers who want to be in the middle of a bustling big city. All western downtown sights are just steps away. Breakfast is served on a rooftop terrace with views of the famous boulevard. **www.ahc-hotels.com**

Hotel-Pension Elite 🛗 €

Rankestrasse 9, 10789 **Tel** *881 53 08* **Fax** *882 54 22* **Rooms** *14* **Map** *10 E1*

The small Pension on quiet Rankestrasse, not far away from bustling Breitscheidplatz, features late-Classicist, turn-of-the-19th-century rooms with an elegant ambience. Some rooms come with private bathrooms, while the cheaper rooms have shared ones. **www.berolinahotels.de**

Art'otel City Center West 🛗 🅿 🍴 €€

Lietzenburger Strasse 85, 10719 **Tel** *887 77 70* **Fax** *887 777 777* **Rooms** *91* **Map** *10 D2*

Just steps away from Kurfürstendamm is one of Germany's top art and designer hotels, filled with art reproductions of Andy Warhol's work. Rooms are individually designed and feature state-of-the-art furniture. This is a great place to stay if you like design, bright colours and a western city centre location. **www.artotels.com**

Art Nouveau Hotel 🛗 🅿 🏋 €€

Leibnizstrasse 59, 10629 **Tel** *327 74 40* **Fax** *327 744 40* **Rooms** *14* **Map** *9 B1*

Tucked away in a 19th-century mansion, this typical Berlin *Hotelpension* has incredibly high, individually designed rooms with original stucco, featuring only a few modern pieces, such as futon-like beds. Many guests like the elegant "yellow room" best. **www.hotelartnouveau.de**

Key to Price Guide *see p220* **Key to Symbols** *see back cover flap*

Belmondo Am Kurfürstendamm

€€

Joachimsthaler Strasse 39-40, 10623 **Tel** *889 110* **Fax** *889 111 50* **Rooms** *138*　　　　**Map** *10 D1*

This hotel, centrally located at one of Berlin's busiest street corners on Kurfürstendamm, makes a great impression with its magnificent lobby, but somehow disappoints with the uninspired rooms. Nevertheless, this is a good alternative to the more expensive big hotels. **www.azimuthotels.com**

Berlin Excelsior Hotel S.A.

€€

Hardenbergstrasse 14, 10623 **Tel** *315 50* **Fax** *315 510 02* **Rooms** *316*　　　　**Map** *3 C5*

The Excelsior, once a first-class hotel, still exudes an elegant, international flair but lacks the service and amenities you would expect. Nevertheless, the large, stylishly decorated rooms with a view of quaint Steinplatz are appealing. Students' bars and cafés are footsteps away. **www.hotel-excelsior.de**

Crowne Plaza Berlin City

€€

Nürnberger Strasse 65, 10787 **Tel** *210 070* **Fax** *213 20 09* **Rooms** *423*　　　　**Map** *10 E2*

This luxurious hotel is located near Kaiser-Wilhelm-Gedächtnis-Kirche and Tauentzienstrasse. It has a swimming pool, a good restaurant, large rooms with all amenities and a pleasing amosphere. It offers special weekend rates combined with sightseeing tours. **www.cp-berlin.com**

Hecker's Hotel

€€

Grolmannstrasse 35, 10623 **Tel** *889 00* **Fax** *889 02 60* **Rooms** *69*　　　　**Map** *9 C1*

Situated in the very heart of town, this low-key, private hotel caters not only for its guests' needs but tries for a more individual approach. The plain façade hides a more sophisticated interior, with simple furniture in the style of Frank Lloyd Wright, and displays of contemporary art. **www.heckers-hotel.com**

Hotel Askanischer Hof

€€

Kurfürstendamm 53, 10707 **Tel** *881 80 33* **Fax** *881 72 06* **Rooms** *16*　　　　**Map** *9 B2*

One of the few hotels that survived World War II. The interior is decorated in the style of 1920s and the rooms are cosy and comfortable, some have canopy beds and are surprisingly spacious. Authors Franz Kafka and Arthur Miller used to stay here. It also has an intimate little bar. **www.askanischer-hof.de**

Hotel Astoria

€€

Fasanenstrasse 2, 10623 **Tel** *312 40 67* **Fax** *312 50 27* **Rooms** *32*　　　　**Map** *4 D5*

Managed by the same family for three generations, this intimate hotel occupies a 19th-century building and is considered to be one of the best of its kind in town. The rooms are comfortable and the lack of a restaurant is made up for by the hotel's proximity to Savignyplatz. **www.hotelastoria.de**

Hotel Gates

€€

Knesebeckstrasse 8-9, 10623 **Tel** *311 060* **Fax** *312 20 60* **Rooms** *104*　　　　**Map** *3 C5*

Offering varying prices and standards, this art hotel presents original modern art, besides a stylish, private bathroom, minibar and TV in every room. The location in the most authentic Charlottenburg neighbourhood is a great plus, while the Ku'damm is just a few steps away. **www.hotel-gates.com**

Hotel Pension Augusta

€€

Fasanenstrasse 22, 10719 **Tel** *883 50 28* **Fax** *882 47 79* **Rooms** *47*　　　　**Map** *10 D1*

This relatively inexpensive guesthouse is located in the very heart of Berlin. As it is based in a 19th-century building, the rooms are spacious and quiet. Some rooms lack en suite bathrooms and so are much cheaper. There is no hotel restaurant, but there are many good places to eat nearby. **www.hotel-augusta.de**

Hotel Pension Dittberner

€€

Wielandstrasse 26, 10707 **Tel** *881 64 85* **Fax** *885 40 46* **Rooms** *22*　　　　**Map** *3 B5*

One of the charming old-style Hotelpensionen, once typical in Berlin, it promises a personal, if somewhat disorganized, service in a 19th-century setting. Rooms are large, with slightly moth-eaten furniture. The prime location off Kurfürstendamm and the flair of old Berlin more than make up for this. **www.hotel-dittberner.de**

Ku'Damm Art'otel Berlin

€€

Joachimstaler Strasse 29, 10719 **Tel** *884 470* **Fax** *884 477 00* **Rooms** *133*　　　　**Map** *10 D2*

The Art'otel can be easily recognized from a distance by the figure of a discus-thrower on the façade. Its interiors are boldly designed in a colourful, ultra-modern style. The decor might evoke a mixed response from the guests, but they are nonetheless impressed by the service. **www.artotels.com**

NH Berlin Kurfürstendamm

€€

Grolmannstrasse 41-43, 10623 **Tel** *884 260* **Fax** *884 265 00* **Rooms** *167*　　　　**Map** *9 C1*

The building of this welcoming hotel is modern and some of its rooms have extra-long beds for taller guests. There is a roof terrace and during summer, dinner is served in the inner courtyard. Try to get a reservation for a calm front or a courtyard room. **www.nh-hotels.com**

Propeller Island City Lodge

€€

Albrecht-Achilles Strasse 58, 10709 **Tel** *891 90 16* **Fax** *891 87 21* **Rooms** *30*

Situated in a 19th-century apartment block in one of the quiet streets off Kurfürstendamm, the Propeller is known as an art hotel. Each room is differently – and often outrageously – themed, with real works of art. An ideal place for those looking for a memorable stay. **www.propeller-island.de**

Bleibtreu Hotel
Bleibtreustrasse 31, 10707 **Tel** *884 740* **Fax** *884 744 44* **Rooms** *60*   **Map** *9 B2*

This hotel occupies a restored 19th-century building located on a quiet street. The sophisticated interiors are made of natural materials. The restaurant serves mainly organic food from farms outside Berlin. In summer, the inner garden in the pretty courtyard comes into its own. **www.bleibtreu.com**

Ellington Hotel Berlin
Nürnberger Strasse 50–55, 10789 **Tel** *683 150* **Fax** *683 155 555* **Rooms** *285*   **Map** *10 E2*

The Ellington offers affordable, stylish rooms in an historic, 1920s Bauhaus building, just a few steps away from busy Tauentzien and Kurfürstendamm. The great location and perfect service make up for the rooms being smaller than those in other city hotels. **www.ellington-hotel.com**

Hotel am Zoo
Kurfürstendamm 25, 10719 **Tel** *884 370* **Fax** *884 377 14* **Rooms** *136*   **Map** *10 D1*

The small but elegant Hotel Zoo is a charming, intimate combination of a modern, upmarket hotel with timeless furniture and large, very peaceful rooms, hidden in one of the few great old mansions left standing on Kurfürstendamm. Perfect for a stroll down the boulevard. **www.hotelzoo.de**

Hotel Mondial
Kurfürstendamm 47, 10707 **Tel** *884 110* **Fax** *884 111 50* **Rooms** *75*   **Map** *9 B2*

Wonderfully located near George-Grosz-Platz, close to several restaurants, this friendly hotel offers high-standard service. It is recommended for the disabled, as it is wheelchair-accessible and one quarter of the rooms have special facilities for disabled guests. **www.hotel-mondial.com**

Hotel Residenz Berlin
Meinekestrasse 9, 10719 **Tel** *884 430* **Fax** *882 47 26* **Rooms** *77*   **Map** *10 D2*

A restored 19th-century building, with many Art Nouveau features, this appealing establishment is in a side street close to Kurfürstendamm. First-class suites are available as well as apartments with a kitchen. Special prices are available for long stays. **www.hotel-residenz-berlin.com**

Ku'Damm 101 Hotel
Kurfürstendamm 101, 10711 **Tel** *520 05 50* **Fax** *520 055 555* **Rooms** *170*   **Map** *9 A2*

On the most elegant part of Kurfürstendamm, this designer hotel is striking in its use of clear forms, sparse furnishings, abstract paintings, a lot of glass, steel and beautiful wood. Every room has wireless LAN and spacious desks. Business lounge and a rooftop breakfast room with scenic views of Berlin. **www.kudamm101.com**

Swissôtel Berlin
Augsburgerstrasse 44, 10789 **Tel** *220 100* **Fax** *220 102 222* **Rooms** *316*   **Map** *10 D1*

One of the few first-class hotels on Ku'damm, the impressive building overlooks a busy cross section of the boulevard, making it perfect for sightseeing. The modern rooms are large, decorated in brown colours with comfortable lounge chairs, thick carpets and curtains. **www.swissotel.com**

Hotel Palace Berlin
Budapester Strasse 45, 10789 **Tel** *250 20* **Fax** *250 21 119* **Rooms** *119*   **Map** *10 E1*

The uninspiring shape of the building hides its charming interior, which is full of discreet elegance. The hotel is distinguished by the intimate atmosphere. Guests have included Julia Roberts and Isabella Rossellini. Rooms range from double to presidential suites. **www.palace.de**

Hotel Steigenberger Berlin
Los-Angeles-Platz, 10789 **Tel** *212 70* **Fax** *212 71 17* **Rooms** *397*   **Map** *10 E2*

With a very good location this hotel offers cosy rooms and several categories of apartments and suites. The hotel's facilities include a swimming pool, sauna, massage, a bar and good Berlin cuisine in the hotel restaurant, Berliner Stube. **www.berlin.steigenberger.de**

Kempinski Hotel Bristol Berlin
Kurfürstendamm 27, 10719 **Tel** *884 340* **Fax** *883 60 75* **Rooms** *301*   **Map** *10 D1*

One of Berlin's most famous and historic hotels, the Kempinski has a classic and elegant interior. Its luxurious rooms, with modern touches, are very comfortable, and 18 rooms have wheelchair access. Its famous restaurant, Kempinski-Grill, serves international cuisine. **www.kempinski-berlin.de**

Louisa's Place
Kurfürstendamm 160, 10709 **Tel** *631 030* **Fax** *631 031 00* **Rooms** *47*   **Map** *9 A2*

This 5-star luxury boutique hotel radiates old-world charm with its classy and elegant interior. All the spacious suites come with kitchens, some with balconies. In-house pampering available – sauna, massages, beauty treatments. Located directly on Kurfürstendamm, near all the famous designer shops. **www.louisas-place.de**

Savoy Hotel
Fasanenstrasse 9-10, 10623 **Tel** *311 030* **Fax** *310 33 33* **Rooms** *125*   **Map** *10 D1*

Rated among the most beautiful hotels in Berlin, the Savoy's comfortable rooms and friendly atmosphere attract an exclusive clientele. The suites on the sixth floor offer good views. Facilities include babysitting, theatre ticket service and the city's first cigar bar. **www.hotel-savoy.com**

Key to Price Guide *see p220* **Key to Symbols** *see back cover flap*

Hotel Brandenburger Hof

Eislebener Strasse 14, 10789 **Tel** *214 050* **Fax** *214 051 00* **Rooms** *72*
Map *10 E2*

An intimate family atmosphere, impeccable service and quiet, luxurious rooms make this one of the most desirable top-notch hotels in Berlin. The enchanting building has been restored and rooms feature Bauhaus furniture. The Michelin-awarded restaurant is a must. **www.brandenburger-hof.com**

Hotel Concorde Berlin

Augsburgerstrasse 41, 10789 **Tel** *800 99 90* **Fax** *800 999 99* **Rooms** *311*
Map *10 D1*

This hotel in the heart of the western downtown area welcomes guests with the sophisticated charm of French "savoir vivre". It offers minimalist architecture, understated but comfortable, large rooms, a French restaurant, impeccable service and great views of the bustling streetlife on Kurfürstendamm. **www.berlin.concorde-hotels.com**

AROUND SCHLOSS CHARLOTTENBURG

Art Hotel Charlottenburger Hof

Stuttgarter Platz 14, 10627 **Tel** *329 070* **Fax** *323 37 23* **Rooms** *46*
Map *9 A1*

A must for any individual traveller looking for a real Berlin experience, the Charlottenburger Hof is a successful version of a traditional *Hotelpensionen* for young tourists. The individually designed rooms are decorated with art by Mondrian. The staff here are very helpful. **www.charlottenburger-hof.de**

Comfort Hotel an der Oper

Bismarckstrasse 100, 10625 **Tel** *315 830* **Fax** *315 831 09* **Rooms** *49*
Map *3 A4*

Located near the opera house in Charlottenburg. Although some rooms overlook the noisy Bismarckstrasse, windows have been soundproofed. The pastel-coloured rooms are fairly large and have basic furniture. There is an Italian restaurant serving Mediterranean food. Check as there is often a 4-night minimum stay. **www.hotel-an-der-oper.de**

Hotel Econtel Berlin

Sömmeringstr. 24-26, 10589 **Tel** *346 810* **Fax** *346 810 63* **Rooms** *205*
Map *3 A2*

A large, family-oriented hotel that somehow lacks character but is the best deal for families in town. Provides many baby and toddler services, children-oriented rooms and large family apartments, all tastefully yet functionally decorated. The quiet location is yet another advantage. **www.econtel.de**

Schlossparkhotel

Heubnerweg 2a, 14059 **Tel** *326 90 30* **Fax** *326 903 600* **Rooms** *40*
Map *2 D2*

The modern Schlossparkhotel is part of a private clinic and is known as a very pleasant and small, but top-class, hotel near the beautiful gardens of Schlosspark Charlottenburg, making this the only downtown hotel in a green setting. The S-Bahn Westend is nearby. Request a room with a balcony overlooking the gardens. **www.schlossparkhotel.de**

FURTHER AFIELD

Die Fabrik

Schlesische Strasse 18, 10997 **Tel** *611 71 16* **Fax** *618 29 74* **Rooms** *45*

Set in an old factory building in the heart of alternative Kreuzberg, this youth-hostel type offers shared bathrooms and and simple furnishings, but its easy-going atmosphere appeals to all tastes. Very well-kept single, double and cheap dormitory rooms available. **www.diefabrik.com**

Eastern Comfort

Mühlenstrasse 73–77, 10243 **Tel** *667 63 806* **Fax** *667 63 805* **Rooms** *24*

The Eastern Comfort may be Berlin's most unusual hotel as it is set on an historic, meticulously restored, wooden houseboat, moored on the banks of the river Spree in Friedrichshain. There are three types of room, with the best located on the upper deck. Most offer a great view of the Oberbaumbrücke. **www.eastern-comfort.com**

East-Side Hotel

Mühlenstrasse 6, 10243 **Tel** *293 833* **Fax** *293 835 55* **Rooms** *36*
Map *8 F5*

The East-Side Hotel is located opposite the East-Side-Gallery, in a building that was formerly used to house workers. It opened in 1996, and has big, bright rooms with modern facilities and spacious bathrooms. The hotel has a comfortable family atmosphere. **www.eastsidehotel.de**

Holiday Inn Berlin City Center East

Prenzlauer Allee 169, 10409 **Tel** *446 610* **Fax** *446 616 61* **Rooms** *123*

The hotel calls itself an art hotel, and there is some original art to be found both in the public areas and rooms. Nonetheless, this Holiday Inn is primarily a standard business hotel with competitive prices. Rooms are quite clean and comfortable, though lacking in individuality. **www.hi-berlin.com**

Hotel Schöneberg ▨ 🅿 €

Hauptstrasse 135, 10827 **Tel** *780 96 60* **Fax** *780 966 20* **Rooms** *31*

This three-star hotel is away from many tourist sights, yet a good choice for its unbeatable prices and nice setting. Hotel Schöneberg is located in a beautiful Art Nouveau building. All the rooms of the three different categories are large, yet furnished with 1990s decor. Friendly service. **www.hotel-schoeneberg.de**

Michelberger Hotel ▨ 🅿 ⅋ 🚶 €

Warschauer Strasse 39/40, 10243 **Tel** *297 785 90* **Fax** *297 785 929* **Rooms** *119*

A very funky hotel in Friedrichshain – for a first impression, visit their website! The red-brick listed building close to the East Side Gallery offers basic budget rooms of different sizes, quirky decorations, a bar with live music and a beer garden. Great location with good transport links, free Internet and friendly staff. **www.michelbergerhotel.com**

Forsthaus Paulsborn ⅋ €€

Am Grunewaldsee/Hüttenweg 90, 14193 **Tel** *818 19 10* **Fax** *818 191 50* **Rooms** *10*

Peaceful location, deep in the Grunewald, makes it better suited to visitors with cars. Stained-glass windows and a fireplace in the lobby add character to this stylish former hunting lodge that also has a nice restaurant serving char-broiled meat dishes. Rooms are nicely decorated in a country-style mix. **www.paulsborn.de**

Frauenhotel Artemisia €€

Brandenburgische Strasse 18, 10707 **Tel** *873 89 05* **Fax** *861 86 53* **Rooms** *12*

Frauenhotel Artemisia caters exclusively for women and is often visited by business travellers. Men are allowed into the conference room. Some of the nice rooms, with many green plants, share modern bathrooms. The hotel has its own art gallery, while its breakfast room has a delightful terrace. **www.frauenhotel-berlin.de**

Hotel Müggelsee Berlin ▨ 🅿 ⅋ 🍴 ▤ €€

Müggelheimer Damm 145, 12559 **Tel** *658 820* **Fax** *658 822 63* **Rooms** *176*

This is an excellent hotel, far from the hustle and bustle of the city. Tucked away in the greenery on the Müggelsee in Köpenick, it is perfect for a relaxed stay. Rooms are fairly spacious, and all of the three guest floors are decorated differently in Italian, Asian and German styles. **www.hotel-mueggelsee-berlin.de**

Hotel-Pension Kastanienhof ▨ 🅿 €€

Kastanienallee 65, 10119 **Tel** *44 30 50* **Fax** *443 051 11* **Rooms** *35*   **Map** *1 B3*

The Kastanienhof is a budget *Pension* hidden in a fully restored, typical Berlin tenement house. Its location is perfect for exploring the clubbing scene in Prenzlauer Berg. Rooms are surprisingly nice, though, and come equipped with a hairdryer, minibar and safe. **www.kastanienhof.biz**

Hotel Sylter Hof Berlin ▨ 🅿 ⅋ ▤ €€

Kurfürstenstrasse 114-116, 10787 **Tel** *212 00* **Fax** *212 02 00* **Rooms** *178*   **Map** *10 F1*

Once one of Berlin's leading first-class hotels, the Sylter Hof is still a good choice. Entering the hotel feels like stepping back into the late 1960s. Once inside the rooms, you will be pleasantly surprised by Classicist furniture, upscale bathrooms and modern amenities such as Wi-Fi. **www.sylterhof-berlin.de**

Jurine ▨ 🅿 €€

Schwedter Strasse 15, 10119 **Tel** *443 29 90* **Fax** *443 299 99* **Rooms** *53*

This small hotel is located in a side street near Senefelderplatz, in the centre of Prenzlauer Berg. The nearby U-Bahn station gives easy access to the town centre. The rooms are of a high standard and there is a surprisingly green hotel garden behind the house. **www.hotel-jurine.de**

Villa Toscana 🅿 €€

Bahnhofstrasse 19, 12207 **Tel** *768 92 70* **Fax** *773 44 88* **Rooms** *16*

This quiet hotel is situated in an Italian-style villa, dating from the late 19th century. It's more convenient for tourists who have their own transport as the hotel is far from the centre and from any S- and U-Bahn stations. The rooms are well furnished and the marble bathrooms are elegant. **www.villa-toscana.de**

Ackselhaus & Bluehome ⅋ 🚶 €€€

Belforter Strasse 21, 10405 **Tel** *443 376 33* **Fax** *441 611 6* **Rooms** *35*

Located in a late 19th-century townhouse in Berlin's trendiest area and yet an oasis of peace, Ackselhaus provides individually styled studios and suites. Ranging in style from maritime to oriental and equipped with kitchenettes, all the apartments are easy to fall in love with. There's also a lovely back garden. **www.ackselhaus.de**

Albion Spreebogen Waterside Hotel ▨ 🅿 ⅋ 🏊 🏋 ▤ €€€

Alt-Moabit 99, 10559 **Tel** *399 200* **Fax** *399 209 99* **Rooms** *224*   **Map** *4 F1*

Beautifully located on the bank of the Spree river, the hotel is surrounded by modern tower blocks close to the Tiergarten. The building was an old dairy. Some stylishly-designed rooms have views of the river and the hotel has its own yacht for trips along the river. In summer, its restaurant has a great terrace. **www.hotel-spreebogen.de**

Estrel Hotel & Convention Center ▨ 🅿 ⅋ 🏊 🏋 ▤ €€€

Sonnenallee 225, 12057 **Tel** *683 10 0* **Fax** *683 123 45* **Rooms** *1125*   **Map** *14 F5*

The biggest hotel in continental Europe, the Estrel opened in 1994 to house major conferences. It is also popular among tourists, being conveniently linked by S-Bahn to the town centre. In summer, you can enjoy a beer in the garden along the canal. The affordable rates and great service are add-ons. **www.estrel.com**

Key to Price Guide *see p220* **Key to Symbols** *see back cover flap*

Hotel Seehof Berlin
🖥️ 🅿️ 🍴 ♨️ 👥 📋   €€€

Lietzenseeufer 11, 14057 **Tel** *320 020* **Fax** *320 022 51* **Rooms** *75*   **Map** *2 D5*

An amazing hotel, only ten minutes on foot from Messegelände, the complex of trade fair halls. Given the modern structure, the stylish interiors and large rooms come as something of a surprise. Its lovely restaurant, Au Lac, is one of the few places where you can dine with a view of a lake – the Lietzensee. **www.hotel-seehof-berlin.de**

Villa Kastania
🖥️ 🅿️ 🍴 ♨️ 📺 📋   €€€

Kastanienallee 20, 14052 **Tel** *300 00 20* **Fax** *300 002 10* **Rooms** *45*   **Map** *1 A5*

A warm and intimate establishment with a high standard of service. It is located in a quiet street, a few minutes on foot from the complex of trade fair halls, Messegelände, and with excellent links to the centre. All rooms have balconies and standard rooms have kitchenettes. **www.villakastania.com**

Schlosshotel im Grunewald
🖥️ 🅿️ 🍴 ♨️ 📺 📋   €€€€€

Brahmsstrasse 10, 14193 **Tel** *895 840* **Fax** *895 848 00* **Rooms** *54*

This exclusive hotel was formerly a palace, built in 1912 for Walter von Pannwitz, the Kaiser's personal lawyer. The contemporary interiors were created by Karl Lagerfeld. There is a breathtaking lobby with a magnificient coffered ceiling and decorative woodcarving. **www.schlosshotelberlin.com**

GREATER BERLIN

Art'otel Potsdam
🅿️ 🍴 📋   €€

Zeppelinstrasse 136, 14471 **Tel** *0331 981 50* **Fax** *0331 981 55 55* **Rooms** *123*

Part of this luxurious hotel on the bank of Havel river occupies an old 19th-century granary, where rooms have beautiful ceilings with restored beams and designer furniture. The best features of rooms in the modern wing are the balconies overlooking the Havel. **www.artotel-potsdam.com**

Hotel am Luisenplatz
🖥️ 🅿️   €€

Luisenplatz 5, 14471 Potsdam **Tel** *0331 971 900* **Fax** *0331 971 9019* **Rooms** *38*

Overlooking Potsdam's most charming square, this private four-star hotel is tastefully decorated in warm shades of brown and blue. Rooms are fairly large and equipped with all modern necessities. Apartments, which come for 20 euros more, are even better, and the suites (€50–60 more) are finer still. **www.hotel-luisenplatz.de**

NH Voltaire Potsdam
🅿️ 🍴 👥 📺   €€

Friedrich-Ebert-Strasse 88, 14467 **Tel** *0331 231 70* **Fax** *0331 231 71 00* **Rooms** *143*

This is a top-quality hotel with a restaurant and bar in the centre of town, adjacent to the famous Dutch quarter. The comfortably furnished and surprisingly elegant rooms have individual colour schemes. The modern part of the building is joined to a converted Baroque palace. **www.nh-hotels.com**

Steigenberger MAXX Hotel Sanssouci
🖥️ 🅿️ 🍴 📋   €€

Allee nach Sanssouci, 14471 Potsdam **Tel** *0331 909 10* **Fax** *0331 909 19 09* **Rooms** *137*

This small-town hotel has all the business amenities you would expect from a Steigenberger hotel. The quieter rooms are decorated with non-kitschy Hollywood movie themes of the 1940s and 50s, combined with country-style furniture. The hotel has a restaurant and a bar. **www.potsdam.steigenberger.de**

Hotel Schloss Lübbenau
🖥️ 🅿️ 🍴 👥   €€€

Schlossbezirk 6, 3222 Lübbenau **Tel** *03542 873 0* **Fax** *03542 873 666* **Rooms** *46*

In the heart of the unique Spreewald landscape (1.5 hours from Berlin) and surrounded by a 22-acre English garden, this neo-classical castle hotel takes you back in time. Built in 1818 and well renovated, it is ideal for conferences and weddings or a relaxing weekend get-away. Excellent restaurant specializes in regional cuisine. **www.schloss-luebbenau.de**

Relexa Schlosshotel Cecilienhof
🅿️   €€€

Neuer Garten, 14469 **Tel** *0331 370 50* **Fax** *0331 370 52 21* **Rooms** *41*

A treat for history-lovers, the hotel, furnished in an elegant British country style, occupies most of the Cecilienhof palace. In the evening, when the daytrippers have left, hotel guests can take a stroll in the gardens or a boat trip on the lake. The hotel restaurant serves fine regional fare. **www.relexa-hotel.de**

Travel Charme Hotel am Jaegertor
🖥️ 🅿️ 🍴 👥 📋   €€€

Hegelallee 11, 14467 Potsdam **Tel** *0331 201 110 0* **Fax** *0331 201 133 3* **Rooms** *62*

Charming 4-star boutique hotel in the old town of Potsdam, between Sanssouci castle and the Dutch Quarter – the perfect location for exploring the city. Mediterranean-style terrace, beautifully appointed rooms; free Internet in the lobby, for charge in the guest rooms. The two restaurants serve regional and international cuisine. **www.travelcharme.com**

Zur Bleiche Resort & Spa
🅿️ 🍴 👥 📺   €€€

Bleichestrasse 16, 03096 Burg im Spreewald **Tel** *03560 3620* **Fax** *03560 3602 92* **Rooms** *91*

Travellers looking for relaxation after a tiring day in the city will indulge in this exclusive, yet relaxed, spa resort set in a historic country house. Rooms range from rustic to elegant, there are extensive wellness packages and fitness services available. The restaurant is considered to be one of East Germany's best. **www.hotel-zur-bleiche.com**

RESTAURANTS, CAFÉS AND BARS

Shield of the Forst-haus Paulsborn restaurant

Given that Berlin is so cosmopolitan, you will find a wider range of restaurants here than in any other city in Germany. This includes Indian, Greek, Chinese, Thai and Turkish as well as Alsatian and Cambodian. Recently, new places have been opened by famous chefs, which maintain high European standards of international-style cuisine. There are also plenty of restaurants specializing in local dishes: the food can be a little heavy, but it is usually very tasty and served in large portions. Wherever you are in Berlin, you won't have to travel far to find somewhere to eat – every area has its own cluster of restaurants, cafés and bars, covering a range of styles and prices. Some of the best places are listed on pages 236–43. These have been chosen for their delicious food and/or good value. The listings on pages 244–9 should help those who would like a bite to eat but want the more relaxed setting of a café or bar.

The elegant interior of Margaux *(see p236)*

WHERE TO GO

Although good restaurants and cafés can be found all over Berlin, some of the best gourmet restaurants tend to be located in exclusive hotels, including **Facil** in the Mandala *(see p223)* or **Fischer's Fritz** in the Regent *(see p221)*. Alternatively, some good restaurants, such as the excellent **Margaux** *(see p236)*, can also be found on quiet streets.

The largest concentrations of restaurants are in a number of well-known districts. In the former West Berlin, for example, the most famous restaurants are clustered around Savignyplatz. Good places to eat in the centre can be found in and around Oranienburger Strasse. One of the recent top spots in Berlin that is popular with young people is Prenzlauer Berg, near Kollwitzplatz.

Despite all the changes that have taken place in the eastern part of Berlin over the past few years, restaurants in Kreuzberg (particularly along Oranienstrasse) are among the busiest in the city. The places in these areas are all consistently good and offer a wide choice in style and price.

WHAT TO EAT

In the morning, nearly all eateries, including those in most hotels, will offer a substantial breakfast. This usually consists of eggs, ham or cold cuts and different kinds of cheese. On Sundays some places also serve a German buffet-style brunch (breakfast combined with lunch) until 2pm. At lunchtime, one can easily find an elaborate salad or a bowl of steaming soup almost anywhere. In addition many restaurants may also offer their standard menus with slightly reduced prices.

The options for an evening meal are practically unlimited. In a restaurant serving local food one can have, for example, a tasty pork knuckle or potato soup *(see pp232–3)*. Lovers of Italian cuisine can easily find a good pizzeria or a restaurant serving sophisticated regional Italian dishes. Fans of Oriental food can choose between many Asian national cuisines, a great variety of which are situated along Prenzlauer Berg and around Savignyplatz. Berlin also has very good Mexican restaurants, particularly around Oranienburger Strasse and in

Outside Oxymoron *(see p238),* **in the Hackesche Höfe**

Outside Dressler Unter den Linden *(see p236)*

Kreuzberg, and the food served at Greek restaurants is usually quite good and very inexpensive. Vegetarians can easily find something suitable at almost every restaurant; however places that offer a significant choice of meat-free dishes are specially marked in the restaurant listings *(see pp236–43).*

PRICES AND TIPPING

Menus, showing meals and their prices, are usually on display outside restaurants and cafés. Prices can vary a great deal. It is possible to eat a three course meal, without alcohol, for €15, but in the centre of Berlin the price rises to €20–€25. In a top-notch establishment the cost of a meal can be over €80. The price of alcohol varies as well, but the most popular and cheapest drink is beer. Although prices include service and tax, many Germans will round up the bill. In more expensive restaurants a 10 per cent tip is customary. Some restaurants have begun to add "service not included" to their menus and bills. Although it is not legal to demand a tip, it is polite to leave some extra for the waiting staff.

EATING HOURS

In general, cafés open at 9am and restaurants at noon; the latter sometimes also close between 3 and 6pm. However, there are a lot of places that stay open very late, sometimes

until 2 or 3am. Some of the most expensive and best restaurants are only open in the evening and are sometimes closed on one day during the week as well.

BOOKING

In the most up-market restaurants, reservations are almost certainly required – in popular places it is advisable to book well in advance. For the majority of good restaurants it is necessary to book only for Friday or Saturday evenings, when all restaurants are at their busiest. If you do not have a reservation, look for a street or square with a large concentration of restaurants – there is bound to be an empty table among these.

DISABLED DINERS

In order to avoid any problems in advance, you should discuss wheelchair access when booking. Bear in mind, however, that even if a dining room may be accessible on the ground floor, the toilets may be up or down stairs or through a narrow corridor.

CHILDREN

Casual restaurants usually welcome children, though this may not be the case in more upmarket establishments. Those that do cater for children may provide high chairs as well as light dishes, particularly during lunchtime. Some places will offer a separate

children's menu with small portions. Children are also allowed in pubs and bars.

READING THE MENU

Menus are often written out in German and English, and some restaurants will provide menus in French as well. If you find yourself in a casual restaurant or bar, where the menu is perhaps hand-written, ask a waiter for help. Many restaurants offer a menu of the day with seasonal dishes or the chef's specials, which are always worth considering.

The stylish Bocca di Bacco *(see p236)*

SMOKING

Smoking was banned in all public places, including restaurants, bars, pubs and clubs in 2008. A handful of restaurants have a separate smoking area or room. In some parts of Berlin, such as Kreuzberg and Friedrichshain, the ban appears to have been ignored.

The elegant interior of Facil *(see p239)*

What to Eat in Berlin

To treat your senses in Berlin, you need do nothing more than stroll through the street markets, historic market halls and speciality food shops. Spicy, hot sausages such as *Currywurst* or *Thüringer* will lure you into the traditional German butcheries. The scent of freshly baked rolls and breads wafts from the corner bakeries. Fresh herbs, typical German garden vegetables such as red or green cabbage, and wild mushrooms are spectacularly displayed. Freshwater fish from the region's many lakes and rivers glisten on their beds of ice; particularly popular are pike-perch, eel, trout and even sweet river crabs.

Harzer Roller and Emmenthaler cheeses

Wild mushrooms, one of the region's most famous products

BERLIN'S HEARTY HERITAGE

Historically, Berlin has never been a gourmet capital, and neither has the surrounding, rural Brandenburg region. The Hohenzollern court focused more on its army than on culture and cuisine. But the Great Electors were formidable hunters, and game such as wild boar, rabbit, and duck, as well as goose and birds of prey were (and remain) an integral part of Berlin's cuisine. Later, in the 19th century, both the evolving Prussian well-to-do and the working class preferred hearty and simple food over fine dining – not only because Berlin was then a comparatively poor city, but also because of the long and hard winters and generally inclement weather.

BREAD AND POTATOES

There is an enormous variety of breads and rolls to be found on today's menus. Many are unique to Berlin, such as the wholewheat and rye, dark, crusty *Schuster-jungen* ("shoemaker's boy") or *schrippen*, the cheap roll eaten daily at every meal.

Potatoes were introduced by Frederick the Great. They appear at most German meals,

Mehrkornbrötchen (mixed grain roll)   **Berliner Landbrot (mild rye bread)**
Laugenbrötchen (salty sourdough rolls)
Graubrot (sourdough rye bread)   **Semmel (milk-dough roll)**

Selection of typical German loaves and bread rolls

LOCAL DISHES AND SPECIALITIES

Berliners have many ways of preparing pork, making it the most popular main dish. As *Kasseler*, created by Berlin butcher Cassel in the late 19th century, the meat is salted and then dried before being served with sauerkraut, mashed potatoes and very spicy mustard. Berlin's traditional pork knuckle, also accompanied by sauerkraut and potatoes, isn't complete without a portion of split pea purée (called *Erbspuree* in Berlin). Pork sausages include *Currywurst* – a post-World War II invention by Berlin Imbiss (food stall) owner Hedwig Mueller – which are served with a spicy sauce of curry, tomatoes and chili along with a roll or French fries. You can find this filling snack at Imbisse throughout the city.

Zanderfilet, *or Havel-Zander, is pan-fried pike-perch with a vegetable sauce and onions, served with mashed potatoes.*

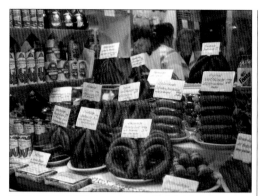

Display of traditional German sausages in a Berlin butcher's shop

alongside fish or meat or cooked in a broth for dishes such as *Kartoffelsuppe*.

THE BRANDENBURG INFLUENCE

Berlin's restaurants only rediscovered the region's true heritage after the fall of the Wall, absorbing culinary traditions from the Mark Brandenburg, the suddenly re-accessible rural country-side surrounding Berlin with its thick forests, rivers and lakes. Today, the fresh produce provided by the region's farms are an integral part of Berlin's cuisine. Old recipes have returned to modern kitchens. Freshwater fish like pike-perch, or game such as wild boar or duck, are flavoured with fresh herbs such as dill and parsley, and the famous

Brandenburger Landente (Brandenburg country duck), stuffed with apples, onions and herbs, slowly roasted and coated with a honey-oil to make it perfectly crusty, is once again a favourite on Berlin menus.

Fresh vegetables from the Mark Brandenberg region

BERLIN'S FINE DINING REVOLUTION

With the city's reunification came a new international influence, which gave birth to many Michelin-starred and other gourmet restaurants. Restaurants often prepare Berlin signature dishes with a more healthy or an exotic twist, giving traditional dishes a modern flavour. One of the Mark Brandenberg's most im-portant products, fresh wild mushrooms, such as *Pfiffer-linge* or *Steinpilze*, figure prominently, and classic ingredients like sauerkraut, cabbage and beet may be paired with Mediterranean fish or Asian spices.

BEST LOCAL FOOD

Restaurants: Altes Zollhaus (*p240*); Leibniz-Klause (*p241*); Reinhard's (*p238*); Lorenz- Adlon-Gourmet (*p236*); Zur letzten Instanz (*p238*); Mutter (*p242*); Dressler (*p236*).

Shops and markets: Marheineke-Markthalle; Turkish Market, Maybachufer; KaDeWe gourmet food floor (*p258*); Rogacki Gourmet Centre (*p259*); Butter Lindner delicatessen chain.

Imbisse (food stalls): Konnopke (below train tracks, Eberswalder Strasse subway, Prenzlauer Berg); Ku'damm 195 Imbiss, Kurfürstendamm; Currywurstbude, Wittenberg-platz, Charlottenburg.

Kasseler Nacken *is salted and dried pork served with sauerkraut or green cabbage and mashed potatoes.*

Berliner Leber *is veal or pork liver on a bed of mashed potatoes, with fried onions and pan-fried apple slices.*

Brandenburger Landente *is stuffed duck served with red cabbage and potato dump-lings or mashed potatoes.*

What to Drink in Berlin

In Berlin, as throughout the rest of Germany, beer is the most widely drunk alcoholic beverage. There are no productive vineyards around Berlin, but wines from the Rhine and Mosel regions are always popular. As an *aperitif*, or with pork dishes, Berliners often enjoy a shot of rye vodka *(Korn)*, sometimes flavoured with herbs. With dessert, a glass of herbal liqueur often fits the bill.

Engelhardt brewery logo

Pilsner beers from Berlin breweries

LAGER *(PILSNER)*

Berliners drink beer on every occasion, and Germany's many beers are some of the best and purest in the world. Some of the best-known Berlin breweries are Schultheiss, Berliner Kindl, Berliner Pils and Engelhardt, but beers brewed in other parts of Germany are just as popular. Although beer is available in all sorts of venues and *"Ein Bier bitte"* can be heard in pubs, cafés and restaurants, it is worth experiencing the atmosphere of an old-fashioned beerhouse, or *Kneipe*. The most highly esteemed beer is draught beer, drawn from the cask *(vom Fass)* and poured slowly into tall glasses. Pouring in a thin trickle is essential to achieve a thick head of foam, and a good barman will take a few minutes to fill your glass. Berliners drink mostly lager *(Pils)*, but other beers are also popular.

Strong, dark Bock beer

OTHER BEERS

In addition to the usual light, Pilsner-type beers, Berlin's breweries, many of them small and independent, also make a number of more adventurous brews. Dark, sweetish beer, known as *Schwarzbier* or black beer, is becoming more and more popular and has rather more than the standard four per cent alcohol. *Weizenbier* is made from wheat rather than barley, and is usually served in half-litre (one pint) glasses wth a slice of lemon. Another unusual drink is *Bock*, an especially strong beer made with barley. *Maibock* is a special version, available only in May.

A *Brezel* makes a good snack with beer

BERLINER WEISSE MIT SCHUSS

A Berlin speciality, called *Berliner Weisse mit Schuss*, is a light, newly-fermented wheat beer that continues fermenting in the bottle. On its own, it is not very palatable as it is rather watery and sour, but when mixed with raspberry cordial it becomes fruity and delicious. Mixing with sweet woodruff syrup gives it a vivid green colour and a slightly medicinal flavour. *Berliner Weisse mit Schuss* is served in large wine glasses with a straw, and makes a very refreshing drink, particularly popular during the hot summer months.

Berliner Weisse, a light malted-wheat beer

Berliner Weisse with raspberry and woodruff cordials

WINE

No wine is produced around Berlin as the climate here is too cold for vines, but a variety of wines from Germany's southern and western regions are available in Berlin. The most famous are the white wines, particularly those made from Riesling grapes. Most expensive are those from the Rheingau region. The northern climate dictates that most German wines are white, but lovers of red wine can try the Rhine Assmanshausen Spät-burgunder, made from Pinot Noir grapes. Although there is no regional system of classification like the French *Appellation d'Origine Contrôlée,* a national quality control system divides German wines into three categories: *Tafelwein* or table wine is the most basic; next comes *Qualitätswein,* and the highest is *Qualitätswein mit Prädikat,* which includes wines made from specially selected grapes. *Trocken* means dry, *halbtrocken* means medium dry and *süss* means sweet. You can also find some very good sparkling wines known as *Sekts.*

A prize-winning bottle of German red wine

Riesling from Schloss Vollrads

OTHER ALCOHOLIC BEVERAGES

Vodka is often drunk with more substantial meals, particularly those based on pork. Especially recommended is one of the rye vodkas, such as *Weizendoppelkorn,* that are popular in Berlin. Many establishments also serve brandies, known generically as *Weinbrand.* In addition, various digestive liqueurs and vodkas flavoured with plant extracts are quite popular, particularly *Kümmerling, Jägermeister* and, a Berlin favourite, *Kaulzzdorferkräuter Likör.* In many restaurants you will come across a speciality honey liqueur from east Prussia known as *Bärenfang.* More of an acquired taste is *Goldwasser* from Danzig, a traditional herbal liqueur containing flakes of gold leaf. It is made according to a secret 16th-century German recipe.

Weizendoppel-korn rye vodka **Herbal digestive liqueur** **Bitter-sweet Jägermeister liqueur**

NON-ALCOHOLIC COLD DRINKS

Although Berlin tap water is safe to drink, it is not usually served with restaurant meals. If you want water you should order a bottle of mineral water *(Mineralwasser)* adding *"ohne Kohlen-Säure"* if you prefer still water. A wide variety of canned sparkling soft drinks, ubiquitous across Europe and the US, are popular in Berlin. Fruit juices are also widely drunk and a wide selection is available in every restaurant and café. Another popular soft drink is *Apfelschorle,* apple juice mixed in equal proportions with sparkling mineral water.

Apfelschorle

COFFEE AND TEA

Coffee is very popular in Berlin and is served in a variety of ways. The most usual is filter coffee, served by the cup or the pot, generally with condensed milk and sugar. If you prefer something stronger and more aromatic you should go for an espresso. It is also easy to enjoy a good cup of tea in Berlin, herbal or otherwise. Germans drink a lot of herbal teas, two of the most common being peppermint *(Pfefferminz-tee)* and camomile *(Kamillentee).* If you want a cup of non-herbal tea, you can make a point of ordering *Schwarzen Tee.* If you want milk with your tea, then ask for *Tee mit Milch.*

Peppermint and camomile, two widely available herbal teas

Choosing a Restaurant

The restaurants in this guide have been selected because of their good value, good food and attractive interiors. The chart below lists restaurants in Berlin area by area, and the entries are alphabetical within each price category. Some of the specialities served at the restaurants have been mentioned in the listings.

PRICE CATEGORIES
For a three-course meal per person, including tax and service but not alcohol:

€ Under €25
€€ €26–35
€€€ €36–45
€€€€ €46–55
€€€€€ Over €56

AROUND UNTER DEN LINDEN

Nante-Eck   €
Unter den Linden 35, 10117 **Tel** *22 48 72 57*   **Map** *6 F3, 15 C3*

Here's your chance to enjoy a currywurst in a sit-down setting, watching life go by on Berlin's most famous crossing. Named after a city original, this typical old-Berlin Kneipe-style place offers excellent value. Dishes are hearty and simple and include all the Berlin specialities – *Eisbein* and *Sauerkraut*, *Sülze* and *Erbssuppe*. Affordable set lunches.

XII Apostel   €
Georgenstrasse 2 (S-Bahnbögen 177-180), 10117 **Tel** *201 02 22*   **Map** *7 A2, 16 D2*

Picturesquely situated in the old arcade of an S-Bahn railway bridge near Museum Island, this restaurant offers popular Italian cuisine. The thin, crispy pizza creations fresh from a stone oven are a speciality here, named after the twelve apostles. Ironically, Judas is the most sumptuous.

Bocca Di Bacco   €€
Friedrichstrasse 167/168, 10117 **Tel** *206 728 28*   **Map** *7 A4, 16 D3*

One of Western Berlin's oldest and most traditional upmarket Italian restaurants, the elegant Bocca attracts the rich and the famous. Tom Hanks and Spielberg are among its fans. Chef Lorenzo Pizetti has earned 14 Gault Millau points, and delights his patrons with probably the best pasta and fresh fish dishes outside Italy.

Dressler   €€€
Unter den Linden 39, 10117 **Tel** *204 44 22*   **Map** *6 E4, 15 A3*

Dressler is the perfect setting for a quick dinner before or after a theatre visit. Serves traditional German and French cuisine in an Art Deco-designed dining hall. In season, it has some of the city's best seafood. In winter, try their hearty German fare, such as oven-roasted duck with red cabbage and dumplings.

Lutter & Wegner   €€€
Charlottenstr. 56, 10117 **Tel** *202 95 40*   **Map** *7 A4*

The first restaurant to start the revitalization of the gourmet scene in the historic centre of Eastern Berlin. A fine German champagne brand until today, it now serves delicious German-Austrian food. The huge *Wiener Schnitzel* with potato salad, best served luke-warm, is a delight as are the rabbit and veal specialities.

Borchardt   €€€€
Französische Strasse 47, 10117 **Tel** *818 862 62*   **Map** *6 F4, 15 C3*

One of the few restaurants in Berlin with an original interior, including marble columns, mosaics and patterned floors in the Wilhelmine style. Good food, such as the French *steak et frites*, comes reasonably priced. Weekends are crowded so don't forget to make a reservation.

Lorenz-Adlon-Gourmet   €€€€€
Unter den Linden 77, 10117 **Tel** *226 119 60*   **Map** *6 E4, 15 A3*

This establishment is worthy of the hotel in which it is located, the Adlon. From the day it opened, this restaurant has been rated among Berlin's best. Under the guidance of its chef, Thomas Neeser, Lorenz-Adlon has managed to maintain its top reputation. It now serves light nouvelle cuisine. Closed Sun & Mon.

Ma Tim Raue   €€€€€
Behrenstrasse 72, 10117 **Tel** *30 11 17 333*   **Map** *6 E4, 15 A3*

The Ma's cuisine is Chinese-inspired and light, using no carbs and milk products. Chef de cuisine Tim Raue was awarded one Michelin and 18 Gault Milleu stars for his innovative work. The Shochu Bar next door serves Chinese and Japanese spirits exclusively, combined with fresh herbs and juices. Exquisite ambience. Closed Sun, Mon and most of Aug.

Margaux   €€€€€
Unter den Linden 78, 10117 **Tel** *226 526 11*   **Map** *6 E4, 15 A3*

The stylish and urban Margaux represents the new Berlin better than any other gourmet restaurant, even though it has lost some of its class after being taken over by different management. Classic yet creative French dishes are served. The restaurant also offers an extensive wine list and affordable lunch specials. Closed Sun.

Key to Symbols *see back cover flap*

Parioli
P ♿ ⬛ 🗐   €€€€€

Behrenstrasse 37, 10117 **Tel** *460 60 912 01*   **Map** *7 A4*

The Parioli is a quiet, stylish Italian restaurant in the luxury Hotel de Rome. Diners are always greeted with a selection of breads served with excellent virgin oils and balsamic vinegar. Pasta and risotto dishes are a speciality, but the set menus with several courses offer the best deal. In summer, guests can dine more casually in the small courtyard.

Vau
€€€€€

Jägerstrasse 54-55, 10117 **Tel** *202 97 30*   **Map** *6 F4, 15 C4*

This restaurant stands out with its elegant and unpretentious interiors. The excellent and imaginative Austrian- and French-based dishes are created by Berlin's star chef, Kolja Kleeberg. The service is welcoming and there is a selection of good wines. The small courtyard is used during lunch. Closed Sun.

MUSEUM ISLAND

Brauhaus Georgbräu
♿ ⬛   €

Spreeufer 4, 10178 **Tel** *242 42 44*   **Map** *7 C3*

At first sight, this restaurant looks like a typical tourist trap – large tables, big dining halls and masses of people. If you are not a fan of sausages, try *Brauhausknüller*, a Berlin dish with pork knuckle, mashed split peas, *Sauerkraut* and potatoes with cold beer.

The Factory & Bar
€€€

Wallstrasse 70-73, 10179 **Tel** *240 629 03*   **Map** *7 C4*

Good regional cuisine in a modern style, with a Mediterranean flair. The restaurant is part of the gastronomic complex of Art'otel and is situated in a stylishly decorated basement. After a good fill of beef filet with fried potatoes and green beans, or green salad with filled rabbit neck, enjoy a cocktail at the bar counter.

Heat
P ♿ ⬛   €€€

Karl-Liebknecht-Strasse 3, 10178 **Tel** *238 283 472*   **Map** *7 B2, 16 F2*

Heat is Berlin's latest fusion-cuisine restaurant, serving an eclectic mixture of Asian, Indian and Mediterranean dishes. A lunch restaurant, its light cuisine consists mainly of fresh fish and salads. In summer, a table on the terrace, just above the Spreekanal, is one of the nicest restaurant spots in Mitte.

EAST OF THE CENTRE

Blaues Band
P ♿   €

Alte Schönhauser Strasse 7/8, 10119 **Tel** *283 850 99*   **Map** *7 C1*

Despite its location in the trendy Mitte district, the Blaues Band is a secret to many Berliners. The ambience is friendly and relaxed, and the food delicious. It offers specialities from a specific country or region. German cuisine is particularly recommended. The menu has fresh asparagus in early summer and duck and goose in winter.

Brauhaus Mitte
♿ ⬛   €

Karl Liebknecht Strasse 13, 10178 **Tel** *308 789 89*   **Map** *7 C2*

This Brauhaus, a rustic mixture of microbrewery and traditional Berlin *Kneipe*, is opposite busy Alexanderplatz and is the perfect spot to relax after sightseeing in the eastern downtown area. The menu offers mostly heavy but delicious Berlin specialities such as pork knuckle with sauerkraut and mash, or *Bouletten*, Berlin-style, cold hamburger balls.

Monsieur Vuong
♿ ⬛   €

Alte Schönhauser Strasse 46, 10119 **Tel** *992 969 24*   **Map** *7 C1*

This tiny Vietnamese restaurant is one of the most popular eateries among the young, stylish Mitte crowd. It offers inexpensive yet delicious Asian and Vietnamese dishes, primarily excellent soups and snacks. Monsieur Vuong, whose black-and-white photograph is in the restaurant, is the father of current owner, chef Doug Vuong.

Zum Nussbaum
€

Am Nussbaum 3, 10178 **Tel** *242 30 95*   **Map** *7 C3*

Situated in an alley in the Nicolaiviertel, this is a reconstruction of a 16th-century country inn, serving traditional Berlin cuisine, with tender pork knuckle, rollmops or *Berliner Boulette*, a spicy hamburger pattie without a bun. In summer, dine in its garden and enjoy the various brands of local beer.

Zur letzten Instanz
P   €

Waisenstrasse 16, 10179 **Tel** *242 55 28*   **Map** *8 D3*

Berlin's oldest restaurant dating back to 1621, this used to be a meeting place for lawyers. Today, almost every visiting head of state pays homage to this pub. It specializes in traditional German food, such as pork knuckle (*Eisbein*) and beef olive (*Rinderroulade*) and big mugs of German beer. Closed Sun.

Oxymoron €€
Rosenthaler Str. 40-41, 10178 **Tel** *283 918 86*   **Map** *7 B2*

This fashionable restaurant, with its distinctive red-and-gold interior reminiscent of a 19th-century salon, has mainly Mediterranean and light German dishes on the menu. For lunch, dine at a table in the courtyard, the most beautiful inside historic Hackesche Höfe, and enjoy a small fare at a reasonable price.

Zoe 🗐 🅿 🚻 ♿ €€
Rochstrasse 1, 10178 **Tel** *240 456 35*   **Map** *7 C 2*

Zoe is a highly successful combination of German nouvelle cuisine and Asian dishes. The menu changes daily, but there is always a roasted, pan- or deep-fried meat, fish and vegetable creation, served with noodles, mushrooms and salads, in delicious Asian sauces. German recipes are more creative.

Reinhard's 🚹 €€€
Poststrasse 28, 10178 **Tel** *238 42 95*   **Map** *7 C3*

The interior of this enchanting place is decorated in style of the Roaring Twenties. The food is excellent. The speciality is *Das Geheimnis aus dem Kaiserhof* (the secret of the Kaiser's court), a succulent steak served with a sauce that was apparently created for Max Liebermann.

NORTH OF THE CENTRE

Kamala €
Oranienburger Strasse 69, 10117 **Tel** *283 27 97*   **Map** *7 A1*

Though this small restaurant has simple furnishings, the service is prompt and the quality of food is high. The menu features standard Thai dishes, prepared with a very careful use of spices, as well as excellent soups flavoured with delicate Thai flowers. The Kamala is part of the Mao Thai chain, a group of Berlin's four best Thai restaurants.

Nolle 🚹 €
Georgenstrasse, S-Bahnbogen Nr. 203, 10117 **Tel** *208 26 45*   **Map** *7 A3*

The Nolle is a pleasantly decorated, 1920s-style Berlin restaurant tucked away under the S-Bahn tracks. The lush greenery around the place, the elegantly appointed tables, and candlelights make a perfect setting for international and German dishes. The *schnitzel* selection is impressive.

Orange €
Oranienburger Strasse 32, 10117 **Tel** *283 852 42*   **Map** *7 A1*

Diners sit in a pleasing interior in the style of a café-restaurant, offering Italian and international dishes. Try a leisurely three-course meal or a snack. The Orange, a good location for starting a tour through Scheunenviertel, is also recommendable for its great breakfast selection.

Yosoy 🚹 €
Rosenthaler Strasse 37, 10787 **Tel** *283 912 13*   **Map** *7 B2*

A pleasant and inexpensive restaurant with a large selection of Spanish wines and dishes. The tapas are excellent, you can choose from 20 different creations presented *comme il faut* behind glass. A good deal is the *Yosoy-Tapasplatte*, a sampler of the best tapas for just €7.50.

Hackescher Hof €€
Rosenthaler Strasse 40/41, 10178 **Tel** *283 52 93*   **Map** *7 B2*

A very popular spot, this café-restaurant, divided into a bar and pub and a dining hall, serves breakfast from early morning, followed by inexpensive fixed-price lunches and Italian fare in the evenings. The food is excellent and the dishes are creative. In summer, the best tables are outside. Book ahead.

Kellerrestaurant im Brecht-Haus €€
Chausseestrasse 125, 10115 **Tel** *282 38 43*   **Map** *6 E1*

This restaurant is located in the cellar of the house where Bertolt Brecht used to live. The mostly hearty dishes served here are prepared according to the recipes of Helene Weigel, the wife of the famous writer. A very good creation is *Tafelspitz*, a boiled and marinated rump steak.

Ganymed Brasserie €€€
Schiffbauerdamm 5, 10117 **Tel** *285 990 46*   **Map** *6 F2, 15 C1*

A good-quality brasserie restaurant in charming surroundings with a small garden and views of the Spree river. The chef favours fish dishes, including Berlin fish specialities, but also offers traditional French fare such as *Steak Tartare*, fresh scallops sautéed in white wine, and a good cheese selection.

San Nicci €€€€
Friedrichstrasse 101, 10117 **Tel** *30 64 54 980*   **Map** *6 F3, 15 C2*

Conveniently located in the historical Admiralspalast building next to Friedrichstrasse station, stylish San Nicci combines fine dining and celebrity-spotting. This is where the city's in-crowd samples Italian-inspired food. After a home-made pasta dish, the walnut-filled *panzarotti* will melt in your mouth. Culinary *dolce vita* in the heart of Berlin!

Grill Royal
€€€€€

Friedrichstrasse 105, 10117 **Tel** *28 87 92 88*
Map *6 F2, 15 C1*

Reservations are a must at this trendy place frequented by the likes of Claudia Schiffer and Quentin Tarantino. This is one of the few places in Germany serving Kobe beef, though service is not quite up to the quality of the steaks. The best tables overlook the river (outside in summer). There is a beautiful smokers' lounge.

Weinbar Rutz
€€€€€

Chausseestrasse 8, 10115 **Tel** *246 287 60*
Map *6 E1*

Having earned a Michelin star, Weinbar Rutz is one of Berlin's leading gourmet restaurants. Fresh and imaginative cuisine that mixes traditional German dishes with Mediterranean fare is served. The excellent wine selection makes Weinbar Rutz a perfect, centrally located alternative to the stuffier gourmet temples of the Mitte district.

TIERGARTEN

Desbrosses
🅿 🛉 🛅 🎵   €€€

Potsdamer Platz 3 (in Beisheim Center am Potsdamer Platz), 10785 **Tel** *337 763 40*
Map *6 D5*

Desbrosses has the most authentic French brasserie interior in all of Berlin. Dark wood-panelled walls, comfortable, plush leather banks, bistro chairs, an open show kitchen and music by Piaf, all make for a real French experience. A must here is the seafood platter.

Midtown Grill
🅿 🛉 🛅   €€€

Eberstrasse 3, 10785 **Tel** *220 005 411*
Map *6 E5*

Steak and fresh seafood are the order of the day at this restaurant. While waiting for your dinner, you can watch the chefs in the open show kitchen, enjoy vintages from one of Berlin's best overseas wine menu and listen to jazz. Service is very friendly, though somewhat slow when the restaurant is full.

Oktogon Fusion Restaurant
🛉 🛅   €€€

Leipziger Platz 10, 10117 **Tel** *206 428 64*
Map *6 E5*

The cuisine and service here are on level with top, first-class restaurants, though the prices are still affordable. The menu reads like a trip around the world, with a mouthwatering array of specialities from nearly every continent, presented in creative combinations.

Käfer im Bundestag
🛉   €€€€

Reichstag, Platz der Republik, 10557 **Tel** *226 29 90*
Map *6 D3*

A favourite dining place of the Mitte district, thanks to its unique location on the rooftop of the Reichstag, right next to Sir Norman Foster's cupola. The German cooking is creative and true to the owner, German catering star Käfer. Service is impeccable. Book ahead for lunch.

Facil
🅿 🛉 🛅   €€€€€

Potsdamer Strasse 3, 10785 **Tel** *590 051 234*
Map *6 D5*

Germany's finest (and most affordable) Michelin-starred restaurant, Facil delights both food and interior design connoisseurs. A seven-course dinner with French and German dishes is a feast for the eye. The food is served in a sleek, elegant rooftop dining hall. In summer the restaurant front opens onto a small garden. Closed Sat & Sun.

Hugo's
🅿   €€€€€

Budapesterstrasse 2, 10787 **Tel** *260 20*
Map *10 F1*

This restaurant located in the Inter-Continental hotel is one of the best in Berlin. Unusual French and international dishes are prepared with a German influence. The fish and seafood dishes are proof of the chef's real mastery. An attraction is the restaurant's rooftop location with great views. Reservations necessary. Closed Sun.

Vox
🅿 🛉 🛅 🎵   €€€€€

Marlene Dietrich Platz 2, 10785 **Tel** *255 317 72*
Map *6 D5*

The Grand Hyatt's leading hotel-restaurant is undoubtedly one of the town's finest. The exquisite food is a sleek, modern fusion of Asian and international dishes, with an emphasis on Japanese (sushi) recipies and French-Italian creations. The show kitchen was one of the first in Berlin and is a major attraction. Reservations necessary.

KREUZBERG

Defne
🍽 🛉 🛅   €

Planufer 92c, 10967 **Tel** *817 971 11*
Map *14 D3*

This intimate place has been voted as Berlin's best Turkish restaurant, probably because it is different from the area's other Turkish eateries. It serves fresh, slightly modernized versions of traditional meat and fish dishes. The emphasis is on top-quality produce. In summer, the garden terrace with a view of the canal is very inviting.

Hasir

⊟ P 🚶 ♿   €

Adalbertstrasse 10, 10999 **Tel** *614 23 73*   **Map** *14 E2*

One of the city's oldest and most traditional Turkish restaurants, now part of a chain by the same name, this is where it all started.The Hasir offers one the most extensive Turkish-Arabian menus to be found in town. Apart from the various traditional *kebab* dishes, the soups are exceptionally good.

Osteria No. 1

€€

Kreuzbergstraße 71, 10965 **Tel** *786 91 62*   **Map** *12 E4*

This Osteria was one of the first in Berlin and thus quickly gained its reputation as the hippest Italian restaurant in town. Those days are gone, but patrons can still enjoy the well-prepared, brick-oven pizzas. Main dishes such as rabbit or lamb are particularly good as are the fresh salads and exquisite pasta creations.

Sale E Tabacchi

P 🚶   €€

Rudi-Dutschke-Strasse 23, 10969 **Tel** *252 11 55*   **Map** *13 A1*

The Sale E Tabacchi offers reliable Italian food (but almost never pizza) in a dark, cosy Kreuzberg interior. In summer, the courtyard is the preferred dining area, mostly frequented by politicians and journalists from the neighbouring newspaper companies. For lunch, try one of the inexpensive three-course meals.

Altes Zollhaus

P 🚶   €€€€

Carl-Herz-Ufer 30, 10961 **Tel** *692 33 00*   **Map** *13 B3*

This restaurant is situated on the picturesque bank of the Landwehrkanal in what used to be a border control point. Excellent gourmet-style German food is served here without the usual heavy sauces. Dishes based on wild mushrooms, when in season, are delicious. Closed Sun & Mon.

E.T.A. Hoffmann

🚶 ♿   €€€€

Yorckstrasse 83, 10965 **Tel** *780 988 09*   **Map** *12 F4*

Always a leader on Berlin's gourmet scene, this restaurant's chef, Thomas Kurt, has reinvented German cuisine with fresh produce and international touches. Light fish dishes accented with carefully composed sauces and veggies, are summer signature dishes; hearty German fare can be enjoyed in winter. Closed Tue.

AROUND KURFÜRSTENDAMM

Ali Baba

🚶 ♿   €

Bleibtreustrasse 45, 10623 **Tel** *881 13 50*   **Map** *9 B1*

A long-time favourite among Berlin's students, the small, budget Italian pizzeria is open until the wee hours of the morning, mostly serving two different kinds of pizza by the slice – cheese or salami. These and all other freshly-baked stone-oven pizzas are simply delicious and affordable. No reservations.

Francucci's

🚶 ♿ ▤   €

Kurfürstendamm 90, 10711 **Tel** *323 33 18*   **Map** *9 A2*

One of Berlin's best-kept secrets and a favourite among locals, this upscale restaurant on upper Kurfürstendamm offers excellent, hearty Tuscan country cooking. Specialities include home-made pasta dishes prepared to your liking, meat dishes such as Italian wild boar and their signature pizza, served by the slice.

Good Friends

€

Kantstrasse 30, 10623 **Tel** *313 26 59*   **Map** *9 B1*

Packed for dinner each night, a mixed crowd of tourists, students and other locals relish the authentic Cantonese and other Oriental delicacies at Good Friends. The interior is somewhat tacky, the service not particularly friendly, and the noise is too loud. But the food is worth it.

Kuchi

€

Kantstrasse 30, 10623 **Tel** *315 078 15*   **Map** *9 B1*

Kuchi, one of the best-value Japanese restaurants in Berlin, offers excellent sushi and regional dishes. A simple, unpretentious Asian interior and a welcoming service make it the ideal venue for a dinner for two. The dim sum rotation and the sampler are particularly tasty. Reservations advised.

Lubitsch

🚶   €

Bleibtreustrasse 47, 10623 **Tel** *882 37 56*   **Map** *9 B1*

This popular restaurant is in one of the liveliest streets around Savignyplatz. A wide variety of German and international dishes is on the menu, with very reasonable prices at lunchtime. For dinner, try one of their two- or three-course meals – one of the best deals in town.

Marché

€

Kurfürstendamm 14, 10719 **Tel** *882 75 78*   **Map** *10 D1*

A self-service restaurant under the Mövenpick umbrella, Marché caters for the many tourists visiting Kaiser-Wilhelm-Gedächtniskirche. Choose from meat, poultry and fish dishes, plenty of desserts, beer and wine. All food is freshly prepared at market-like stalls. The nicer tables are upstairs.

Key to Price Guide *see p236* **Key to Symbols** *see back cover flap*

XII Apostel

🍴 🅿 🚹   €

Bleibtreustrasse 49, 10623 **Tel** *312 14 33*   **Map** *9 B1*

The Italian food served is available nearly 24 hours, but this place is always busy. The menu includes all types of pastas and pizza creations fresh from a stone oven. Choose between a cosy dining room and dining tent or, in summer, outside in a picturesque alley. Reservations for dinner strongly advised.

Zing

🚹 ♿   €

Grolmanstrasse 21, 10623 **Tel** *375 91 339*   **Map** *9 C1*

This relaxed Asian restaurant serves delicious fusion cuisine, mainly from China and Thailand, in a warm, elegant ambiance. All dishes emphasize their fresh ingredients, many are hot and spicy. Favourites include the appetizer dish for two and the General Tso chicken. In summer, the outside tables are a great spot from which to people-watch.

Austeria Brasserie

€€

Kurfürstendamm 184, 10719 **Tel** *881 84 61*   **Map** *9 B2*

A popular fish and oyster restaurant. During lunchtime, it's usually visited by people working around the Ku'damm. Good seafood influenced by German and French cuisine. On summer nights, the four tables on the tiny terrace are one of the most pleasant "people-watching" spots.

Café Einstein

€€

Kurfürstenstrasse 58, 10785 **Tel** *261 50 96*   **Map** *11 A2*

This Berlin landmark is located in an elegant villa once owned by a German movie star. The old-fashioned waiters are dressed in black suits and bow-ties, while the fine Viennese food has fin-de-siècle Austrian charm. All the traditional dishes are good, but *Wiener Schnitzel* and *Gulasch* are exceptional.

Cassambalis Taverna

🅿 🚹 ♿ 🎵   €€

Grolmanstrasse 35, 10623 **Tel** *885 47 47*   **Map** *9 C1*

The Cassambalis exudes the flair of an upscale Greek tavern with a big, open buffet table dominating the dining room. Apart from Greek and Turkish delicacies, it also serves Italian fare, such as freshly-made pasta, various kinds of fish and all kinds of salads and beef dishes.

El Borriquito

🍴 🚹 ♿ 🎵   €€

Wielandstrasse 6, 10625 **Tel** *312 99 29*   **Map** *9 B1*

A small dining room stuffed with Iberian memorabilia and an authentic staff make this a charming place. Seafood and meat dishes are very good here; the best is probably the lamb, served with a home-made sauce. Almost every night, a guitar player gives a soulful recital. In summer, tables are put out on the street.

Florian

€€

Grolmannstrasse 52, 10623 **Tel** *313 91 84*   **Map** *3 C5*

The daily specials in this restaurant, frequented by filmmakers and actors, vary with the seasons. The best dishes are created during the asparagus and wild mushroom seasons. Also on offer is a wide selection of wines. Reservations required.

Leibniz-Klause

🚹   €€

Leibnizstrasse 46, 10629 **Tel** *323 70 68*   **Map** *6 D5*

One of the few good restaurants that exclusively serve Berlin dishes, this is a traditional German neighbourhood restaurant where you still get large portions for your money. *Eisbein, Berliner Leber, Havelzander, Wurst,* and *Sauerbraten,* served along with red or green cabbage or *Sauerkraut,* are always on the menu.

Marjellchen

🚹 🅿   €€

Mommsenstrasse 9, 10629 **Tel** *88 32 676*   **Map** *9 B1*

Marjellchen is a small and cosy neighbourhood restaurant that serves specialities from former German territories. On offer are *Schlesisches Himmelreich* (smoked meat with baked fruits and dumplings) and other such temptations. Starters are the size of entrees elsewhere; the dark interior reminds one of pre-war Berlin. Closed Sun.

Nu

🚹 ♿   €€

Schülterstrasse 55, 10629 **Tel** *887 098 11*   **Map** *9 B1*

Among locals, Nu is one of the most popular Asian-inspired fusion restaurants in the western downtown area. Thanks to its fascinating mix of Thai, Chinese, Singaporean and Vietnamese dishes, served on huge tables and to be shared with other diners, Nu attracts a young and very hip clientele. DJs play smooth lounge music on weekend nights.

Ottenthal

€€

Kantstrasse 153, 10623 **Tel** *313 31 62*   **Map** *10 D1*

The simple interior is adorned by a clock from the Ottenthal Church in Austria and the background music is mainly Mozart. Fine Austrian cuisine and heavenly desserts are served with a fantastic wine list with more than 150 vintages from the Alps. Reservations required.

Paris Bar

€€

Kantstrasse 152, 10623 **Tel** *313 80 52*   **Map** *9 C1*

This is an exclusive bistro frequented by artists and politicians. Fairly expensive, and the food is good – particularly meat dishes such as blood sausage with potatoes *(Blutwurst mit Kartoffeln)* are recommended. Book ahead. If you don't get your table on time, have a drink at the neighbouring Le Nouveau Bar du Paris.

Shaan II
🏃   €€

Marburger Strasse 14, 10789 **Tel** *634 206 56*   **Map** *10 E1*

This superb Indian restaurant prepares authentic, but not overly spicy, dishes based on ancient royal recipes. The chef only uses fresh produce and rare spices, often imported directly from India. Among the top-rated dishes are tandoori creations fresh from from the earthenware oven.

Bacco
🏃   €€€€

Marburger Strasse 5, 10789 **Tel** *211 86 87*   **Map** *10 E1*

An intimate restaurant, with a modern interior and marvellous food from Tuscany. This a more quiet and relaxed version of the now famous, upscale Bocca di Bacco in Mitte. Prices are fairly high and the portions are small, but the quality makes it worthwhile. Closed Sun in summer.

Die Quadriga
€€€€€

Eislebener Strasse 14, 10789 **Tel** *214 050*   **Map** *10 E1*

Hotel Brandenburger Hof's most obvious attraction is this gourmet restaurant, one of Berlin's best. This cosy establishment serves unusual French dishes accompanied by perfect service. Master chef Sauli Kemppainen has been awarded a Michelin star. Closed Sun.

First Floor
🅿   €€€€€

Budapester Strasse 45, 10787 **Tel** *250 210 20*   **Map** *10 E1*

An elegant restaurant of the highest-quality German cuisine, run by Berlin star chef Matthias Buchholz. The Michelin-starred restaurant offers traditional food as well as unrivalled creations with fish, crayfish and truffles. The menu changes according to season, and at times the dishes can be quite heavy. Book in advance. Closed Sun & Mon.

AROUND SCHLOSS CHARLOTTENBURG

Le Piaf
🏃 ♿ 🎵   €€€€

Schlossstrasse 60, 14059 **Tel** *342 20 40*   **Map** *2 E3*

A small French restaurant-cum-bistro, typical for this kind of well-to-do neighbourhood. The down-to-earth cooking is a fine mixture of Alsatian and traditional French recipes, presented by the very personal and friendly staff or owner, Mr. Claude Trendel. In summer, there is a leafy beer garden right in front of the restaurant. Closed lunch & Sun.

Ana e Bruno
€€€€€

Sophie-Charlotten-Strasse 101, 14059 **Tel** *325 71 10*   **Map** *2 D3*

One of the best Italian restaurants in Berlin. An elegant interior creates the perfect atmosphere to sample the magnificent creations prepared by the chef. Everything is delicious, including the roasted sturgeon in Mediterranean sauce. Menus given to women omit prices, but provide a calorie count for each dish.

GREATER BERLIN

DAHLEM: Diekmann im Chalet Suisse
€€

Clayallee 99, 14195 **Tel** *832 63 62*

Occupying a picturesque old wooden building, this is a perfect place for a rest after walking in the Grunewald forest. Now run by the Diekmann restaurant chain, it offers an impeccable service. The menu is often imaginative. There is a large selection of Swiss and German dishes. Serves a *Crème brulée* to die for.

FRIEDRICHSHAIN: Umspannwerk Ost
🅿 🏃 ♿ 🎵   €€

Palisadenstrasse 48, 10243 **Tel** *428 094 97*

Set in a beautifully converted old transformer station, Umspannwerk's ambience and impressive room dimensions provide a literally electrifying dining experience. The show kitchen delivers a wide range of seasonal food that comes with carefully selected wines and occasional dinner shows ranging from dramatic theatre to flamenco.

GRUNEWALD: Forsthaus Paulsborn
€€

Hüttenweg 90, 14195 **Tel** *818 19 10*

This excellent restaurant is on the ground floor of a former hunting palace – now used as a lodge – located deep in the forest. In summer, the Forsthaus extends into the garden. The food is magnificent. On weekends, it also has a great brunch buffet. Home-made cakes and pastries are served every afternoon. Closed Mon.

GRUNEWALD: Vivaldi
🅿 🏃   €€€€€

Brahmsstrasse 10, 14193 **Tel** *895 840*

A luxurious restaurant in the expensive Schlosshotel. The interior, designed by Karl Lagerfeld, features panelled walls, gold leaf and chandeliers. Due to the many changes in hotel management, the restaurant has lost its gourmet standard, but still makes for a pleasant evening with exquisite French food. Book ahead. Closed Tue & Wed.

Key to Price Guide *see p236* **Key to Symbols** *see back cover flap*

NEUKÖLLN: Merhaba

Wissmannstrasse 32, 12049 **Tel** *692 17 13*

People from all over Berlin come to this charming restaurant to join the local Turks and Germans who enjoy the food served here. Even if you are not particularly hungry, you will not be able to resist the various appetizers. There is outdoor dining in summer and belly dancing on Fridays and Saturdays.

PRENZLAUER BERG: Mao Thai

Wörtherstrasse 30, 10405 **Tel** *441 92 61*

This is one of Berlin's best Thai restaurants, with an interior filled with beautiful antiques. The menu offers a full range of aromatic dishes, toned down to suit European tastes. Fresh and top-quality vegetables, carved into creative forms, are a speciality here. Reservations for dinner strongly advised.

PRENZLAUER BERG: Pasternak

Knaackstrasse 22-24, 10405 **Tel** *441 33 99*

Comfortable armchairs, sofas, and food from St. Petersburg can be found here. A mixed clientele of Russian expats and German students and artists come here for the joyous atmosphere and tasty but heavy food. Specialities include: beetroot soup *(borscht)*, blinis and *beef stroganov*. Vodka and caviar are available for brunch.

PRENZLAUER BERG: Gugelhof

Kollwitzstrasse 59, 10435 **Tel** *442 92 29*

Gugelhof is one of the most popular restaurants in town. This is even more the case since Bill Clinton spent an evening there. The wine list is equally impressive and affordable and the boisterous atmosphere of this neighbourhood venue make it inviting to locals and visitors alike.

PRENZLAUER BERG: Restauration 1900

Husemannstrasse 1, 10435 **Tel** *442 24 94*

One of the oldest and most traditional in this part of Berlin, this restaurant welcomes its guests into a simple dining room with a outstanding historic bar counter and other antiques. It offers light cuisine with some dishes of German origin and a large selection for vegetarians. The terrace looks over to Husemannstrasse.

SCHÖNEBERG: Pranzo e Cena

Goltzstraße 32, 10781 **Tel** *216 35 14*　　　　　　　　　　　　　　　　　　　　**Map** *11 A3*

This neighbourhood Italian pizzeria, set in a simple but cosy old-style Berlin pub, is a trendy hangout for the Schöneberg scene. The selection of freshly-made pasta is impressive. Try *Tris di Pasta*, a combination of three pasta dishes. There is a standard wine selection of German and Italian vintages. Reservations are a must.

WEDDING: Maxwell

Bergstrasse 22, 10115 **Tel** *280 71 21*

This highly regarded, upmarket, but very well-known, restaurant offers exquisite Berlin and German food with Mediterranean influences. The Maxwell always guarantees a laid-back and unpretentious atmosphere with a friendly, helpful service. There is a cheaper menu for lunch but only a few affordable wines.

WILMERSDORF: Bieberbau

Durlacherstrasse 15, 10715 **Tel** *853 23 90*

Stephan Garkisch turned this legendary nightspot into a brilliant gourmet restaurant. Lovers of Berlin food will find a typical dish like *Eisbein* or *Berliner Leber*, creatively served with a salad and Pommery potatoes (instead of *Sauerkraut* and mashed split peas). Reservations advised.

ZEHLENDORF: Wirtshaus Moorlake

Moorlakeweg 6, 14109 **Tel** *805 58 09*

Situated on the secluded bank of the Havel river, this historic restaurant serves German dishes. Though it is worth trying all the game dishes on its menu, the most highly recommended are game ragout with cranberries and buttered *spaetzle*, and the barbecue sampler, *Moorlake* with pork filets and sauce Bearnaise. Closed Mon–Tue (Jan–Feb only).

ZEHLENDORF: Blockhaus Nikolskoe

Nikolskoer Weg 15, 14109 **Tel** *805 29 14*

This restaurant is an old *dacha* (Russian-style log cabin) built by Prussian king Friedrich Wilhelm III for his daughter who married Tsar Nicholas I. The terrace has views of the lake. Fresh game and fish dishes are particularly recommended. The menu also offers German dishes and tasty cakes.

ZEHLENDORF: Waldhaus

Onkel-Tom-Strasse 50, 14169 **Tel** *813 75 75*

Set in leafy surroundings, the Waldhaus is a lovely place to spend an evening enjoying the barbecue, a speciality it is famous for. Pork, beef and fish are grilled on charcoal to order. In winter, the menu offers mostly German dishes, such as duck, goose and venison. The meat comes fresh from Berlin's state forests.

ZEHLENDORF: Goldene Grief im Schloss Klein-Glienicke

Königstrasse 36 (Klein-Glienicke), 14109 **Tel** *805 40 00*

This is an ideal place for an elegant meal on the outskirts of Berlin. Now run by Franz Raneburger, one of Berlin's mmost prominent chefs, the restaurant offers excellent German cuisine, with perch, crayfish and game, all prepared with a dose of imagination. The restaurant is also a good choice for lunch. Closed Mon & Tue.

Light Meals and Snacks

There are many popular fast-food bars and restaurants in Berlin that serve the all-pervading burgers, French fries and pizzas, some of them run by well-known international chains. By way of contrast, many of the self-service places specialize in local foods. The city's cafés are ideal stopping places for a quick meal and always offer something on the menu that will fill you up. Even more convenient are the many bars on wheels or small kiosks – *Imbissbuden* – that serve the traditional Berlin *Currywurst (see p232)*.

Vietnamese specialities. There are also many restaurants offering Indian food, mainly along Grolmanstrasse. Nearby, in Wielandstrasse, the Italian **Briganti** deserves a special recommendation.

Berlin's Japanese restaurants tend to be of the more exclusive type but still offer excellent soups and sushi. The best are **Sushi Bar Ishin**, **Saganoxpress**, **FUKU Sushi** and **Musashi**.

IMBISSBUDEN AND SNACK BARS

The classic *Imbissbude* is a simple little kiosk selling drinks and a few light snacks, such as *Currywurst* or French fries *(Pommes)* served with mayonnaise or ketchup (or both). The former is a genuine Berlin speciality consisting of grilled, sliced sausage *(Bratwurst)*, topped with a spicy sauce, and served on a paper plate with a plastic fork. These kiosks are usually located in convenient sites near the S-Bahn or U-Bahn stations, or on busy streets and junctions. **Ku'damm 195** and **Konnopke** are considered the best places to experience traditional *Currywurst*, which is served with home-made spicy sauce instead of the now standard tomato ketchup sprinkled with curry powder and fiery paprika.

Other popular snacks sold on the streets include various grilled sausages, collectively referred to as *Bratwurst*. The most common types are frankfurters *(Wienerwurst)* and a thicker kind of sausage known as *Bockwurst*. These are heated in hot water. The German variation on the hamburger theme is called *Boulette*.

Unfortunately there are few places similar to the *Imbiss-bude* that offer food from other regions of Germany. One of the exceptions is **Weizmann**, which is in an arcade under the S-Bahn railway bridge near Bellevue station. Short, thick noodles called *Spätzle* feature heavily on its typically southern German menu. **Spätzleexpress** also offers southern German dishes such as *Spätzle*, *Knödel* and *Maultaschen*.

SPECIALITIES FROM AROUND THE WORLD

Traditional Berlin specialities are facing stiff competition from further afield. Turkish restaurants serving excellent *Döner Kebab* are on every corner. Typically a kebab is a piece of warmed flat *pitta* bread stuffed with hot sliced meat, lettuce, cucumber, and tomatoes, and covered with a thick, aromatic, yogurt-based sauce. Obviously the best kebabs are made by the Turks living around Kreuzberg, but you can also have an excellent version of this dish in most of the other Berlin districts. The restaurants worth trying are **Maroush** or indeed any of the places around Kottbuser Tor or Oranienstrasse.

Vegetarians should try *falafel*, a Middle Eastern speciality widely available in Berlin. Balls of chickpeas and coriander or parsley are rolled in breadcrumbs and deep fried, then served stuffed inside flat bread with salad and yogurt sauce. The best places to try this excellent snack are around Winterfeldt-platz, for example, **Habibi**, **Dada Falafel** and **Baharat Falafel**, or **Hasir** in the eastern part of the city.

Fragrant Thai dishes are offered by **Fish & Vegetables** in Goltzstrasse, while those with a passion for Chinese food should eat at **Pagode** in Kreuzberg on Bergmann-strasse. If you wish to try Korean cuisine, then pay a visit to **Korea-Haus** on Danziger Strasse, which servers a good-value "all you can eat" Korean buffet. A visit to **Vietnam Imbiss** is a good opportunity to try out some

LIGHT SNACKS

Those with an appetite for more traditional snacks are catered for in the establish-ments around S- and U-Bahn stations and along the main streets offering fresh baguettes filled with ham or cheese.

For an instant solution to hunger pangs, try one of the bakeries that offer delicious freshly baked croissants or excellent *Brezeln* (pretzels) covered with coarse salt. During lunchtime, the popular **Nordsee** chain of restaurants offers fish sandwiches to take away, as does the stylish **Let's Go Sylt**. Some sandwich bars, such as **Fressco** in Kreuzberg, offer mouth-watering quiches and tarts alongside baguettes and rolls.

If a traditional American-Jewish bagel bar is what you fancy, then **Bagels & Bialys** in Rosenthaler Strasse or **Salomon Luna Bagels** in Joachimstaler Strasse are the places to go, where the variety of fillings is quite staggering.

Some places also specialize in one particular kind of dish or food. For example **Soup-Kultur** and **Intersoup** serve only soup, but in a multitude of varieties – hot, cold, exotic, spicy or mild. Garlic lovers should visit **Knofel** in Prenzlauer Berg. **Diekmann im Weinhaus Huth** is an upscale bistro tucked away in the Weinhaus Huth. Also worth mentioning are **Deli 31** and **Deli Street**.

Another way to ensure a quick and inexpensive fill-up are self-service pizzerias such as **Piccola Italia**. A great alter-native are the lighter pizza breads at **La Focacceria** served with any topping you like.

EATING IN SHOPPING CENTRES

One of the problems for the dedicated shopper is that eating can seriously cut down on shopping time. Fortunately, many snack bars in shopping centres have put the emphasis on fast service. Some, however, such as **KaDeWe** manage this in stylish surroundings. A visit to this enormous shop features on most tourists' list of things to do, and its self-service café is therefore very popular. Lunch at one of the tables with a view of Wittenbergplatz is a very pleasant adjunct to a Berlin shopping trip. **The Duke** is another good choice and is just around the corner from KaDeWe and Peek & Cloppenburg, off Taventzien-strasse. The stylish restaurant serves light German and American fare, making it a popular lunch spot.

Another equally busy venue is the self-service café situated in the basement of the chic **Galeries Lafayette** in Friedrichstrasse.

For those reluctant shoppers who put more emphasis on the food, a new oasis of bars and cafés has opened near to Potsdamer Platz, in the **Arkaden** shopping centre. As well as a branch of Salomon Bagels, this centre provides a taste of the Orient in Asia Pavillon, while fans of potatoes should pay a visit to Pomme de Terre. Here, the humble potato becomes the star of the meal and is served in a myriad of guises and with just as many different fillings.

For short stops, both the dedicated and the reluctant shopper should visit the classic **Wiener Café** for coffee and cakes and the **Caffé e Gelato** for delicious ice cream.

EATING IN MUSEUMS

As a city offering a wealth of culture, many of Berlin's museums have established fascinating cafés and bistros. **Café im Zeughaus** at the Deutsches Historisches Museum offers a great breakfast with views of the river Spree, while **Liebermanns** is a snack bar serving Jewish specialities at the Jüdisches Museum. **Bistro Sarah Wiener**, adjacent to the Brandenburg Gate, has some great German cakes, and **Café Dix** at the Berlinische Galerie is one of the city's most enjoyable art cafés.

CAFÉS

Berlin is well served by cafés that provide a wide range of light snacks or cakes to suit everyone's budget and tastes. They are normally open from 9 or 10 in the morning until late at night. In the mornings they serve breakfast, either à la carte or as a buffet. After that the regular café menu comes into force, although breakfast items are often still available. Main meals on the menu might include several salads, several hearty soup-type stews (*Eintöpfe*) and a few simple hot dishes. Prices are quite reasonable, not greater than ten euros. Invariably, every café has a great choice of desserts, ice creams and cakes, as well as a range of alcoholic drinks.

Around the Technical University, **Café Hardenberg** is popular with students, and near Kantstrasse you can visit **Schwarzes Café**, which is open 24 hours a day. If you are on Savigny-platz you might want to try **Café Aedes**, which has two good branches, one by the architecture gallery and the other in the second courtyard of Hackesche Höfe in Mitte. **Café am Neuen See** is situated near the lake in the Tiergarten Park. **Patisserie Buchwald**, in Hansaviertel, offers a wide range of *Baumkuchen* (so-called "tree cakes" that resemble tree stumps).

Kreuzberg's Oranienstrasse has an array of good cafés, including **Milch und Zucker** and **Pfeiffers**. You can also explore Graefestrasse, where you'll find the delightful **Café Matilda**.

Other renowned cafés include the charming **Café Wintergarten**, located in the Literaturhaus on Fasanen-strasse, and the Viennese-style **Café Einstein**. Here you can enjoy coffee made with beans fresh from their own roasting room. The original café, in Kurfürstenstrasse, has been joined by another branch in Mitte, on Unter den Linden, whose cakes are almost as refined as those at the **Opernpalais** (*see p259*).

While taking a walk around Checkpoint Charlie, you could drop in to **Sale e Tabacchi**, an excellent Italian restaurant.

There are many places that offer light lunches and coffee around Oranienburger Strasse and Alte and Neue Schönhauser Allees. In the evening they attract livelier crowds in search of decent music and good beer. You can stop by **Die Eins**, an atmospheric café.

An interesting evening can be spent investigating the options in Prenzlauer Berg. Join the in-crowd at **Anita Wronski** then move on to **Tantalus**, which serves great pancakes. If you prefer somewhere cosy, try **Chagall**, with its welcoming open fire and Russian ballads. On hot days a good spot to enjoy the sun is on the terrace in **November** or at **Seeblick**, which is a good place to eat.

Other reliable cafés that are well worth looking out for include **Atlantic**, **Keyser Soze**, **Rathauscafé**, **Telecafé** and **Voltaire**.

COFFEE BARS AND TEA ROOMS

There are not many coffee bars in Berlin, but they are easily spotted as they tend to be run by well-known coffee producers such as Eduscho or Tschibo. **Barcomi's** is a real treat, an American-style coffee bar with its own roasting room and a large selection of coffees. If you need more sustenance than coffee and muffins, try **Barcomi's Deli** where you can build your own sandwiches.

If you want a good cup of tea, then you should go to **Tadschikische Teestube**, or **TTT (Tee, Tea, Thé)**, where the choice is quite amazing.

DIRECTORY

IMBISSBUDEN AND SNACK BARS

Konnopke
Schönhauser Allee 44a
(U-Bahnhof Eberswalder Str.)
Tel 442 77 65.
◯ *6am–8pm Mon–Fri,
noon–7pm Sat.*

Ku'damm 195
Kurfürstendamm 195.
Map 9 B2.
◯ *11am–5am Mon–Thu,
11am–6am Fri & Sat,
noon–5am Sun.*

Spätzleexpress
Wiener Strasse 14a,
Kreuzberg. **Map** 14 F3.
Tel 69 53 44 63.
◯ *noon–10pm daily.*

Weizmann
Lüneburger Strasse 390.
Map 5 A3. *Tel 394 20 57.*
◯ *6–11pm Mon–Sat.*

SPECIALITIES FROM AROUND THE WORLD

Baharat Falafel
Winterfeldstrasse 37.
Map 11 B3.
Tel 216 83 01.
◯ *11am–2am daily.*

Briganti
Wielandstrasse 15.
Map 9 B1. *Tel 323 53 62.*
◯ *11am–7pm Tue–Fri,
10am–4pm Sat.*

Dada Falafel
Linienstrasse 132. **Map**
6 F1. *Tel 27 59 69 27.*
◯ *10am–2am Sun–Wed,
10am–3am Thu–Sat.*

Fish & Vegetables
Goltzstrasse 32. **Map** 11
A3. *Tel 215 74 55.*
◯ *noon–10pm daily.*

FUKU Sushi
Rosenthaler Strasse 61.
Map 7 B1. *Tel 28 38 77
83.* ◯ *noon–11pm
Mon–Fri, 4–11pm
Sat & Sun.*

Habibi
Goltzstrasse 24.
Map 11 A3. *Tel 215 33
32.* ◯ *11am–3am Sun–
Thu, 11am–5am Fri & Sat.*

Hasir
Oranienburger Strasse 4.
Map 7 B2.
Tel 28 04 16 16.
◯ *11:30am–1am daily.*

Korea-Haus
Danziger Strasse 195.
Tel 423 34 41.
◯ *noon–10pm daily.*

Maroush
Adalbertstrasse 93.
Map 14 E2.
Tel 69 53 61 71.
◯ *10am–11pm daily.*

Musashi
Kottbusser Damm 102.
Map 14 E3. *Tel 693 20
42.* ◯ *noon–10:30pm
Mon–Sat, 7–10pm Sun.*

Pagode
Bergmannstrasse 88.
Map 13 A4. *Tel 691 26 40.*
◯ *noon–midnight daily.*

Saganoxpress
Wilmersdorferstrasse 94.
Map 9 A2. *Tel 88 77 38
87.* ◯ *noon–midnight
Mon–Sat.*

Sushi Bar Ishin
Schlossstrasse 101.
Map 2 E4. *Tel 797 10 49.*
◯ *11am–8pm Mon–Sat.*

Sushi Imbiss
Pariser Strasse 44.
Map 9 B2. *Tel 881 27 90.*
◯ *noon–11pm Mon–Sat,
4–11pm Sun.*

Vietnam Imbiss
Damaschkestrasse 30.
Tel 324 93 44.
◯ *noon–9pm Mon–Sat.*

LIGHT SNACKS

Bagels & Bialys
Rosenthaler Strasse
46–48. **Map** 7 B2.
Tel 283 65 46.
◯ *8am–1am daily.*

Diekmann im Haus Huth
Alte Potsdamer Str. 5.
Map 6 D5. *Tel 25 29 75
24.* ◯ *noon–1am daily.*

Deli 31
Bleibtreustrasse 31.
Map 9 B2. *Tel 88 47 46
02.* ◯ *8am–10pm Mon–
Sat, 8am–8pm Sun.*

Deli Street
Chauseestrasse 4.
Map 6 F1. *Tel 28 09 28
33.* ◯ *8:30am–4:30pm
Mon–Fri.*

Fressco
Zossener Strasse 24.
Map 13 A4.
Tel 69 40 16 13.
◯ *5:30pm–1am Tue–Sun.*

Intersoup
Schliemannstrasse 31.
Map 6 F1.
Tel 23 27 30 45.
◯ *5pm–midnight daily.*

Knofel
Wichertstrasse 33.
Tel 447 67 17. ◯ *6pm–
late Mon–Sat, 2pm–late
Fri, 1pm–late Sun.*

La Focacceria
Fehrbellinerstrasse 24.
Map 6 F1. *Tel 44 03 27
71.* ◯ *11am–11pm daily.*

Nordsee
Spandauer Strasse 4.
Map 7 C3, 16 F2.
Tel 24 26 881.
◯ *10am–9pm daily.*

Piccola Italia
Oranienburger Strasse 6.
Map 7 B2. *Tel 283 58 43.*
◯ *11am–1am Mon–Thu,
11am–3am Fri–Sun.*

Salomon Luna Bagels
Joachimstaler Strasse 13.
Map 10 D2. *Tel 8870 26
17.* ◯ *9am–6pm
Mon–Sat.*

Soup-Kultur
Kurfürstendamm 224.
Map 10 D1. *Tel 88 62
92 82.* ◯ *noon–7:30pm
Mon–Sat.*

EATING IN SHOPPING CENTRES

Duke
Nurnbergerstrasse 50-55.
Map 10 A2.
Tel 68 31 54 00.
◯ *11:30am–11pm daily.*

Galeries Lafayette
Französische Strasse 23.
Map 6 F4, 15 C3.
Tel 20 94 80.
◯ *10am–8pm Mon–Sat.*

KaDeWe
Tauentzienstrasse 21–24.
Map 10 E1.
◯ *10am–8pm Mon–Fri,
9:30am–8pm Sat.*

Karstadt
Kurfürstendamm 231.
Map 10 D1. *Tel 880 030.*
◯ *10am–8pm Mon–Thu,
10am–10pm Fri,
10am–8pm Sat.*

Potsdamer Platz Arkaden
Alte Potsdamer Strasse 7.
Map 6 D5.
◯ *10am–9pm Mon–Sat.*

EATING IN MUSEUMS

Bistro Sarah Wiener
Akademie der Künste,
Pariser Platz 4. **Map** 6 E3.
◯ *10am–6pm daily.*

Café Dix
Berlinische Galerie,
Alte Jakobstrasse 128.
Map 7 C5. ◯ *10am–7pm
Wed–Mon.*

Café im Zeughaus
Deutsches Historisches
Museum, Unter den
Linden 2.
Map 7 A3 and 16 E2.
◯ *10am–6pm daily.*

Liebermanns
Jüdisches Museum,
Lindenstrasse 9–14.
Map 13 A2. ◯ *noon–
8pm daily (10pm Mon).*

CAFES

Anita Wronski
Knaackstrasse 26–28.
Tel 442 84 83.
◯ 9am–2am daily.

Atlantic
Bergmannstrasse 100.
Map 12 F4. *Tel 691 92 92.* ◯ 9am–1am daily.

Buchwald
Bartningallee 29.
Map 4 F2. *Tel 391 59 31.*
◯ 9am–6pm Mon–Sat.
10am–6pm Sun.

Café Aedes
Rosenthaler Strasse 40–41
(Hackesche Höfe, second courtyard). **Map** 7 B2.
Tel 28 58 275.
◯ 10am–midnight daily.
Aedes West at Savignyplatz
(arcade under the S-Bahn bridge). **Map** 9 C1.
Tel 31 50 95 35.
◯ 8am–8pm daily.

Café am Neuen See
Lichtensteinallee 1.
Map 4 F5. *Tel 254 49 30.*
◯ Apr–Nov: 10am–
11pm daily; Dec–Mar:
10am–10pm Mon–Fri,
10am–11pm Sat–Sun.

Café Cinema
Rosenthaler Strasse 39.
Map 7 B2. *Tel 280 64 15.*
◯ noon–2am daily.

Café Einstein
Kurfürstenstrasse 58. **Map**
11 A2. *Tel 261 50 96.*
◯ 8am–midnight daily.
Unter den Linden 42.
Map 6 F3, 15 C3.
Tel 204 36 32.
◯ 7am–10pm daily.

Café Hardenberg
Hardenbergstrasse 10.
Map 3 C5. *Tel 312 26 44.* ◯ 9am–1am daily.

Café Lebensart
Unter den Linden 69–73.
Map 6 E3, 15 B3.
Tel 229 00 18.
◯ 8am–9pm Mon–Fri,
10am–midnight Sat & Sun.

Café Matilda
Graefestrasse 12. **Map** 14
D4. *Tel 81 79 72 88.*
◯ 9am–1am daily.

Café Morgenrot
Kanstanienallee 85. *Tel 44
31 78 44.* ◯ noon–1am
Tue–Thu, 11am–3am Fri &
Sat, 11am–11pm Sun.

Café Oliv
Münzstrasse 8. **Map** 7 C2.
Tel 89 20 65 40.
◯ 8:30am–7pm Mon–
Sat, 10am–4pm Sun.

Café Ständige Vertretung
Schiffbauerdamm 8.
Tel 282 39 65.
◯ 10:30am–1am daily.

Café Tomasa
Motzstrasse 60.
Map 10 F3. *Tel 213 23
45.* ◯ 8am–midnight
Mon–Fri, 8am–1am Sat,
9am–midnight Sun.

Café Wintergarten im Literaturhaus
Fasanenstrasse 23. **Map**
10 D1. *Tel 882 54 14.*
◯ 9:30am–1am daily.

Chagall
Kollwitzstrasse 2.
Tel 441 58 81.
◯ 10am–1am daily.

Deli Lama
Quartier 205,
Friedrichstrasse 68.
Map 6 F4.
Tel 609 80 69 12.

Die Eins
Wilhelmstrasse 67A
(eingang Reichstagsufer).
Map 6 E3.
Tel 22 48 98 88.
◯ 9am–midnight Mon–
Sat, 10am–midnight Sun.

Dolores
Rosa-Luxemburg-Strasse 7.
Map 7 C2. *Tel 28 09 95
97.* ◯ 11:30am–10pm
Mon–Sat, 1–10pm Sun.

Filmbühne am Steinplatz
Hardenbergstrasse 12.
Map 4 D5. *Tel 312 65
89.* ◯ 9am–1am daily.

Kaffeestube am Nikolaiplatz
Poststrasse 19. **Map** 7 C3.
Tel 24 63 06 41.
◯ 9am–midnight daily.

Keyser Soze
Tucholskystrasse 33. **Map** 7
A1. *Tel 28 59 94 89.*
◯ 8am–3am daily.

Kleine Orangerie
Spandauer Damm 20.
Map 2 E3. *Tel 322 20 21.*
◯ 9am–9pm daily
(10am–8pm in winter).

Milch und Zucker
Oranienstrasse 37. **Map**
14 D2. *Tel 61 67 14 97.*
◯ 7am–7pm Mon–Fri,
9am–7pm Sat,
10am–6pm Sun.

November
Husemannstrasse 15.
Tel 442 84 25.
◯ 10am–2am Mon–Fri,
9am–2am Sat & Sun.

Operncafé
Unter den Linden 5. **Map**
7 A3, 16 E3. *Tel 20 26 83.*
◯ 9am–midnight daily.

Pfeiffers
Oranienstrasse 17.
Map 14 E2. *Tel 61 65
86 09.* ◯ 8:30am–
midnight daily.

Sale e Tabacchi
Kochstrasse 18.
Tel 252 11 55.
◯ noon–midnight daily.

San Remo
Falckensteinstrasse 46.
Tel 74 07 30 88.
◯ 4pm–2am Mon–Fri,
3pm–2am Sat & Sun.

Schwarzes Café
Kantstrasse 148. **Map** 9
C1. *Tel 313 80 38.*
◯ 24 hours daily.

Seeblick
Rykestrasse 14. *Tel 442
92 26.* ◯ noon–late daily.

Let's Go Sylt
Kurfürstendamm 212.
Map 9 C2. *Tel 88 68
28 00.* ◯ 11am–
midnight Mon–Sat.

Telecafé
Alexanderplatz (TV Tower).
Map 8 D2. *Tel 242 33 33.*
◯ 10am–midnight daily.

COFFEE BARS AND TEA ROOMS

Balzac Coffee
Knesebeckstrasse 1.
Map 3 C5.
Friedrichstrasse 125.
Map 15 C4 & 6 F4.
◯ 7:30am–8pm Mon–
Fri, 9am–6:30pm Sun.

Barcomi's
Bergmannstrasse 21.
Map 13 A5.
Tel 694 81 38.
◯ 8am–9pm Mon–Sat,
9am–9pm Sun.

Barcomi's Deli
Sophienstrasse 21
(second courtyard).
Map 7 B1. *Tel 28 59 83
63.* ◯ 9am–9pm Mon–
Sat, 10am–9pm Sun.

Einstein Coffeeshop
Friedrichstrasse 166.
Map 15 C4.
◯ 7am–8:30pm Mon–
Fri, 7:30am–8:30pm Sat,
9am–6pm Sun.
Friedrichstrasse185.
Map 6 F4.
◯ 7.30–8:30pm Mon–
Sat, 9am–8pm Sun.
Savignyplatz 11.
Map 9 C1.
◯ 7:30–8pm Mon–Fri,
9am–8pm Sat, 9am–
6pm Sun.

Tadschikische Teestube
Am Festungsgraben 1.
Map 7 A3, 16 E2.
Tel 204 11 12.
◯ 5pm–midnight
Mon–Fri, 3pm–midnight
Sat & Sun.

TTT – Tee, Tea, Thé
Goltzstrasse 2.
Map 11 A4.
Tel 21 75 22 40.
◯ Oct–Apr: 9am–10pm
Mon–Fri, 9am–8pm Sat,
10am–8pm Sun; May–
Sep: 9am–8pm Mon–Sat,
10am–8pm Sun.

Bars and Wine Bars

Trying to make a clear distinction between wine bars, bars, pubs and *Bierstuben* or giving a precise definition for the word *Kneipe* is practically impossible. However, regardless of the nuances behind all these names, they do share some basic characteristics: they are places where drinking is the primary activity, although eating is sometimes possible; they are usually open from late afternoon or early evening but do not close till late at night or even till morning, if the atmosphere is lively.

KNEIPEN

In general terms, a *Kneipe* means a cosy sort of place which serves beer (although other drinks are available, too) and where you can have something to eat. The typical *Alberliner Kneipe* is a dark room with panelled oak walls, a big bar and buffet with snacks such as *Buletten* (made from pork), *Soleier* (pickled eggs), *Rollmöpse* (marinated herring) and a selection of cold meats, black pudding (blood sausage) and patés. This kind of traditional pub can still be found in the less affluent districts of Berlin – in Moabit, Kreuzberg and in Neukölln, for example, but they are not as common in the city centre. Among the most popular are **Zur Kneipe** and **Ranke 2**, as well as several *Kneipen* in Mitte around the Nikolaiviertel, including **Zum Nussbaum**.

Each *Kneipe* has its own character. More and more of them are choosing modern and inventive interiors, often specializing in less traditional kinds of food: Italian, French or Oriental. Whatever the blend, however, a relaxed atmosphere and a big choice of alcoholic beverages seem to be common features. Many *Kneipen* are evolving into a fashionable mix of *Kneipe*, bar, lounge and beer garden. One such is **Reingold** in Mitte. In Savignyplatz, you might want to visit **Dicke Wirtin**, where you can try a hearty *Eintopf* (a rich soup-type stew). The majority of these fashion-able places are situated in Kreuzberg and in Prenzlauer Berg – especially around Kollwitzplatz, which is dotted with all sorts of bars and pubs. At **Ankerklause** students and political activists come together to drink, dance and put the world to rights.

BIERGARTEN

A *Biergarten* is an outdoor venue only open during the summer months, and usually located somewhere scenic, maybe in a park or by a lake. In addition to the usual food and drinks, it completes the outdoor experience with a barbecue. **Golgatha** and **Schleusenkrug** provide a much welcome breath of fresh air in the centre of Berlin; or if you are exploring Prenzlauer Berg, try the **Prater**. After enjoying the views in Tiergarten, the **Café am Neuen See** is a pleasant place to end the day.

A Berlin trend is the open-air beach bar situated on one of the city's waterways, the most popular of these being **Bundespressestrand**.

WINE BARS

Berlin wine bars tend to have a Mediterranean feel to them. Interiors are often quite rustic in style, but there are exceptions. They open from early evening and stay open late. As for food, menus feature predominantly Italian, Spanish and French cuisine, while the bar serves a huge selection of wines by the glass, bottle or carafe. **Vienna Bar**, a wine bar with an established reputation, features French food and wine. If you are visiting Prenzlauer Berg you might want to try **Weinstein** which offers French and Spanish food and wine. By way of contrast, at **Lutter & Wegener** in Mitte you can match German-Austrian food with appropriate, native wines, or sample a selection of American snacks and cocktails at **Billy Wilder's**.

BARS

A Berlin bar is a good place to finish your evening, and the dedicated barfly is spoiled for choice. You should not count on food but you can drink till late, as most bars do not open until 8pm or later. Although there is no strict dress code, scruffy clothes are not really appropriate. The **Riva Bar**, one of the city's most elegant and hip bars, is tucked away under the S-Bahn viaduct, and serves some of the best cocktails in town. A Latin American atmosphere is created at **Roter Salon** by tango, salsa and all the fantastic dancers. You might step in to **Vox Bar** to try one of its huge range of cocktails in a pre-war movie setting. Don't forget to visit some of the hotel bars which are among the best late-night venues in the city. Two worthy of mention are **Harry's New York Bar** (the later the better), in the Hotel Esplanade and the **Newton Bar**.

GAY AND LESBIAN BARS

Berlin has a unique tradition of nightlife for homosexuals, dating back to the 1920s, when its cabarets and bars, especially around Nollendorfplatz, were the most outrageous in Europe. Today that hardcore legacy remains, but there are also bars to suit every taste. Some, like **Café Seidenfaden**, are for women only, while **Roses** is exclusively for men. Many, like **Haus B**, are frequented by both gays and lesbians. For a more mixed ambiance, the friendly attitude of bars such as **Heile Welt** or **So 36** means they are popular with both gay and straight visitors alike.

DIRECTORY

KNEIPEN

Ankerklause
Maybachufer 1.
Map 14 E3.
Tel 693 56 49.

Dicke Wirtin
Carmerstrasse 9.
Map 3 C5.
Tel 312 49 52.

Diener Tattersall
Grolmanstrasse 47.
Map 9 C1.
Tel 881 53 29.

Gasthaus Lenz
Stuttgarter Platz 20.
Tel 324 16 19.

Meilenstein
Oranienburger Strasse 7.
Map 7 B2, 16 F1.
Tel 282 89 95.

Ranke 2
Rankestrasse 2.
Map 10 E1.
Tel 883 88 82.

Reingold
Novalisstrasse 11.
Map 6 F1.
Tel 28 38 76 76.

Restaurant Zur Gerichtslaube
Poststrasse 28.
Map 7 C3.
Tel 241 56 97.

Slumberland
Goltzstrasse 24.
Map 11 A3.
Tel 216 53 49.

Zum Nussbaum
Am Nussbaum 3.
Map 7 C3.
Tel 242 30 95.

Zum Patzenhofer
Meinekestrasse 26.
Map 10 D1.
Tel 882 11 35.

Zur Kneipe
Rankestrasse 9.
Map 10 D2.
Tel 883 82 55.

BIERGARTEN

Bundespressestrand
Kapelle-Ufer 1. **Map** 6 D2.
Tel 28 09 91 19.

Café am Neuen See
Lichtensteinallee 2. **Map** 4 F5. *Tel* 25 44 93 00.

Golgatha
Dudenstrasse 40, in Viktoriapark.
Map 12 E5.
Tel 78 52 453.

Prater
Kastanienallee 7–9.
Map 1 A5, 1 B3.
Tel 448 56 88.

Schleusenkrug
Müller-Breslau-Strasse/at Tiergartenschleuse.
Map 4 E4.
Tel 313 99 09.

WINE BARS

Billy Wilder's
Potsdamer Strasse 2.
Map 6 D5.
Tel 26 55 48 60.

Lutter & Wegener
Charlottenstrasse 56.
Map 7 A4, 16 D4.
Tel 202 95 40.

Vienna Bar
Kantstrasse 152.
Map 10 D1.
Tel 313 80 52.

Vox Bar at the Grand Hyatt
Marlene-Dietrich-PLatz 2.
Map 6 D5.
Tel 030 2553 1772.

Weinstein
Lychener Strasse 33.
Tel 441 18 42.

BARS

Altes Europa
Gipsstrasse 11.
Map 7 B1.
Tel 28 09 38 40.

Ballhaus Berlin
Chausseestrasse 102
Map 6 F1. *Tel* 282 75 75.

Bar am Lützowplatz
Lützowplatz 7.
Map 11 A1.
Tel 262 68 07.

b-flat
Rosenthaler Strasse 13.
Map 7 B1. *Tel* 283 31 23.

Gainsbourg – Bar American
Savignyplatz 5.
Map 9 B1 and 9 C1.
Tel 313 74 64.

Green Door
Winterfeldtstrasse 50.
Tel 215 25 15.

Haifischbar
Arndtstrasse 25.
Map 13 A5.
Tel 691 13 52.

Harry's New York Bar
Lützowufer 15 (in Hotel Esplanade). **Map** 11 A1.
Tel 25 47 88 633.

Kumpelnest 3000
Lützowstrasse 23.
Map 11 B1.
Tel 26 16 918.

Newton Bar
Charlottenstrasse 57.
Map 16 D4.
Tel 20 29 54 21.

Riva Bar
Dircksenstrasse,
S-Bahnbogen 142.
Map 7 C2.
Tel 24 72 26 88.

Roter Salon
Rosa-Luxemburg-Platz 2.
Map 7 C1.
Tel 24 06 56 24.

Times Bar (cigar bar)
Fasanenstrasse 9–10.
Map 10 D1.
Tel 31 10 33 36.

Trompete
Lützowplatz 9.
Map 11 A1.
Tel 23 00 47 94.

Zur Fetten Ecke
Schlesische Strasse 16.
Tel 44 65 16 99.

GAY AND LESBIAN BARS

Ackerkeller
Bergstrasse 68.
Tel 36 46 13 56.

Café Seidenfaden
Dircksenstrasse 47.
Map 7 C3.
Tel 283 27 83.

Haus B
Mühlenstrasse 11–12.
Tel 296 08 00.

Heile Welt
Motzstrasse 5.
Map 11 A2.
Tel 21 91 75 07.

Möbel Olfe
Dresdnerstrasse (am ende).
Map 14 D2.
Tel 23 27 46 90.

Roses
Oranienstrasse 187.
Map 14 E2.
Tel 615 65 70.

So 36
Oranienstrasse 190.
Map 13 B1, 14 D1.
Tel 61 40 13 06.

SHOPPING IN BERLIN

With a shopping centre in every district, each selling a wide variety of merchandise, Berlin is a place where almost anything can be bought, so long as you know where to look. The most popular places are Kurfürstendamm and Friedrichstrasse, but the smaller shops in Prenzlauer Berg, Friedrichshain, Schöneberg and the Tiergarten are also worth a visit. Small boutiques selling flamboyant Berlin-style clothes crop up in unexpected courtyards, while the top fashion houses offer the latest in European elegance. Early on Saturday morning is often the best time to visit the city's various markets, the most popular of which – with their colourful stalls full of hats, bags and belts – can be found on Museum Island and at the Tiergarten. The Galeries Lafayette, KaDeWe and any of the city's numerous bookshops all make ideal venues for a pleasant afternoon's window shopping.

Inside the modern, multi-level Europa-Center *(see p150)*

OPENING HOURS

The majority of shops are open Monday to Friday from 10am to 8pm (10am to 6pm or 8pm on Saturday), but some department stores open as early as 9am. The larger stores may open until 10pm or midnight on Friday and Saturday.

Generally, there are no lunch breaks unless the shop is a one-person business. During the six weeks before Christmas, shops stay open until late on Saturdays. Most shops close on Sundays. If you are in need of groceries or food, try one of the main train stations. You'll find supermarkets open at Hauptbahnhof, Friedrichstrasse and Ostbahnhof.

DEPARTMENT STORES

Kaufhaus Des Westens, better known as **KaDeWe** at Wittenbergplatz *(see p155)*, is undoubtedly the biggest and the best department store in Germany. Only products of the highest quality are sold in these luxurious halls, where virtually everything you need is on sale – from unusual perfumes and elegant underwear to *haute couture*, all sold in a system of shops-within-shops. The food hall on the sixth floor is legendary for its restaurant overlooking Tauentzienstrasse.

Galeries Lafayette on Friedrichstrasse is nothing less than a slice of Paris placed in the heart of Berlin. Perfumes, domestic accessories and clothing attract an enormous clientele, many of whom also visit the food counter which offers a wide range of French specialities. An extraordinary glass cone rises through the middle of the store, reflecting the interiors of the shops.

Another very popular store is **Karstadt** on the Ku'damm.

A typical street-side stall, brimming with souvenirs for visitors

Although its range of goods is not as broad as the range at Galeries Lafayette, there is still an enormous choice and the top-floor restaurant offers excellent views over the city.

SHOPPING CENTRES

In addition to the two biggest shopping districts in town – the Ku'damm and Friedrichstrasse – shopping

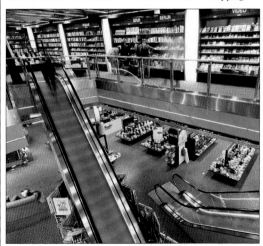

The spacious interior of the Hugendubel department store

Milano tie shop on Kurfürstendamm

DIRECTORY

DEPARTMENT STORES

Galeries Lafayette
Französische Strasse 23.
Map 7 A4.
Tel 20 94 80.

KaDeWe
Tauentzienstrasse 21-24.
Map 10 F2.
Tel 21 21 0.

Karstadt
Kurfürstendamm 231.
Map 10 D1.
Tel 88 00 30.

SHOPPING CENTRES

Alexa
Alexanderplatz.
Tel 269 340. **Map** 8 D3.

Das Schloss
Schlossstrasse 34. **Tel** 66 69 120.

Potsdamer Platz Arkaden
Alte Potsdamer Strasse 7.
Tel 255 92 70. **Map** 6 E5.

Shopping Guide
www.berlin-shopper.com

centres are constantly being built, usually conveniently situated close to S-Bahn stations. These massive three-level structures, resembling huge arcaded passageways, contain an enormous number of shops, ranging from supermarkets and chemists to bars, high-street fashion and bookshops. Like most of the shops in Berlin they stay open until 8pm during the week. One of the newest shopping centres is the **Potsdamer Platz Arkaden**. It is very popular both as a shopping mall and a meeting place. It is visited by thousands of tourists and Berliners every day.

Of a similar character, although smaller yet still upmarket, are the glitzy shopping mall **Das Schloss** and the budget-oriented Forum Steglitz, both on Schlossstrasse in the southern district of Steglitz. **Alexa** on Alexanderplatz is a huge shopping centre with some 180 stores spread over five levels, a large food court and extensive underground parking. Major international clothing retailers, bookshops, electronics outlets and toy shops are all represented.

SEASONAL SALES

All shops in Berlin empty their racks and shelves in the sale, or *Schlussverkauf*, which takes place twice a year. At the end of January, before the new year's collections are displayed in shop windows, you can buy winter clothes for as little as 50 per cent of their original price. During the summer sales (*Sommerschlussverkauf*), which take place at the end of July, you can find similarly-reduced summer outfits. Goods bought in a sale are officially non-returnable, but if you are really keen to take an item back, there is no harm in at least trying to negotiate with the shop assistant.

A number of shops sell a variety of articles marketed as "second season" items. These are always new articles, albeit stocked for the previous season, and they are offered at often generously-reduced prices. You will also find that various shops specialize in top-brand jeans, selling them at much-reduced rates owing to what are often very minor defects. These represent excellent value for money.

HOW TO PAY

When it comes to paying for goods you may find that some small shops still insist on cash. In the centre of Berlin there should be a suitable cash machine not too far away *(see p284)*. Larger shops and department stores will also accept most major credit cards.

SHOPPING GUIDE

If you are planning to do some serious shopping in Berlin, and are worried about getting lost among the many possibilities, you may want to use the services of a "shopping guide". These are specialists who will tell you what is currently on offer in both the big department stores and in the smaller boutiques.

A shop-floor display in the lobby of KaDeWe *(see p155)*

Clothes and Accessories

There are many shopping centres in Berlin, and nearly every district has its own high street where residents do their shopping. If it's luxury, elegance and a wide variety of goods you are after, however, then head for the shops on Kurfürstendamm, Friedrichstrasse and Potsdamer Platz. This is where all the major fashion houses and perfume makers have their shops, right in the heart of the city. Alternatively, if you want to explore the smaller boutiques of some lesser-known designers, make your way to Hackescher Markt in the Mitte district, or to Prenzlauer Berg.

WOMEN'S FASHIONS

The most famous fashion houses are on the Ku'damm (Kurfürstendamm) and its side streets, particularly in the area around the quietly elegant Fasanenstrasse. Among the many famous names doing business here are **Yves Saint Laurent**, **Max Mara**, **Sonia Rykiel**, **Bogner**, **Louis Vuitton**, **Chanel** and **Gucci**. Simplicity is the order of the day in the **Designer Depot** shop, making it the ideal place to buy a straightforward dress with exquisite accessories. Gucci has two shops in the area, one in Fasanenstrasse and another in the fashionable Quartier 206 on Friedrichstrasse. The latter shares the street with many other fashion houses that specialize in women's clothes: **Evelin Brandt**, **Department Store 206**, **Strenesse**, **Strenesse Blue** and **ETRO**, to name a few. The city's first international fashion concept store, **The Corner Berlin**, offers a mix of rare designer clothes by stars such as Roland Mouret and John Galliano, accessories, beauty products and even art in a minimalist, ultra-stylish setting.

MEN'S FASHIONS

For the full range of the latest in fashion for men, on or near Kurfürstendamm is the place to go shopping, for this is where various retailers sell clothing straight from Europe's best-known fashion houses. **Patrick Hellmann** is certainly worth a visit with its wide choice of the best designer labels around.

Clothes by Giorgio Armani, Helmut Lang, Christian Dior and Dolce E Gabbana can all be found here. Also very popular are **Anson's** and the more upmarket **Mientus**, which has a second outlet on Wilmersdorfer Strasse. **Peek & Cloppenburg**, Germany's second largest speciality store, sells its own budget labels as well as designer clothes by Boss, Armani and Joop. **Zegna** on Kurfürstendamm is a flagship store for men. This Italian company sells some of the finest-quality suits in Germany.

CHILDREN'S CLOTHING

Shops selling children's clothes can generally satisfy any taste, depending on how much you are willing to spend. **I Pinco Pallino** offers *haute couture* for all ages. Alternatively, the Prenzlauer Berg district, which has the highest birth rate in the whole of Germany, is dotted with small children's boutiques offering both brand names and handmade clothes.

YOUNG DESIGNERS

A number of galleries, studios and boutiques specialize in the so-called Berlin style, the collections on sale usually consisting of short-series items that are produced in strictly limited numbers. At one time it was possible to find shops like this across the whole of the city, but now they are concentrated mainly in the northern part of the Mitte area, where a unique fashion centre is firmly established. **NIX** offers timeless clothes made from heavy, dark fabrics and cut in classical fashion.

Among the other shops in Mitte, **Fishbelly** on Sophienstrasse is noted for its unique range of erotic underwear, designed by Jutta Teschner. At **Molotow**, in Kreuzberg, the choice is more classical than the trendy name might suggest. Another very popular place to buy clothes is **Chapeaux**, in Charlottenburg, while **Lisa D**. offers classic and elegant dresses by one of Berlin's top female designers. Young fashion hunters looking for the latest underground trends should head to **Apartment** and **Redspective**, both in the trendy fashion district Mitte.

SHOES AND ACCESSORIES

One of the largest shoe shops in Berlin is **Schuhtick**, which has three branches in the city, though the highest quality can be found in the **Budapester Schuhe** chain. A good selection can also be found at the **Görtz** outlets around Kufürstendamm. The latest Italian designs are available at **Riccardo Cartillone**.

Penthesileia on Tucholskystrasse offers an amusing range of handbags, which come in all kinds of shapes and sizes. If it's a hat you are after, then you need go no further than **Hut Up**, in the Heckmannhöfen. All kinds are headgear are available here, from typical Russian *shlapas* to party hats with Rastafarian dreadlocks.

PERFUMES

All of the large department stores, including **KaDeWe** and **Galeries Lafayette**, offer a sizeable selection of the best-known perfumes, but there are also a number of specialist shops dotted around the city. The **Douglas** chain, which has numerous outlets, has a wide range of perfumes at very reasonable prices. **Quartier 206** has a good selection of the better-known perfumes, but if you are looking for something unusual, then **Harry Lehmann** is the place to visit. This unique store is a perfume-lover's paradise, where Mr Lehmann himself continues an 80-year-long family tradition of mixing your very own perfume from a variety of 50 scents. He also stocks long-forgotten brands. The **Body Shop** group is popular in Berlin. Natural perfumes of all kinds can be bought here, and its policy of no animal testing is popular with customers. It also encourages the return of its containers for recycling.

DIRECTORY

WOMEN'S FASHION

Bogner
Kurfürstendamm 42.
Map 9 C2.
Tel 88 71 77 80.

Chanel
Kurfürstendamm 188.
Map 9 C3.
Tel 885 14 24.

Department Store Quartier 206
Friedrichstrasse 71.
Map 6 F4.
Tel 20 94 68 00.

Designer Depot
Rochstrasse 2.
Map 7 C2.
Tel 28 04 67 00.

ETRO
Friedrichstrasse 71.
Map 6 F3.
Tel 20 94 61 20.

Evelin Brandt
Savignyplatz 6.
Map 9 C1.
Tel 313 80 80.

Gucci
Kurfürstendamm 190–192.
Map 9 C2.
Tel 885 63 00.

Friedrichstrasse 71.
Map 6 F3.
Tel 201 70 20.

Louis Vuitton
Friedrichstrasse 71.
Map 6 F4.
Tel 20 94 68 68.

Max Mara
Kurfürstendamm 178.
Map 10 D1.
Tel 885 25 45.

Sonia Rykiel
Kurfürstendamm 186.
Map 9 A2.
Tel 882 17 74.

Strenesse & Strenesse Blue
Friedrichstrasse 71.
Map 6 F3.
Tel 20 94 60 35.

The Corner Berlin
Französische Strasse 40.
Map 7 A4.
Tel 20 67 09 40.

Yves Saint Laurent
Kurfürstendamm 52.
Map 9 A2.
Tel 883 39 18.

MEN'S FASHIONS

Anson's
Schlossstrasse 34.
Tel 79 09 60.

Mientus
Wilmersdorfer Strasse 73.
Map 2 F3, 3 A5, 9 A1.
Kurfürstendamm 52.
Map 9 A2.
Tel 323 90 77.

Patrick Hellmann
Kurfürstendamm 190–192. **Map** 10 D2.
Tel 884 87 711.

Peek & Cloppenburg
Tauentzienstrasse 19.
Map 10 E1.
Tel 21 29 00.

Zegna
Kurfürstendamm 185.
Map 9 B2.
Tel 887 190 90.

CHILDREN'S CLOTHING

H&M Kinder
Friedrichstrasse 78/80.
Map 6 F4. *Tel* 201 20 10.

Pinco Pallino
Kurfürstendamm 46.
Map 10 D1.
Tel 881 28 63.

YOUNG DESIGNERS

Apartment
Memhardstrasse 8 10178.
Map 7 C2.
Tel 28 04 22 51.

Chapeaux
Bleibtreustrasse 51.
Map 9 B1.
Tel 312 09 13.

Fishbelly
Sophienstrasse 7a.
Tel 28 04 51 80.

Lisa D.
Hackesche Höfe,
Rosenthaler
Strasse 40–41.
Map 7 B2.
Tel 28 29 061.

Molotow
Gneisenaustrasse 112.
Map 13 A4.
Tel 693 08 18.

NIX
Oranienburger
Strasse 32.
Map 7 A2.
Tel 281 80 44.

Redspective
Rosa-Luxemburg-Strasse
18. **Map** 7 C1.
Tel 27 59 54 09.

SHOES AND ACCESSORIES

Budapester Schuhe
Kurfürstendamm 43 &
199. **Map** 10 D1.
Tel 88 11 707.

Bleibtreustrasse 24.
Map 9 B1.
Tel 62 95 00.

Görtz
Kurfürstendamm 13-14.
Map 10 D1.
Tel 88 68 37 52.

Hut Up
Oranienburger Strasse 32.
Map 7 A2.
Tel 28 38 61 05.

Penthesileia
Tucholskystrasse 31.
Map 7 A2, 16 D1.
Tel 282 11 52.

Riccardo Cartillone
Savignyplatz 4.
Map 9 C1.
Tel 312 97 01.

Schuhtick
Savignyplatz 11.
Map 9 C1.
Tel 315 93 80.

Potsdamer Platz Arkaden,
Alte Potsdamer Strasse 7.
Map 6 D5.
Tel 25 29 33 58.

PERFUMES

Body Shop
(in the main hall of
Zoologischer Garten
railway station).
Map 10 D1.
Tel 31 21 391.

Douglas
Kurfürstendamm 216.
Map 10 D1.
Tel 881 25 34.

Galeries Lafayette Parfümerie
Französische Strasse 23.
Map 6 F4. *Tel* 20 94 80.

Harry Lehmann
Kantstrasse 106.
Map 9 A1.
Tel 324 35 82.

KaDeWe Parfümerie
Tauentzienstrasse 21–24.
Map 10 E1. *Tel* 21 210.

Quartier 206
Friedrichstrasse 71.
Map 6 F3.
Tel 20 94 68 00.

Gifts and Souvenirs

Whether it is a piece of the Wall or a Prussian tin soldier, Berlin souvenirs are easy to come by. While most needs can be met on one of the main shopping thoroughfares, there are more exclusive options. If you are looking for something elegant, a piece of china made by Königliche Porzellan-Manufaktur Berlin (see p133) might be a good idea. Other good sources are the museum shops, notably the one in the Bauhaus Museum with its designer household objects. For a child, a teddy bear is always an option — after all, the bear is the city's emblem. For handmade jewellery or contemporary art, head for Berliner Kunstmarkt Unter den Linden on a Sunday. In December, find the most beautifully crafted gifts on the numerous Christmas markets all over the city, the one on Gendarmenmarkt being particularly worthwhile.

BOOKS AND MUSIC

The best places to buy books on art are the shops at major museums, where you will also find a good selection of cards, posters and general souvenirs. The best of these are in **Hamburger Bahnhof** (see pp110–11), **Gemälde-galerie** (see pp122–5), **Museum Berggruen** (see p164), **Schloss Charlottenburg** (see pp160–61) and **Altes Museum** (see p75).

The **Bücherbogen** chain offers a huge choice of books and has several outlets in the city. Other good stores include **Autorenbuchhandlung** or, if you want to combine shopping for books and art appreciation, **Artificium** has a gallery attached.

For English-language books or papers, **Books in Berlin** and **Saint Georges** are the places to go with their wide choice of both English and American literature. **Prinz Eisenherz** also has a good selection of gay literature. For second-hand books try **Another Country** in Kreuzberg, which also operates a book exchange system. **Do You Read Me?!** in Mitte and **Motto Bookshop** in Kreuzberg both sell a wide range of fascinating magazines, including rare, small-distribution independent press. In all of these shops the staff are usually very helpful.

Music lovers should head for **Artificium** in Schloss-strasse, **Cover Music** near the Ku'damm or, if it is classical music you are after, then **L & P Classics** has one of the finest selections. For something avant-garde don't miss **Gelbe Musik** on Chauseestrasse. If you happen to be short of funds there is always the option of flicking through the second-hand CDs on offer at the Sunday antique market on Strasse des 17 Juni (see p256). The market is always crammed with souvenirs and is a great hunting-ground for collectors of old vinyl records.

TOYS

You won't have to travel far to buy a typical Berlin teddy bear – you can find them in stores all over the city, especially the gift shops in the Nikolaiviertel. If you're after a wider variety of toys, then **KaDeWe** (see p155) is the place to go. Like all the major department stores, KaDeWe (see p155) offers a whole range of toys for children of all ages, but its teddy bear section is second to none in Berlin. From the highly portable half-inch bear to the life-size 2-metre model, every kind of bear you can imagine is on sale here, so you shouldn't be disappointed. Also, the store can arrange a delivery to your home, so if your child has always dreamed of having an enormous teddy bear, this is a perfect opportunity to fulfil the dream.

Small manufacturers still make old-style wooden toys, from doll's house furniture to traditional jigsaw puzzles, and these make excellent gifts to take home. **Heidi's Spielzeugladen** on Kantstrasse, **Original Erzgebirgs-Kurst** on Sophienstrasse and **Spielen** on Hufelandstrasse are the best places to go for souvenirs of this kind. Train lovers hoping to extend their tracks and build more depots and stations should visit **Michas Bahnhof** on Nürnberger Strasse, the city's top provider of model train set accessories. An amazing range of goods is available here.

As an old Prussian capital, Berlin is also a good place to find Germanic lead soldiers; the best place to look is **Berliner Zinnfiguren Kabinett**. While most of the soldiers available are designed for children, collecting them is a popular hobby among adults, and the rarities often fetch very high prices on the market.

FLOWERS

It is very easy to find a nice bouquet in Berlin. Flower shops stand on nearly every street corner and the majority of them are open for business on Sundays. **Blumen-Koch** in Wilmersdorf offers an amazing selection of beautiful and colourful plants and is famous for its bouquets of exotic flowers which are always arranged and wrapped with real artistry.

CHINA AND CERAMICS

The history of European china started in Germany in 1708. The alchemist Böttger, while searching for the secret of making gold, discovered instead how to make Chinese-style porcelain. Berlin soon became a major producer. **KPM (Königliche Porzellan-Manufaktur Berlin)** (see p133) is still in operation, and its products will satisfy even the most choosy of porcelain collectors. Plenty of newly made china is available, but if you are looking for something older, then an afternoon could be spent in some of the city's antique shops *(see pp256–7)*. Currently manufactured pieces can be bought in the KPM factory shop. Those who prefer Meissen porcelain will be able to find it in several shops along the Ku'damm.

While porcelain is expensive, an equally precious gift can be made of a ceramic dish or breakfast set, traditionally manufactured in Thuringia. With their characteristic blue and white patterns, a wide choice of exquisite Thuringian ceramics can be found in **Bürgel-Haus** on Friedrichstrasse.

SPECIALIST SHOPS

If you are determined to find something unique, or even quirky, you might want to visit some of the interesting specialist shops – like **Knopf Paul**, which specializes in extraordinary buttons, or **Bären-Luftballons**, which offers a delightful variety of colourful and amusing balloons. There are also a number of shops which specialize in teas and tea-time accessories. **Tee Gschwendner** and **Berliner Teesalon** offer the best selection in this field.

Smart letter paper and good pens can be bought in **Papeterie**, but if you're still stuck for ideas, there's no harm in browsing through the specialist departments in **KaDeWe** *(see Toys)* where there's always something guaranteed to catch the eye. For gifts and clothing designed by local artists, visit **Berlinomat** in Frankfurter Allee.

DIRECTORY

BOOKS AND MUSIC

Another Country
Riemannstrasse 7.
Map 13 A4.
Tel 69 40 11 60.

Artificium
Rosenthalerstrasse 40/41.
Map 7 B1.
Tel 30 87 22 80.

Autorenbuch-handlung
Carmerstrasse 10.
Map 3 C5.
Tel 313 01 51.

Books in Berlin
Goethestrasse 69.
Map 3 B5.
Tel 31 31 233.

Bücherbogen
Savignyplatz.
Map 9 C1.
Tel 31 86 95 11.

Cover Music
Kurfürstendamm 11.
Map 10 D1.
Tel 88 55 01 30.

Do You Read Me?!
Auguststrasse 28.
Map 7 A1.
Tel 69 54 96 95.

Gelbe Musik
Chausseestrasse 128.
Map 6 F1.
Tel 211 39 62.

Gemäldegalerie
Matthäikirchplatz 8.
Map 5 C5.
Tel 266 424 242.

Grober Unfug
Zossener Strasse 33.
Map 13 A3.
Tel 69 40 14 90.

Hamburger Bahnhof
Invalidenstrasse 50/51.
Map 6 D1.
Tel 266 424 242.

Hugendubel
Tauentzienstrasse 13.
Map 10 E1.
Tel (01801) 48 44 84.

Lehmann's
Hardenbergstrasse 5.
Map 3 C4.
Tel 61 79 110.

Kulturkaufhaus Dussmann
Friedrichstrasse 90.
Map 15 C2.
Tel 202 51 111.

L & P Classics
Knesebeckstrasse 33-34.
Map 9 C1.
Tel 88 04 30 43.

Motto Bookshop
Skalitzer Strasse 68.

Museum Berggruen
Schlossstrasse 1.
Map 2 E3.
Tel 266 424 242.

Prinz Eisenherz
Lietzenburger Strasse 9a.
Map 9 B2. *Tel 313 99 36.*

Saint Georges
Wörther Strasse 27,
Prenzlauer Berg.
Tel 81 79 83 33.

TOYS

Berliner Zinn-figuren Kabinett
Knesebeckstrasse 88.
Map 3 C5.
Tel 315 70 00.

Heidi's Spielzeugladen
Kantstrasse 61.
Map 2 F5.
Tel 323 75 56.

Original Erzgebirgs-Kurst
Sophienstrasse 9.
Map 7 B1.
Tel 282 67 54.

Michas Bahnhof
Nürnberger Strasse 24.
Map 10 E2, 10 F2.
Tel 218 66 11.

FLOWERS

Blumen Damerius
Potsdamer Platz
Arkaden. *Tel 45 38 005.*

Blumen-Koch
Westfälische Strasse 38.
Map 9 A4.
Tel 896 69 00.

CHINA AND CERAMICS

Bürgel-Haus
Friedrichstrasse 154.
Map 6 F3, 15 C3.
Tel 204 45 19.

KPM
Wegelystrasse 1.
Tel 39 00 92 15.
Kurfürstendamm 27.
Map 10 D1.
Tel 88 62 79 61.

SPECIALIST SHOPS

Bären-Luftballons
Kurfürstenstrasse 31/32.
Map 9 C1.
Tel 26 97 50.

Berlinomat
Frankfurter Allee 89.
Tel 42 08 14 45.

Knopf Paul
Zossener Strasse 10.
Map 13 A4.
Tel 692 12 12.

Papeterie
Uhlandstrasse 28.
Map 9 C2.
Tel 881 63 63.

Tee Gschwendner
Kurfürstendamm 217.
Map 10 D1.
Tel 881 91 81.

Berliner Teesalon
Invalidenstrasse 160.
Tel 28 04 06 60.

Antiques and Objets d'Art

The antique and art markets in Berlin are booming. New galleries are opening all the time, particularly in the eastern areas of town. Spandauer Vorstadt is full of antique shops and contemporary art galleries, but the northern part of Mitte (the area around East of the Centre) is the focus of the Berlin art market. Constantly raising their standards, the galleries attract numerous art dealers and collectors, while non-commercial exhibitions organized by art societies like NGbK, NBK and Kunst-Werke add to the creative atmosphere. As for the antique trade, a walk through any of the city's main thoroughfares should show that it is active in just about every district.

AUCTION HOUSES

Berlin's oldest and most prestigious auction houses are **Gerda Bassenge** and **Villa Grisebach**, both of which organize sales at the start of the year and in the autumn. Bassenge specializes in graphic art, and a month before each sale an auction of books and autographs is held. A photographic auction takes place a few days after the main sale of graphic art. The prices are usually higher at Grisebach which deals mainly in 19th-century paintings. Expressionists and modern classics often go under the hammer here. Another good auctioneer is **Kunst-Auktionen Leon Spik** on Ku'damm.

GALLERIES

If you are pressed for time, Spandauer Vorstadt in the northern part of Mitte might be the place to go. Since the fall of the Berlin Wall, some 30 galleries have been set up in the Linienstrasse, August-strasse, Sophienstrasse and Gipsstrasse areas. Among these are **Arndt & Partner** and **Eigen & Art**, both on August-strasse, **Contemporary Fine Arts**, **Gebauer**, **Max Hetzler**, **Mehdi Chouakri** and **Wohn-maschine**. **Galerie & Buchladen Barbara Wien** and **Neugerrie-menschneider** are both on Linienstrasse. On so-called "open days" three or four times a year, all the galleries open at the same time to exhibit the new collections. One is always in early October, when the Art Forum Berlin fair is held, providing a chance to spot

the changing trends in contemporary art. It can also be enjoyable to walk this district on a Friday evening, when many galleries have opening parties (*Vernissages*).

The galleries near Kurfürsten-damm, such as **Brusberg**, offer high-quality art in a quieter atmosphere. Other galleries include **Hartmann & Noé** on Knesebeckstrasse, as well as **Anselm Dreher**, **Barbara Weiss**, **Franck & Schulte**, **Poll** and **Galerie Stühler**. The latter offers a crossover of paintings, design and jewellery.

ANTIQUE SHOPS

Antique shops can be found in every district of Berlin. Near Kurfürstendamm and around Ludwigkirchplatz there are a number of high-class shops offering expensive *objets d'art*, from Chinese furniture in **Alte Asiatische Kunst** to Secession trinkets in **ART 1900**.

Furniture specialists can be found in Suarezstrasse in Charlottenburg, where orig-inal Thonets can be bought as well as modern steel items by well-known designers. For a slightly lower grade of antique, the best place to go is Berg-mannstrasse in Kreuzberg. In its mildly Oriental atmosphere you can often find valuable pieces among masses of junk. **Das Zweite Büro** in Zossener Strasse specializes in trading old desks, cupboards and filing cabinets, which don't come cheap, but the quality of the merchandise is excellent. Standing opposite Das Zweite Büro is **Radio Art** with its

extensive collection of old radios and record players. Some other interesting shops to try are **Bleibtreu Antik** and **Art Déco**. There's a real market atmosphere in the arcades of the S-Bahn railway bridge near Friedrichstrasse where a host of street traders sell all kinds of knick-knacks, from clothes and books to cutlery and domestic accessories.

FLEA MARKETS

Many Berliners spend their Saturday and Sunday mornings at flea markets, and after a coffee go for a stroll in the Tiergarten or to a museum. Trödel- und Kunstmarkt, on Strasse des 17 Juni near Tier-garten S-Bahn station, is the most popular market in town. It is divided into two parts, and the antique section deals with books and magazines as well as pricey rarities. If you have the time and patience to sift through the enormous amount on offer, you are likely to find some great bargains. Arts and crafts trading takes place on the other side of Charlotten-burger Brücke, and the goods on offer range from leather items and ceramics to colour-ful silk clothes and jewellery. Shops from all over Berlin are usually represented here.

From **Berliner Kunst- und Nostalgiemarkt an der Museumsinsel**, it is only a few steps to the museums. The stalls along Kupfergraben stand opposite the Pergamon- and Altes Museum, and art objects, books, records and other antiques are always on display around the Zeughaus.

Young tourists and locals flock to the **Flohmarkt am Mauerpark**, occupying a stretch of land where the Berlin Wall once stood. This lively market offers antiques, curiosities, clothing, arts and crafts and homemade items every Sun-day, and Saturdays in the summer. It's worth a visit just for the celebratory atmosphere with live music and street per-formers. Also worth a Sunday visit is the **Flohmarkt Box-hagener Platz** in Friedrich-shain, one of the best small markets. For fabrics, as well as food, try the **Turkish Market** on Maybachufer in Neükolln each Tuesday and Friday.

The flea market operating in the car park near the Fehrbelliner Platz U-Bahn station opens at the weekends at 8am. You would do well to get there as early as possible as it is full of experienced collectors who only need a few minutes to spot something valuable. If you are after memorabilia from the former GDR, you should try the stalls around Potsdamer Platz and Leipziger Platz. However the quality and authenticity of what is on sale is often questionable.

The **Treptower Hallentrödel** market on Eichenstrasse offers everything under one roof, from old telephones and army boots to bathroom accessories and piles of very cheap books (5 for €2). The hall, a former bus depot, is worth visiting for its interesting architecture alone. Other flea markets to visit include **Antik & Trödelmarkt am Ostbahnhof**.

DIRECTORY

AUCTION HOUSES

Gerda Bassenge
Erdener Strasse 5a.
Tel 89 38 02 90.
🕒 10am–6pm Mon–Thu, 10am–4pm Fri.

Kunst-Auktionen Leo Spik
Kurfürstendamm 66.
Map 10 D1.
Tel 883 61 70.

Villa Grisebach
Fasanenstrasse 25.
Map 10 D2.
Tel 885 91 50.

GALLERIES

Anselm Dreher
Pfalzburger Strasse 80.
Map 9 C2.
Tel 883 52 49.
🕒 2–6pm Tue–Fri, 11am–2pm Sat.

Arndt & Partner
Invalidenstrasse 50–51.
Map 6 D1.
Tel 280 81 23.
🕒 11am–6pm Tue–Sat.

ATM Gallery
Brunnenstrasse 24. **Tel** 0176 62 55 58 10.
🕒 1–7pm Tue–Sat.

Barbara Weiss
Zimmerstrasse 88–91.
Map 7 A5.
Tel 262 42 84.
🕒 11am–6pm Tue–Sat.

Brusberg
Kurfürstendamm 213.
Map 9 C1.
Tel 882 76 82.
🕒 10am–6pm Tue–Fri, 10am–2pm Sat.

C/O Berlin
Oranienburger Strasse 35–36. **Map** 7 A1.
Tel 28 09 19 25.

Contemporary Fine Arts
Am Kupfergraben 10.
Map 7 A2.
Tel 28 87 870.
🕒 11am–6pm Tue–Fri, 11am–4pm Sat.

Eigen & Art
Auguststrasse 26.
Map 7 B1.
Tel 280 66 05.
🕒 11am–6pm Tue–Sat.

Galerie Crystal Ball
Schönleinstrasse 7.
Map 14 E4.
Tel 600 52 828.
🕒 3–8pm Tue, Fri & Sun.

Galerie Poll
Anna-Louisa-Karsch Strasse 9. **Tel** 261 70 91.
🕒 11am–6pm Tue–Fri, 11am–4pm Sat.

Galerie Stühler
Fasanenstrasse 69.
Map 10 D1.
Tel 881 76 33.

Galerie und Buchladen Barbara Wien
Linienstrasse 158.
Map 7 C1.
Tel 28 38 53 52.
🕒 1–6pm Tue–Fri, noon–6pm Sat.

Gebauer
Markgrafenstrasse 67.
Map 7 A4.
Tel 24 00 86 30.
🕒 11am–6pm Tue–Sat.

Max Hetzler
Oudenarder Strasse 16–20. **Map** 6 F5.
Tel 229 24 37.
🕒 11am–6pm Tue–Sat.

Mehdi Chouakri
Schlegelstrasse 26.
Map 7 B1.
Tel 28 39 11 53.
🕒 11am–6pm Tue–Sat.

Michael Schultz
Mommsenstrasse 34.
Tel 31 99 130.
🕒 11am–7pm Tue–Fri, 10am–4pm Sat.

Neugerriemschneider
Linienstrasse 155.
Map 7 A1.
Tel 28 87 72 77.
🕒 10am–6pm Tue–Fri, 11am–6pm Sat.

Thomas Schulte
Charlottenstrasse 24.
Map 7 A3.
Tel 20 60 89 90.
🕒 noon–6pm Tue–Sat.

Wohnmaschine
Invalidenstrasse 50–51.
Map 6 D1.
Tel 87 20 15.
🕒 11am–6pm Tue–Sat.

ANTIQUE SHOPS

Alte Asiatische Kunst
Fasanenstrasse 71.
Map 10 D1.
Tel 883 61 17.

Art Déco
Grolmanstrasse 51.
Map 3 C5.
Tel 31 50 62 05.

ART 1900
Kurfürstendamm 53.
Map 9 B2.
Tel 01578 212 22 00.

Bleibtreu Antik
Schlüterstrasse 54.
Map 9 B1.
Tel 883 52 12.

Das Zweite Büro
Zossener Strasse 6.
Map 13 A3.
Tel 693 07 59.
🕒 10am–6pm Mon–Fri.

Lakeside Antiques
Neue Kantstrasse 14.
Map 2 E5.
Tel 25 45 99 30.

Radio Art
Zossener Strasse 2.
Map 13 A3.
Tel 693 94 35.
🕒 noon–6pm Thu & Fri, 10am–1pm Sat.

FLEA MARKETS

Antik & Trödelmarkt am Ostbahnhof
Erich-Steinfurth-Strasse.
🕒 10am–5pm Sun.

Berliner Kunst- und Nostalgiemarkt an der Museumsinsel
Museumsinsel & Kupfergraben.
Map 7 A2, 16 D1.
🕒 11am–5pm Sat & Sun.

Flohmarkt Boxhagener Platz
Boxhagener Platz.
🕒 10am–6pm Sun.

Flohmarkt am Mauerpark
Bernauer Strasse 63–64.
🕒 7am–7pm Sun.

Treptower Hallentrödel
Puschkinallee.
🕒 10am–6pm Sat & Sun.

Turkish Market
Maybachufer Neukölln.
🕒 11am–6:30pm Tue & Fri.

Food Products

Food specialities from all over the world can be found in Berlin, a fact which is due partly to the city's own lack of traditional cuisine. Gone are the days when local fare was restricted to pork knuckle with cabbage, cutlets, *Currywurst* and potatoes. Today the side-streets and thoroughfares are teeming with the shops and restaurants of many nationalities – Italian, Greek, Turkish, Spanish and French as well as Mexican, American, Japanese, Chinese and Thai. As befits any major European capital, the food is of the highest quality, and there are more and more shops providing organic products, from vegetables and wholemeal bread to various wines and beers.

PATISSERIES AND SWEET SHOPS

Berliners certainly have a sweet tooth for there are plenty of patisseries and sweet shops all over the city, and a wide range of cakes is available. A typical speciality is a doughnut known simply as a *Berliner*, but the majority of places offer a whole range of cakes along with French pastries and fruits. **Buchwald** is renowned for producing some of the best cakes in town, mainly to take away, but there are also a number of patisseries, or *Konditoreien* Among the best of these is **Opernpalais**.

Delicacies from Vienna can be bought in **Wiener Conditorei Caffeehaus**, while **Leysieffer** shops, with their exquisite chocolates and pralines, are a serious temptation for chocoholics. Visitors with a sweet tooth should also try the large stores: **KaDeWe's Feinschmecker Etage** and **Galeries Lafayette's Gourmet** departments both have a wonderful range of confectioneries.

CHEESES

The largest selection of cheeses in Berlin can be found at the Gourmet in Galeries Lafayette which has a particularly broad choice from France. KaDeWe's cheese department also offers a wide variety, while Maître Philipe sells only select cheeses from small producers. You won't find any fridges here but the whole shop is air-conditioned and the aroma whets the appetite. A huge assortment of cheeses can also be found at **Giovanni's Käsekellerei**. **Einhorn** specializes in international products, mainly sandwiches, pasta, meats and a wide variety of cheeses. **Salumeria** is also a must for cheese lovers.

WINES

Between them, **KaDeWe** and **Galeries Lafayette** have the biggest wine cellars, while smaller businesses usually specialize in wines from a particular region. **Der Rioja-Weinspezialist**, for example, sells only wines originating from northern Spain, while **Vendemmia** specializes in Tuscan wines. A wide selection of German wines is available at **Viniculture**.

MEATS, COLD CUTS AND FISH

Berliners eat quite a lot of meat and meat products – the latter in particular are real German specialities. So if you are not vegetarian you should try something from the bewildering range of sausages and meat rolls. As well as the well-stocked departments in the big stores **KaDeWe** and **Galeries Lafayette**, small shops offer excellent quality products. **Neuland Fleischerei Bachhuber** is good. It specializes in chemical- and hormone-free meats, while a broad selection of fish (both fresh- and salt-water) and game is offered in KaDeWe's delicatessen. **Rogacki** is another good fishmonger and **Kropp Delikatessen und Feinkost** is a well-stocked delicatessen where you can buy a variety of prepared meats.

FOOD HALLS

The old 19th-century food halls are not as important today as they were before World War II, when they were the chief source of produce. The biggest of them all was on Alexanderplatz. The place used to teem with people 24 hours a day, but the hall wasn't rebuilt after sustaining damage during World War II. The GDR authorities had no use for such a large food hall, and with the advent of supermarkets, there was no need for it.

Today there are only three food halls in operation; **Arminiushalle** in Moabit, the **Markthalle am Marheinekeplatz** in Kreuzberg and **Domäne Dahlem Hofladen**. All of these are usually open all day six days per week – Monday to Saturday. Typically, Berliners use the food halls to pick up the one or two speciality items they can't find in the supermarkets. Shopping in these halls is a good opportunity to try traditional German *Currywurst*: the outlets in these food halls are regarded as the best in town.

MARKETS

Markets offer an additional way of shopping for food. They take place twice a week, and one of the best is the **Winterfeldtmarkt** which takes place on Wednesdays from 8am until 2pm and on Saturdays from 8am until 6pm. On Saturdays the opening hours are extended if the crowd is big, which it often is. You can buy everything from high quality fruits, through vegetables and cheeses from all over the world to clothing and domestic accessories. Fast-food outlets offer *falafel* or grilled sausages, and the place is surrounded by bars and cafés full of clients and traders relaxing with a glass of beer. The atmosphere and range of goods on offer is truly international.

Türkisher Markt am Maybachufer is a big Turkish market which opens on Tuesdays and Fridays. It is popular with Turks living in Kreuzberg and Neukölln. The stalls offer all kinds of Turkish specialities. There are also markets in the city centre on

Kollwitzplatz – the **Ökomarkt** and **Neuer Markt** on Thursdays and Saturdays and the **Markt am Wittenbergplatz** on Thursdays. In fact, Thursday is the day when Wittenbergplatz is invaded by farmers from all over the region offering a variety of products. You won't find any exotic fruits at these, but if you have had enough of tasteless supermar-

ket tomatoes and apples then they should provide a good alternative. Depending on the season, you can buy pickled gherkins (*Salzgurken*) from the Spreewald, asparagus from the Beelitz region and delicious, sweet aromatic strawberries. **Domäne Dahlem Ökomarkt** offers a good selection of organic foods on Wednesdays and Saturdays.

DIRECTORY

DEPARTMENT STORES WITH FOOD HALLS

KaDeWe's Feinschmecker Etage
Tauentzienstrasse 21-24.
Map 10 E2.
Tel 21210.

Galeries Lafayette Gourmet
Friedrichstrasse 23.
Map 6 F4.
Tel 20 94 80.

PATISSERIES AND SWEET SHOPS

Buchwald
Bartningallee 29.
Map 4 F3.
Tel 391 59 31.

Caffeehaus Am Roseneck
Hohenzollerndamm 92.
Tel 89 59 69 22.

Fassbender & Rausch
Charlottenstrasse 60.
Map 7 A4.
Tel 20 45 84 43.

Kolbe & Stecher Bonbonmacherei
Heckmann Höfe,
Oranienburger Strasse 32.
Map 7 A1.
Tel 4405 52 43.

Leysieffer
Kurfürstendamm 218.
Map 10 D1.
Tel 885 74 80.

Leysieffer
Quartier 205,
Friedrichstr. 68
Map 15 C4.
Tel 20 64 97 17.

Opernpalais
Unter den Linden 5.
Map 7 A3, 16 E3.
Tel 20 26 83.

Wiener Conditorei Caffeehaus
Hagenplatz 3.
Tel 89 72 93 60.

CHEESES

Einhorn
Wittenbergplatz 5–6.
Map 10 F2.
Tel 218 63 47.

Giovanni's Käsekelleri
Monbijouplatz 2.
Map 7 B2.
Tel 030 33 77 10 51.

Maître Philippe
Emser Strasse 42.
Map 9 B3, 9 C3.
Tel 88 68 36 10.

Salumeria
Windscheidstrasse 20.
Map 2 E5.
Tel 324 33 18.

WINES

Der Rioja-Weinspezialist
Akazienstrasse 13.
Tel 782 25 78.

Vendemmia
Akazienstrasse 20.
Tel 787 125 35.

Viniculture
Grolmanstrasse 44–45.
Tel 883 81 74.

MEATS, COLD CUTS AND FISH

Kropp Delikatessen und Feinkost
Karl-Marx-Strasse 82.
Map 14 F5.
Tel 623 1090.

Neuland Fleischerei Bachhuber
Güntzelstrasse 47.
Map 9 C4.
Tel 873 21 15.

Rogacki
Wilmersdorfer Strasse 145–146.
Map 2 F4.
Tel 343 82 50.

FOOD HALLS

Arminiushalle
Arminiusstrasse 2-4.
Map 4 E1. 🕐 7:30am–6pm Mon–Thu, 7:30am–7pm Fri, 7:30am–2pm Sat.

Domäne Dahlem Hofladen
Königin-Luise-Strasse 49,
Dahlem. **Tel** 66 63 00 12.

Markthalle am Marheinekeplatz
Marheinekeplatz.
Map 13 A5.
🕐 8am–8pm Mon–Fri, 8am–6pm Sat.

Markthalle Tegel-Center
Gorkistrasse 13–17.
Tel 43 43 849.
🕐 8am–7pm Mon–Fri, 8am–6pm Sat.

MARKETS

Domäne Dahlem ökomarkt
Königin-Luise-Strasse 49,
Dahlem.
Tel 666 3000.
🕐 noon–5pm Wed, 8am–1pm Sat.

Markt am Wittenbergplatz
Wittenbergplatz.
Map 10 F2.
🕐 10am–6pm Thu.

Ökomarkt am Kollwitzplatz
Prenzlauer Berg.
🕐 noon–7pm Thu.

Neuer Markt am Kollwitzplatz
Prenzlauer Berg.
🕐 9am–4pm Sat.

Türkischer Markt am Maybachufer
Maybachufer.
Map 14 E3, F4.
🕐 11am–6:30pm Tue & Fri.

Winterfeldtmarkt
Winterfeldplatz.
Map 11 A3.
🕐 8am–2pm Wed, 8am–6pm Sat.

ENTERTAINMENT IN BERLIN

With so much on offer, from classical drama and cabaret to variety theatre and an eclectic nightclub scene, it is possible to indulge just about any taste in Berlin. During the summer months many bars and restaurants set up outdoor tables, and the area around Unter den Linden, the Kurfürstendamm, Kreuzberg and Prenzlauer Berg in particular, seems to turn into one large social arena. The city really comes into its own at night, when its clubs, all-night cafés and cocktail bars give you the chance to dance till dawn. The city has many night-life centres, each with a slightly different character. Prenzlauer Berg is best for mainstream bars, cafés and clubs, while Friedrichshain has a bustling nightlife, and Kreuzberg has a vibrant gay scene. The Mitte district (see East of the Centre) offers a true mixture, its opera house and classical theatre surrounded by lively and inexpensive bars. On a Sunday, a quiet trip down the river or along the canals offers a pleasant way to unwind.

Flute player in costume

The Berlin Philharmonic Orchestra

PRACTICAL INFORMATION

There are so many things going on in Berlin that it can be difficult to find what you're looking for. The Information Centre offers basic information (see p278), but for greater detail you can buy a copy of the listings magazines *Tip* or *Zitty* which offer the widest range of suggestions. Information on festivals, sports events, cinema programmes, theatre schedules, cabarets and concerts can be found on websites www.berlinonline.de and www.visitberlin.de.

But if you've only just arrived in town and haven't made it yet to an Internet café or a kiosk, the chances are the bar you're sitting in, or your hotel foyer, has leaflets on the wall to point you in the right direction. And there is no end of posters around town telling you what's on offer.

GUIDES

You won't be short of cultural guides in Berlin. The fortnightly listings magazines *Tip* and *Zitty*, which cover the widest choice of events, are issued on Wednesdays, while the daily newspaper *Berliner Morgenpost* has daily culture pages, as do the other major newspapers *Taz*, *Berliner Zeitung* and *Tagesspiegel*. All of these can be bought at news kiosks.

For culture information in English, pick up a copy of the *Exberliner* magazine, which has feature stories and listings. It can be found at English-language bookshops, as well as a few cafés.

The monthly magazine *Kunst* (Art) is a dual-language guide to galleries and exhibitions. It also has an informative website (www.kunstmagazinberlin.de).

TICKETS

Tickets can usually be bought two weeks before an event, and you can buy them directly at theatre box offices or make a telephone booking. Reserved tickets have to be picked up and paid for at least half an hour before a show. Students,

The Admiralspalast entertainment complex (see p69)

Berlin's Jazzfest features traditional jazz music *(see p268)*

pensioners and the disabled are entitled to a 50 per cent discount, but you will need to present appropriate documentation. You can also pre-book tickets at special outlets all over Berlin but they charge a 20 per cent commission. All the major theatres and concert halls have special wheelchair access, but the number of places for the disabled is limited; make it clear when buying a ticket that you need an appropriate place. Tickets to some theatres include a pass for public transport.

If a performance has sold out, you can always try to find tickets just before the show, for some of the pre-booked tickets may not have been collected. One agency which specializes in these last-minute purchases is called **Hekticket Theaterkassen**. You can buy tickets on the day, even an hour before a performance. If someone has already returned their ticket, you might be able to buy it at a 50 per cent discount.

Other agencies to contact for tickets are **Interklassik**, on Friedrichstrasse, and **Koka 36** on Oranienstrasse in Kreuzberg.

INFORMATION FOR THE DISABLED

In all the guides to theatres and concert halls the availability of wheelchair access is noted by a distinctive blue sign. The majority of the bigger theatres, halls and opera houses have special places for wheelchairs and seats reserved for people with walking difficulties. When buying a ticket you must specify your need as the number of places is limited.

If you are disabled you should be able to commute without restriction on public transport, as the majority of U- and S-Bahn stations have lifts, and they are clearly marked on maps of the underground. Many buses now have special ramps and facilities for wheelchairs, but if you experience any difficulty members of the BVG staff will always help.

PUBLIC TRANSPORT AT NIGHT

The last U-Bahn trains run just before 1am, but buses and trams continue running every half an hour, making Berlin's night-time transport one of the most efficient in

Ornate Elephant Gate at the Zoo Berlin *(see p150)*

Germany. Bus and tram timetables are linked, and there are two major interchange points: one on Hardenbergplatz, near the Zoo railway station, and the other on Hackescher Markt. On Friday and Saturday nights you can also use all U-Bahn lines (except 4 and U55), which operate every 15 minutes throughout the night. Some S-Bahn lines also work at night over the weekend. Every ticket office and information point in town has brochures with details about night-time public transport.

Afternoon with the children in the Museumsdorf Düppel *(see p180)*

DIRECTORY

TICKET AGENTS

Hekticket Theaterkassen
Hardenbergstrasse 29d.
Map 10 D1.
Tel 230 99 30.

Alexanderplatz 8.
Map 7 D2.
Tel 230 99 30.

Interklassik
im Maritim proArte Hotel,
Friedrichstrasse 150–152.
Map 6 F3.
Tel 204 45 40.

Koka 36
Oranienstrasse 29.
Map 14 E2.
Tel 61 10 13 13.
www.koka36.de

Theatres

Thanks to Reinhardt and Brecht, Berlin became a landmark in the European theatre scene in the 1920s, and its success continues to this day. During the years of Nazi rule, many people working in the business were killed or forced to emigrate as the stage became a propaganda machine, but after World War II a revival spread through Berlin's theatres. At the heart of this revival were Bertolt Brecht and his Berliner Ensemble, and Peter Stein who ran the Schaubühne.

MODERN HISTORY

Following the construction of the Berlin Wall, the number of venues doubled as each part of the divided city worked to build its own theatres. The Volksbühne in the East had its equivalent in the West called the Freie Volksbühne, and the eastern acting school, the Academy, was matched by a second Academy in the west.

The economic difficulties caused by the reunification of Germany forced a number of places to shut down, but the theatres of East Berlin managed to survive. In the west, the Freie Volksbühne and the Schiller-Theater (the largest stage in Germany) had to close, but the Volksbühne, under Frank Castorf, and the Deutsches Theater, led by Thomas Langhoff, continued to do well. Independent theatres have fared equally well in both parts of the city.

The theatre season runs from September to July, with its peak in May during Berliner Theatertreffen (Berlin Theatre Forum), when many other German theatre groups are invited to stage their plays. There are also a number of youth theatres which produce the work of young writers, and these follow the seasons of the major venues.

Repertoires are published in the listings magazines *Tip* and *Zitty*, and also displayed on yellow posters in U-Bahn stations and throughout Berlin. Leaflets are available in many restaurants around the city.

MAJOR STAGES

The **Deutsches Theater** and its small hall **Kammerspiele** on Schumannstrasse is a top-class theatre and offers a varied repertoire of productions with very professional modern stagings. From the Greek classics to the modern classics and contemporary plays, the Deutches Theater has successfully staged them all. Tickets for these plays can be difficult to obtain, but it is worth persevering.

At **Volksbühne** you can see interesting performances of classical plays in modern settings, as well as adaptations of books or films or pieces written by young writers. Concerts, lectures and dance evenings are organized in the Red and Green Salon of the theatre, and with so much going on the Volksbühne now seems more of a cultural centre with a multimedia character than just a stage.

Although it was particularly important for German theatre in the 1970s and 80s, **Schaubühne am Lehniner Platz** is no longer as popular as it was, which is a shame, for production values don't get any higher than this. The close attention to detail – on everything from the sets and scenery to the choice of music and the editing of the printed programme – is extraordinary, and distinguishes it from the other theatres in town.

The **Berliner Ensemble** (or BE for short) has been managed by such influential dramatists as Bertolt Brecht from 1949 and then Heiner Müller in 1970. The spectacles created by these two are still performed today. The whole theatre is magnificent, and it has some superb architecture including the stage; after each performance you can meet the actors in the canteen in the courtyard. Another venue well worth visiting is **Hebbel am Ufer, Hau Eins** – an ambitious place with a programme that includes contemporary plays and modern dance.

Other major venues include the **Maxim Gorki Theater** and the **Renaissance-Theater**. The **Schlosspark Theater** is a former state theatre that is now a private enterprise with an interesting repertoire.

SMALL STAGES AND ALTERNATIVE THEATRE

There are a number of alternative theatres in Berlin, each enthusiastically playing the works of what are generally lesser known authors. **Hebbel am Ufer, Hau Eins** is devoted to avant-garde theatre and dance and is considered to be the city's best alternative stage. The smaller boulevard theatres, like **Theater am Kurfürstendamm** or **Komödie am Kurfürstendamm**, offer different, lighter programmes.

Among other small theatres are **Bat-Studiotheater** and **Kleines Theater**. There are many other notable venues, including **Theater 89**, **Heimathafen Neukölln** and the **Vagantenbühne**.

To enjoy theatre in English, head to the **English Theatre Berlin**, which produces many of its own original productions, as well as classics and improvisational pieces.

MUSICALS, REVIEWS AND CABARETS

There are four main musical theatres in Berlin, in addition to the many small venues which fit musicals into their more general repertoire. **Friedrichstadtpalast** and the historic **Admiralspalast**, both in the eastern part of the city, stage many of the new major shows as well as musicals and variety shows. A smaller stage at Friedrichstadtpalast hosts cabaret. The **Theater des Westens** in Charlottenburg is more traditional, while the **Theater am Potsdamer Platz** is a modern theatre set up in 1999.

As for cabaret, there are probably as many acts in Berlin today as there were in the 1920s, usually performed by small itinerant groups which rely on the hospitality of theatres for a venue. **Distel**, in Friedrichstrasse, continues its success from GDR times, and **Stachelschweine** celebrates its popularity in western Berlin.

There are many more venues for musicals, reviews and cabarets. Among these are **Bar jeder Vernunft, Chamäleon Variété, Shake! Das Zelt am Ostbahnhof, Scheinbar, Wintergarten Varieté** and **Die Wühlmäuse**.

TICKETS

It is usually possible to pre-book tickets two weeks before a performance. You can buy them directly from the box office of the theatre or by telephone booking. There are also ticket vendors all over town, but they usually charge a per cent commission. Even if the theatre or concert has been sold out, there is still a chance of buying something just before the performance, provided that not all pre-booked tickets have been collected.

Hekticket Theaterkassen specializes in this kind of last-minute ticket. If you are lucky enough to pick up a ticket on the day of performance, you may find it has been returned and reduced to half its former price.

DIRECTORY

MAJOR STAGES

Berliner Ensemble
Bertold-Brecht-Platz 1.
Map 6 F2, 15 C1.
Tel 28 408 155.

Deutsches Theater
Schumannstrasse 13a.
Map 6 E2, 15 A1.
Tel 28 44 12 25.

Hebbel am Ufer
Hau Eins
Stresemanstrasse 29.
Hau Zwei
Hallesches Ufer 32.
Hau Drei
Tempelhofer Ufer 10.
Map 12 F2.
Tel 259 00 40.
www.hebel-am-ufer.de

Maxim Gorki Theater
Am Festungsgraben 2.
Map 7 A3, 16 E2.
Tel 20 22 11 15.

Renaissance-Theater
Hardenbergstrasse 6.
Map 3 C5.
Tel 312 42 02.

Schaubühne am Lehniner Platz
Kurfürstendamm 153.
Tel 89 00 23.

Schlosspark Theater
Schlossstrasse 48
Map 2 E4.
Tel 789 566 71 00.

Volksbühne
Rosa-Luxemburg-Platz.
Map 8 D1.
Tel 30 24 0655.

SMALL STAGES AND ALTERNATIVE THEATRE

Bat-Studiotheater
Belforter Strasse 15.
Tel 755 41 77 77.

English Theatre Berlin
Fidicinstrasse 40.
Map 12 F5.
Tel 693 56 92.

Heimathafen Neukölln
Karl-Marx-Strasse 141.
Tel 56 82 13 33.

Kleines Theater
Südwestkorso 64.
Tel 821 20 21.

Sophiensaele
Sophienstrasse 18.
Map 7 B1.
Tel 283 52 66.

Theater 89
Torstrasse 216.
Map 6 F1.
Tel 282 46 56.

Theater und Komödie am Kurfürstendamm
Kurfürstendamm 206/209.
Map 9 C2.
Tel 88 59 11 88.

Vagantenbühne
Kantstrasse 12a.
Map 10 D1.
Tel 312 45 29.

MUSICALS, REVIEWS & CABARETS

Admiralspalast
Friedrichstrasse 101.
Map 6 F2 and 15 C1.
Tel 47 99 74 99.

Bar jeder Vernunft
Schaperstrasse 24.
Map 10 D2.
Tel 883 15 82.

BKA Theater
Mehringdamm 34.
Map 12 F4.
Tel 202 20 07.

Chamäleon Variété
Rosenthaler Strasse 40–41.
Map 7 B2.
Tel 40 00 59 30.

Die Wühlmäuse
Pommernallee 2–4.
Map 1 B5.
Tel 30 67 30 11.

Distel
Friedrichstrasse 101.
Map 6 F2, 15 C1.
Tel 204 47 04.

Friedrichstadtpalast
Friedrichstrasse 107.
Map 6 F2, 15 C1.
Tel 23 26 23 26.

Kalkscheune
Johannisstrasse 2 (behind Friedrichstadtpalast).
Map 6 F2.
Tel 59 00 43 40.

Scheinbar
Monumentenstrasse 9.
Map 11 C5.
Tel 784 55 39.

Shake! Das Zelt am Ostbahnhof
Am Postbahnhof 1.
Tel 290 47 84 12.

Stachelschweine
Europa-Center.
Map 10 E1.
Tel 261 47 95.

Theater am Potsdamer Platz
Marlene-Dietrich-Platz 1.
Tel (0180) 544 44.

Theater des Westens
Kantstrasse 12.
Map 2 E5, 9 A1, 10 D1.
Tel (0180) 54 444.

Wintergarten Varieté
Potsdamer Strasse 96.
Map 11 C2.
Tel 588 43 40.

TICKETS

Hekticket Theaterkassen
Hardenbergstrasse 29d.
Map 10 D1.
Tel 23 09 930.

Alexanderplatz 8.
Map 7 D2.
Tel 230 99 30.

Cinema

Berlin has always been the capital of German cinema, and it is likely to remain so. In November 1895, exactly two months after the Lumière Brothers presented their first moving pictures in France, brothers Emil and Max Skladanowsky showed a series of short films to a spellbound German public. Wintergarten Varieté-theater was the place where you could go to see those famous pioneering films of kangaroos fighting, acrobats tumbling and children performing folk dances. By 1918 there were already some 251 cinemas with 82,796 seats available in Berlin, and by 1925 the number of people involved in the film industry had reached 47,600. The history of UFA (Universal Film AG), established in 1917, is intimately linked to that of Berlin, for the company has its two studios here.

BIG SCREENS AND BIG FILMS

Many cinemas can be found around Breitscheidplatz, near the Ku'damm, Tauentzien-strasse and Alexanderplatz. After the fall of the Berlin Wall, many new multiplex cinemas were built, the biggest being the **CinemaxX Potsdamer Platz** and the **Cinestar Sony Center**. At the Cinestar, mainstream Anglo-American movies are dubbed, rather than subtitled, but you can also see films in their original language here. The Cinemaxx, with a total of 19 screens, is the city's largest multiplex. Here cinema-goers can see all the latest Hollywood and German blockbusters. Next to the Cinestar, the Cinemaxx offers the best cinema technology, but it can get rather crowded on weekend nights.

Next door to CinemaxX is the **IMAX** cinema – the biggest screen in Germany. It can only show films that are shot with an Imax camera, but the spectacle is always breathtaking. Its huge curved screen is 27 m (89 ft) across and covers approximately 1000 sq m (10,750 sq ft). It shows a range of films including natural history, travel and underwater features, as well as a selection of 3D films that require special viewing glasses.

Each February, Potsdamer Platz is taken over by the **Berlin International Film Festival**, or Berlinale. Hundreds of films are screened, and Berliners often queue for hours to get hold of the popular tickets. You can also buy tickets online at the festival's website.

Three other areas of Berlin are known as cinema centres: East of the City, in Friedrich-shain and in Prenzlauer Berg. For those curious about the days of the GDR, the **International** on Karl-Marx-Allee, built in 1963, is typical of cinemas built in the communist era. It's pretty austere and only has 551 seats.

STUDIO CINEMAS

There are plenty of small studio cinemas scattered across town, and it is in these that new independent films and retrospectives of particular actors and directors are shown. Cinemas like **Hackesche Höfe Kino** or **Central**, situated near Hackescher Markt, offer a pleasant break from the bustle of modern city life, and most have bars of their own. The café at Hackesche Höfe Kino offers light snacks as well as a wonderful 5th-floor view over the neighbourhood.

The **Arsenal**, on Potsdamer Platz, belongs to the Freunde der Deutschen Kinemathek (Friends of German Cinema), and is ideal for lovers of German film for this is where you can see all the national classics. The venue has a detailed monthly programme which includes four screen-ings per day, many of which come with a small introductory lecture. Copies of the programme are distributed in bars all over town.

If you're interested in origi-nal language movies, **Cinéma Paris** in Charlottenburg is the place to go for French films, while the **Odeon** in Schöne-berg specializes in English and American films.

There are also many tiny neighbourhood cinemas and kino-bars, which have their own charm. Among the best are the **Tilsiter Lichtspiele** in Friedrichshain, and the **Lichtblick Kino** in Prenzlauer Berg, which plays *Casablanca* at midnight every Saturday.

OPEN-AIR CINEMA

Open-air cinemas start operating as soon as the weather allows. They can be found in parks and open spaces all across town. Some of the nicest are the **Freiluftkinos** Kreuzberg and Friedrichshain, as well as the **Openair** inside the Schloss Charlottenburg. All of these outdoor venues show a selec-tion of current first-run films as well as the established classics. Screenings start when it starts to grow dark, around 9pm during summer.

NON-COMMERCIAL FILMS

Although most people tend to go to the cinema nowadays to see the latest blockbuster movie from Hollywood, it is still possible to track down some of the venues which show less popular films including documentaries and other non-commercial films.

The **Zeughauskino**, which has recently reopened its doors, specializes in non-commercial films. It co-ordinates its interesting and informative repertoire with exhibitions in the Deutsches Historisches Museum (the German Historical Museum), as well as showing its own series of documentaries.

PRICES

Cinema tickets usually cost between €8–11 and students and senior citizens don't always receive a discount. Many cinemas declare Tuesday or Wednesday as Cinema Day, when tickets are €1–2 cheaper. Some cinemas also organize so-called "Blue Mondays" when tickets are reduced to as little as €4.

In most cinemas there are usually three shows per evening, the first at 6pm, the last at around 10pm. Some cinemas accept telephone bookings, but you have to turn up to pay for your ticket at least half an hour before a show, otherwise it may go to somebody else. Most ticket offices don't take credit cards, so have cash in hand. Twenty minutes of commercials precede most screenings, although some venues use this time to show short films by up-and-coming directors.

THE FILM BUSINESS

If you're interested in the business of film production then you will want to visit Studio UFA in Babelsberg, Potsdam. A must for all cinema fans, the **Studiotour Babels-berg** allows you to see a live film crew working on a current production (see p205). You will also get a chance to see some classic film sets – some going back to the days of Marlene Dietrich – as well as samples of the latest technical wizardry.

A wide variety of books, in many different languages, about cinema and film can be found in **Bücherbogen** under the arcade of the S-Bahn railway bridge at Savignyplatz. Alternatively you can try **Bücherstube Marga Schoeller** at 33 Knesebeckstrasse, near Kurfüstendamm.

DIRECTORY

BIG SCREENS AND BIG FILMS

CinemaxX Potsdamer Platz
Potsdamer Strasse 5.
Map 6 D5.
Tel (0180) 524 63 62 99.

Cinestar Sony Center
Potsdamer Strasse 4.
Map 6 D5.
Tel 26 06 62 60.

IMAX
Potsdamer Strasse 4.
Tel 26 06 62 60.

Kino International
Karl-Marx-Allee 33
(corner of Schillingstrasse).
Map 8 E3. **Tel** 24 75 600.

STUDIO CINEMAS

Arsenal 1–2
Potsdamer Strasse 2/Sony Center.
Map 10 F2.
Tel 26 95 51 00.

Central
Rosenthaler Strasse 39.
Map 7 B1.
Tel 28 59 99 73.

Cinéma Paris
Kurfürstendamm 211.
Map 9 A2, 10 D1.
Tel 881 31 19.

Hackesche Höfe Kino
Rosenthaler Strasse 40-41.
Map 9 C2.
Tel 283 46 03.

Lichtblick Kino
Kanstanienallee 77.
Tel 44 05 81 79.

Odeon
Hauptstrasse 116.
Map 11·B5.
Tel 78 70 40 19.

Tilsiter Lichtspiele
Richard-Sorge-Strasse 25a.
Tel 426 81 29.

OPEN-AIR CINEMA

Freiluftkino Friedrichshain
Volkspark Friedrichshain.
Map 8 F1.
Tel 29 36 16 29.

Freiluftkino Kreuzberg
Adalbertstrasse 73.
Map 14 E1.
Tel 29 36 16 20.

Openair Schloss Charlottenburg
Spandauer Damm 10.
Map 2 E2.
Tel (1805) 44 70 111.

FILM FESTIVALS

Berlin International Film Festival
Every February,
Potsdamer Platz.
Tel 259 200.
www.berlinale.de

THE FILM BUSINESS

Bücherbogen am Savignyplatz
Stadtbahnbogen 593.
Tel 31 86 95 11.

Studiotour Babelsberg
August-Bebel-Str. 26–53,
Potsdam (entrance Grossbeerenstrasse).
Tel (0331) 721 27 50.

FAMOUS FILMS ABOUT BERLIN

Berlin Alexanderplatz
Germany 1931, directed by Phillip Jutzi, based on Alexander Döblin's book.

Berlin Alexanderplatz
GDR 1980, directed by Rainer Werner Fassbinder.

Berlin, Chamissoplatz
GDR 1980, directed by Rudolf Thome.

Berlin – Ecke Schönhauser
GDR 1957, directed by Gerhard Klein.

Berliner Ballade (Berlin Ballad)
American Occupied Zone 1948, directed by Robert Stemmle.

Berlin Calling
Germany 2008, directed by Hannes Stöhr.

Berlin, die Symphonie einer Grossstadt (Berlin, Symphony of a Great City)
Germany 1927, directed by Walter Ruttmann.

Cabaret
USA 1972, directed by Bob Fosse.

Coming Out
GDR 1988/1989, directed by Heiner Carow.

Der Himmel über Berlin (Wings of Desire)
GDR/France 1987, directed by Wim Wenders.

Die Legende von Paul und Paula (The Legend of Paul and Paula)
Germany 2003, directed by Wolfgang Becker.

Eins, zwei, drei (One, two, three)
USA 1961, directed by Billy Wilder.

Goodbye Lenin!
Germany 2003, directed by Wolfgang Becker.

Kuhle Wampe
Germany 1932, directed by Slatan Dudow, script by Bertolt Brecht.

Menschen am Sonntag (Men on Sunday)
Germany 1930, directed by Robert Siodmak and Edgar G Ulmer.

Lola rennt (Run, Lola, Run)
Germany 1998, directed by Tom Tykwer.

Sonnenallee
Germany 1998, directed by Leander Haußmann.

Classical Music and Dance

Berlin has one of the world's finest orchestras (the Berlin Philharmonic Orchestra) and two of the most beautiful concert halls (the Philharmonie and the Konzerthaus). The Berlin Philharmonic is pre-eminent among the city's three symphonic orchestras, all of which perform regularly in Berlin. There are three major opera houses to choose from and a smaller one for lovers of the avant-garde. The opera houses have interesting ballet programmes built into their repertoires, performed largely by resident dance companies. Throughout the year, the city also attracts international ballet groups. Apart from regular concerts, the city offers many festivals, two of the most popular being *MaerzMusik* and the *Classic Open Air Festival* on Gendarmenmarkt. Smaller concerts are organized in the city's many churches, halls and palaces.

CONCERT HALLS

The **Philharmonie** is one of Europe's grandest concert halls, with excellent acoustics. It houses the Berlin Philharmonic Orchestra, which was founded in 1882 and achieved great popularity under the conductor Herbert von Karajan. In 1989, the orchestra was taken over by Claudio Abbado, a worthy successor, and since 2002 it has been directed by Sir Simon Rattle, an acclaimed British conductor. Tickets for popular programmes quickly sell out. Chamber orchestras perform in the smaller **Kammermusiksaal** attached to the bigger hall.

With its elegant surroundings, **Konzerthaus Berlin**, formally known as the Schauspielhaus *(see p65)*, is one of the best places to listen to classical music. The building was restored after World War II and now contains a large concert hall and a smaller room for chamber music. Classical concerts are also held at the **Universität der Künste** and the **Staatsbibliothek** (State Library).

Many churches in Berlin also open their doors for concerts throughout the year. Berliner Dom in Mitte is a spectacular venue with an excellent concert programme. For a guide to all these events, look up the listings magazines *Tip* or *Zitty (see p260)*.

OPERA AND CLASSICAL BALLET

Among Berlin's three major opera houses, the **Staatsoper Unter den Linden** *(see p63)*, under the leadership of Daniel Barenboim, is a gem. However, this beautiful building is undergoing major restoration works until the end of 2013. In the meantime, performances take place at Schillertheater (Bismarckstrasse 110, Charlottenburg). The repertoire includes the traditional German classics, Italian opera, classical ballets and to a lesser extent, contemporary pieces.

Komische Oper *(see p68)* is known for its broad range of lighter opera, for which you can nearly always find tickets. The ballet produced here is particularly innovative.

Opera productions at the **Deutsche Oper Berlin** are often modern and intriguing. The repertoire includes music ranging from major Italian operas and Mozart to Wagner and Saint Saëns.

The **Neuköllner Oper** in the Neukölln district is an innovative and productive stage.

MODERN DANCE

Modern dance productions are held in **Hebbel am Ufer** on Stresemannstrasse or Hallesches Ufer. In recent years, however, **Tanzfabrik** in Kreuzberg and **Sophiensaele** and **Radialsystem** in Mitte have become equally dynamic centres of avant-garde dance, as has the International Choreographic Theater of Johann Kresnik in the Volksbühne *(see p263)*.

CONTEMPORARY MUSIC

The Berlin organization **Initiative Neue Music Berlin e.V.** publishes a website with information about current performances of contemporary music. It always includes **BKA** near Mehringdamm with its weekly programme of **Unerhörte Musik**.

FESTIVALS

The *Berliner Festwochen* festival has been divided into **Musikfest Berlin** held throughout September and **spielzeiteuropa**, a theatre and dance festival stretching from October to December. Each festival promises a range of events and attracts famous orchestras and soloists from around the world.

Contemporary music festival **MaerzMusik**, held every March, sees numerous world premieres of newcomers and established composers alike.

The *Young Euro Classic* festival is a platform for the best young symphony orchestras from all over the world who convene in Berlin's prestigious Konzerthaus every August.

Once a year for *Berlin Night of Theatres and Operas*, around 60 of the capital's stages, connected by shuttle buses, open late and offer short productions to touring visitors.

Berlin Klassiktage is an annual summer festival of classical music with evening concerts held in historic settings all over the city.

A real treat for music lovers is the wonderful *Classic Open Air Festival* featuring opera and concerts that is held every summer on an open stage on Gendarmenmarkt, which is built especially for the occasion. Another musical feast is the *Bach-Tage* festival in Potsdam, which takes place every year in September.

OPEN-AIR CONCERTS

Classical open-air concerts are staged at **Waldbühne**, located in a beautiful leafy setting near the Olympiastadion. The venue seats 20,000 and once a year features the Berlin Philharmonic Orchestra. The atmosphere is relaxed and informal, with kids running around while parents eat and drink during the shows. After sunset, when the crowds light candles brought for the occasion, the atmosphere becomes magical.

MUSIC IN PALACES AND NOTABLE BUILDINGS

During music festivals, recitals are often held in Berlin's beautiful historic buildings, and a concert in the Berliner Dom (see p77), the Orangerie in Schloss Charlottenburg (see pp160–61) or Schloss Friedrichsfelde (see p174) can be an unforgettable and delightful experience.

VARIOUS

The **Musikinstrumenten Museum** offers entertaining concerts on selected Sunday mornings, and as a part of the *Alte Musik Live* scheme you can listen to the music of old masters played on their original instruments. A special booklet covering the museum's various musical events is available from all theatres, concert halls and music shops.

The Konzerthaus Berlin and Komische Oper have regular classical concerts, tours and demonstrations for children. Find a calendar of all classical music events in Berlin. at the website www.klassik-in-berlin.de (English version is available).

The **Kulturkaufhaus Dussmann** shop offers the widest range of music in Berlin, with a stock of over 50,000 titles, and competent staff always ready to help you. Literary readings, lectures, and other special cultural events are also staged at the store. **Gelbe Musik** is also more than a shop; it is a gallery specializing in contemporary music and co-ordinates many concerts and recitals.

DIRECTORY

CONCERT HALLS

Konzerthaus Berlin
(Schauspielhaus)
Gendarmenmarkt 2.
Map 7 A4, 16 D4.
Tel 203 09 21 01/02.
www.konzerthaus.de

Philharmonie & Kammermusiksaal
Herbert-von-Karajan-Strasse 1.
Map 6 D5.
Tel 25 48 89 99.

Staatsbibliothek
Potsdamer Strasse 33.
Tel 2660.

Universität der Künste
Hardenbergstrasse 33.
Map 4 E3.
Tel 31 85 23 74.

OPERA AND BALLET

Deutsche Oper Berlin
Bismarckstrasse 34–37.
Map 3 A4.
Tel 343 84 01.

Komische Oper
Behrenstrasse 55–57.
Map 6 F4, 15 C3.
Tel 47 99 74 00.

Neuköllner Oper
Karl-Marx-Strasse 131–133, Neukölln.
Map 14 F5.
Tel 688 90 777.

Staatsoper Unter den Linden
Unter den Linden 7.
Map 7 A3, 16 D3.
Tel 20 35 45 55.
(Until 2013:
Bismarckstrasse 110.
Map 3 A4.)

MODERN DANCE

Hebbel am Ufer
Hau Eins
Stresemannstrasse 29.
Hau Zwei
Hallesches Ufer 32.
Map 12 F2.
Tel 259 00 40.
www.hebel-am-ufer.de

Radialsystem
Holzmarktstrasse 33.
Map 8 F5.
Tel 288 788 50.

Sophiensaele
Sophienstrasse 18.
Map 7 B1.
Tel 283 52 66.

Tanzfabrik
Möckernstrasse 68.
Map 12 E4.
Tel 786 58 61.

CONTEMPORARY MUSIC

Initiative Neue Musik Berlin e.V.
Klosterstrasse 68–70.
Map 8 D3.
Tel 242 45 34.
www.inm-berlin.de

Unerhörte Musik (BKA)
Mehringdamm 34.
Map 12 F3.
Tel 202 20 07.

FESTIVALS

Musikfest Berlin/spielzeiteuropa
Berliner Festspiele GmbH
Schaperstrasse 4.
Map 10 D2.
Tel 25 48 91 00.

MaerzMusik
Berliner Festspiele GmbH
Schaperstrasse 24.
Map 10 D2.
Tel 25 489 100.

OUTDOOR CONCERTS

Waldbühne
Glockenturmstrasse 1.
Tel (01805) 33 24 33.

VARIOUS

Gelbe Musik
Chausseestrasse 128.
Map 6 F1.
Tel 211 39 62.

Kulturkaufhaus Dussmann
Friedrichstrasse 90.
Tel 202 50.

Musikinstrumenten Museum
Tiergartenstrasse 1.
Map 6 D5.
Tel 25 48 10.

TICKETS

Hekticket
Reduced and last-minute tickets only.
Tel 230 99 30.

KaDeWe Theaterkassen
KaDeWe department store (6th floor),
Tauentzienstrasse 21.
Map 10 F2.
Tel 212 122 77.

Karstadt
Karstadt department store (ground floor),
Kurfürstendamm 231.
Map 10 D1.
Tel 88 00 30.

Rock, Jazz and World Music

To music lovers Berlin can mean anything from techno to the Berlin Philharmonic Orchestra, for the city has a thriving and multi-faceted music industry. Between its classical and ultra-modern extremes the full spectrum of musical taste is catered for, from bar-room blues to rock'n'roll and international pop. Whether it's a major event by a world-famous band or a small-scale evening of jazz improvization, you needn't look far to find what you want. The biggest events take place in sports halls and stadiums, but most of the action can be found in discos, bars and the city's various clubs (see pp270–71). There are also a number of cultural centres where you can stop by to listen to modern music. The best way to find something for yourself is to get hold of a copy of the listings magazines *Zitty* or *Tip*, and look out for flyers and leaflets in bars.

BIG CONCERTS

Berlin is always high up on the list when major pop, rock or jazz bands go on tour. While people flock from all over the country to attend these events, there are a number of smaller events which attract an equally devoted audience. Since the closure of the huge Deutschlandhalle, the big events take place in **Max-Schmeling-Hall** and the Velodrom (see p273). For the really big crowds, events are usually held at the **Olympiastadion** (see p184) which has seating for 100,000. The **Waldbühne** next door has a capacity of 20,000 and hosts both classical orchestras and rock bands. **Kindl-Bühne Wuhlheide** is another equally flexible venue. Concerts and plays are also organized at the popular **Arena** in Treptow – a very large music hall, dating from the 1920s, which used to be a local bus depot. In 2008, the massive **O2 World** arena opened in Friedrichshain. It hosts many of the large touring pop concerts, as well as sport events and other productions. For detailed information about what's on and where, consult the websites berlinonline.de and berlin.de or the listings magazines *Zitty* and *Tip*.

OTHER MUSICAL EVENTS

There are plenty of smaller venues in Berlin where concerts are held. Among them are **Lido** and the famous **SO 36** in Kreuzberg. The future of this legendary venue is uncertain, due to the gentrification of the area. See it before it disappears.

Schöneberg was notorious in the 1980s for its punk rock scene, but while those days are now over, there are still plenty of exciting things on offer here today. One of the most popular places in town is **Tempodrom** (check listings magazines for up-to-the-minute details).

Columbia Halle, which is located near Columbiadamm, is a well-known location for medium-size events, and so is the **Knaack Club**, a multi-sited venue on Greifswalder Strasse. If you are looking for particularly atmospheric concerts, try the **Passionskirche**, a church in Kreuzberg. Another good location to check out is the large **Kulturbrauerei** complex in Prenzlauer Berg. This former brewery now houses dozens of venues, playing a mix of world, rock and electronic music.

JAZZ

Jazz lovers from all over the world descend on Berlin for the **Jazzfest Berlin**, and its accompanying **Total Music Meeting**, both of which are held each year. The former is more traditional, but the latter is devoted to modern experimental work. "Jazz across the Border" takes place in July; it is a festival at which all kinds of borders are crossed, not least those of musical inhibition.

As far as regular clubs are concerned, jazz is still very popular in Berlin, in spite of the pull of its perhaps better known electronic and techno discotheques. The **A Trane** and **b-flat** are classical jazz bars where you can listen to small bands just about every night of the week.

Another great venue is **Quasimodo** on Kantstrasse, which has a relaxed and intimate atmosphere. Its concerts only start after 10pm when performances at Theater des Westens have finished; the vibrations would otherwise disturb the neighbouring audience. The acoustics at Quasimodo are also excellent and many big names in jazz have performed on its stage. Another good venue for enjoying jazz is **Bilderbuch**, on Akazienstrasse.

Apart from the typical, classical jazz clubs, jazz can also be heard in many of the city's smaller bars, like **Kunstfabric Schlot** on Kastanienallee. If it's a mixture of soul, rap and jazz you want to listen to then head for the **Junction Bar** in Kreuzberg. The **Badenscher Hof Jazzclub** on Badensche Strasse is another great place for jazz. It has a varied programme of mainstream jazz, modern jazz and blues.

WORLD MUSIC

As a broadly cosmopolitan city with an increasingly multi-national population, Berlin is home to a wide variety of music. Lovers of world music should visit Berlin in May, when the large and lively Karneval der Kulturen takes place. The main event is an exciting street parade through Kreuzberg featuring marching bands and dance troupes playing an extremely diverse array of music. The presence of music from all parts of the world is never that far away.

The **Haus der Kulturen der Welt** on John-Foster-Dulles-Allee is an institution set up by the Berlin Upper Chamber to support this cosmopolitanism, and its main aim is to make non-European cultures more accessible to Germany. As music is one of the best ways of bridging cross-cultural differences, the Haus der Kulturen der Welt organizes all kinds of concerts at its own **Café Global** – one of the best Saturday evening venues for listening to and dancing to music from all over the world. Details of the bands on offer can be found in a booklet which should be available in bookshops and restaurants around town.

A similar organization is the **Werkstatt der Kulturen** on Wissmannstrasse which has been staging all kinds of cultural events for some years

now. These include regular concerts and music festivals. Between them, the Haus der Kulturen der Welt and the Werkstatt are the most reliable providers of world music in town, but you can also find a number of bars and clubs that specialize in the music of one particular nation. Details of these can be found in the listings magazines *Zitty* and *Tip*, and on flyers all over town.

Latin American discos are becoming ever more popular throughout Berlin – **Havanna** in Schöneberg is one of the city's most popular and largest.

Irish music is also well represented in the city, and all you have to do is visit a few pubs. Live music is played in **Wild at Heart** on almost every night of the week.

TICKETS

The price of tickets for major pop concerts can be astronomical, particularly if you want to secure a good seat. At the other extreme, you should be able to get into smaller clubs for €5–12, but again, if a famous person or band is playing you will have to pay a good deal more. Often you will find the ticket price includes a drink at the bar.

Tickets for major events are likely to sell out quickly and should be booked well in advance; there are numerous ticket offices in the busier parts of town *(see p261)*.

If you just want to spend the night at a club you should have no trouble buying a ticket at the door.

DIRECTORY

BIG CONCERTS

Arena
Eichenstrasse 4.
Tel 533 73 30.

O2 World
Mühlenstrasse 12.
Tel 20 60 70 88 44.

Waldbühne
Glockenturmstrasse 1.
Tel (01805) 33 24 33.

OTHER MUSIC EVENTS

Columbia Halle and Columbia Club
Columbiadamm 13–21.
Tel 780 99 810.

Kindl-Bühne Wuhlheide
An der Wuhlheide 187.
Tel 857 58 10.

Knaack Club
Greifswalder Strasse 224.
Tel 442 70 60.

Lido
Cuvrystrasse 7.
Map 6 E5.
Tel 695 66 840.

Meistersaal
Köthener Strasse 38.
Map 6 E5.
Tel 325 999 710.

Passionskirche
Marheineckeplatz 1-2.
Map 13 A5.
Tel 69 40 12 41.

SO 36
Oranienstrasse 190.
Map 14 E2.
Tel 61 40 13 06.

Tempodrom
Am Anhalter Bahnhof,
Möckernstrasse 10.
Map 12 E1.
Tel 747 370.

Tipi am Kanzleramt
Grosse Querallee,
Tiergarten. **Map** 5 C3.
Tel (0180) 327 93 58.

UFA Fabrik
Victoriastrasse 10–18.
Tel 75 50 30.

Wild at Heart
Wiener Strasse 20
(Kreuzberg).
Tel 610 747 01.

JAZZ

A Trane
Pestalozzistrasse 105.
Map 3 C5.
Tel 313 25 50.

Aufsturz
Oranienburger Strasse 67.
Map 7 A1.
Tel 280 474 07.

Badenscher Hof Jazzclub
Badensche Strasse 29.
Map 10 D5.
Tel 861 00 80.

b-flat
Rosenthaler Strasse 13.
Map 7 B1.
Tel 283 31 23.

Bilderbuch
Akazienstrasse 28.
Map 11 A5.
Tel 78 70 60 57.

Jazzfest Berlin
Schaperstrasse 24.
Map 10 D2.
Tel 25 48 90 .

Junction Bar
Gneisenaustrasse 18.
Tel 694 66 02.

Kunstfabric Schlot
Edisonhöfe,
Chausseestrasse 18.
Map 1 A4. *Tel 448 21 60.*

Quasimodo
Kantstrasse 12a.
Tel 312 80 86.

Yorckschlösschen
Yorckstrasse 15.
Map 12 E4.
Tel 215 80 70.

WORLD MUSIC

Haus der Kulturen der Welt & Café Global
John-Foster-Dulles-
Allee 10.
Map 5 C3. *Tel 39 78 70.*

Havanna
Hauptstrasse 30.
Map 11 A5.
Tel 784 85 65.

Kulturbrauerei
Schönhauser Allee 36.
Tel 443 52 60.

Werkstatt der Kulturen
Wissmannstrasse 32.
Map 14 E5.
Tel 60 97 700.

Clubs

Berlin is considered the clubbing capital of Europe. Countless clubs with an atmosphere from trashy to classy attract visitors from all over the world. The years after the fall of the Wall provided a limitless supply of new locations, from old bank vaults to abandoned power stations, though some of these have closed to make way for more profit-oriented uses. Still, the city parties on and the endurance of Berlin's late-night scene is stunning. Parties rarely get going before mid-night, and after-work and after-hours parties serve as a connection to the next night out. Few clubs specialize in a particular kind of music but rather reserve certain days of the week for different styles; find out what you are in for online, or through free copies of *Partysan* and flyers distributed widely in bars.

TECHNO

Although the legendary Love Parade that used to lure over a million devotees into town has moved on, Berlin still considers itself to be the techno capital and looks on its clubs, with their striking locations, as cultural assets. In 2009, British *DJ Mag* named **Berghain** the world's best techno club. Combined with its upstairs **Panorama Bar**, the former power station is a unique Saturday night cathedral of techno and house but is not always easy to get in to due to its selective door policy. **Tresor**, Berlin's first techno club, moved from its old bank vaults to a post-industrial location in Mitte. The somewhat eerie place can absorb several thousand people and is open Wednesdays to Saturdays.

Watergate in Kreuzberg, is located right beside the beautiful Oberbaumbrücke bridge on the banks of the Spree and is favoured by techno, D&B, minimal and house DJs from all over the world. Both sound system and visual effects are spectacular at this temple of hedonism that also sports a floating outside terrace.

On Thursdays, popular **Sage Club** in Mitte has mostly rock, less techno and house; it features live acts, DJs and theme nights. One of the dancefloors is adorned with a fire breathing dragon and instead of air-conditioning, an outdoor pool provides welcome relief in the summer.

DISCOS

If it's a good old-fashioned disco you're looking for, with happy tunes and a little less of the techno, then **Sophienclub** is the place to go. It was famous even before the fall of the Wall and attracts a mixed crowd that is into classic and independent rock, soul, R&B, dance and pop. **FritzClub im Postbahnhof**, a multi-floor party and disco venue in two former mail cargo halls that accommodates up to 1,200 guests, is favoured by an under-25 student crowd that couldn't care less about dress codes. Also in Friedrichshain, **Matrix** is a booming club and disco, its vaulted brick catacombs bustling with a young crowd. **Narva Lounge** next door is a little more refined, with two dance floors, a cocktail bar and white leather booths. **Ritzy Adagio** at Potsdamer Platz is styled like a medieval castle and attracts a good mix of young and a little more mature party-goers. A stunning location with high ceilings, chandeliers and a dress code is **Goya**, favoured by thirty-somethings eager to dance.

TRENDY AND ALTERNATIVE CLUBS

Twelfth-floor **WeekEnd** at Alexanderplatz is a beautifully designed bar cum rooftop terrace club with a stunning view over downtown east Berlin. Resident and visiting DJs spin mostly hip-hop, electro, deep-house and funk. The most grown-up feature here is the prices.

For the quintessential Berlin experience, try retro-style **Kaffee Burger** where the legendary "Russendisko" was born. Parties, often featuring Russian bands and DJs, are wild; the interior is a mix of 1950s Germany and Soviet realism. **Maria am Ostbahnhof**, with **Joseph** as a club-floor spin-off, has a programme spanning from techno raves to rock concerts to digital culture festivals, where experts in digital art, music and animation present their work to the public –culminating in a digital musica party. **K17** is a rather dark "goth", punk and electro club playing different music on each of its four floors.

Bohannon is an unpretentious but nicely styled soul and oldies club with two bars in Mitte. It is frequented by a friendly and open-minded thirty-something crowd. Also located near Hackescher Markt, low-key **Dante** club doubles as a restaurant in day-time and excellent cocktail bar in the evening. Later, even on Mondays and Wednesdays, it turns into a chill-out club, featuring mainly soul and house. **Felix Club Restaurant** at the backside of Adlon Hotel may be as posh as the location suggests – but the symbiosis of Italian cuisine and relaxed clubbing works for Berlin's fashionable and wealthy.

For a more underground experience, try the **Cassiopeia** in trendy Friedrichshain (good for electro, house, funk, ska, old school rap and reggae) that apart from dance floors, features an outdoor rock climbing tower. **SO36** in Kreuzberg is a classic and still worth a visit for a Karaoke or ballroom-dancing night, a punk or rock concert or one of the regular oriental gay parties.

The front part of **Oscar Wilde**, in the location of a popular 1920s dance hall on Friedrichstrasse, is an Irish pub, while the backroom has wild soul and hip-hop parties. There are also a couple of surviving old dance halls to go and waltz. Among the oldest is **Clärchens Ballhaus** in Mitte, shared by patrons of all ages dancing to an eclectic mix of German classics, chart hits and the Beatles.

LOUNGES

For those not sure whether they feel like dancing the night away, Berlin's lounges are good for a relaxed evening. In contrast to the clubs, they tend to be open every day. **PURO Sky Lounge** near the KaDeWe on Tauentzien is a very stylish fully glazed rooftop club with great sunset views. Elegant **Solar** near Potsdamer Platz offers great views from the 17th floor. **40seconds** serves as a restaurant and bar before the DJs get going after 11pm. This exclusive penthouse venue also has incredible 360 degree views of the Potsdamer Platz area. **Spindler und Klatt** in Kreuzberg is a former grain warehouse now sporting lounge beds to sprawl on, one-stop dining (specializing in Asian food) and clubbing. In summer, the riverside terrace is a huge bonus.

GAY AND LESBIAN CLUBS

Berlin has a very tolerant attitude to people with different sexual orientations. A big day for the whole city is the gigantic parade on Christopher Street Day, which takes place annually at the end of June. Berlin Pride Festival is celebrated for three weeks preceding the CSD. Berlin's gay community meets at countless bars, clubs and discos, many of them found around Nollendorfplatz in Schöneberg, or in gay-friendly clubs like **Berghain/Panorama Bar**.

The city's most popular gay discos are **SchwuZ**, on Mehringdamm, and **Connection** on Fuggerstrasse. Many clubs usually frequented by straight people also have regular gay nights.

For lesbians the best clubs in Berlin are **Ackerkeller** and Café Fatal at **SO36**. The latter also admits gay men to its popular Sunday tea dance.

SPECIAL INTEREST

You want to check the dress/undress code before heading out to legendary **Kit-Kat Club**. On most nights, guests are requested to shed most of their clothes on entering this adult playground. The techno and trance club has plenty of room to dance but also to lie down and relax – which is practiced by clubbers of all sexual persuasions.

DIRECTORY

TECHNO

Berghain/ Panorama Bar
Am Wriezener Bahnhof. (Friedrichshain).
Tel 290 005 97.

Sage Club
Köpenicker Strasse 76–78.
Tel 278 50 52.
Map 8 D5.
Tel 278 98 30.

Tresor
Köpenicker Strasse 70.
Map 8 E5.
Tel 229 06 11.

Watergate
Falckensteinstrasse 49 (Kreuzberg).
Tel 612 803 95.

DISCOS

Adagio
Marlene-Dietrich-Place 1.
Map 6 D5.
Tel 259 29 550.

FritzClub im Postbahnhof
Strasse der Pariser Kommune 8.
Tel 698 2 80.

Goya
Nollendorfpl. 5.
Map 11 A2.
Tel 419 939 000.

Matrix
Warschauer Platz 18 (U/S Warschauer Strasse).
Tel 293 699 920

Narva Lounge
Warschauer Platz 18.
Tel 293 699 918.

Sophienclub
Sophienstrasse 6.
Map 7 B1.
Tel 282 45 52.

TRENDY & ALTERNATIVE

Bohannon
Dircksenstrasse 40.
Map 7 C2.
Tel 695 05 287.

Cassiopeia
Revaler Strasse 99.
Tel 226 855 05.

Clärchens Ballhaus
Auguststrasse 24.
Map 7 A1.
Tel 282 92 95.

Dante
Am Zwirngraben 8-10.
Map 7 B2, 16 F1.
Tel 247 27 401.

Felix Club Restaurant
Behrenstrasse 72.
Map 2 F3, 6 E4.
Tel 301 117 152.

Kaffee Burger
Torstrasse 60.
Map 7 C1.
Tel 280 455 39.

Maria/Josef am Ostbahnhof
An der Schillingbrücke 33–34.
Map 8 F5.
Tel 212 38 190.

Oscar Wilde
Friedrichstr. 112a.
Map 6 F1.
Tel 282 81 66.

SO36
Oranienstrasse 190.
Map 14 E2.
Tel 614 013 06.

WeekEnd
Am Alexanderplatz 5.
Map 8 D2.
Tel 246 31 676.

LOUNGES

40seconds
Potsdamer Strasse 58.
Map 11 C2.
Tel 89 06 42 41.

PURO Sky Lounge
Tauentzienstrasse 9-11.
Map 10 E1.
Tel 263 678 75.

Solar
Stresemannstrasse 76.
Map 12 E1.
Tel 0163 765 27 00.

Spindler und Klatt
Köpenicker Strasse 16 (Kreuzberg).
Tel 695 667 75.

GAY AND LESBIAN

Ackerkeller
Bergstrasse 68.
Tel 36 46 13 56.

Connection
Fuggerstrasse 33.
Map 10 F2.
Tel 218 14 32.

SchwuZ
Mehringdamm 61.
Map 12 F4.
Tel 629 08 80.

SO36 (see Trendy & Alternative)

SPECIAL INTEREST

Kit-Kat Club
See Sage Club, Fri–Sun.
Tel 787 18 96.

Sport and Recreation

Berlin is a sports-loving town, and every year the major sports events attract a growing number of fans and competitors. The Berlin Marathon, run in September, is now the third largest in the world, its 42-km (26-mile) distance tackled by runners and roller-skaters – able-bodied and disabled alike. The Bundesliga (German football league) cup final takes place in May in the Olympia Stadion. Crowds of each team's supporters converge on the city a few days before the game, and after the match they all join a huge party for the winners along the Ku'damm. The world tennis élite battle it out during the German Open championship every April.

CYCLING

The flat terrain, numerous parks and countless special routes for cyclists – which reach a total of 850 km (530 miles) – make Berlin a cycle-friendly city. Outside rush hour you can take your bike on S- or U-Bahn trains, which provide easy access to the three most popular routes – along the Havel river, around the Grunewald forest, and around the Müggelsee.

There are many places all over Berlin where you can rent a bike for €5–12 per day (see p293), provided you leave a deposit, either as cash or a cheque. The best hotels in town also hire out their own bikes for guests. The route from the historic centre of Mitte to the Ku'damm via Tiergarten can be an unforgettable experience.

In January those lovers of two wheels meet during Berliner Sechs-Tage-Rennen in the **Velodrom** on Paul-Heyse-Strasse. You might have some problems buying a ticket as the event is very popular, so give them a call beforehand. For information concerning routes, events, tours, or anything else you may need to know about cycling in Berlin, contact the **ADFC (Allgemeiner Deutscher Fahrrad-Club)**.

GOLF

Just about every sporting discipline is catered for in Berlin, and golfing is no exception. The Driving Range golf club is situated in the centre of the town on Chausseestrasse, and during spring and summer it is open from noon until sunset. Entrance to the course is free, but you have to leave a deposit on hiring golf clubs. A bucket of 30 balls costs only €1.50. Golf coaching is available either for individuals or in a group.

There are two golf courses within Berlin: the **Golf und Landclub Berlin-Wannsee**, which has a large 18-hole course and a smaller one with 9 holes, and **Berliner Golfclub-Gatow** which only has a 9-hole course. There are a total of 15 golf clubs around Berlin, most of which have excellent restaurants and are situated close to hotels.

SWIMMING POOLS

Public swimming facilities in Berlin are extremely clean and you can always swim there safely. Some of the best places to try are on the Havel river and the city's lakes. Swimming on natural beaches is free, but there are no changing rooms or toilet facilities.

Berlin also has a number of artificial beaches which are all manned by lifeguards. The best known is the **Strandbad Wannsee**, which was built in the 1920s and remains very popular today. Other excellent spots can be found around Müggelsee.

One of the most beautiful swimming pool complexes is **Olympiastadion** (see p184) which was a venue for the 1936 Berlin Olympic Games. A special pool for diving has a 10-m (33-ft) tower with a lift. Alternatively, you can simply sunbathe on the steps and admire the view.

The three most beautiful swimming pools are situated in Mitte, Neukölln and Wilmersdorf. **Stadtbad Mitte**, on Gartenstrasse, is a painstakingly restored building which dates from the 1930s. It has a 50-m (164-ft) pool designed for sporting events as well as recreational swimming. **Stadtbad Charlottenburg**, on the other hand, offers a smaller pool which is more appropriate for relaxation than serious swimming; it is also beautifully decorated with Secessionist paintings. But if it's a swim in luxurious surroundings you want, then take a dive at the **Stadtbad Neukölln**; the extraordinary decorative mosaics, frescos, and marble-and-bronze ornamentation is enough to make you forget why you came here in the first place.

Two equally stunning experiences are guaranteed at the **Badeschiff Arena** on the river Spree in Treptow. In summer, the arena is a floating, open-air swimming pool on the river bank. In winter, it is transformed into a space-like, enclosed swimming hall. The **Tropical Islands** water and fun park, southeast of Berlin, is a huge, artificial paradise set in a vast construction hall once built for zeppelins.

BADMINTON, SQUASH AND TENNIS

You won't have to travel far in Berlin to find facilities to play badminton, squash or tennis as numerous courts are scattered all over town, from local parks to sophisticated sports centres. It is customary to bring your own sports shoes, but rackets are almost always available to rent.

The entrance fee in most cases includes the use of a sauna, and at **Sportoase** there are 18 badminton courts in addition to 8 squash courts. **City Sports** offers an opportunity to play tennis on any of its five courts. Other addresses can be found in the telephone directory.

OTHER SPORTS

Every weekend in August, John-Foster-Dulles-Allee in Tiergarten is closed to traffic to become a genuine paradise for rollerblade and in-line skaters. If you fancy trying this yourself, there are plenty of shops in the area offering skates and safety equipment at reasonable rates.

If you fancy a boat trip, rowing boats are available for hire at many places along the banks of the lakes. In the Tiergarten you can rent them near Café am Neuen See and around Schlachtensee; the price is usually somewhere around €7–10 per hour.

FITNESS

There are always new gyms opening and others closing down in Berlin, so your best bet is to check the telephone directory for the most up-to-date listings. At many gyms you can buy a daily card, rather than becoming a member. But if your visit to Berlin is a long one, it may be worth joining. **Ars Vitalis** is the best

independent fitness club and spa for men and women. **Fitness First** is one of the best options for women; it has five studios across the city and they are all large and well equipped. The main one is on Tauentzienstrasse and has a pleasant terrace overlooking town. A one-day ticket costs €25.

SPECTATOR SPORTS

As a rule, Berlin's sports teams tend to be among the country's best, and rank highly in each of their respective leagues. Football matches of Hertha BSC take place in the Olympia Stadion and tickets are usually available at approximately €6–18.

Alba Berlin is among the top basketball teams in Germany, and its matches in **Max-Schmeling-Halle** can be attended by up to 8,500 fans. For international events it's best to pre-book tickets well in advance, and these can vary between €10 and €52, depending on the match. Berlin has two very good hockey teams: Berlin-Capitals

and Eisbären Berlin – both of whose matches always sell out of tickets very quickly.

HORSE RACING

Lovers of horse racing have two tracks to choose from in Berlin. **Trabrennbahn** in Mariendorf is open all year and the races held here are strictly commercial. **Galopp-rennbahn Hoppegarten**, on the other hand, has a more approachable feel.

MARATHON

Marathon running isn't everyone's cup of tea, but when you see the enormous crowds gathered to run the **Berlin-Marathon** in August, you may well wish you were one of the pack.

The route is one of the fastest in the world, attracting top sponsors and athletes alike; the world record was broken here in 1998. Thousands of viewers gather en route to cheer the runners, rollers and disabled athletes – the latter having their own group which starts before the others.

DIRECTORY

CYCLING

ADFC
Brunnenstrasse 28.
Tel 448 47 24.

Velodrom
Paul-Heyse-Strasse.
Tel 44 30 45.

GOLF

Berliner Golfclub-Gatow
Sparnecker Weg 100.
Tel 365 00 06.

Golf und Landclub Berlin-Wannsee
Golfweg 22.
Tel 806 70 60.

SWIMMING

Badeschiff Arena
Eichenstrasse 4.
Tel 533 20 30.

Stadtbad Charlottenburg
Krumme Strasse 9.
Tel 34 38 38 65.

Stadtbad Mitte
Gartenstrasse 5.
Plan 7 A1. Tel 308 80 90.

Stadtbad Neukölln
Ganghoferstrasse 3.
Tel 68 24 98 12.

Strandbad Wannsee
Wannseebadweg 25.
Tel 70 71 38 33.

Tropical Islands
Tropical Islands Allee 1D, 15910 Krausnick.
Tel (035477) 605 050.

BADMINTON, SQUASH, TENNIS

City Sports
Brandenburgische Strasse 53. *Tel 873 90 97.*

Sportoase
Stromstrasse 11–17.
Plan 4 F1, 4 F2.
Tel 390 66 20.

Squash Factory
Warener Strasse 5.
Tel 563 85 85.

MARATHON

Berlin-Marathon
Hanns-Braun-Strasse/
Adlerplatz.
Tel 30 12 88 10.

SPECTATOR SPORTS

Max-Schmeling-Halle
Am Falkplatz.
Tel 44 30 45.

FITNESS

Ars Vitalis
Hauptstrasse 19.
Map 11 A5.
Tel 311 65 94 70.

Fitness First
Tauentzienstrasse 13.
Map 10 E1.
Tel 2145 94 42.

HORSE RACING

Galopprennbahn Hoppegarten
Goetheallee 1.
Tel (03342) 389 30.
◻ *4–10pm Sat & Sun.*

Trabrennbahn Mariendorf
Mariendorfer Damm 222, Tempelhof.
Tel 740 12 12.
◻ *1:30pm Sun, 6:30pm Mon.*

CHILDREN'S BERLIN

When it comes to entertainment, people of all ages are catered for in Berlin, and children are no exception. There are numerous shops, theatres and cinemas to keep them occupied, not to mention circuses and zoological gardens. Additionally, there is the Deutsches Technikmuseum

One of Berlin's young roller skaters

(German Museum of Technology), the Museumsdorf Düppel, or the Kinder- und Jugendmuseum, all of which encourage children to take part in the displays. Tickets for children under 14 are almost always reduced, and very young children are often admitted for free. Restaurants often have special areas for toddlers.

The Potsdam train, always a favourite among children

INFORMATION

Berlin is very welcoming to its younger visitors. Families with children are entitled to public transport discounts, and children can travel free or at a reduced rate, depending on their age. For detailed information on the discounts and opportunities for children, contact **Berlin Tourismus Marketing GmbH**. This organization offers several discount cards which entitle the holder to public transport use and entry to various museums and attractions. Some versions of these cards are valid for one adult and up to three children. Ask about the Berlin WelcomeCard and the CityTourCard (see p279).

ZOOLOGICAL GARDENS

One of Berlin's zoological gardens can be visited the moment you arrive in town, as it is located opposite the Zoo railway station. The **Zoo Berlin** offers extensive parkland and many animal enclosures, as well as an excellent aquarium with the biggest collection of aquatic fauna in the world.

The second zoo, **Tierpark Berlin** in Friedrichsfelde, isn't quite so convenient but it is much bigger and can still be reached by U-Bahn. Covering a wide area around Schloss Friedrichsfelde, the Tierpark is the largest park in Europe.

Apart from these zoological gardens, a lot of the parks in Berlin contain mini-zoos where many different kinds of animals can be seen. In a garden behind the Märkisches Museum, for example, you can see a family of bears.

As well as the more exotic animals, however, it is also possible to see the familiar favourites. Small children will love the **Kinderbauernhof Auf dem Görlitzer**, which has a collection of domestic animals. Here geese, pigs and rabbits run happily around the Görlitzer Park.

MUSEUMS

Generally speaking, Berlin's museums are well set up for children. Perhaps the most entertaining is the **Deutsches Technikmuseum** (see p144) where children can take part in all kinds of experiments. The **Ethnologisches Museum** (see p178) also prepares

special exhibitions for children. On some days you can take part in a game with Mexican papier-mâché dolls, on others you can participate in a Japanese ceremonial bath. A visit to the **Museumsdorf Düppel** is an excellent way to show a child the workings of a medieval village. The Museum für Naturkunde (see p109) is another fun place for children, particularly the dinosaur sections and the dioramas of animals in their natural habitats. The **Kinder-museum Labyrinth** is another favourite.

Another great place to visit is the **Puppentheater-museum**, which is always lively, and offers a chance for children to take part in minor performances.

THEATRES

Established in 1969, **Grips Theater** is probably the most interesting theatre for children and teenagers. Its independent and ambitious programme attracts many spectators and one of its performances,

Children admiring Neptune's Fountain by the Town Hall

A visit to the medieval village at Museumsdorf Düppel

Linie 1, was made into a film. Other venues worth trying are the **Theater an der Parkaue**, **Theater o.N.**, **Zaubertheater Igor Jedlin** and the **Puppentheater Berlin**. Another option is to go to one of the city's many circuses, all of which prepare their programmes with children in mind.

SPORTS

Ice-skating in winter and roller-skating in summer are popular in Berlin, and football and swimming are popular year-round. You can swim in rivers, lakes and swimming pools (Hotline **Berliner Bäderbetriebe**

offers useful information). Each district has its own ice-skating rink, but the **Horst-Dohm-Eisstadion** is outstanding with its 400-m (1,312-ft) run and large ice-hockey rink. **FEZ Berlin** offers a special daily programme for kids.

OTHER ENTERTAINMENT

Berlin is full of wonderfully equipped children's playgrounds. Each neighbourhood has at least one, usually complete with climbing frames, ping-pong tables and mini soccer courts.

An ascent of the Fernsehturm (television tower) at

Alexanderplatz *(see p93)* is a great way to treat a child, perhaps for afternoon tea. You can buy cake and juice in the tower's rotating café. A lift in the Funkturm (radio tower) in the Messegelände *(see p183)* offers an excellent view of the city, from a slightly lower height.

Cabuwazi is a children's circus-training group that offers workshops and performances. It operates five permanent big-top tents, the main one being at Görlitzer Park in Kreuzberg. **The Story of Berlin** is a fun way for both parents and children to experience the history of Berlin in a thrilling multimedia exhibit. And the **Berliner Gruselkabinett** (Room of Fear) is enough to frighten anybody.

For an out-of-the-ordinary experience, you can't go wrong at either the **Zeiss-Planetarium** or the **Planetarium am Insulaner**, where fascinating shows allow you to explore the known universe and to have a good look at the stars.

DIRECTORY

INFORMATION

Berlin Tourismus Marketing GmbH
Am Karlsbad 11.
Tel 25 00 25.
www.visitberlin.de

Berlin mit Kindern
www.berlin-with-children.com

ZOOLOGICAL GARDENS

Kinderbauernhof Auf dem Görlitzer
Wiener Strasse 59.
Tel 611 74 24.

Tierpark Berlin
Am Tierpark 125,
Lichtenberg.
Tel 51 53 10.

Zoo Berlin
Hardenbergplatz 9,
Charlottenburg.
Tel 25 40 10.

MUSEUMS

Kindermuseum Labyrinth
Osloer Strasse 12.
Tel 800 93 11 50.
🕐 *1–6pm Fri–Sat,*
11am–6pm Sun.

Museumsdorf Düppel
Clauertstrasse 11.
Tel 862 11 80.
🕐 *Apr–Oct: 3–7pm Thu,*
10am–5pm Sun and
holidays.

Puppentheater-Museum Berlin
Karl-Marx-Strasse 135.
Tel 687 81 32.
🕐 *9am–4:30pm Mon–*
Fri, 11am–4:30pm Sun.

THEATRES

Theater an der Parkaue
Parkaue 29.
Tel 55 77 520.

Grips Theater
Altonaer Strasse 22.
Tel 39 74 74 77.

Puppentheater Berlin
Gierkeplatz 2.
Tel 342 19 50.

Theater o.N.
Kollwitzstrasse 53.
Tel 440 92 14.

Zaubertheater Igor Jedlin
Roscherstrasse 7.
Tel 323 37 77.

SPORTS

Berliner Bäderbetriebe
Tel (01803) 10 20 20.

Horst-Dohm-Eisstadion
Fritz-Wildung-Strasse 9.
Tel 824 10 12.

FEZ Berlin
Strasse zum FEZ 2.
Tel 53 07 10.

OTHER ENTERTAINMENT

Berliner Gruselkabinett
Schöneberger Strasse 23a.
Map 12 E1.
Tel 26 55 55 46.

Cabuwazi Circus
Wiener Strasse 59H.
Tel 530 00 40.
www.cabuwazi.de

Planetarium am Insulaner
Munsterdamm 90.
Tel 790 09 30.

The Story of Berlin
Kurfürstendamm 207–208.
Map 9 A2.
Tel 88 72 01 00.

Zeiss-Großplanetarium
Prenzlauer Allee 80.
Tel 42 18 450.

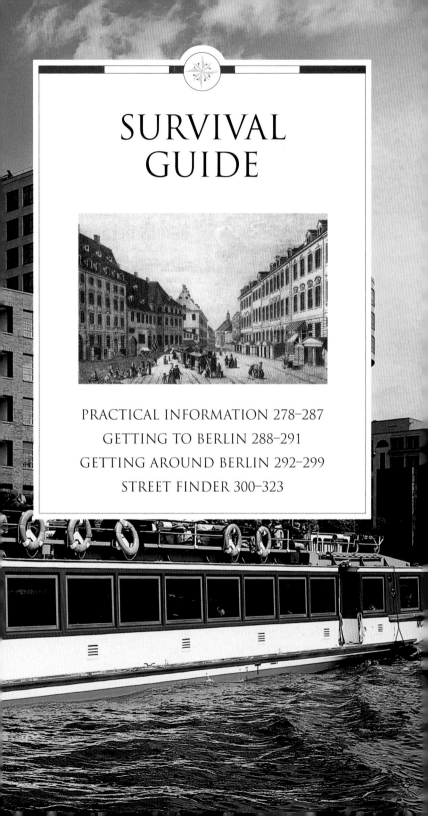

SURVIVAL
GUIDE

PRACTICAL INFORMATION

Berlin is a tourist-friendly city, so you shouldn't have too much difficulty getting around. Many Germans speak English and Berliners are usually welcoming to newcomers. Cash machines, telephones and parking meters all have clear instructions, and public transport is of the highest standard *(see pp292–3)*. For reduced fares on public transport, buy

Berlin tourist information sign

yourself a daily or weekly travel card, or a BerlinWelcomeCard which also gives you reduced access to many museums. There are plenty of information centres in the busiest areas of town and a number of different listings magazines and brochures are available. If you have Internet access, VisitBerlin.de is a good information source.

VISA AND CUSTOMS

A valid passport is necessary for all visitors to Germany. Visas are not required for citizens of EU countries. A list, available from all German embassies, specifies other countries whose nationals do not need a visa for visits of less than 90 days. Non-EU citizens wishing to stay in Germany longer than three months will need a visa, available from German consulates. These must be obtained in advance. All visitors should check requirements before travelling.

On arrival in Germany, you will not be charged duty on personal articles. As in other European countries, no drugs or weapons may be brought across the border. The amount of cigarettes and alcohol allowed in or out of the country is restricted. Adults resident outside the EU can bring up to 200 cigarettes (50 cigars, or 250g of tobacco), one litre of spirits (or four litres of wine), and up to €430 worth of personal goods (including perfumes and electronic items). You may be asked to pay extra tax on items deemed to be worth more than your personal allowance.

EMBASSIES AND CONSULATES

Most large countries have embassies in Berlin. They are spread across different parts of the city, a result of the period when Germany was divided. Some of the newer embassies are wonderful examples of modern architecture, such as the Nordic countries' joint mission in Tiergarten, while some older embassies retain the design ethos of the divided period, such as the Czech Republic Embassy on Wilhelmstraße.

TOURIST INFORMATION

There are many excellent tourist information centres in Berlin. The two biggest are at the **Neues Kranzler Eck** and the **Brandenburg Gate**, but others can be found at **Hauptbahnhof** and in the **ALEXA** shopping centre near Alexanderplatz. The **Potsdam Tourismus Service** office is in central Potsdam, on Brandenburger Strasse.

For up-to-the-minute news, turn to the Internet; **Visit Berlin.de**, which is managed by **Berlin Tourismus Marketing**, is a very reliable source of information for tourists.

OPENING HOURS

Offices in Berlin usually open from 9am to 6pm, with an hour's lunch break. Smaller shops open from 9:30 or 10am to 8pm, and on Saturdays most shops close at 4 or 5pm. Shops are closed on Sundays due to Germany's religious traditions. However, those in the main train stations remain open on Sundays; you can find supermarkets at Hauptbahnhof, Friedrichstrasse and Ostbahnhof.

Trading rules are relaxed in the month before Christmas, when shops open every day and for longer hours. For typical bank opening hours, *see p284*.

SchauLUST Museen Berlin pass, for unlimited 3-day entry to museums

MUSEUMS AND HISTORIC BUILDINGS

There are over 150 museums and galleries in Berlin, but exhibitions change and collections move continually. This guide covers the most important places, but plenty of information is also available on lesser-known museums and galleries. Tourist information offices can provide up-to-the-minute details.

A good information line is the **Info-Telefon der Staatlichen Museen zu Berlin** and its associated website, and there

Tourist information centre in Berlin

◁ **Hotel Spreebogen on the River Spree**

Sight-seeing boat tour along the Spree

are also information centres devoted to the Pergamon-museum and the Sanssouci complex in Potsdam. Contact the **Stiftung Preussische Schlösser und Gärten Berlin-Brandenburg**, which is the authority in charge of most major gardens and castles in the region.

Museums and historic buildings are usually open 10am to 5pm (sometimes 6pm) Tuesday to Sunday. Some museums, however, close on another day instead of Monday, and many museums are open late on Thursdays, and often allow free entry during these hours.

For reduced entrance prices, you may want to get hold of the SchauLUST Museen Berlin pass, which allows three days' unlimited access to the major museums. This pass is sold at official tourist information centres. It can be used at all the national museums, including the whole Museum Island complex, the Kulturforum, Museen Dahlem and several additional institutions in Charlottenburg.

Other options for getting value for money are the Berlin Welcome Card (see www.VisitBerlin.de) and the **CityTourCard**, which both offer you public transport for three days, and discount entry to a long list of attractions. The conditions and attractions offered by both vary, so it's best to check which is most suitable for you.

Check event listings for the biannual Lange Nacht der Museen, held at the end of January and August, when many museums stay open until midnight, with special shuttle buses to transport visitors between them.

GUIDED TOURS

There are many bus tours available in Berlin, each of which, in 3 or 4 hours, introduce you to the city's chief historic buildings. A single ticket usually allows you to get off at any stage and rejoin the tour at different stops. However, if you want to save some money, the double-decker public transport bus No. 100 follows a similar route (see p295).

If you would rather go on foot, walking tours are also possible – these provide a more leisurely view of the city, stopping at all the major landmarks and museums.

A variety of cycling tours, or tours by Segway (two-wheeled electronic vehicles), provide fun ways to see the sights.

There are many different companies offering tours; some ask you to pay in advance, wheras others offer "free" tours, but may request a tip at the end (the tour guides often earn very little for their work).

If you are in Potsdam (see pp190–205) you can ride a train around town, which starts outside the Kutscherhaus Inn in Sanssouci.

Guided bus tour offering an overview of Berlin and its environs

SOCIAL CUSTOMS AND ETIQUETTE

Older Germans are quite formal upon first meeting, and may introduce themselves with their surname and a stiff handshake. Younger Germans tend to be more casual.

As in most of Europe, smoking is technically illegal inside public buildings, cafés, restaurants, bars and nightclubs. However, there are many establishments in Berlin which circumvent these laws by naming themselves a *raucher kneipe* or smoking pub. It is quite common for people to smoke in public locations, and although this is increasingly discouraged, it is rarely punished.

LANGUAGE

German is the official language, but many places have signs in English. Most staff and locals speak some English, but Berlin is a good place to try German (see pp350–52), as the locals are used to hearing their language spoken in many accents.

A refurbished antique public convenience in Kreuzberg

PUBLIC CONVENIENCES

There are plenty of public toilets in Berlin, but you can also use the facilities in museums, stores and cafés. In some places the convenience comes with a charge, usually 50 cents.

Men's toilets are marked by the word *"Herren"* or a triangle with the vertex pointing downwards; ladies', by the word *"Damen"* or *"Frauen"*, or a triangle with its vertex pointing upwards.

TRAVELLERS WITH SPECIAL NEEDS

Not all of Berlin's streets and shops have been altered to cater for the disabled, but the majority of theatres, galleries and other sights do have the required facilities, such as wheelchair access. Detailed information about accessibility can be obtained from **Mobidat Infoservice**. Two other organizations to consult are the **Berliner Behinderten-verband** and **Der Landesbeauft-ragte für Menschen mit Behinderung**. Both of these organizations can be contacted if you need to hire a wheelchair, a special bus, or even someone to help assist for the day.

GAY AND LESBIAN TRAVELLERS

Berlin is a relaxed and toler-ant city, and is home to one of the largest and most diver-sified gay communities in Europe. There are many vibrant gay scenes across the city, with numerous bars, cafés and clubs. Areas which are recommended are the district near Nollendorfplatz U-Bahn station in Schöneberg, around Mehringdamm and Oranienstrasse in Kreuzberg, as well as much of Prenzlauer Berg and Mitte. The magazine *Siegessaeule* is good for up-to-date information.

The Berlin Pride Festival is held at the end of June, and there are many other events and festivals held throughout the year. The **Schwules Museum** contains an exhibition about the development of gay rights and the gay community.

Revellers at the Berlin Pride Festival

An ISIC card (International Student Identity card)

TRAVELLING ON A BUDGET

By European standards, Berlin is one of the cheapest cities and it is possible to get by with very little money. Travellers wishing to save can purchase a meal for a few euros at one of the many *volksküchen*, or "people's kitchens", which can be found in a number of former squat buildings in the eastern districts. For a full directory check www.stressfaktor.squat.net.de.

If eligible, before arriving in Berlin it is worth getting hold of an **ISIC** card (or Intern-ational Student Identity Card). This entitles you to a 50 per cent reduction on some museum entrance fees and to occasional discounts on theatre, plane and rail tickets. Another discount card, **EURO<26**, is available for people up to the age of 30. These cards are only valid in Europe, but can provide many discounts.

Germany's excellent *mitfah-rer,* or car-pooling systems, provide a free or cheap way to get between cities. The main one is www.mitfah-rgelegenheit.de. Free accom-modation-sharing schemes can be found at www.couchsurfing.com and www.hospitalityclub.org.

TIME

Germany is in the Central-European time zone, which means that Berlin is 1 hour ahead of Greenwich Mean Time; 6 hours ahead of US Eastern Standard Time, and 11 hours behind Australian Eastern Standard Time. From late March to late October, clocks are set forward 1 hour.

ELECTRICAL EQUIPMENT

Most electrical sockets carry 220V, although in bathrooms the voltage may be slightly lower for safety reasons. Plugs are the standard continental type, with two round pins. Buy a European travel adap-tor before you leave home.

A stall at Öko-markt in Kollwitzplatz – an organic market

RESPONSIBLE TOURISM

Germany is among the most ecologically aware countries in Europe, with many well-established systems in place to help reduce negative environmental impact. About 15 per cent of the country's energy comes from renewable sources, a percentage expected to increase. The Green Party is one of Berlin's major parties, and one of the strongest in Europe. There are often many independent demonstrations on environ-mental and political grounds.

Most Berliners are passion-ate cyclists, recyclers, and "bio" food consumers. Given the extent of environmental awareness, it's quite easy to participate in impact-reducing schemes whilst visiting Berlin. Recycling bins can be found at many public locations, such as train stations. It's possible to eat ecologically by visiting one of the many outdoor organic markets across the city (the **Öko-markt** in Kollwitz-platz on Thursdays and Saturdays is regarded as one of the best). Here you can be sure of the food's origin and buy locally sourced produce. Many restaurants also choose to serve organic food.

To see green building practices in action in the city, visit Potsdamer Platz, where many of the office buildings have grass roofs and water recycling schemes. The modern Reichstag building (*see pp134–5*) is successfully powered by renewable energy.

There are a number of hotels in Berlin which claim to operate on ecological principles, using less-harmful cleaning products, recycled and non-toxic furniture, or renewable electricity. Some

accreditation schemes are available to help guide guests opting for the green choice, for example **Green Key**. Check the green credentials of a hotel before booking – your query may encourage other hotels to adapt their practices.

Berlin is surrounded by nature reserves and there are many accommodation options located in forests with good connections to the city centre. Camping is possible, near Hauptbahnhof, for those wanting the greenest option.

DIRECTORY

EMBASSIES

Australian Embassy
Wallstrasse 76-79.
Map 7 C4.
Tel *880 08 80.*

British Embassy
Wilhelmstrasse 70.
Map 6 A4, 15 A3.
Tel *20 45 70.*

Canadian Embassy
Leipziger Platz 17.
Map 6 E5, 15 A5.
Tel *20 31 20.*

New Zealand Embassy
Friedrichstrasse 60.
Map 6 F2, 15 C1.
Tel *20 62 10.*

South African Embassy
Tiergartenstrasse 18.
Tel *22 07 30.*

US Embassy
Neustädtische Kirchstrasse 4-5. **Map** 6 F3, 15 B2. **Tel** *830 50.*

RELIGIOUS SERVICES

American Church
Lutherkirche, Bülowstrasse 71-72. **Tel** *813 20 21.*

Anglican Church
St Georg, Preussenallee 17–19. **Tel** *304 12 80.*

Jewish
Oranienburger Strasse 29.
Map 7 A1. **Tel** *88 02 80.*

Muslim
Berliner Moschee, Brienner Strasse 7–8.
Map 9 A5. **Tel** *87 357 03*

Protestant
Berliner Dom, Lustgarten,
Map 7 B3.
Tel *202 691 36.*
Kaiser-Wilhelm-GedächtnisKirche, Breitscheidplatz.
Map 10 E1.
Marienkirche, Karl-Liebknecht-Strasse.
Map 7 C3. **Tel** *242 44 67.*

Roman Catholic
St-Hedwigs-Kathedrale, Bebelplatz.
Map 7 A3, 16 D3. **Tel** *20 348 10.*

Huguenot
Französischer Dom, Friedrichstadtkirche, Gendarmenmarkt.
Map 7 A4.
Tel *892 81 46.*

TOURIST INFORMATION

ALEXA Shopping Center
Alexanderplatz, Grunerstrasse 20.
Map 8 D3.
⏲ *10am–8pm Mon–Sat.*

Berlin Tourismus Marketing
Am Karlsbad 11.
Tel *25 00 25 (24-hour).*
Fax *25 00 24 24.*
www.visitberlin.de

Brandenburg Gate
Pariser Platz, southern building. **Map** 6 E3, 15 A3. ⏲ *10am–6pm daily.*

Hauptbahnhof
Europaplatz 1, level 0, northern entrance. **Map** 6 D1. ⏲ *8am–10pm daily.*

Neues Kranzler Eck
Kurfürstendamm 21. **Map** 10 D1. ⏲ *10am–8pm Mon–Sat.*

Potsdam Tourismus Service
Brandenburger Strasse 3.
Tel *(0331) 27 55 80.*
Fax *(0331) 275 58 29.*

MUSEUM INFORMATION

CityTourCard
www.citytourcard.com

Info-Telefon der Staatlichen Museen zu Berlin
Tel *24 74 97 00.*
www.smb.museum

Stiftung Preussische Schlösser und Gärten Berlin-Brandenburg
Tel *(0331) 969 42 02.*
www.spsg.de

GUIDED TOURS

Segway Tours
Tel *240 479 91.*
www.citysegwaytours.com/berlin

TRAVELLERS WITH SPECIAL NEEDS

Berliner Behinder-tenverband
Jägerstrasse 63d.
Tel *204 38 47.*

Mobidat Infoservice
Tel *747 771 12.*
www.mobidat.net

Der Landesbeauf-tragte für Menschen mit Behinderung
Oranienstrasse 106.
Tel *90 28 29 17.*

GAY AND LESBIAN TRAVELLERS

Schwules Museum
Mehringdamm 61, Kreuzberg.
Tel *69 59 90 50.*
www.schwulesmuseum.de

Siegessaeule
www.siegessaeule.de

TRAVELLING ON A BUDGET

EURO<26
www.euro26.org.de

ISIC
www.isiccard.com

RESPONSIBLE TOURISM

Green Key
www.green-key.org

Öko-markt
Kollwitzplatz, Prenzlauer Berg.
⏲ *12–7pm Thu, 9am–4pm Sat.*

Personal Security and Health

Berlin police insignia

Berlin is a relatively safe cosmopolitan city, with few serious security concerns. Crime isn't usually directed at tourists; the most serious incidents, such as car burnings (for which the city has a reputation for), are usually targeted at rich residents living in formerly poor neighbourhoods. Nevertheless, as with all major European destinations, you should always be careful with your belongings, particularly during rush hours. If you do run into trouble, or need advice, you can always get help from the police.

Policeman   **Policewoman**

POLICE (HOW TO REPORT A CRIME)

For serious crimes in progress, call the emergency police number, **110**. For all other crimes, you should call the non-emergency police number and ask to speak to an English-speaking officer. They will inform you of the address of the nearest police station and give you basic information about what to do next.

At the police station, you will be asked some questions and may have to sign a statement. The officer may ask for specific details, such as serial numbers or pictures of stolen items. If it is a more serious matter you may be asked to return to give evidence; smaller problems might be resolved in your absence.

If you are accused of a crime, you have the right to request that police contact your embassy (see p281), which should then provide basic assistance and may give you legal support or suggest a lawyer to represent you. You are not obliged to answer any questions and any interviews that are conducted must be done in the presence of a translator.

WHAT TO BE AWARE OF

Berlin, like most major cities, has a number of beggars who hassle tourists. It is common to be approached by women carrying cards written in English which request money. These people are often more of a nuisance than a threat. If you wish to help the homeless, it's more helpful to donate direct to a charity (www.berliner-stadtmission.de). Pickpockets can also be a problem.

Kottbusser Tor U-Bahn station is notorious for its drug pushers, so be careful there late at night. Like most big cities, few of the S- and U-Bahn stations are pleasant after dark, but they are often patrolled by guards – if you need help, you can approach them. Panic buttons on platforms can also be used in an emergency.

IN AN EMERGENCY

The first number to call in an emergency is **112**, which connects you to the emergency call centre for medical, fire or police assistance. The police also operate a separate emergency number, 110.

If you spot a fire, phone the emergency number and ask for the **Fire Brigade**, or *Feuerwehr*, or use one of the emergency alarm buttons located in public areas.

Ambulances are operated by many different companies, but the emergency call centre will dispatch the nearest ambulance unit available. In less urgent circumstances you can request an ambulance or a doctor by calling the **Medical Services** number, which may take up to 2 hours to respond to a call.

On S- and U-Bahn platforms there are panic buttons that connect you to an operator who will call the appropriate emergency service.

A special Chemist Information number is available (see p283) offering information about chemists, which is helpful when searching for a pharmacist after hours. Another option is to contact your embassy, which should be able to inform you which doctors are able to speak your language. Other helplines include a **Poisons** emergencies service and a **Confidential Helpline for Women**.

LOST AND STOLEN PROPERTY

A public fire alarm

There is one central bureau for lost property in Berlin (the **Zentrales Fundbüro**) and this is where anything left in public is deposited. It is worth noting, however, that the BVG (Berliner Verkehrs-betriebe) has its own office (the **Fundbüro der BVG**) for items left on buses or trams or on the U-Bahn system. Some items left on S-Bahn trains may also be sent to the **Zentrales Fundbüro der Deutschen Bahn** in Wuppertal.

Unfortunately, tourists are more frequently targeted by thieves than any other group, which is why all valuables should ideally be kept in a hotel safe. Thankfully, serious robberies are rare in Berlin, but pickpockets are active, particularly on the U-Bahn system.

A German fire engine

German police van, a common sight

If you are unlucky enough to be the victim of street crime, you should report it to the police straight away. Remember to obtain a statement confirming what items were stolen – you will need this when it comes to making any insurance claims.

If you are travelling by car, don't leave photographic equipment or luggage in open view, and try to use a secure car park or hotel garage whenever possible.

PHARMACIES AND HOSPITALS

It's never hard to find a pharmacy, or *apotheke*. There is one on almost every city block, and they are marked by large distinctive signs bearing the letter "A".

Symbol for *Apotheke* (pharmacy)

Pharmacies are generally open from 8am to 6pm Mon–Sat. At least one pharmacy in each district is open after hours and on Sundays and public holidays. The

addresses are usually posted near the door of any pharmacy, or can be easily obtained by calling the **Chemist Information** hotline.

When visiting an after-hours pharmacy, you will be served through a window in the door and will have to wait outside while your prescription is provided. You may need a doctor's prescription to obtain certain pharmaceuticals and the pharmacist can inform you of the closest doctor's practice. Visitors who require prescribed medication should ensure they take enough to cover their stay, in case it is not available.

There are many so-called "*drogerie*" shops, such as the chain stores Rossmann and DM, which look like pharmacies but sell only cleaning and beauty products. Only *apothekes* are authorized to sell pharmaceutical products.

There are several major hospitals in Berlin, all equipped with casualty units. The most central hospital is **Charitie Mitte Campus** in Mitte. Call the emergency Medical Services number for information about your nearest hospital. When visiting a hospital or using an ambulance, you may be charged a €10 consultation fee even if you have health insurance.

TRAVEL AND HEALTH INSURANCE

All EU nationals holding a European Health Insurance Card (EHIC) are entitled to use the German health service. Patients must pay for any treatments and then reclaim most of the cost from the health authorities. All tourists should have insurance for travel and personal possessions.

DIRECTORY

IN AN EMERGENCY

Confidential Helpline for Women
Tel 615 42 43.

Fire Brigade and Ambulance
Tel 112.

Medical Services
Tel 31 00 31.

Poison Helpline
Tel 192 40.

Police
Tel 110 (Emergency).
Tel 4664 4664 (Non-Emergency).

LOST PROPERTY

Fundbüro der BVG
Potsdamer Strasse 180–182.
Tel 194 49.

Zentrales Fundbüro der Deutschen Bahn AG
Döppersberg 37, 42103 Wuppertal.
Tel 01805 990 599.

Zentrales Fundbüro
Platz der Luftbrücke 6.
Tel 90277 31 01.

PHARMACIES AND HOSPITALS

Charitie Mitte Campus
Schumann Strasse 20-21.
Tel 450 50.

Chemist Information
Tel 11 880.

An independent chemist in Berlin's city centre

Banking and Local Currency

Logo of ReiseBank

Unlike in many other countries, it is quite hard to travel around in Germany without cash. Credit card use is not prevalent, although it has increased slightly in recent years. Many retailers – including major supermarkets – still refuse credit cards or foreign bank cards, as do smaller shops, cafés and bars. However, ATMs are easy to find in most areas if you need to withdraw cash using a credit or debit card.

BANKS AND BUREAUX DE CHANGE

Most visitors use debit cards for safety. Cash can be exchanged at banks and bureaux de change *(Wechselstuben)*. The major banks, such as **Deutsche Bank** and **ReiseBank**, usually have similar rates of exchange, but some charge a commission; ask how much before commencing your transaction. Bank opening hours vary from branch to branch, but generally are as follows: 9am to 4pm (Monday, Wednesday, Friday) and 9am to 6pm (Tuesday and Thursday).

Bureaux de change are often located close to railway stations and airports. **Exchange AG** and Reisebank AG are among the most reliable places for exchanging cash or traveller's cheques. Others can be found downtown, around Joachimsthaler Strasse in the west and Friedrichstrasse in the east. You can also exchange cash at hotel reception desks, but rates are often poor. Given the high commission rates sometimes charged by banks and bureaux de change, the most economical way to get cash can be to withdraw from an ATM.

ATM – a convenient method for accessing cash while in Berlin

ATMS

ATMs are easy to find and use. Most are operated by banks and are accessible 24-hours a day, in well-serviced lobbies.

Most ATMs have multiple-language menu options and accept all major credit and debit card systems, including Maestro, Cirrus, VISA and MasterCard. Less commonly accepted are American Express, Diners Club and other cards. Check the machine for the corresponding logos.

Note that some ATMs are operated by private companies which charge large fees, and some banks may charge you extra for using an international terminal.

Always exercise caution while using ATMs; be aware of anyone standing close to you when using one and shield the numbered keypad when entering your PIN.

DEBIT AND CREDIT CARDS

You may find it difficult to get by using only a credit card. Cards are accepted in some hotels, shops and restaurants, but not all. A sign on the door should tell you if cards are accepted, and which brands they take – **VISA** and **Master-Card** are most frequently accepted, and sometimes **American Express** and **Diners Club** as well.

Some cafés and restaurants require a minimum purchase to use a credit card. If you are only ordering a snack, check that you have some cash in case your card is not accepted.

Many shops accept Electronic Cash cards, or EC cards, which are issued by German banks. Your regular bank debit card may be accepted in shops, but check before relying on this method of payment.

DIRECTORY

BANKS AND BUREAUX DE CHANGE

Deutsche Bank
www.deutsche-bank.de

Exchange AG
Friedrichstrasse 172.
Tel 20 45 57 21.

ReiseBank
www.reisebank.de

LOST CARDS AND CHEQUES

American Express
Tel (069) 97 97 10 00.

Diners Club
Tel 0800 5070 719.

MasterCard
Tel 0800 819 1040.

VISA
Tel 0800 811 8440.

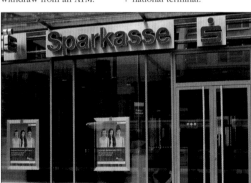

One of the city's many banks where money can be exchanged

THE EURO

The Euro (€) is the common currency of the European Union. It went into general circulation on 1 January 2002, initially for 12 participating countries. Germany was one of those 12 countries, and the German mark was phased out in 2002. EU members using the Euro as sole official currency are known as the Eurozone. Several EU members have opted out of joining this common currency.

Euro notes are identical throughout the Eurozone countries, each one including designs of fictional architectural structures. The coins, however, have one side identical (the value side), and one side with an image unique to each country. Both notes and coins are exchangeable in all participating Euro countries.

Bank Notes

Euro bank notes have seven denominations. The €5 note (grey in colour) is the smallest, followed by the €10 note (pink), €20 note (blue), €50 note (orange), €100 note (green), €200 note (yellow) and €500 note (purple). All notes show the stars of the European Union.

5 euros

10 euros

20 euros

50 euros

100 euros

200 euros

500 euros

2 euros

1 euro

50 cents

20 cents

10 cents

Coins

The euro has eight coin denominations: €1 and €2; 50 cents, 20 cents, 10 cents, 5 cents, 2 cents and 1 cent. The €2 and €1 coins are both silver and gold in colour. The 50-, 20- and 10-cent coins are gold. The 5-, 2- and 1-cent coins are bronze.

5 cents

2 cents

1 cent

Communications and Media

Logo for Deutsche Telekom

The postal and telecommunications networks and services in Germany are very efficient. Letters addressed within the country are usually delivered within 24 hours. Public telephones are becoming rare, though they can be found at train stations and in some busy public areas. Mobile telephone coverage is excellent, and you can buy a cheap pre-paid SIM card to use during your visit. Internet facilities are widely available, with Internet cafes in many locations. News and information services are excellent in Germany. There is a plethora of good quality newspapers, magazines, and television and radio channels. For English-language news and information, the best place to turn is the Internet. The website VisitBerlin.de is a good information source and will keep you up-to-date with what is happening across the city.

A typical Deutsche Telekom public telephone booth in Berlin

INTERNATIONAL AND LOCAL TELEPHONE CALLS

Although the number of public phone booths is constantly being reduced, Deutsche Telekom still operates a network across Berlin and Germany. Some accept coins, but more common are phones that take credit cards as payment. It is also possible to buy a pre-paid telephone card from newspaper kiosks, post offices and tourist offices. A small number of telephone boxes for long-distance calls are operated by other companies. These normally accept coins and credit cards.

If you are staying in a hotel, making telephone calls from your room is usually the least economical option. For long-distance calls, the cheapest option is often to visit an Internet and telephone café.

Internet and telephone centres often sell international calling cards, which can be used from any phone. The quality and value of such cards varies greatly. It is worth requesting a receipt upon purchase in case your card is faulty.

MOBILE PHONES

If you are travelling with a mobile phone it can be a good idea to buy a local SIM card with a German telephone number. This can help reduce the costs of using

public or hotel telephones to call local numbers. Having a mobile is advisable in case of emergencies, for calling ahead to confirm bookings, or to find addresses. There are many companies offering cheap pre-paid SIM cards, for example **Base**, which you can insert into your mobile telephone (check with your regular mobile service provider about possible restrictions that might prevent this). You can find SIM card packages on sale at most supermarkets and convenience stores.

To add credit, buy a credit voucher from the cashier. Sometimes you will be asked to enter your phone number into a point-of-sale machine at the cashier, or you may be given a voucher with instructions on entering a code into your handset.

To call local numbers using your mobile phone, you will

have to enter the local area code, 030 for Berlin and 0331 for Potsdam. If using an international mobile phone, you may need to add the national calling code (+49), remove the first zero, then complete the number as listed.

THE INTERNET AND EMAIL

Internet centres are common throughout Berlin, particularly in areas of high ethnic diversity, such as Kreuzberg. They can be an economical way to check your email, and many locations offer printing services as well. Most Internet centres ask you to pay at the end of your computer session. Rates can vary greatly, so it's best to check before using a terminal.

Berlin is trialling free public Wi-Fi access in the city centre. Expect to find it at many cafés, libraries and other public places. Most wireless networks are password-controlled, and an access code is required, although it is usually provided free of charge to the customer.

A bustling Internet café in Berlin

IMPORTANT NUMBERS

- Germany country code 49.
- Berlin area code 030.
- Potsdam area code 0331.
- National directory inquiries 11 8 33.
- International directory inquiries 11 8 34.
- Emergency 112.

- To make an international call, dial 00 followed by the country code, area code and number, omitting the initial 0. Country codes: UK 44; Eire 353; Canada and US 1; Australia 61; South Africa 27; New Zealand 64.

German magazines on display at a street vendor stall

POSTAL SERVICES

German post offices are easy to spot with their distinctive yellow **Deutsche Post** signs. Mailboxes, too, are an eye-catching yellow.

As in other European countries, you can send registered letters, parcels and money orders from post offices. They also offer stamps, telephone cards and the usual variety of postal stationery, as well as some banking services. If the office is closed, you can use automatic stamp and package machines, which have instructions in multiple languages.

When posting a letter, always check the labels on the mailbox. Some boxes are divided, with one side accepting mail for within Berlin only, and the other accepting everything else.

Opening times can vary widely, but most post offices in Berlin are usually open from 8am to 6pm on weekdays, and until 1pm on Saturdays. Those with extended hours, including Sundays, are at major railway stations and central areas, such as **Bahnhof Friedrichstrasse** in Georgenstrasse.

Information about collection times

Slot for non-local letters

Slot for local letters

Typical Berlin-style mailbox found on street corners

Poste restante letters can be collected from a number of post offices, depending on the post code they are addressed to. For the central Friedrichstrasse post office, the post code is 10117, and for the Joachimstaler Strasse post office in West Berlin, use the post code 10623.

As well as the nationalized Deutsche Post, Germany also has a private mail network, known as **PIN Mail**, which offers competitive prices for domestic mail and package delivery services. You can find their distinctive green-coloured offices in various locations across the city, and their mailboxes can be found in some newsagents.

NEWSPAPERS AND MAGAZINES

Newspapers can be bought in shops all over Berlin, but mostly they are sold by the city's numerous street vendors. In the evenings you may also find them on sale in bars and cafés. The most popular titles are the *Berliner Zeitung*, *Der Tagesspiegel*, the *Berliner Morgenpost* and *BZ*. Foreign-language papers can be found all over the city, especially at airport and railway kiosks. Some of the major department stores also have a good range of newspapers and magazines.

The two best magazines devoted to cultural events are *Zitty* and *Tip*, which cover the major (as well as minor) concerts, exhibitions and lectures held throughout Berlin. The very latest news can also be obtained from tourist information centres and the Internet. For visitors, VisitBerlin.de is essential for keeping up-to-date with events.

TELEVISION AND RADIO

You may find yourself spoilt for choice when it comes to television channels in Germany. Apart from the national ARD and ZDF there are many regional and private channels. Berlin has its very own channel, RBB, alongside national channels RTL, RTL2, SAT1 and PRO7. You can also pick up special interest channels, like DSF for sport and VIVA or MTV for all things music.

In addition to these there is even an option for Turkish programmes in Berlin, and thanks to cable and satellite television you can easily tune into foreign programmes in English, American, French and many other languages. In hotels, television channels mainly cover the news, music and sport. For radio news in English, tune into the BBC World Service (90.2 MHz).

DIRECTORY

MOBILE PHONES

BASE
www.base.de

INTERNET

Internet Café
Schönhauser Allee 188, Mitte.
◐ 8–4am daily.

POSTAL SERVICES

Deustche Post
www.deutschepost.de

PIN Mail
www.pin-ag.de.

Post Office
Bahnhof Friedrichstrasse, Georgenstrasse 12.
◐ 6am–10pm Mon–Fri, 8am–10pm Sat & Sun.

GETTING TO BERLIN

Berlin lies at the heart of Europe and has excellent rail and air links with the rest of the continent. Its airports receive regular flights from major European cities as well as North America, the Middle East and southeast Asia. Likewise Lufthansa, the German national carrier, offers flights to destinations around the world. The railway network

A Lufthansa aeroplane

is as good as anywhere in Europe, and takes you to the centre of Berlin. One of the cheapest ways to travel to the city is by international coach, although this is usually the slowest form of transport. If you are travelling by car, the *Autobahn* (motorway) leads to the Berliner Ring (Berlin Circular Road), from where a number of exits are signposted to the city centre.

Airport information signs, directing passengers to various services

ARRIVING BY AIR

Although Berlin receives numerous flights from destinations throughout Europe, North America and Asia, Frankfurt is still Germany's chief intercontinental airport. However, the construction of the new Berlin Brandenburg airport at Schönefeld may change this. The airport, which will informally be named after Willy Brandt, the former Berlin mayor and German chancellor, will significantly increase the city's capacity to receive international flights. Until the new airport is fully functional (scheduled for late 2011 completion), however, Tegel Airport will still be Berlin's busiest air traffic terminal.

The most frequent flights are by **Lufthansa** and **British Airways,** offering flight connections from all over Europe and beyond. From North America, **Delta** and **United** fly to Tegel from New York. **EasyJet** offers daily connections from London Luton and Gatwick airports, and **Ryanair** flies from London Stanstead three times daily. **Air Berlin** and **German Wings** offer indirect connections to London and North America.

TICKETS AND FARES

When planning your trip to Berlin, it is worth shopping around as prices can vary enormously. Some of the best deals are offered by inclusive tour operators such as **Tuifly** and **Thomas Cook**; see your local travel agent for details. Air fares are usually cheaper when booked well in advance, and discounts are available for children and students. Low-cost airlines, such as Ryanair and EasyJet, can only be booked via the Internet. A useful source of up-to-date information on schedules and fares to Berlin is www.opodo.com, a site operated by a consortium of European airlines including Lufthansa. Another helpful site is www.skyscanner.net. If you are willing to travel at short notice, you may be able to find a last-minute bargain.

TEGEL AIRPORT

Tegel airport is located within Berlin, only 5 miles (8 km) from the city centre. It is scheduled to close once the

Destinations listings on the departures board

new Berlin Brandenburg airport is open and functional (late 2011). It has several terminals connected by walkways. In the main terminal you can find a bank with bureau de change, a post office and several shops.

The city centre is reached easily by bus or taxi, both of which stop in front of the main hall. Express bus No. X9 takes you to Kurfürstendamm, while TXL buses take you quickly to Unter den Linden and Alexanderplatz. Bus No. 128 links the airport with U-Bahn station Kurt-Schumacher-Platz on the U6 line, while Bus No. 109 links to Jakob-Kaiser-Platz station on the U7 line, and continues to Bahnhof Zoologischer Garten. A trip

The busy main hall at Tegel Airport

![Tegel Airport, currently the main international airport serving Berlin]

Tegel Airport, currently the main international airport serving Berlin

by bus from the airport to the city centre usually takes 25–30 minutes. A single ticket costs €2.10. If travelling by taxi, a trip to the centre of Berlin can cost between €20 and €30.

SCHÖNEFELD AIRPORT

Located about 12 miles (20 km) south of the city centre, Schönefeld airport is set to be incorporated into the city's new Berlin Brandenburg airport. Its terminals will close and all air traffic will be handled at the new terminals nearby. Until it closes, there are a number of options for travelling to and from the city centre. Schönefeld serves mostly low-cost and charter airlines, but not exclusively.

The Flughafen Berlin Schönefeld railway station is located a short walk from the airport terminal. From here, you can catch the Airport Express and fast regional trains (RE7 and RB14) that take you to the Hauptbahnhof in less than 30 minutes. These services operate daily from 4.30am to 11pm. For these trips, you can use a normal public transport ticket (*see p296*). Schönefeld airport is located in public transport zone C, so purchase tickets accordingly. A single journey costs €2.80.

You can also take the S-Bahn, travelling on the S9 or S45 and change to other lines at connecting stations. On weekdays, the S-Bahn operates until just after midnight. If arriving late, you may have to take a series of night buses to get into the city.

Other options are to take buses No. 171 or X7 to the Rudow U-Bahn station on the U7 line. The SXF1 is a coach

service that provides a connection to Sudkreuz railway station, departing every 20 minutes from 5am to 11pm. A single journey costs €6 (the S45 travels the same journey for less than half the cost, though may take longer).

A taxi ride from Schönefeld airport to the centre of Berlin is quite expensive at €30–40.

BERLIN BRANDENBURG AIRPORT

Berlin's new international airport (due to open late 2011) which will be located next to the current Schönefeld airport site, will have its own railway station beneath the main terminal. The public transport facilities that currently service the Schönefeld terminal will be relocated here, except for the regional trains (RE7 and RB14) which will stop at Flughafen Berlin Schönefeld station. The Airport Express will depart from the new station three times an hour. Eventually, ICE trains (*see p290*) will provide fast connections from the airport across Germany.

Airport check-in counter for First Class passengers

DIRECTORY

AIRLINES

Air Berlin
Saatwinkler Damm 42.
Tel (01805) 73 78 00.
www.airberlin.com

British Airways
Budapesterstrasse 18b.
Tel (01805) 26 65 22.
www.ba.com

Delta
www.delta.com

EasyJet
www.easyjet.com

German Wings
Tel (0900) 19 19 19.
www.germanwings.com

Lufthansa
Friedrichstrasse 185-190.
Tel (01805) 805 805.
www.lufthansa.com

Ryanair
www.ryanair.com

United
www.united.com

TICKETS AND FARES

Thomas Cook
www.thomascook.com

Tuifly
www.tuifly.com

AIRPORTS

Tegel Airport
Tel (01805) 00 01 86.

Schönefeld Airport
Tel (01805) 00 01 86.
www.berlin-airport.de

The engine of an ICE (Inter City Express) train

ARRIVING BY TRAIN

The standards of European public transport are generally very high, particularly in central Europe, so whichever rail link you take to Berlin your journey is bound to be comfortable. The city has excellent connections with most major German and European cities. There are direct services between Berlin and Zürich, Brussels, Prague, Amsterdam, Paris and Warsaw. Besides these lines, there are many convenient international routes to choose from, via other German cities.

Deutsche Bahn, the national railway company, operates a famously efficient service that criss-crosses the country. The Regional Bahn (RB) and Regional Express (RE) trains operate routes around the greater Berlin and Potsdam area, while longer distances are served by Inter City (IC) and European City (EC) trains. For a luxurious experience, take an Inter City Express (ICE) service; these sleek trains are the most expensive mode of rail transport, but are also extremely fast and comfortable.

If you are thinking of staying in Germany for quite a while, and are keen to travel around a lot by train, one of the cheapest options is an **InterRail** card. This can be bought by persons of any age, from any European country (and a variety of neighbouring countries), and gives the traveller unlimited access to rail transport in a selection of European countries. Tickets can be bought online. North American visitors can enquire into **Eurail** cards, which are available through travel agents or online. The prices vary depending on your age and the number of countries you want to visit, and the duration of the pass; the younger the visitor, and the more limited number of countries you wish to visit, the cheaper the card.

At various times of the year, but especially in summer, there are often special deals offering discounted travel. Among these are weekend tickets and family tickets. It pays to visit the information desk and ask about the different fares currently on offer.

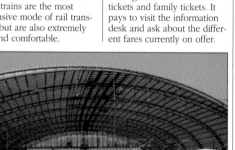

DB

Logo of Deutsche Bahn
(German Railways)

There are also discounts available by booking online, for travelling in groups and for those under 26 years of age.

Berlin's central railway station, **Hauptbahnhof**, opened in 2006 and is one of Europe's biggest rail traffic hubs. With its two soaring glass and steel office towers and a vast main hall, the station is a spectacular sight. The Hauptbahnhof is the main station for all Deutsche Bahn trains with German and international destinations or origins. Several S-Bahn routes (S3, S5, S7 and S75) link the station with the city. A short U-Bahn line, the U55, travels from here to the Bundestag and Brandenburger Tor, and there are plans to extend this line to meet the U5 at Alexanderplatz. The station also has a Deutsche Bahn Customer Centre, a tourist office, a lost and found bureau, shops, restaurants, rental car agencies, a bank, late-night services and a supermarket that is open on Sundays.

The former West Berlin central railway station, the Bahnhof Zoo (now called Zoologischer Garten), has become a regional railway station, but with many U- and S-Bahn lines connecting here, it is still an important traffic hub in the western downtown area. The best place to obtain information about public transport is the BVG pavilion on Hardenbergplatz (see p295).

Some trains coming from destinations in the south or east arrive in Ostbahnhof, a convenient station where you can easily exchange money and send mail. Ostbahnhof is linked to other districts in Berlin via S-Bahn.

Remember that the ticket for your journey to Berlin is also valid on all S-Bahn connections to other stations, providing you use it immediately on arrival. For details of train times and destinations call the **Deutsche Bahn Information** line.

Covered platforms at the airy, modern Hauptbahnhof

COACH TRAVEL

Wherever you can travel by train, the chances are you can also travel by coach (long-distance bus), and Germany is no exception. On international routes, the fast network of *Autobahnen* (motorways) enables coaches to nearly match the speed of trains. Some try to raise the level of comfort by showing videos and serving light refreshments, but coaches generally are less roomy and less comfortable than trains. It is often a question of cost; coach travel is nearly always cheaper than rail travel.

After you have visited Berlin, you may decide to take a coach trip to another German city or further afield. If so, the place to go is the **Zentral-Omnibus-Bahnhof**, situated near the Internationales Congress Centrum in the west of the city, best reached via the Messe Nord/ICC S-Bahn station. This is the city's largest long-distance bus station, and you will find connections to towns all over Germany, as well as links to other major European cities.

The main coach companies that stop in Berlin are **Eurolines**, **Berlin Linien Bus**, **Student Agency Bus** and **Ecolines**. Some coach companies, on overnight journeys, offer more comfortable sleeper seats for a small extra charge.

TRAVELLING BY CAR

Berlin is surrounded by a circular *Autobahn* or motorway (the Berliner Ring), which is linked to *Autobahnen*, leading to Dresden, Nürnberg, Munich, Hannover, Hamburg and beyond. Numerous exits from the ring road are signposted into the city centre, but the road is so long that it is sometimes quicker to cut through town to get to wherever you're going (although not during rush hour).

While driving around the city, keep an eye on your speed; the police are extremely vigilant at doing speed checks. Less-experienced drivers may feel a little

One of the many coach services available in Berlin

uneasy on the *Autobahn* as German drivers tend to zoom along at speeds reaching 200 km/h (125 mph). Keep to the right, unless you are overtaking. Always remember to check your side- and rear-view mirrors before switching to a left-hand lane. If you want to overtake, make sure there's nobody coming up behind. The speed at which fast cars come up behind you can be surprising. On some stretches of the *Autobahn*, lower speed limits are imposed depending on weather and road conditions. For assistance on the road call ADAC Auto Assistance (*see p293*).

Driving licences from all European countries are valid in Germany. Visitors from other countries need an international licence. You must also carry your passport and the standard documentation (including insurance certificate or "green card") if driving your own car. To rent a car you will need a credit card. There are several places to rent vehicles around the city, including the major train stations and airports (*see p293*).

As in most countries, German law is tough on drinking and driving. In the event of an accident, or being pulled over by the police, you may find yourself in serious trouble if alcohol is found in your bloodstream. It is better not to take the risk in the first place, and abstain from drinking.

Typical road signs indicating the *Autobahn* and sights within Berlin

DIRECTORY

TRAINS

Deutsche Bahn Information
Tel 0180 5 99 66 33.

Deutsche Bahn UK Booking Centre
Tel +44 (0) 8718 80 80 66.
www.bahn.de

Eurail
www.eurail.com

Hauptbahnhof
Service point at northern entrance, ground floor.
Map 6 D1.
Tel 29 70.

InterRail
www.interrailnet.com

COACHES

Berlin Linien Bus
Mannheimer Str. 33/34.
Tel 861 93 31.
www.berlinlinienbus.de

Ecolines
Tel (069) 401 59 055.
www.ecolines.net

Eurolines
Tel (069) 7903 501.
www.eurolines.com

Student Agency Bus
www.studentagencybus.com

Zentral-Omnibus-Bahnhof (Cental Bus Station)
Am Funkturm, Masurenallee 4–6.
Map 1 C5.
Tel 301 03 80.

GETTING AROUND BERLIN

Getting around Berlin is easy and enjoyable, thanks to the wonderfully efficient public transport system. It's also a great city to experience by bicycle or foot. Most of its main sights are located in the

Exploring Berlin by Velo Taxi

city centre and can easily be reached by cycling or walking. More peripheral areas can be reached by public transport. U- and S-Bahn trains systems are by far the quickest way to travel, but the trams and

buses are also reliable. If you happen to get a double-decker, they are excellent for sightseeing. Drivers, however, may find that Berlin isn't the easiest of cities to drive in, largely because of the endless road works. Building sites are scattered all over the city, and the number of parking spaces is inadequate in central areas, so congestion is bad and driving should be avoided if possible.

Lights at a pedestrian crossing indicating when it's safe to cross

GREEN TRAVEL

There is almost no reason to use a car in Berlin, as public transport is extensive and efficient, even to the outer reaches of the city. You can buy day-, week- or month-long passes to make your visit cost effective (see p294). For long distance trips, there are many fast train connections, as well as safe and effective *Mitfahrer* car-pooling schemes that stretch across Europe (www. mitfahrgelegenheit.de).

The best way to see Berlin is by bicycle. There are more than 600 km (372 miles) of dedicated bicycle lanes, and drivers give cyclists respect when sharing the road. It's easy to hire a bike for a day, a week, or even an hour through DB Call-A-Bike, the public cycling scheme operated by Deutsche Bahn (see p293).

There are several hundred *Umwelt Taxis* (Environmental Taxis) operating in Berlin. They carry a sign to indicate that they use *Erdgas*, or natural gas, which is slightly less polluting than other fossil fuels.

Other green travel systems include Segway tours (see p279) and Velo Taxi (see p293).

WALKING

German drivers are generally careful and watch out for pedestrians, but vigilance is still needed. Cyclists travelling at speed can be dangerous as many cycle routes run along the pavements (sidewalks), only marked by a line or by a different colour (normally red). You can easily be hit, or at least scolded for being in the wrong lane.

When searching for a specific street address, keep in mind that street numbers sometimes increase along one side of the street and then turn around at the end and continue on the other side. Street signs on each corner include the numbers within that particular block.

Disabled visitors should contact **Mobidat Infoservice** or the **Berliner Behindertenverband**

for advice on getting around, including wheelchair rental and other support services.

DRIVING

Driving around Berlin is not as straightforward as it is in some European capitals. Most of downtown Berlin (inside the S-Bahn ring) is a green zone, where only vehicles with an approved environmental badge are allowed. You can buy the badge online at www.umwelt-plakette.de. Most rental cars are covered.

Local drivers are mostly careful and don't break speed limits or enter junctions on yellow lights. You are allowed to turn right on a red light if a green arrow is also showing.

Petrol stations can be found right across the city. Some may require you to pay before your pump is activated.

Stopping and parking prohibited from Monday to Friday

Parking permitted during working hours and at weekends only with a ticket

Parking Meter
Parking meters are used on most streets. You have to pay for parking between 9am and 7pm on weekdays and 9am and 2pm on Saturdays.

Clock indicating date and time

Information in different languages

Ticket is dispensed here

Slot for inserting coins

You won't have a problem hiring a car in Berlin, as long as you show your passport and a valid driving licence; a credit card is the preferred method of payment. There are many hire companies, including **Avis**, **Europcar**, **Hertz** and **Sixt**, with offices at the airports, railway stations and in the city centre.

If you experience any trouble on the road, you should call **ADAC Auto Assistance**.

PARKING

Finding a parking place won't always be easy, especially during lunchtime, but with a bit of luck you should be able to leave your car in the middle lane of the Ku'damm or near Alexanderplatz. There are also parking meters on nearly every street, and many car parks.

Parking your car illegally is not worth the risk; Berlin traffic wardens are constantly on the prowl, and as well as giving you a ticket, they can have your vehicle towed. If your vehicle is towed away, you must call the **Berlin Police**. It can cost up to €250 to locate your vehicle. For a cheaper solution, search nearby streets – cars are sometimes simply moved rather than impounded.

CYCLING

Most of the main roads have designated cycling lanes and traffic lights at intersections. When using bicycle racks, make sure your bike is locked and don't leave it for too long.

You can take your bike on U- and S-Bahn trains and

trams but must enter the carriage by the correct door and leave your bike in the designated space. Bikes are prohibited on buses, except night buses, which can carry up to two at the driver's discretion. For all public transport an additional *Fahrrad* (bicycle) ticket is required.

Deutsche Bahn operates a fantastic public bicycle system. You can find ranks of their specially marked **DB Call-a-Bike** bicycles at train stations and major intersections. To rent one, call the number on the bicycle's instruction panel, give your credit card details, and you'll be given an access code to unlock the bike. You must call each time you begin and end your journey. It costs 8 cents a minute, or up to €9 for 24 hours.

You can also hire bikes at many cycling shops for similar or cheaper rates; one of the most reliable is **Fahrrad-station**. Or take a ride in a **Velo Taxi**. You will be transported in an open-air coach on the back of a bike.

DIRECTORY

WALKING

Berliner Behindertenverband
Jägerstrasse 63d.
Tel 204 38 47.

Mobidat Infoservice
Tel 747 771 12.

DRIVING

ADAC Auto Assistance
Tel (01802) 22 22 22.

Avis
Tel 23 09 370 or (01805) 55 77 55 (International booking).
www.avis.com

Europcar
Tel (01805) 22 11 22.
www.europcar.com

Hertz
Tel 26 11 053.
www.hertz.com

Sixt
www.sixt.com

PARKING

Berlin Police (towed vehicles)
Tel 4664 98 78 00.

CYCLING

DB Call-A-Bike
Tel 07000 522 5522.

Fahrradstation
Dorotheenstrasse 30.
◷ 10am–7pm Mon–Fri, 10am–4pm Sat.
Tel 28 38 48 48.

Velo Taxi
Tel 400 5620.
◷ Apr–Oct. www.velotaxi.com

DB Call-a-Bike bicycles for rent with one easy phone call

Buses, Trams and Taxis

Travelling by bus in Berlin is highly recommended. Buses are efficient, generally on time, and they travel useful routes – although some buses can get crowded during rush hour. Most of the major roads have special bus lanes so buses are punctual even when the main roads are congested. A double-decker bus is worth taking if you're new in town and want to have a good look round (see Useful Bus Routes map on the City Map). Trams are another particularly good option in the central and eastern parts of the city; like the buses and S-Bahn lines they are part of BVG and accept the same tickets.

BVG pavilion on Hardenbergplatz providing transport information

TICKETS

The whole of Berlin is divided into three travel zones: A, B and C. Zone A covers the city centre, Zone B the outskirts of town and Zone C includes Potsdam and its environs. Travel between the zones is simple, with tickets available for each combination of zones.

The most expensive option is to travel by buying a single ticket, which is valid for 2 hours and valid on all forms of public transport, including S- and U-Bahn trains, with as many changes as you need. Travel is allowed in only one direction, so a second ticket is needed for the return journey. Short-trip (*Kurzstrecke*) tickets are cheaper, but can only be used for three stops on trains and six stops on buses or trams.

Tickets can be bought from ticket machines at U- or S-Bahn stations, on board trams, or from the bus driver. You must validate your ticket before you start your journey by inserting it in a red or yellow time-stamping machine found near the ticket machines, at platform entrances and on board buses. Children under 14 years old are entitled to a discount (*Ermässigungstarif*) and those under six can travel for free.

The One-Day Ticket (*Tageskarte*) is valid from the moment it is validated until 3am the next morning. Weekly cards (*7-Tage-Karte*) are valid for seven days, and have the added benefit of allowing you to travel with one extra adult and up to three children for free after 8pm on weekdays, or all hours across the weekend.

Several tourist cards are available that combine public transport with discount entry to museums and attractions. The Berlin Welcome Card and the CityTourCard are both popular (*see p279*). For information about tickets and public transport in general, check the **BVG** website, visit a **BVG Pavilion** for all transport information, or check the **Ticket Information** line.

Berlin WelcomeCard ticket

Bus stops are marked by signs bearing the letter H, for *haltestelle* or stop. All bus routes have a detailed timetable on display at each stop. Inner-city bus stops are equipped with digital screens indicating waiting times. Bus stops are often relocated due to road works. You can always find a replacement stop nearby.

Apart from its number, a bus will also have its destination on show; pay attention to this as some buses shorten their routes outside rush hour. It is not always necessary to flag down buses at stops, but it can help. Enter via the front door and buy a ticket from the driver. If you are transferring and already have a validated ticket, show this.

Approaching stop names are announced automatically and are displayed digitally. Press the "Halt" ("Stop") button to get off; most stops are made "on request" only (especially in the suburbs). To exit, you must press a button to open the doors.

A typical single decker bus

TYPES OF BUS SERVICE

There are several different bus services operating in Berlin, but all use the same ticket tariffs. Regular buses are marked by three-digit route codes and operate every 20 minutes between 5am and midnight. Important routes are serviced by Metro buses, marked by the letter M at the start of their route code. These operate 24 hours a day, and run every 10 to 20 minutes. Express buses, marked by the letter X, run every 5 to 20 minutes.

The night bus service begins operation after midnight and is a very reliable network. These buses are marked by the letter N and tickets can be bought direct from the driver. They operate every half-hour until about 4am, when the U-Bahn service resumes.

ROUTES 100 AND 200

These special routes are served by double-deckers and include the most attractive parts of town. The buses operate between Bahnhof Zoo and Prenzlauer Berg, passing most of the city's interesting historic sights. For the price of a regular bus ticket, you can visit many of the locations as a more expensive tourist bus tour. The buses stop at Museum Island, Unter den Linden, Brandenburg Gate, the Reichstag, Potsdamer Platz, the Tiergarten and Kaiser-Wilhelm-Gedächtniskirche.

The BVG also operates a special historic bus tour called the Zille-Express, which makes a 40-minute circuit around the centre of Berlin, with commentary in German and English. The tour operates between April and October, departing from Brandenburg Gate every hour from 10.30am to 5.30pm. A trip costs €5 and is free for children under the age of ten.

TRAMS

Trams (*Strassenbahn*) operate in Mitte and the eastern parts of the city – a legacy from the city's division, when West Berlin tore up its once-

Modern tram operating in the former East Berlin quarter

Tram Stop

Every tram stop displays the appropriate tram numbers, timetables and maps. Buses sometimes also use the stops and are listed accordingly.

Tram stop symbol: Haltestelle

Bus numbers and names of destinations

Public transport map

Timetable of each route

extensive tram network. Despite servicing only one-third of the city, trams remain a great way to get around, particularly if you are travelling from Mitte to any part of Prenzlauer Berg. The M10 is also a convenient route, connecting Prenzlauer Berg to Friedrichshain.

Important routes are serviced by Metro trams, marked by the letter M at the front of their route code. These trams run every 10 or 20 minutes, 24 hours a day. Other trams operate between 5 or 6 am and midnight, arriving every 20 minutes.

The network runs a mix of modern wheelchair-friendly low-floor trams and old carriages with stairs; look for wheelchair symbols on timetables for guidance on which service is most suitable. Tram tickets can also be used on buses, S- and U-Bahn trains. You can purchase tickets using machines on board.

TAXIS

Taxis are a comfortable but expensive way of getting around Berlin. All taxis are of the same cream colour and have a big TAXI sign on the roof. You can easily hail one on the street or arrange a cab by phone, through **Taxi Funk** or **Wurfelfunk**. You can also get a taxi from a designated rank in popular locations, such as train stations.

The fare is calculated by a meter on the driver's dashboard. If you are travelling 2 km (1 mile) or less, you can request the *kurzstrecke* (short trip) for €4 – but only from taxis hailed in the street, and only if you inform the driver at the start of the trip.

A Berlin taxi with a yellow roof sign

Travelling by U-Bahn, S-Bahn and Regional Trains

U-Bahn display board with U-Bahn platform (Gleis), and destination

While in theory Berlin has two separate train networks – the U-Bahn and S-Bahn systems – in practical terms there is not much difference between them, and commuters use the same tickets for both. Strictly speaking, the U-Bahn operates as a metro system, with most of its trains running underground, while the S-Bahn is a longer-distance commuter service. In practice, however, there is a great deal of overlap between the two systems, and many stations have both S- and U-Bahn platforms. The U-Bahn is owned by BVG and the S-Bahn by Deutsche Bahn.

Train arriving at a station on a U-Bahn platform

U-BAHN

The U-Bahn network is very dense, with numerous stations very close together. Don't be confused by the name – "underground" trains also run on elevated tracks above the street in some sections. During rush hours trains are very frequent, usually arriving every few minutes. There are ten U-Bahn lines in total. The service closes down between around 12.30am and 4am, and is replaced by night buses. On weekends, all lines are open 24 hours, except the two short-line services, the U4 and the U55.

S-BAHN

The S-Bahn is faster than the U-Bahn, with stations spaced further apart. Trains run every 10 or 20 minutes, or more frequently in peak hours. There are a total of 15 S-Bahn lines, all running well beyond the confines of the city; four of them (S3, 5, 7 and 75) travel concurrently along the central line between Westkreuz and Ostkreuz. The Ring service (S41 and 42) is a convenient way to circle the city; it takes one hour to travel a complete circuit.

The S-Bahn has been plagued by problems due to cost-cutting over the years. If on your journey you face delays, it's worth noting you can use your ticket on the large red regional trains (RE and RB), which stop at most stations on the central line between Ostbahnhof and Zoologischer Garten.

TICKETS

Tickets for S- and U-Bahn trains are the same as the tickets used on local buses and trams. The *Kurzstrecke* (short-trip) single ticket is also acceptable, although it is only valid for three stops. Vending machines stand at the entrance to each station, selling single tickets, and one- and seven-day travelcards and other tickets. The red or yellow validation machines can be found next to the ticket machines, or near the entrance to each platform.

You may notice that there are no gates to stop free-riders trying their luck on the trains, but attempting to travel free of charge can be risky. Trains are patrolled by ticket inspectors who always work in plain clothes. They go on their rounds as soon as the train starts moving, and tend not to accept any excuses; fines for not having a ticket start at €40.

SIGNS AND TRAINS

There's no mistaking a U-Bahn station, with its large rectangular sign and trade-mark white U on a blue background; similarly for S-Bahn stations, which have a round sign with a large white S on a green back-ground. On metro maps each line is marked by a different colour and number.

The direction of the train is noted on the train and platform, which always give the final destination. When embarking, always check both the line number and the final destination of the train as it is very easy to confuse your direction. All stations have maps of the local area as well as maps of the entire metro system. Maps of the network are also on view in the train carriages.

Train doors do not open automatically; you must push a flashing button or pull a

An S-Bahn line 5 train heading out to Pichelsberg

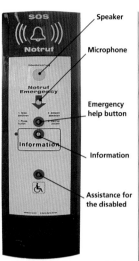

Information and emergency help point for the S-Bahn and U-Bahn

metal handle to open them. An alert sounds when doors are closing and the train conductor will announce "*Zurück bleiben!*" (remain back). During the journey the next station is announced inside the carriage and information is given on electronic screens.

REGIONAL TRAINS

Operated by Deutsche Bahn (*see p290*), the Regional Bahn and Regional Express (RB & RE) trains service the wider Berlin-Brandenburg region and beyond. They are a great way to get to Potsdam (*see pp190–205*) or other smaller towns near Berlin.

Tickets can be bought at automatic machines on station platforms, or from ticket offices. If travelling at the weekend there are special offers available, including a five-person ticket that lasts all day. A normal U- and S-Bahn ticket can be used to ride these trains within Berlin – which is particularly useful when there are delays on the S-Bahn line.

Regional trains depart from only a small number of stations, including Hauptbahnhof, Friedrichstrasse, Alexanderplatz, Ostbahnhof, Zoologischer Garten, Gesundbrunnen and Sudbahnhof.

USING THE U- AND S-BAHN

1 Find the station you want on a map and see which line runs there. Do not forget to make a note of the final destination of the line so you can be sure of travelling in the right direction.

Map of U- and S-Bahn lines
(see inside back cover)

2 Find the type of ticket you require on the touchscreen. After making your selection, the price is displayed and you can insert your coins, notes or credit cards.

Credit card

Bank notes

Tickets and change

3 A ticket from the machine looks different from one bought on a bus or tram, but it will always contain information about its type and price.

Weekly travel card and one-day travel card

4 After entering the station you must validate your ticket in one of the red or yellow stamping machines located on the platform.

Ticket

5 Follow the signs to the appropriate platform and choose the correct side by checking the destinations of departing trains.

Information board indicating the destinations of departing trains

Colour-coded sign for various S-Bahn lines

6 After leaving a train, proceed to the exit marked by the *Ausgang* sign. If there are several exits from the station additional signs will tell you the names of the streets outside.

Sign indicating where to go for these U-Bahn lines

A typical exit sign

Getting Around by Boat

A ship's bell

The river routes of Berlin may not be as dense as those of Amsterdam or Venice, but the Spree and the Havel offer more than just a pleasure cruise in the sun. An extensive system of canals and lakes links the city centre with Potsdam, Spandau, Charlottenburg and the area of Müggelsee. All kinds of water transport are available, from rowing boats to catamarans and barges.

One of many tourist boats on the Spree river

GETTING AROUND BERLIN ON THE WATER

One of the most relaxing ways to spend the afternoon in Berlin is to take a leisurely 3–4 hour journey by boat along the Spree river and the Landwehrkanal. There is no shortage of companies offering this kind of trip. Four of the most reliable are **Reederei Bruno Winkler**, **Stern und Kreis**, **Reederei Hartmut Triebler** and **Reederei Riedel**. Each has its own dock, but the routes they follow are similar. You can admire the historic buildings of Mitte as the boat passes by the Berliner Dom along Museum Island, before heading off to the new government district and the Reichstag. You should have a good view of the Haus der Kulturen der Welt and the new city in Moabit shortly before entering the Landwehrkanal. This runs alongside the Zoological Garden and new city buildings on Potsdamer Platz, and passes through Kreuzberg on its way to the junction with the Spree at Oberbaumbrücke.

Most of the boats available along this route have enclosed lower decks and open upper decks, with a bar serving snacks and drinks. All the sights are explained by a guide along the way; the commentary is usually in German, but some companies can arrange for an English-speaker.

PUBLIC FERRIES

In addition to the many privately operated cruises, there are also six public ferry lines that are integrated into the public transport system. These are marked by a stylized F and use the same tickets as trains and buses. Most of them provide cross-river connections in locations to the east where there are no bridges. However the F10, provides a particularly charming trip from Wannsee (near Potsdam) to the lakeside village of Alt-Kladow – a great budget option for those who don't want to pay a lot for a cruise.

TRIPS ALONG THE SPREE AND HAVEL RIVERS

If you want to try something a little more adventurous there are longer trips to choose from, some of which cover the western lakes as well as the city centre. A pleasant route takes you along the Spree, past the Mitte district, to Treptow, Charlottenburg and Spandau. From here you can carry on along the Havel river to the Grunewald and the Wannsee, then take a trip past Pfaueninsel to Potsdam. To do this, enquire at Stern und Kreis. Companies Reederei Bruno Winkler and Reederei Hartmut Triebler offer similar trips starting at Spandau and Charlottenburg.

Other options include a trip from Tegel port to Spandau and Wannsee, or a journey from Treptow to Köpenick. If you really want to, you can cover the whole of Berlin by boat, starting from Tegel in the north and finishing at Köpenick in the southeast, all within 5 or 6 hours.

LONGER JOURNEYS AROUND BERLIN

For even longer tours, you may decide to take a whole day exploring the rivers, canals and lakes of Berlin. From Treptow you can take a boat to Woltersdorf which takes

Boat moored along the river in the summer

One of the larger boats available on the Spree

you through the charming lakeland area of Müggelsee. This region really is one of Berlin's greatest treasures and is ideal for anyone searching for a quiet place to relax. There are many man-made beaches to choose from, as well as summer gardens and cafés – and a large white fleet of ships to show you around Berlin. Müggelsee is best visited on a warm summer's day when you can easily spend a few hours on one of its beaches.

Reederei Riedel company logo

Another adventurous idea is to take a voyage along the Teltowkanal from Treptow to Potsdam. From here, **Weisse Flotte Potsdam** can take you not only to Wannsee and the other familiar routes around town, but also to Caputh,

Werder and to many other sights to the south and west of Potsdam.

BOAT HIRE

It is possible to charter a small boat to use for several hours or longer. **Bootsverleih Spreepoint**, on the shores of Müggelsee in the east, hires motorboats to those with the appropriate licences, or you can find a chartered boat at the **Solar Boat Pavilion** in Köpenick. For a trip through the centre of the city, the **Spree Shuttle** offers private boat tours of the main sights.

Potsdam and its lakes and rivers teem with boat rental companies; check with the Potsdam Tourismus Information Centre *(see p281)* for contact details.

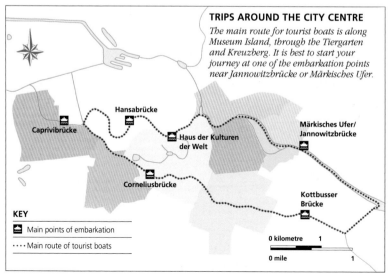

TRIPS AROUND THE CITY CENTRE

The main route for tourist boats is along Museum Island, through the Tiergarten and Kreuzberg. It is best to start your journey at one of the embarkation points near Jannowitzbrücke or Märkisches Ufer.

Hansabrücke

Caprivibrücke

Haus der Kulturen der Welt

Märkisches Ufer/ Jannowitzbrücke

Corneliusbrücke

Kottbusser Brücke

KEY

🛥 Main points of embarkation

···· Main route of tourist boats

0 kilometre   1

0 mile   1

STREET FINDER

Map references given for historic buildings, hotels, restaurants, bars, shops and entertainment venues refer to the maps in this section of the guidebook only. A complete index of street names and all places of interest can be found on the following pages. The key map below shows the area of Berlin covered by the *Street Finder*. The maps include all the major sightseeing areas, historic attractions, railway stations, bus stations and the suburban stations of the U-Bahn and S-Bahn, as well as the ferry embarkation points. The names of the streets and squares in the index and maps are given in German. The word Strasse (Str.) indicates a street, Platz a square, Brücke a bridge and Bahnhof a railway station.

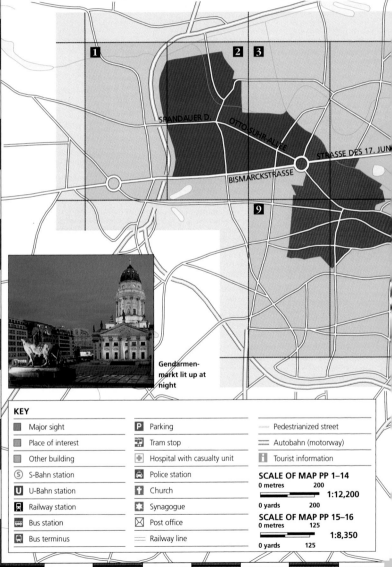

Gendarmenmarkt lit up at night

KEY

Major sight		Parking		Pedestrianized street
Place of interest		Tram stop		Autobahn (motorway)
Other building		Hospital with casualty unit		Tourist information
Ⓢ S-Bahn station		Police station		**SCALE OF MAP PP 1–14**
Ⓤ U-Bahn station		Church		0 metres 200
Railway station		Synagogue		1:12,200
Bus station		Post office		0 yards 200
Bus terminus		Railway line		**SCALE OF MAP PP 15–16**
				0 metres 125
				1:8,350
				0 yards 125

Palm house in the Botanischer Garten

Rococo Chinesisches Teehaus in Park Sanssouci, Potsdam

6 7 8

15 16

KARL-MARX-ALLEE

TER DEN LINDEN

LEIPZIGER STRASSE

12 13 14

POTSDAMER STRASSE

TEMPELHOFER DAMM

SATURN

Modern business centre of
Potsdamer Platz

Street Finder Index

Index

Page numbers in bold type refer to main entries

Acknowledgements

Dorling Kindersley would like to thank the following people whose contributions and assistance have made the preparation of this book possible.

Managing Art Editor
Kate Poole
Editorial Director
Vivien Crump
Art Director
Gillian Allan
Consultant
Gordon McLachlan
Fact Checker
Jürgen Scheunemann
Translators
Magda Hannay, Anna Johnson, Ian Wisniewski
Proofreader
Stewart Wild
Indexer
Hilary Bird

Design and Editorial Assistance
Gillian Andrews, Brigitte Arora, Marta Bescos Sanchez, Tessa Bindloss, Arwen Burnett, Lucinda Cooke, Nicola Erdpresser, Emer FitzGerald, Jessica Hughes, Priya Kukadia, Delphine Lawrance, Jude Ledger, Carly Madden, Catherine Palmi, Franziska Marking, Kate Molan, Ellen Root, Simon Ryder, Sands Publishing Solutions, Sadie Smith, Andrew Szudek, Leah Tether, Helen Townsend, Conrad van Dyk, Hugo Wilkinson

DTP
Samantha Borland, Lee Redmond

Additional Illustrations
Paweł Pasternak

Additional Photography
Amir Akhtar, Francesca Bondy, Claire Jones, Catherine Marshall, Ian O'Leary, Jürgen Scheunemann

Additional Text
Joel Dullroy, Claudia Himmelreich, Jürgen Scheunemann

Special Assistance
Dorling Kindersley would like to thank the staff at the featured museums, shops, hotels, restaurants and other organizations in Berlin for their invaluable help. Special thanks go to the following for providing photographs and pictures: Heidrun Klein of the Bildarchiv Preussischer Kulturbesitz; Frau Betzker and Ingrid Jager of the Bröhan Museum; Margit Billeb of the Centrum Judaicum; Brucke-Museum; Deutsche Press Agency (DPA); Renate Forster of the Deutsches Technikmuseum Berlin; Andrei Holland-Moritz of Forschung- und Gedenkstätte Normannenstrasse (Stasi-Museum); Matthias Richter of Konzerthaus Berlin and the Berlin Symphony Orchestra; Georg Kolbe Museum; Carl Kamarz of Stiftung Preussische Schlösser und Gärten Berlin and the Berlin and Potsdam Palaces; Thomas Wellmann of the Museum of the City of Berlin; Hamburger Bahnhof; Annette Jäckel of DeragHotels for providing photographs of the interiors of DeragHotel Grosser Kurfürst; Reinhard Friedrich; Hans-Jürgen Dyck of Haus am Checkpoint Charlie; Gaby Hofmann of Komische Oper Berlin; Gesine Steiner of Museum für Naturkunde; Ute Grallert of Deutsches Historisches Museum; Elke Pfeil of the Brecht-Weigel-Museum; Ingrid Flindell of the Käthe-Kollwitz-Museum; Sylvia U Moller of Villa Kastania; Manuel Volsk of the Savoy Hotel; Sabine Rogge of the Grand Hotel Esplanade Berlin; Claude Borrmann of the Hotel Palace Berlin; Gerald Uhligow of the Einstein Café; Hotel Adlon; Hotel Brandenburger Hof and Restaurant Die Quadriga; Hotel Kempinski; Rockendorf's Restaurant; The Westin Grand Hotel.

Photography Permissions
Dorling Kindersley would like to thank the following for their kind permission to photograph at their establishments: Margaret Hilmer of the Berliner Dom; Kaiser-Wilhelm-Gedächtniskirche; Galeries Lafayette; KaDeWe; Frau Schneider of BVG (Berlin Underground System); Deutsche Bundes-bahn for allowing photography of the Zoo railway station; Dorotheen-städtischer Friedhof for allowing photographs of the tombs; Flughafen Schönefeld for allowing photography of the airfield; Annie Silbert of the Zoologischer Garten Berlin for allowing photography of the animals and attractions; Hilton Hotel; Carlos Beck of the Sorat Art'otel, Berlin; Manuel Volsk of the Savoy Hotel, Berlin; Sabine Rogge of the Grand Hotel Esplanade; Claude Borrmann of the Hotel Palace Berlin; Gerald Uhligow of the Einstein Café; the Olive restaurant; the Bamberger Reiter restaurant; Sklepo for allowing photography of its interiors and porcelain. Count Lehmann of Senatsverwaltung für Bauen, Wohnen und Verkehr for providing cartographic information as well as copyright for the use of maps; Ms Grazyna Kukowska of ZAIKS for her help in securing permission to reproduce works of art.

34tr, *Woman in a Hat* (1939) Pablo Picasso ©Sucession Picasso/DACS, London 2006 159tl; *First Time Painting* (1961) Robert Rauschenberg ©DACS, London/VAGA, NY 2006 111bl; *Farm in Daugart* (1910) Karl Schmidt-Rottluff ©DACS, London 2006 126tl; *Mao* (1973) Andy Warhol © Licensed by the Andy Warhol Foundation for the Visual Arts, Inc./ARS, NY and DACS, London 2006 111br.

The publisher is grateful to the following individuals, companies and picture libraries for their permission to reproduce their photographs. The works of art have been reproduced with the consent of the copyright owners.

ADMIRALSPALAST: S. Greuner 260br; ALAMY IMAGES: David Crausby 283bl; CroMagnon 10tc; europhotos front endpaper tl, 112; Imagebroker/Hartmut Schmidt 287tr; Leslie Garland Picture Library 134br; Joern Sackerman 11b; ALLSTAR: cinetext 141t; AMJ HOLDING GMBH & Co. KG: Steffen Janicke 65br; ANA E BRUNO 231cr; AKG LONDON: Dieter E Hoppe front cover cl and 166, Lothar Peter front cover cbr; ANTHONY BLAKE PHOTO LIBRARY front cover ccr; BERGER + PARKKINEN ARCHITEKTEN ZIVILTECHNIK GMBH: 42br; BERLIN TOURISMUS MARKETING GMBH: 278bl, 279tl, 280cr, 286br, 292tc; C. Joosten 292tc; visitBerlin.de 278crb; visitBerlin.de/adenis 279tl; visitBerlin.de/Koch 163br; visitBerlin.de/Koch 290bl; visitBerlin.de/Meise 278bl; BERLINER DOM: 76br; BERLINER FESTSPIELE: Bianka Göbel 261t; BERLINER SPARKASSE: 284bl; BERLINER VERKEHRSBETRIEBE (BVG): 294bl, 294cla, 297tr, 297c, 297cr, 297cra; BERLINISCHE GALERIE: *Stadtwandelverlag* (2004) © Florian Bulk and *Dreiheit* (1993) © Brigitte and Martin Matschinsky-Denninghoff 139b; BILDARCHIV PREUSSISCHER KULTURBESITZ 9c, 22–23c, 31tr, 32tr, 32br, 34tr, 34br, 35t, 35b, 54cb, 67b, 73ca, 80ca, 82tl, 82b, 83tl, 85b, 115cra, 118tl, 118tr, 122cb, 123clb, 126t, 158cra, 162t, 165tl, 178tr, 178b; Jorg P Anders 20tc, 20cl, 21t, 29cl, 30cl, 73cra, 114c, 114b, 117t, 122tl, 122tr, 122ca, 122b, 123t, 123cr, 123b, 124t, 124ca, 124b, 125t, 125cb, 125cb, 187b; Hans-Joachim Bartsch 118cla, 118c, 120tl, 121cr; Margarete Busing 34c; Ingrid Geske- Heiden 32tl, 75tr, 121b; Klaus Goken 60t, 33crb, 78t, 80b, 81b; Dietmar Katz 43crb; Johannes Laurentius 75b; Erich Lessing 72t, 80t, 81cb; Jürgen Liepe 33cra, 75cla, 80cb, 82t, 83b, 118b, 164b; Saturia Linke 34tl; Georg Niedermeiser 80t, 81ca; Arne Psille 18tc, 119t, 119b, 120c, 121t, 120b; Steinkopf 114tr; G Stenzel 83tr; Jens Ziehe 110t, 111c; Jürgen Zimmermann 29tl; BRECHT-WEIGEL-GEDENKSTÄTTE 46t, 109b; BRIDGEMAN ART LIBRARY 47c, 175b; BRÖHAN-MUSEUM 165cb; CENTRUM JUDAICUM 20cl; CORBIS: Christian Charisius 280bl; Sygma/Aneebicque Bernard 233t; Adam Woolfitt 232cl; Michael S. Yamashita 233c; DEUTSCHE BAHN AG: 293br; DEUTSCHE PRESS AGENCY (DPA) 10bl, 46ca, 46cb, 46bl, 47t, 47crb, 47b, 48tc, 48cla, 48b, 50t, 50b, 67t, 151bl, 199b; DEUTSCHES HISTORISCHES MUSEUM

(Zeughaus) 8–9, 24cb, 24bl, 25tr, 25b, 25clb, 26–27b, 27tr, 28tl, 28cr, 28cb, 28dp, 29tr, 29bl, 46br, 47cra, 58tl, 58tr, 58ca, 58cb, 58br, 59t, 59ca, 59cb, 59b; DEUTSCHES TECHNIKMUSEUM BERLIN 33bl, 136; EUROPEAN COMMISSION 285; FILMPARK BABELSBERG: 205 cla/crb/bl; FIT TO PRINT, BERLIN: 283tl; GEDENKSTATTE UND MUSEUM SACHSENHAUSEN 169b; GEORG KOLBE MUSEUM 183tr; GULLIVERS BUS GMNH: 291tr; HAMBURGER BAHNHOF 110ca, 110cb, 110b, 111t, 111crb, 111b; HAUS AM CHECKPOINT CHARLIE 39br; HAUS DER WANNSEE-KONFERENZ: 181 tr; HOTEL ADLON 68t; HOTEL PALACE BERLIN 219tr; HAYDER ADAM 233br; IMAGEWORKSHOP BERLIN: Vincent Mosch 131br; JEWISH MUSEUM BERLIN: 143 br; Deutsches Technikmuseum Berlin 143cl; Jens Ziehe, Berlin 142cl; Leo Baeck Institute, New York 142tr; KÄTHE-KOLLWITZ-MUSEUM 154b; KADEWE: 51b; KOMISCHE OPER MONIKA RITTERSHAUS 49b, 68b; KONZERTHAUS BERLIN 65t; MEYER NILS 29crb, 40tr; MUSEUM FUR NATURKUNDE 109t; PRESS ASSOCIATION PICTURE LIBRARY 261tl; PRESSEFOTOSPETERS: 10c; PRESSE- UND INFORMATIONSAMT DES LANDES BERLIN: BTM 294c; BTM/Drewes 45bl; BTM/Koch 45tl, 129 tl; G. Schneider 51c; Landesarchive Berlin 129br; Meldepress/ Ebner 126b; Partner fuer Berlin: FTB-Werbefotografie 128cl, 143cr, 143br; RAINER KIEDROWSKI: Nils Koshofer 30, 112; ROBERT HARDING PICTURE LIBRARY 52–53, 274tc, Walter Rawlings 208cl; ROCCO FORTE HOTEL DE ROME: 216br SCHNEIDER, GUENTER: 41tr, 52–53; SCHIRMER, KARSTEN: 260cl; JÜRGEN SCHEUNEMANN: 49cr, 138tr, 139tl; STA TRAVEL GROUP: 280tc; STAATLICHE MUSEEN ZU BERLIN-PREUSSISCHE KULTURBESITZ/KUNSTGEWERBEMUSEUM: Hans-Joachim Bartsch 119cl; Irmgard Mues-Funke 121tl; STADTMUSEUM BERLIN 23tr, 24t, 26cla, 133tr; Hans-Joachim Bartsch 18, 19b, 20c, 21tl, 21br, 27br, 85t; Christel Lehmann 18tl, 18cb; Peter Straube 88b, 90tr; STASI-MUSEUM 174 cbr; STIFTUNG PREUSSISCHE SCHLÖSSER UND GÄRTEN BERLIN 16t, 21c, 160t, 160c, 161ca, 161c, 161b, 188clb, 194tl, 194cla, 194clb, 194br, 195cra, 195br, 195bl, 198t, 200cla, 200b, 201cra, 201crb, 201bl, 201br; TELEGRAPH COLOUR LIBRARY: Bavaria-Bildagentur front cover cbc, Messerschmidt front cover t; TONY STONE IMAGES: Doug Armand 214; VIEW PICTURES: William Fife 43bl; VILLA KASTANIA 217b; THE WESTIN GRAND 218b; WÓJCIK PAWEL 235bl, STUART N.R. WOLFE (STUART@ SNR-WOLFE.COM): 181tr.

JACKET Front – PHOTOLIBRARY: LOOK-foto/travelstock44. Back – DORLING KINDERSLEY: Dorota and Mariusz Jarymowicz clb; Britta Jaschinski bl, cla; Rough Guides/ Diana Jarvis tl. Spine – PHOTOLIBRARY: LOOK-foto/ travelstock44 t.

MAP COVER – PHOTOLIBRARY: LOOK-foto/travelstock44. All other images © Dorling Kindersley. For further information see: www.dkimages.com

---

SPECIAL EDITIONS OF DK TRAVEL GUIDES

Phrasebook

In an Emergency

Where is the telephone?	Wo ist das Telefon?	voh ist duss tel-e-fone?
Help!	Hilfe!	**hilf**-uh
Please call a doctor	Bitte rufen Sie einen Arzt	**bitt**-uh **roof**'n zee ine-en artst
Please call the police	Bitte rufen Sie die Polizei	**bitt**-uh **roof**'n zee dee poli-**tsy**
Please call the fire brigade	Bitte rufen Sie die Feuerwehr	**bitt**-uh roof'n zee dee **foyer**-vayr
Stop!	Halt!	**hult**

Communication Essentials

Yes	Ja	**yah**
No	Nein	**nine**
Please	Bitte	**bitt**-uh
Thank you	Danke	dunk-uh
Excuse me	Verzeihung	fair-**tsy**-hoong
Hello (good day)	Guten Tag	**goot**-en tahk
Goodbye	Auf Wiedersehen	owf-**veed**-er-zay-ern
Good evening	Guten Abend	goot'n **ahb**'nt
Good night	Gute Nacht	goot-uh **nukht**
Until tomorrow	Bis morgen	biss **morg**'n
See you	Tschüss	chooss
What is that?	Was ist das?	voss ist duss
Why?	Warum?	var-**room**
Where?	Wo?	**voh**
When?	Wann?	**vunn**
today	heute	**hoyt**-uh
tomorrow	morgen	**morg**'n
month	Monat	**mohn**-aht
night	Nacht	**nukht**
afternoon	Nachmittag	**nahkh**-mit-tahk
morning	Morgen	**morg**'n
year	Jahr	**yar**
there	dort	**dort**
here	hier	**hear**
week	Woche	**vokh**-uh
yesterday	gestern	**gest**'n
evening	Abend	**ahb**'nt

Useful Phrases

How are you? (informal)	Wie geht's?	vee gayts
Fine, thanks	Danke, es geht mir gut	dunk-uh, es gayt meer goot
Until later	Bis später	biss **shpay**-ter
Where is/are?	Wo ist/sind…?	voh ist/sind
How far is it to…?	Wie weit ist es…?	vee **vite** ist ess
Do you speak English?	Sprechen Sie Englisch?	shpresh'n zee **eng**-glish
I don't understand	Ich verstehe nicht	ish fair-**shtay**-uh nisht
Could you speak more slowly?	Könnten Sie langsamer sprechen?	**kurnt**-en zee **lung**-zam-er shpresh'n

Useful Words

large	gross	**grohss**
small	klein	**kline**
hot	heiss	**hyce**
cold	kalt	**kult**
good	gut	**goot**
bad	böse/schlecht	**burss**-uh/**shlesht**
open	geöffnet	g'**urff**-nett
closed	geschlossen	g'**shloss**'n
left	links	**links**
right	rechts	**reshts**
straight ahead	geradeaus	g'**rah**-der-**owss**

Making a Telephone Call

I would like to make a phone call	Ich möchte telefonieren	ish mer-shtuh tel-e-fon-**eer**'n
I'll try again later	Ich versuche es später noch einmal	ish fair-zookh-uh es **shpay**-ter nokh ine-mull
Can I leave a message?	Kann ich eine Nachricht hinterlassen?	kan ish **ine**-uh nakh-risht hint-er-**lahss**-en
answer phone	Anrufbeantworter	an-roof-be-**ahnt**-vort-er
telephone card	Telefonkarte	tel-e-**fohn**-kart-uh
receiver	Hörer	**hur**-er
mobile	Handy	han-dee
engaged (busy)	besetzt	b'zetst
wrong number	Falsche Verbindung	falsh-uh fair-**bin**-doong

Sightseeing

library	Bibliothek	bib-leo-**tek**
entrance ticket	Eintrittskarte	ine-tritz-**kart**-uh
cemetery	Friedhof	**freed**-hofe
train station	Bahnhof	**barn**-hofe
gallery	Galerie	**gall**-er-ree
information	Auskunft	**owss**-koonft
church	Kirche	**keersh**-uh
garden	Garten	**gart**'n
palace/castle	Palast/Schloss	pallast/shloss
place (square)	Platz	**plats**
bus stop	Haltestelle	**hal**-te-shtel-uh
national holiday	Nationalfeiertag	nats-yon-**ahl**-fire-tahk
theatre	Theater	tay-**aht**-er
free admission	Eintritt frei	ine-tritt fry

Shopping

Do you have/ Is there…?	Gibt es…?	geept ess
How much does it cost?	Was kostet das?	voss **kost**'t duss?
When do you open/ close?	Wann öffnen Sie/ schliessen Sie?	vunn **off**'n zee **shlees**'n zee
this	das	**duss**
expensive	teuer	**toy**-er
cheap	preiswert	**price**-vurt
size	Grösse	**gruhs**-uh
number	Nummer	**noom**-er
colour	Farbe	**farb**-uh
brown	braun	brown
black	schwarz	**shvarts**
red	rot	**roht**
blue	blau	**blau**
green	grün	**groon**
yellow	gelb	**gelp**

Types of Shop

antique shop	Antiquariat	antik-**var**-yat
chemist (pharmacy)	Apotheke	appo-**tay**-kuh
bank	Bank	**bunk**
market	Markt	**markt**
travel agency	Reisebüro	**rye**-zer-boo-roe
department store	Warenhaus	**vahr**'n-hows
chemist's, drugstore	Drogerie	droog-er-**ree**
hairdresser	Friseur	freezz-**er**
newspaper kiosk	Zeitungskiosk	tsytoongs-kee-osk
bookshop	Buchhandlung	**bookh**-hant-loong

bakery	Bäckerei	beck-er-**eye**
post office	Post	posst
shop/store	Geschäft/Laden	gush-**eft**/**lard**'n
film processing shop	Photogeschäft	**fo**-to-gush-**eft**
self-service shop	Selbstbedienungs-laden	selpst-bed-**ee**-nungs-lard'n
shoe shop	Schuhladen	shoo-lard'n
clothes shop	Kleiderladen, Boutique	klyder-lard'n boo-**teek**-uh
food shop	Lebensmittel-geschäft	**lay**-bens-mittel-gush-eft
glass, porcelain	Glas, Porzellan	**glars, Port-sellahn**

Staying in a Hotel

Do you have any vacancies?	Haben Sie noch Zimmer frei?	harb'n zee nokh **tsimm**-er-fry
with twin beds?	mit zwei Betten?	mitt tsvy bett'n
with a double bed?	mit einem Doppelbett?	mitt ine'm **dopp**'l-bet
with a bath?	mit Bad?	mitt **bart**
with a shower?	mit Dusche?	mitt **doosh**-uh
I have a reservation	Ich habe eine Reservierung	ish **harb**-uh ine-uh rez-er-**veer**-oong
key	Schlüssel	shlooss'l
porter	Pförtner	**pfert**-ner

Eating Out

Do you have a table for...?	Haben Sie einen Tisch für...?	harb'n zee tish foor
I would like to reserve a table	Ich möchte eine Reservierung machen	ish **mer**-shtuh ine-uh rezer-**veer**-oong makh'n
I'm a vegetarian	Ich bin Vegetarier	ish bin vegg-er-**tah**-ree-er
Waiter!	Herr Ober!	hair **oh**-bare!
The bill (check), please	Die Rechnung, bitte	dee **resh**-noong bitt-uh
breakfast	Frühstück	**froo**-shtock
lunch	Mittagessen	**mit**-targ-ess'n
dinner	Abendessen	**arb**'nt-ess'n
bottle	Flasche	**flush**-uh
dish of the day	Tagesgericht	**tahg**-es-gur-isht
main dish	Hauptgericht	**howpt**-gur-isht
dessert	Nachtisch	**nahkh**-tish
cup	Tasse	**tass**-uh
wine list	Weinkarte	vine-kart-uh
tankard	Krug	khroog
glass	Glas	**glars**
spoon	Löffel	**lerff**'l
teaspoon	Teelöffel	tay-lerff'l
tip	Trinkgeld	**trink**-gelt
knife	Messer	**mess**-er
starter (appetizer)	Vorspeise	**for**-shpize-uh
the bill	Rechnung	**resh**-noong
plate	Teller	**tell**-er
fork	Gabel	**gahb**'l

Menu Decoder

Aal	**arl**	eel
Apfel	**upf**'l	apple
Apfelschorle	**upf**'l-shoorl-uh	apple juice with sparkling mineral water
Apfelsine	**upf**'l-seen-uh	orange
Aprikose	upri-**kawz**-uh	apricot
Artischocke	arti-**shokh**-uh	artichoke
Aubergine (eggplant)	or-ber-jeen-uh	aubergine
Banane	bar-**narn**-uh	banana
Beefsteack	**beef**-stayk	steak
Bier	beer	beer
Bockwurst	**bokh**-voorst	a type of sausage
Bohnensuppe	burn-en-zoop-uh	bean soup
Branntwein	brant-vine	spirits
Bratkartoffeln	brat-kar-toff'ln	fried potatoes
Bratwurst	brat-voorst	fried sausage
Brötchen	bret-tchen	bread roll
Brot	brot	bread
Brühe	bruh-uh	broth
Butter	**boot**-ter	butter
Champignon	**shum**-pin-yong	mushroom
Currywurst	**kha**-ree-voorst	sausage with curry sauce
Dill	**dill**	dill
Ei	**eye**	egg
Eis	**ice**	ice/ ice cream
Ente	**ent**-uh	duck
Erdbeeren	ayrt-**beer**'n	strawberries
Fisch	**fish**	fish
Forelle	for-**ell**-uh	trout
Frikadelle	Frika-dayl-uh	rissole/hamburger
Gans	ganns	goose
Garnele	**gar**-nayl-uh	prawn/shrimp
gebraten	g'**braat**'n	fried
gegrillt	g'**grilt**	grilled
gekocht	g'**kokht**	boiled
geräuchert	g'**rowk**-ert	smoked
Geflügel	g'**floog**'l	poultry
Gemüse	g'**mooz**-uh	vegetables
Grütze	**grurt**-ser	groats, gruel
Gulasch	**goo**-lush	goulash
Gurke	**goork**-uh	gherkin
Hammelbraten	hamm'l-**braat**'n	roast mutton
Hähnchen	haynsh'n	chicken
Hering	**hair**-ing	herring
Himbeeren	him-beer'n	raspberries
Honig	**hoe**-nikh	honey
Kaffee	kaf-**fay**	coffee
Kalbfleisch	kalp-flysh	veal
Kaninchen	ka-**neensh**'n	rabbit
Karpfen	**karpf**'n	carp
Kartoffelpüree	kar-toff'l-poor-ay	mashed potatoes
Käse	**kayz**-uh	cheese
Kaviar	**kar**-vee-ar	caviar
Knoblauch	**k'nob**-lowkh	garlic
Knödel	**k'nerd**'l	noodle
Kohl	**koal**	cabbage
Kopfsalat	**kopf**-zal-aat	lettuce
Krebs	**krayps**	crab
Kuchen	**kookh**'n	cake
Lachs	**lahkhs**	salmon
Leber	**lay**-ber	liver
mariniert	mari-neert	marinated
Marmelade	marmer-**lard**-uh	marmalade, jam
Meerrettich	may-re-tish	horseradish
Milch	**milsh**	milk
Mineralwasser	minn-er-**arl**-vuss-er	mineral water
Möhre	**mer**-uh	carrot
Nuss	**nooss**	nut
Öl	**erl**	oil
Olive	o-**leev**-uh	olive
Petersilie	payt-er-**zee**-li-uh	parsley
Pfeffer	**pfeff**-er	pepper
Pfirsich	**pfir**-zish	peach
Pflaumen	**pflow**-men	plum
Pommes frites	pomm-**fritt**	chips/ French fries
Quark	kvark	soft cheese
Radieschen	ra-**deesh**'n	radish
Rinderbraten	**rind**-er-brat'n	joint of beef
Rinderroulade	**rind**-er-roo-lard-uh	beef olive
Rindfleisch	**rint**-flysh	beef
Rippchen	**rip**-sh'n	cured pork rib
Rotkohl	roht-koal	red cabbage
Rüben	rhoob'n	turnip
Rührei	**rhoo**-er-eye	scrambled eggs
Saft	**zuft**	juice
Salat	zal-aat	salad

Salz	**zults**	salt
Salzkartoffeln	zults-kar-toff'l	boiled potatoes
Sauerkirschen	zow-er-**keersh**'n	cherries
Sauerkraut	zow-er-krowt	sauerkraut
Sekt	**zekt**	sparkling wine
Senf	**zenf**	mustard
scharf	sharf	spicy
Schaschlik	shash-lik	kebab
Schlagsahne	shlahgg-zarn-uh	whipped cream
Schnittlauch	shnit-lowhkh	chives
Schnitzel	**shnitz**'l	veal or pork cutlet
Schweinefleisch	**shvine**-flysh	pork
Spargel	**shparg**'l	asparagus
Spiegelei	shpeeg'l-eye	fried egg
Spinat	shpin-art	spinach
Tee	**tay**	tea
Tomate	tom-art-uh	tomato
Wassermelone	vuss-er-me-lohn-uh	watermelon
Wein	**vine**	wine
Weintrauben	vine-trowb'n	grapes
Wiener Würstchen	veen-er voorst-sh'n	frankfurter
Zander	**tsan**-der	pike-perch
Zitrone	tsi-trohn-uh	lemon
Zucker	**tsook**-er	sugar
Zwieback	tsvee-bak	rusk
Zwiebel	**tsveeb**'l	onion

Numbers

0	null	**nool**
1	eins	**eye'ns**
2	zwei	**tsvy**
3	drei	**dry**
4	vier	**feer**
5	fünf	**foonf**
6	sechs	**zex**
7	sieben	**zeeb**'n
8	acht	**uhkht**
9	neun	**noyn**
10	zehn	**tsayn**
11	elf	**elf**
12	zwölf	**tserlf**
13	dreizehn	**dry**-tsayn
14	vierzehn	**feer**-tsayn
15	fünfzehn	**foonf**-tsayn
16	sechzehn	**zex**-tsayn

17	siebzehn	**zeep**-tsayn
18	achtzehn	**uhkht**-tsayn
19	neunzehn	**noyn**-tsayn
20	zwanzig	**tsvunn**-tsig
21	einundzwanzig	**ine**-oont-tsvunn-tsig
30	dreissig	**dry**-sig
40	vierzig	**feer**-sig
50	fünfzig	**foonf**-tsig
60	sechzig	**zex**-tsig
70	siebzig	**zeep**-tsig
80	achtzig	**uhkht**-tsig
90	neunzig	**noyn**-tsig
100	hundert	**hoond**'t
1000	tausend	**towz**'nt
1 000 000	eine Million	**ine**-uh **mill**-yon

Time

one minute	eine Minute	**ine**-uh min-**oot**-uh
one hour	eine Stunde	**ine**-uh **shtoond**-uh
half an hour	eine halbe Stunde	**ine**-uh hullb-uh **shtoond**-uh
Monday	Montag	**mohn**-targ
Tuesday	Dienstag	**deens**-targ
Wednesday	Mittwoch	**mitt**-vokh
Thursday	Donnerstag	**donn**-ers-targ
Friday	Freitag	**fry**-targ
Saturday	Samstag/ Sonnabend	**zums**-targ zonn-ah-bent
Sunday	Sonntag	**zon**-targ
January	Januar	**yan**-ooar
February	Februar	**fay**-brooar
March	März	**mairts**
April	April	april
May	Mai	my
June	Juni	**yoo**-ni
July	Juli	**yoo**-lee
August	August	ow-**goost**
September	September	zep-**tem**-ber
October	Oktober	ok-toh-ber
November	November	no-**vem**-ber
December	Dezember	day-**tsem**-ber
spring	Frühling	**froo**-ling
summer	Sommer	**zomm**-er
autumn (fall)	Herbst	**hairpst**
winter	Winter	**vint**-er

Berlin U-Bahn and S-Bahn